NO-FAULT
AUTOMOBILE INSURANCE IN ACTION:
THE EXPERIENCES IN MASSACHUSETTS, FLORIDA, DELAWARE AND MICHIGAN

ALAN I. WIDISS

RANDALL R. BOVBJERG

DAVID F. CAVERS

JOSEPH W. LITTLE

ROGER S. CLARK

GERALD E. WATERSON

THOMAS C. JONES

Published for the Council on Law-Related Studies

1977 OCEANA PUBLICATIONS, INC. DOBBS FERRY, NEW YORK

Chapter 2. "Accident Victims Under No-Fault Automobile Insurance:
A Massachusetts Survey" reprinted, by permission, from the
Iowa Law Review, Volume 61, Number 1, ©1975 by the Uni-
versity of Iowa.

Chapter 3. "Massachusetts No-Fault Automobile Insurance: Its Impact
on the Legal Profession" reprinted, by permission, from the
Boston University Law Review, Volume 56, Number 2, © 1976
by Boston University.

Chapter 4. "The Impact of No-Fault Auto Insurance on Massachusetts
Courts" reprinted, by permission, from the *New England Law
Review,* Volume 11, Number 2, ©1976 by the New England
School of Law.

Chapter 7. "No-Fault Auto Reparation in Florida: An Empirical Examina-
tion of Some of Its Effects" reprinted, by permission, from the
University of Michigan Journal of Law Reform, Volume 9,
Number 1, ©1975 by the University of Michigan.

Chapter 8. " "No Fault" in Delaware" reprinted, by permission, from the
Rutgers-Camden Law Journal, Volume 6, Number 2, ©1974
by the Rutgers School of Law, Camden.

Library of Congress Cataloging in Publication Data

No-fault automobile insurance in action.

Includes index.
1. Insurance, No-fault automobile — United States —
States. I. Widiss, Alan I., 1938-
KF1219.5.N6   346'.73'086   77-71283
ISBN 0-379-00391-0

Manufactured in the United States of America

CONTRIBUTORS

PART I. THE MASSACHUSETTS STUDY

Alan I. Widiss
Professor of Law
University of Iowa

Randall R. Bovbjerg
Research Attorney
Duke University

David F. Cavers
Professor of Law
Harvard University

PART II. THE FLORIDA STUDY

Joseph W. Little
Professor of Law
University of Florida

Part III. THE DELAWARE STUDY

Roger S. Clark
Professor of Law
Rutgers University

Gerald E. Waterson
Director
Camden Center for Computer
and Information Services

PART IV. THE MICHIGAN STUDY

Thomas C. Jones
Commissioner of Insurance
State of Michigan

iii

CONTENTS

FOREWORD

In recent years, the gradual processes of legal change have begun to accelerate, but few innovations in law have been more abrupt than the sudden emergence of no-fault automobile insurance, a sharp departure from the fault-based common law doctrines that had governed motorists' liability for accidents since the horseless carriage first appeared. Yet no-fault insurance had been preceded by an extended search for solutions to the problems that traditional modes of accident compensation had long been creating for accident victims, for car owners and their insurers, and for the judicial system. This search had led to a number of studies of auto accident compensation supported by the Walter E. Meyer Research Institute of Law, the foundation which created the Council on Law-Related Studies, sponsor of this volume.

Among the dozen or more auto compensation studies funded in whole or in part by the Meyer Institute was that conducted by Professor Robert E. Keeton and Jeffrey O'Connell, co-authors of *Basic Protection for the Traffic Victim*. The no-fault plan they advanced in that volume, substantially modified in the legislative process, suddenly—indeed, unexpectedly—became the law of Massachusetts, effective January 1, 1971. This no-fault law was soon followed by a not dissimilar law in Florida and by a quite dissimilar law in Delaware, one that sought to provide both no-fault and fault bases of reparation.

To the Council on Law-Related Studies, these developments came as a call to carry forward the research program which the Meyer Institute had begun. Seeking to evaluate these experiments in "the laboratory(ies) of the states," the Council's Board approved studies designed to cast light on the new laws' early operations in the three pioneering states.

The need for an early beginning led the Council to undertake the Massachusetts study directly instead of seeking out some other institution to assume the task. In the summer of 1971, an arrangement was made with Professor Alan I. Widiss, of the University of Iowa College of Law, author of a treatise on *Uninsured Motorist Coverage*, to serve as director of the study with Randall Bovbjerg, a recent Harvard Law School graduate, as associate director. Treatment of all aspects of the Massachusetts law in operation being impracticable, it was decided to leave its impact on rates and insurers' earnings to economic analysts. Empirical studies were directed to four facets of the law in action: the making of claims by accident victims, claims processing by insurance companies, the bar's adjustment to the new regime, and the law's effect on the state's over-burdened courts. These are reported in the four articles following Professor Widiss' introduction.

The Florida no-fault law resembles the Massachusetts law enough to make comparison possible, yet their terms and the states' past claims experience differ sufficiently so that comparisons may prove significant. Fortunately, Professor Joseph W. Little of the University of Florida College of Law, director of an earlier Council-supported study, was willing to examine the Florida experience, focusing his inquiry on the no-fault law's impact on reparation lawsuits in two Florida counties and on claims processing there by two insurers. Data had been gathered as to both bodily injury and property damage claims when the Florida Supreme Court struck down the property provisions, a sequence permitting Professor Little to deal with both aspects of the original Florida law. He has also prepared an addendum reporting recent changes in the Florida law.

In Delaware, the coupling of compulsory first-party no-fault bodily injury insurance coverage of $10,000 with freedom to sue in tort for any damages, including pain and suffering, not recoverable under the no-fault insurance, led to a dispute whether a law thus designed could properly be termed "no-fault." In any event, the Delaware law had many champions, especially in the bar, and it soon emerged as a serious rival to legislation along Massachusetts lines. It seemed appropriate, therefore, to couple studies of the Massachusetts and Florida experiences with that of Delaware. A Council grant to the Rutgers-Camden University School of Law has led to a study by Professor Roger S. Clark of the effect which the availability of no-fault protection has had on the bringing of tort suits for additional damages by injured persons and on the work of the legal profession. Professor Clark has updated his published study through 1975 in an addendum dealing with the tort caseload.

When planning its research program, the Council hoped to cover the newly-enacted, far-reaching Michigan no-fault law. However, litigation delayed the law from becoming operational so long as to preclude a Council-supported study. Then, just as copy was about to go to the publisher, we learned that a preliminary study of Michigan's law in action was being completed by Thomas C. Jones, Commissioner of Insurance. Happily, he has consented to adapt it for inclusion here, too late for indexing but in time to add another significant dimension to the volume.

Plainly no-fault automobile insurance, already adopted in twenty-three states, has become an American legal institution. Yet its design and dimensions are still fluid. The experience reflected in these articles should prove useful in shaping the no-fault laws of the future. The Council is indebted to the five law school periodicals whose cooperation made it possible to place this body of experience within a single volume and so within the convenient reach of those responsible for charting the course of no-fault legislation in the years ahead.

David F. Cavers
President, Council on
Law-Related Studies

Cambridge, Massachusetts

PART I
THE MASSACHUSETTS STUDY

ALAN I. WIDISS
Director

RANDALL R. BOVBJERG
Associate Director

THE MASSACHUSETTS STUDY

PREFACE

This study is the result of the interest of the Council on Law-Related Studies in supporting analysis of the ways in which compensation is or is not provided for persons injured in automobile accidents, and is a continuation of a program established by the Council's predecessor, the Walter E. Meyer Research Institute of Law, Inc. In this instance, the Council retained the author to serve as director, and Mr. Randall Bovbjerg as associate director of a broadly based empirical investigation on how the implementation of no-fault automobile insurance affected the compensation system in the Commonwealth of Massachusetts.

As the primary investigator and author, I want to particularly acknowledge the contributions of Professor David Cavers, who has been the President of the Council since its inception and throughout the course of this project. To state that the genesis of the study is attributable to Professor Cavers is only to implicitly indicate that he maintained the continuing interest and support of a "parent". Professor Cavers was always available to provide counsel, advice, and assistance. Yet, it would be misleading if I did not also state that he invariably waited to be asked, allowing me to fully exercise my own discretion.

Any undertaking of this type could not have been completed without the cooperation of both public and private institutions and individuals. From the first contact in 1971, Governor Francis Sargent supported the idea of such a study and made the governor's good offices available in ways that aided us in securing the assistance of other government agencies which was essential to the project. Throughout this study, the cooperation of the then Massachusetts Commissioner of Insurance, John Ryan, helped to make the study possible, and Commissioner Ryan's staff was repeatedly generous in making relevant information available. The same acknowledgment is due to Mr. Lemuel Devers, who is Director of the Massachusetts Rating Bureau, and to Mr. Devers' staff at the Rating Bureau.

During the course of this project, many persons responded to requests for aid, counsel, or comments on various aspects of the study design or article drafts. At this point, it is not possible to identify every person who made such a contribution. However, there have been several persons whom I have repeatedly called on, and I do want to both acknowledge their assistance and express a note of appreciation to each of them.

Mr. Roy Anderson, Allstate Insurance Company
Professor David Baldus, University of Iowa
Professor George R. Boyton, University of Iowa
Professor David Caplovitz, City University of New York
Professor Roger S. Clark, Rutgers University
Professor Alfred E. Conard, University of Michigan
Professor Robert E. Keeton, Harvard University
Dr. Jack Fowler, Survey Research Program
Professor Lloyd E. Ohlin, Harvard University
Professor Geoffrey Palmer, Victoria University of Wellington
Professor William Schwartz, Boston University
Dr. Wayne Sorrenson, State Farm Mutual Automobile
   Insurance Co.
Mr. Robert L. Stephens, American Mutual Insurance Alliance

In addition, a special note of acknowledgment is more than justified to Mr. James Grifhorst who supervised almost all phases of the preparation of the survey data for the computer analysis and who did the computer programming for the data analysis conducted at the University of Iowa. I am also especially indebted to Dr. Wayne Sorrenson and his staff at the State Farm Mutual Automobile Insurance Company Computer Center who provided much assistance in regard to the computer analysis of data from both DOT and CLRS claims files surveys.

Law students at the University of Iowa have worked on various aspects of the project, often making contributions that were significant as well as essential to the completion of the surveys. These students included: Ms. Marianne Baldrige, Ms. Jane Eikleberry, Ms. Nancy Hauserman, Ms. Joyce Kerber, Mr. William B. King, Mr. James E. Konsky, Mr. William P. Kovacs, Mr. Gary P. Malfeld, Ms. Patricia Neal, Ms. Sherry Newman Ruth, Mr. Donald F. Staas, Mr. John C. Shupe, and Rev. Daniel J. Ward.

In light of my composing and writing style—which often includes extensive text revisions set out in small and barely legible printing in the margins of the manuscript—a special note of thanks is particularly due to Ms. Connie Snyder and Ms. Janet Edwards who did most of the typing on the project. Ms. Snyder and Ms. Edwards were conscientious, proficient, and helpful through the many months that preceded the completion of the study.

Drafts of the chapters in this volume have been sent to insurance executives, lawyers, and academicians who have provided extraordinarily helpful comments and critiques. The articles which appeared in the University of Iowa and Boston University Law Reviews were the subject of effective editing by the article editors and editors-in-chief of those publications. And, of course, Mr. Randall R. Bovbjerg contributed to every phase of the project. To each of those persons I am indebted.

A special note of acknowledgment is reserved for Ellen Magaziner Widiss, who critiqued and edited every portion of the text, and I believe immeasurably improved its readability.

Finally, a short note of dedication of my portion of this book to Deborah Anne Widiss, who was born shortly after the project began. Suffice it to say that since her birth far too often her father has been preoccupied with the task of completing this undertaking.

A.I.W.

Iowa City, Iowa
Summer and Fall, 1976

CHAPTER 1

INTRODUCTION: BACKGROUND AND PERSPECTIVE

1. AUTOMOBILES, ACCIDENTS, AND INSURANCE LEGISLATION

Motor vehicles have produced many vast economic and social changes in the United States during the twentieth century. Undoubtedly, among the most significant has been that the growing number of automobiles has been accompanied by concomitant increases in accidents involving serious personal injuries and deaths as the advent of mass-produced automobiles placed the potential for causing such injuries literally in the hands of millions of persons. Although providing adequate compensation to or reparation for persons who have been injured and killed in highway accidents is a problem that dates from the earliest use of automobiles and other motor vehicles, the adequacy of the then-existing compensation systems first became a major social question in the United States during the 1920's. In the course of the ensuing half century, many aspects of the compensation system have changed. Notably, most drivers acquire liability insurance that at least complies with the minimum amount of the applicable state financial responsibility law. In addition, in many instances persons injured in automobile accidents are indemnified by various types of first party insurance. These include health or medical insurance, wage replacement coverages such as disability insurance, and since 1971, in a growing number of states, no-fault insurance. However, the adequacy of the reparation payments made to automobile accident victims continues to be a subject of significant public concern.

In the years since the 1920's, several different legislative approaches have been developed to deal with the compensation problems created by the ever-increasing number of automobiles on the nation's highways. A brief review of the legislation enacted in the United States over the past half century is useful in providing a perspective from which to examine the nature of no-fault legislation being enacted in the 1970's, and the results of the surveys on the way the no-fault coverages have operated in Massachusetts, Florida, Delaware, and Michigan.

Tort Liability and Financial Responsibility Legislation

In the United States, the right of an individual injured in an automobile accident to be compensated by another person for

1

injuries resulting from such an accident has primarily been predicated on an allocation of fault, in accordance with the principle that the economic cost of injuries to persons or property attributable to the negligence of a given party should be borne by that party. In other words, the right to be compensated by another for injuries resulting from an accident has been predicated on ascertaining who was at fault. Under the fault theory, in instances where responsibility cannot be assessed, a claimant is at least in principle foreclosed from successfully pursuing indemnification by way of a tort suit. Moreover, under the fault theory (absent application of the doctrine of comparative negligence) when an injured person is in some measure contributorily negligent, recovery in a tort action is also theoretically precluded.

When fault can be allocated exclusively to one driver, an innocent accident victim is still not assured indemnification. There have always been "financially irresponsible" motorists who do not possess sufficient personal financial resources to enable them to respond to such damage claims and who have not purchased liability insurance which would provide a source of indemnification for injured persons. From 1925 to 1970, state governments tried to alleviate or at least reduce the problem of financial irresponsibility by enacting laws that were designed either to induce or, in a few states, to require motorists to acquire liability insurance.[1]

The Connecticut financial responsibility law of 1925 was the first financial responsibility legislation enacted in the United States. Under the Connecticut law, motorists were threatened with suspension of driving privileges in the event they were unable to prove that they could satisfy claims arising out of an automobile accident.[2] The Connecticut legislation authorized the State Commissioner of Motor Vehicles to require the operator and the owner of a vehicle involved in an accident causing death or personal injury, or property damages in excess of one hundred dollars, to

---

1. See Murphy and Netherton, *Public Responsibility and the Uninsured Motorist,* 47 GEORGETOWN L. JOURN. 700 (1959). For an early discussion of the first financial responsibility laws, see Heyting, *Automobiles and Compulsory Liability Insurance,* 16 A.B.A. JOURN. 362 (1930). Also see Risjord and Austin, *The Problem of the Financially Irresponsible Motorist,* 24 U. KANSAS CITY L. REV. 82 (1955-56).

An interesting comparative analysis of various legislative enactments dealing with the problem of financial irresponsibility is found in Ward, *The Uninsured Motorist: National and International Protection Presently Available and Comparative Problems in Substantial Similarity,* 9 BUFFALO L. REV. 283-320 (1960).

2. CONNECTICUT PUBLIC ACTS, ch. 183 (1925). The statute also authorized the commissioner to invoke the same penalties for persons convicted of certain criminal offenses, including reckless driving and driving while intoxicated.

prove their "financial responsibility to satisfy any claim for damages, by reason of personal injury to, or death of, any person, of at least ten thousand dollars."[3] During the same year in which the Connecticut legislation was enacted, in Massachusetts proponents of compulsory insurance secured the passage of legislation that required all motorists to acquire liability insurance as a prerequisite to registration of their motor vehicles.[4] For over thirty years, until 1956 when New York adopted a similar compulsory insurance law, Massachusetts remained the only state with such an insurance requirement.[5]

The Connecticut financial responsibility legislation was the prototype for statutes adopted in 27 states during the succeeding decade, and served for thirty years as a model upon which virtually all financial responsibility laws enacted in the United States were patterned.[6] However, by 1937, it was clear that further refinements were needed.[7] As a consequence, first in New Hampshire and then

3. *Id.* In the event that such person was not a resident of the state of Connecticut, the commissioner was empowered to "withdraw from such person the privilege of operation, within this state, of any motor vehicle owned by him, or refuse to register any motor vehicle transferred by him if it shall not appear to such commissioner's satisfaction that such a transfer is a bona fide sale."

4. MASSACHUSETTS ACTS 1925, Ch. 346. The compulsory insurance requirement for Massachusetts took effect on January 1, 1927.

5. Until 1970, only New York in 1956 [NEW YORK VEHICLE & TRAFFIC LAWS § 312 (McKinney 1960)] and North Carolina in 1957 [NORTH CAROLINA GEN. STATS. §§ 20-309 through 20-319 (Supp. 1957)] enacted comparable compulsory insurance requirements. For a general discussion of these statutes see R. Keeton & J. O'Connell, BASIC PROTECTION FOR THE TRAFFIC VICTIM, pp. 76-102 (Little Brown, 1965). An interesting compilation of the proposals for and discussions of compulsory insurance up to 1936 may be found in Braun, *The Financial Responsibility Laws,* 3 LAW & CONTEMP. PROBL. 505 (1936).

During the period from 1925 through 1970, there was considerable debate over the desirability of compulsory automobile liability insurance. For example, see A. Ehrenzweig, "FULL AID" INSURANCE FOR THE TRAFFIC VICTIM, pp. 9-11 (1954); W. Blum & H. Kalven, PUBLIC LAW PERSPECTIVES ON A PRIVATE LAW PROBLEM: AUTO COMPENSATION PLANS (Little Brown, 1965); DOLLARS, DELAY AND THE AUTOMOBILE VICTIM: STUDIES IN REPARATION FOR HIGHWAY INJURIES AND RELATED COURT PROBLEMS (Bobbs-Merrill Co., Inc. 1968); G. Calabresi, THE COSTS OF ACCIDENTS (Yale University Press, 1970); E. Sullivan, WHERE DID THE $13 BILLION GO? (Prentice-Hall, Inc., 1971); Marx, *Compensation Insurance for Automobile Accident Victims: The Case for Compulsory Automobile Insurance,* 15 OHIO ST. L. REV. 134 (1954); McVay, *The Case Against Compulsory Automobile Insurance,* 15 OHIO ST. L. REV. 150 (1954); Risjord and Austin, *The Problem of the Financially Irresponsible Motorist,* 24 UNIV. OF KANSAS CITY L. REV. 82, 83-84 (1955-56); *Compulsory Automobile Insurance: The Massachusetts Experience,* 438 INSURANCE L. JOURN. 404 (1959).

Also see E. L. Bowers (Editor), SELECTED ARTICLES ON COMPULSORY AUTOMOBILE INSURANCE: LIABILITY AND COMPENSATION FOR PERSONAL INJURIES (H. W. Wilson, 1929); *Symposium on Financial Protection for the Motor Accident Victim,* 3 LAW AND CONTEMP. PROBLEMS (October, 1936); James, *Accident Liability Reconsidered: The Impact of Liability Insurance,* 57 YALE L. JOURN. 549 (1948); and James & Dickinson, *Accident Proneness and Accident Law,* 63 HARVARD L. REV. 769 (1950).

6. Murphy and Netherton, *Public Responsibility and the Uninsured Motorist,* 47 GEORGETOWN L. JOURN. 700, 702 (1959).

7. If the motorist was unable to prove his or her ability to respond to a judgment up to the specified limit, the commissioner was empowered to suspend the registration of such motor vehicle

elsewhere, legislatures began to require that all motorists involved in accidents resulting in death, personal injury, or property damage exceeding a specified amount, had to automatically and within some specified time provide proof of their financial responsibility to pay any claims arising from the accident up to the limits specified in the financial responsibility law of the state (as well as to report the circumstances of the accident).[8] This approach, known as a "security type" law, eliminated the discretion to invoke the law which had been vested in some public official under the earlier Connecticut-type law. Although the application of this type of law to a particular driver still awaits an accident, once an accident occurs a driver must demonstrate financial responsibility in order to retain his or her license to operate motor vehicles. The automatic compliance feature first adopted by New Hampshire was subsequently incorporated into financial responsibility legislation throughout the United States.[9] For most motorists, acquisition of liability insurance in advance of an accident is the most practical method of being prepared to comply with the financial responsibility requirement. And in those states where the requirements were vigorously enforced, these laws induced most motorists to secure liability insurance coverage in at least the minimum amounts specified by the

or refuse thereafter to register any motor vehicles owned by such person. While technically, under the terms of the statute, the commissioner of motor vehicles (or some other designated public official) had the power to demand that such proof be provided whenever an accident occurred, in point of fact in most states state officials apparently did not take any action following an accident unless a complaint was filed by an aggrieved party. This meant that not only were motorists allowed at least one accident before the state questioned their financial responsibility, but in instances where the injured party did not complain to the commissioner's office, even the first accident did not serve to invoke the law's operation. See Corstvet, *The Uncompensated Accident and Its Consequences*, 3 LAW & CONTEMP. PROBL. 466 (1936); and the Columbia University Council for Research in the Social Sciences, REPORT BY THE COMMITTEE TO STUDY COMPENSATION FOR AUTOMOBILE ACCIDENTS, pp. 97-108, 206-08 (1932). The Columbia Report, which was released seven years after the enactment of the Connecticut future proof statute, concluded that the future proof variety of legislation was greatly ineffective, being little better an answer to the problem of the automobile tort victim's compensation than standard civil litigation. Also see Stoeckel, *Administrative Problems of Financial Responsibility Laws*, 3 LAW & CONTEMP. PROBL. 531 (1936) and Grad, REPORT FOR THE LEGISLATURE DRAFTING RESEARCH FUND (Columbia Law School, 1949), reprinted in the 1953 SEMI-FINAL REPORT OF CALIFORNIA ASSEMBLY COMM. ON FINANCE AND INSURANCE (1953).

8. NEW HAMPSHIRE LAWS 1927 § 54.1; NEW HAMPSHIRE REV. STAT. ANN. § 268.1 (1955).

9. See Murphy and Netherton, *Public Responsibility and the Uninsured Motorist*, 47 GEORGETOWN L. JOURN. 700, 706-07 (1959). A compilation of citations to state financial responsibility may be found in Ward, *New York's Motor Vehicle Accident Indemnification Corporation: Past, Present and Future*, 8 BUFFALO L. REV. 215 at 218-220, nn. 8 through 17 (1959). For an excellent discussion on the general operation of the security type statute, see R. Keeton and J. O'Connell, BASIC PROTECTION FOR THE TRAFFIC VICTIM, pp. 105-09 (1965). Also see Vorys, *A Short Survey of Laws Designed to Exclude the Financially Irresponsible Driver From the Highways*, 15 OHIO ST. L. JOURN. 101, 102-104 (1954).

respective state financial responsibility laws.[10]

By the mid-1950's, however, new pressures began to develop for additional legislation that would assure compensation for all persons injured by negligent motorists. Particularly in New York there was substantial support for the enactment of a compulsory insurance law. There was also considerable interest in New York, as well as in several other states, in proposals for the creation of an unsatisfied judgment fund from which accident victims could secure reparation if indemnification was not available from negligent motorists who were uninsured.[11] In addition, some persons sought the adoption of a compensation plan that would indemnify all accident victims without regard to fault, thereby incidentally eliminating, or at least substantially reducing, the problem of financial irresponsibility.[12]

In January, 1956, Governor Harriman delivered a special message to the New York legislature in which he outlined a comprehensive program to deal with the problem of the uncompensated traffic accident victim. The Harriman proposals included both a

10. The National Bureau of Casualty Underwriters has compiled estimates of private passenger cars insured in the United States for the years 1956, 1962 and 1963. Also see Murphy and Netherton, *Public Responsibility and the Uninsured Motorist*, 47 GEORGETOWN L. JOURN. 700, 704-07 (1959).

11. This approach to the problems created by the uninsured motorists was pioneered in the Canadian province of Manitoba, which created a state-sponsored fund to indemnify traffic accident victims injured by financially irresponsible motorists. Similar legislation has been enacted in the provinces of Alberta, British Columbia, Newfoundland, Nova Scotia, Ontario, and Prince Edward Island. North Dakota was the first state to follow suit by enacting legislation in 1947 requiring each owner of a motor vehicle to pay a fee of one dollar (in addition to the regular registration charge) for each motor vehicle registered, until a special fund of $100,000 was created. [NORTH DAKOTA CENT. CODE, §§ 39-17-01 (Supp. 1957).] Under the provisions of the North Dakota law, any resident of that state who obtains in any court of the state an uncollectible judgment exceeding $300 for bodily injury or death arising out of a motor vehicle operation within the state, may obtain payments from the fund up to certain specified limits. Although this approach has been widely discussed, only a few American states—including Maryland, Michigan, New Jersey, and New York—established comparable funds. It should be noted that recourse to the fund in each of several states differs from the pattern established in North Dakota in that the injured claimant is not required to first secure a judgment against the uninsured motorist. On this subject, see V. Hallman, UNSATISFIED JUDGMENT FUNDS (S. S. Huebner Foundation, 1968), which includes an extensive bibliography at pp. 315-334. For a shorter explication see Ward, *The Uninsured Motorist*, 9 BUFFALO L. REV. 283 (1960). Also see *Annotation, Unsatisfied Claim and Judgment Fund*, 2 A.L.R. 3d 760 (1965); *Annotation, Unsatisfied Claim Statute—Coverage*, 7 A.L.R. 3d 822 (1966); *Annotation, Uninsured Motorist Fund—Claimant*, 10 A.L.R. 3d 1166 (1966).

12. By the mid-1950's a "compensation without fault" plan had been in effect for several years in the Canadian Province of Saskatchewan. [Saskatchewan Stat. Chap. 11 (1946)]. The Saskatchewan approach basically following the principles suggested in the Columbia Report of 1932. See Columbia University Council for Research in the Social Sciences, REPORT BY THE COMMITTEE TO STUDY COMPENSATION FOR AUTOMOBILE ACCIDENTS (1932). For an interesting appraisal of Saskatchewan Plan, see Lang, *The Nature and Potential of the Saskatchewan Insurance Experiment*, 14 FLORIDA L. REV. 352 (1961). Also see A. Ehrenzweig, "FULL AID" INSURANCE FOR THE TRAFFIC VICTIM. p. 1 (1954).

requirement that every motorist provide proof of adequate financial responsibility when registering an automobile, and that the victims of uninsured motorists should be indemnified from a special fund in the event compensation was not available from the negligent motorist. Representatives of the industry argued that the Harriman plan was no longer needed because a newly available coverage, the uninsured motorist endorsement, could be added to the existing liability coverage. They maintained that this new insurance coverage would be sufficient to deal with the problem of the financially irresponsible motorist.[13] The legislators, however, were persuaded that modifications were necessary, and in 1956—some thirty years after Massachusetts enacted its compulsory insurance law—New York became the second state to adopt a compulsory insurance requirement.[14]

Notwithstanding the action of the New York legislature, the National Bureau of Casualty Underwriters subsequently announced the development and availability throughout the United States of the uninsured motorist coverage.[15] In 1957, New Hampshire became the first state to require that insurance companies include the uninsured motorist coverage in all liability policies delivered in the state or issued upon any motor vehicle principally used or garaged in the state.[16] Similar legislation was subsequently enacted in almost every state so that uninsured motorist coverage is now an integral part of most automobile insurance policies sold in the United States.[17] The

13. See A. Widiss, A GUIDE TO UNINSURED MOTORIST COVERAGE, pp. 12-13 (W. H. Anderson Co., 1969), and the sources cited therein.

14. The compulsory insurance requirement went into effect in New York on February 1, 1957. NEW YORK VEHICLE AND TRAFFIC LAW §§ 93-93K (McKinney 1960). For an excellent account of the legislative history of the New York compulsory insurance legislation, see Netherton and Nabham, *The New York Motor Vehicle Financial Security Act of 1956,* 5 AMERICAN U. L. REV. 37 (1956).

15. National Bureau of Casualty Underwriters, *News Release,* (dated Wednesday, November 14, 1956). The coverage was announced on November 8, 1956 by the National Bureau of Casualty Underwriters who proposed December 12, 1956 as the effective date of coverage under the endorsement to allow the required time to distribute the appropriate materials. General announcement letter sent by the National Bureau of Casualty Underwriters, dated November 8, 1956. Also see A. Widiss, A GUIDE TO UNINSURED MOTORIST COVERAGE, pp. 14-15 (W. H. Anderson Co., 1969), and the sources cited therein.

16. NEW HAMPSHIRE REV. STAT. ANN. § 268.1.

17. In 1958, the terms of the uninsured motorist coverage were redrafted so that the endorsement could be incorporated into the standard automobile liability policy used by the insurance industry. In the following years, every state enacted legislation in some measure governing the terms of the coverage. It should be noted that in most states the uninsured motorist legislation provides that the coverage must be included in all automobile liability insurance policies unless the purchaser rejects the additional coverage. This type of statute is generally referred to as a mandatory offering

uninsured motorist legislation was the last significant legislative development prior to the renewed interest during the 1960's in proposals for no-fault coverages.

Serious consideration of no-fault insurance was rekindled by the publication of the Keeton-O'Connell study of automobile accident compensation systems, and by their proposal for a more extensive non-fault insurance coverage for accident victims.[18] In this study, published in 1965, Professors Keeton and O'Connell concluded that neither the various first-party insurance systems nor the then-existing types of financial responsibility legislation in fact assured that adequate compensation was provided for persons who were seriously injured in automobile accidents.[19] The Keeton-O'Connell study and proposals served as a catalyst, and by the late 1960's there was increasingly significant support in many states for no-fault insurance legislation. Various non-fault or no-fault approaches to providing compensation received widespread support in Massachusetts, and in 1970 a compromise was worked out in the legislature which led to the adoption of the first no-fault law in the United States. In retrospect, the Massachusetts action represented a significant breakthrough, since it was almost immediately followed by legislation in other states. First in Florida, and subsequently in over two dozen other states, laws were enacted that in varying ways provided for insurance payments on a no-fault basis to all persons injured in automobile accidents.[20]

---

requirement. In the other states, the uninsured motorist legislation does not allow the purchaser to reject the coverage, so that in these states the uninsured motorist coverage must be included as part of the insurance package with every automobile liability insurance policy. See A. Widiss, A GUIDE TO UNINSURED MOTORIST COVERAGE, pp. 131-134 (W. H. Anderson Co., 1969), and American Insurance Association, SUMMARY OF SELECTED STATE LAWS AND REGULATIONS RELATING TO AUTOMOBILE INSURANCE, pp. 44-61 (January, 1976).

18. R. Keeton and J. O'Connell, BASIC PROTECTION FOR THE TRAFFIC VICTIM, (Little Brown, 1965). Although the study is perhaps somewhat less known by the public, an excellent analysis and empirical study was completed at about the same time by a research team at the University of Michigan. See A. Conard, J. Morgan, R. Pratt, C. Voltz, and R. Bombaugh, AUTOMOBILE ACCIDENT COSTS AND PAYMENTS: STUDIES IN THE ECONOMICS OF INJURY REPARATION (University of Michigan Press, 1964). Also see DOLLARS, DELAY AND THE AUTOMOBILE VICTIM: STUDIES IN REPARATION FOR HIGHWAY INJURIES AND RELATED COURT PROBLEMS (Bobbs-Merrill Co., Inc., 1968); and the volumes published as a result of the Department of Transportation Automobile Insurance and Compensation Study.

19. R. Keeton and J. O'Connell, BASIC PROTECTION FOR THE TRAFFIC VICTIM, at p. 3-5.

20. See American Insurance Association, SUMMARY OF SELECTED STATE LAWS AND REGULATIONS RELATING TO AUTOMOBILE INSURANCE (January, 1976). Also see Semerad, *The Automobile Accident Reparations Controversy—A Primer for Lawyers and Others*, 35 ALBANY L. REV. 460-488 (1971), in which the author analyses and compares a number of the no-fault plans; and Dinneen, *How Faultless are the No-Fault Statutes?*, 13 BOSTON COLLEGE IND. & COM. L. REV. 935-954 (1972).

2. No-Fault Automobile Insurance in Massachusetts

On January 1, 1971, Massachusetts became the first state to require that persons injured in automobile accidents be afforded the protection of a no-fault insurance that would provide indemnification for medical expenses, lost wages, and the cost of replacement services.[21] This insurance, which is denoted Personal Injury Protection (and is usually referred to by the acronym PIP) provides first party coverage of up to $2,000 for these "out-of-pocket" expenses. The PIP insurance must be included in all automobile insurance policies purchased by Massachusetts motorists.

The PIP coverage is designed to assure compensation for all persons who might be injured in an automobile accident. The legislation requires that each PIP policy cover (a) the named insured, (b) members of the named insured's household, (c) any authorized operator of an insured's vehicle, (d) any authorized passenger in the insured's vehicle including guests, and (e) any pedestrian struck by an insured vehicle.[22] The coverage is thus keyed to both the individual and the insured vehicle. Anyone who is injured while using the insured vehicle is covered unless the person has no right to be in the vehicle. In addition, it should be noted that the PIP coverage is provided to pedestrians, even when the automobile is being used by an unauthorized driver.[23] In other words, the objective of the PIP coverage is to provide indemnification on a no-fault basis for all motorists (drivers and passengers) and all pedestrians injured in any automobile accident, and the injured party is entitled to receive payments up to $2,000 from the appropriate insurance company regardless of who was responsible for the accident.

Coverage for Wage Losses. Compensation for loss of wages is provided only for earnings that are actually lost by reason of the accident, and the insurance payment is limited to 75 percent of the

21. See Compulsory Motor Vehicle Liability Insurance, Massachusetts Gen. Laws Ann. ch. 90, § 34A (Supp. 1975) (originally enacted August 13, 1970), Massachusetts Acts 1970, ch. 670 (Aug. 1970). See generally Ryan, *No-Fault Automobile Insurance* in the 1970 Annual Survey of Massachusetts Law 530-542 (Little Brown, 1971). Also see M. Woodroof, J. Fonseca and A. Squillante, Automobile Insurance and No-Fault Law §§ 11:30-:33, at 329-32 (Lawyers Cooperative Publishing Co., 1974); W. Rokes. No-Fault Insurance (Insurers Press, Inc., 1971); Kenny and McCarthy, *"No-Fault" in Massachusetts Chapter 670, Acts of 1970—A Synopsis and Analysis,* 55 Massachusetts L. Q. 23 (1970); Ghiardi and Kircher, *Automobile Insurance: An Analysis of the Massachusetts Plan,* 21 Syracuse L. Rev. 1135-1147 (1970); and Rafalowicz, *The Massachusetts "No-Fault" Automobile Insurance Law: An Analysis and Proposed Revision,* 8 Harvard Journ. of Legis. 455 (1971).

22. Massachusetts Gen. Laws Ann. ch. 90, § 34A (1975).

23. Massachusetts Gen. Laws Ann. ch. 90 § 34A (Supp. 1975) (by inference).

wages lost.[24] Thus, if a person injured in an accident had an actual wage loss of $1,000, the maximum recovery provided for under the PIP insurance is 75 percent of the $1,000 or $750. If such a claimant had any type of wage continuation plan or sick leave, the no-fault payment would be reduced by the amount of such payments. In the preceding illustration, if the claimant received sick leave payments of $500, the PIP payments would be reduced from $750 to $250. When the claimant's wages have been fully paid under some type of wage continuation plan, sick leave, or are covered by workers' compensation, there can be no recovery under the PIP coverage for lost income.

Coverage for Medical Expenses. The coverage for hospital and medical expenses includes all costs incurred within a two-year period following the accident. The injured party may collect medical expenses from both the automobile insurance company and from any accident or health insurance company, such as Blue Cross/Blue Shield.[25] However, a purchaser of a PIP policy may choose to avoid duplication in payments by opting for PIP coverage with a deductible amount of $100, $250, $500, $1,000, or $2,000.[26] If an insured covered by a policy with a deductible is injured in an accident, the amount of the claim that is paid is reduced accordingly. By electing a PIP policy with a deductible, the purchaser acquires insurance with a lower premium cost than a PIP policy with first dollar coverage. The deductible applies, not only to the purchaser, but also to any other person making a PIP claim under that coverage.

Persons Not Covered by P.I.P. The Massachusetts legislation, and the PIP endorsement form approved by the Insurance Commissioner, provide that no-fault benefits may be withheld in several situations. These exclusions come into operation in the following three situations. First, operators under the influence of alcohol or narcotic drugs are not covered. Second, persons committing a felony or seeking to avoid lawful apprehension or arrest by a police officer are not insured in the event of a motor vehicle accident. Third, the no-fault coverage is excluded for operators of motor vehicles who

24. A 1971 enactment amended the no-fault law by allowing an injured person who receives benefits under a wage continuation plan to later reimburse the plan without loss of standing. By reimbursing the wage continuation plan, an insured's right to benefits are fully restored in regard to amounts and time previously accumulated under the plan. MASSACHUSETTS ACTS 1971, ch. 794 (Sept. 1971); MASSACHUSETTS GEN. LAWS ANN. ch. 90, § 34A (1975).

26. See The Commonwealth of Massachusetts General Court Joint Committee on Insurance, NO-FAULT: ITS EFFECTIVENESS IN MASSACHUSETTS (January, 1973), p. 11. The $100 deductible was added by Chapter 339 of the Massachusetts Acts of 1972.

are injured in a situation where the operators specifically intended to cause injury or damage to themselves or others.[27]

Tort Litigations. Under the Massachusetts legislation, law suits against a negligent motorist are still permitted in several situations. First, if the economic costs sustained by an insured exceed the $2,000 coverage provided by a PIP policy, a tort action for indemnification is permissible for all out-of-pocket costs not covered by the no-fault insurance.[28] For example, if the injured person's medical costs were $400 and the lost wages were $3,100, there would be a total out-of-pocket loss of $3,500. The injured person would recover $2,000 of the $3,500 of out-of-pocket damages sustained as a result of the accident on a no-fault basis from the insured's own insurance company. The insured could then proceed in a tort action for the remaining $1,500 that was not covered by the PIP insurance. The recovery in that tort action would, of course, depend on a showing of negligence. It should be borne in mind that even though this would be a tort action, the injured person in this illustration still would not necessarily be entitled to recover damages for pain and suffering. Claims for pain and suffering are foreclosed unless one of the thresholds specified in the no-fault legislation is satisfied. In this example, the medical costs were $400, $100 less than the threshold of $500 established by the Massachusetts law. Therefore, the injured party in this case could recover damages for pain and suffering only if the injury sustained in the accident caused death, consisted in whole or part of the loss of a body member, consisted in whole or part of permanent and serious disfigurement, resulted in loss of sight or hearing, or consisted of a fracture.

Compulsory Liability Insurance and Tort Claims. The statutory mandate which requires that all motorists have liability insurance still exists in Massachusetts.[29] Under the no-fault law, the first $2,000 of "out-of-pocket" damages arising from a personal injury is collected on a no-fault basis, and claims in excess of $2,000 are determined on the basis of fault, so that liability insurance is still necessary in order to assure compensation to innocent victims beyond the PIP coverage.

---

27. MASSACHUSETTS GEN. LAWS ANN., ch. 90, § 34A (1975).

28. *See* M. Woodroof, J. Fonesca, and A. Squillante, AUTOMOBILE INSURANCE AND NO-FAULT LAW § 15:15 at 450 (1974). The claimant in such an action, however, would not be entitled to recover damages for pain and suffering unless one of the specified thresholds were met.

29. MASSACHUSETTS GEN. LAWS ANN. 90 §§ 1A, 34A-I (1969). Section 1A was originally enacted as MASSACHUSETTS ACTS 1925, ch. 346, § 1 and became effective in 1927.

PIP Coverage: Out-of-State Cars and Out-of-State Accidents. If a person who is insured under a Massachusetts PIP coverage is injured in an accident by an out-of-state car in Massachusetts, the insured is still entitled to receive benefits under the PIP coverage.[30] If a Massachusetts insured is involved in an automobile accident in another state, the insured has the option of collecting under his or her PIP coverage.[31] Alternately, the Massachusetts insured may elect to sue the out-of-state driver in tort, in which case payment of the no-fault personal injury protection benefits might be withheld by the insurer pending the resolution of that tort claim.

Property Protection Insurance. Compulsory no-fault property insurance, called Property Protection Insurance (PPI), went into effect in Massachusetts on January 1, 1972, one year after the personal injury no-fault coverage began.[32] Under PPI, property damage liability insurance was modified so that the liability coverage applied only for damages to vehicles not covered by the Massachusetts no-fault legislation. The fundamental difference introduced by the adoption of the no-fault property system was that the right to bring an action in tort against the owner of another vehicle covered by a Massachusetts policy was foreclosed, and thereby the need for property liability insurance was eliminated for accidents involving Massachusetts drivers. For any accident involving Massachusetts vehicles subject to the law, the no-fault property insurance legislation provided that owners could only collect for property damage from their own insurers. The PPI law provides that insureds may elect one of three coverage options: (1) All Risk [Collision] Coverage, (2) Restricted [Collision] Coverage, and (3) No Coverage for [the Insured's] Own Vehicles.[33] In essence, what is generally known as "collision coverage"—which is, of course, a first party no-fault coverage—became the broadest first party no-fault option for vehicle damage. Originally, subrogation between two Massachusetts-insured private passenger vehicles was also eliminated. However, the law was subsequently changed in 1973 to allow insurance companies to seek subrogation. Although the CLRS Study was not designed to analyze the effects of PPI in

---

30. See Massachusetts General Court Joint Committee on Insurance, NO-FAULT: ITS EFFECTIVENESS IN MASSACHUSETTS (January, 1973), p. 35.

31. *Ibid.*

32. No-fault coverage for property damage became mandatory on January 1, 1972. MASSACHUSETTS GEN. LAWS ANN., ch. 90, § 340 (1975), enacted as MASSACHUSETTS ACTS 1971, ch. 978 on November 3, 1971. It should be noted that in general this study did not investigate the effects or relative merits of the no-fault property coverage.

33. *Ibid.*

Massachusetts, in several instances the survey data provides information on some aspects of the impact of no-fault property insurance.[34]

3. THE C.L.R.S. MASSACHUSETTS NO-FAULT STUDY

The CLRS Massachusetts No-Fault Study is a multifaceted empirical investigation of the effects that no-fault personal injury automobile insurance has had on the automobile accident compensation system in the Commonwealth. The study examined the effect of the no-fault coverage on accident victims, the payment of claims covered by the PIP insurance, the case load in the state's courts, the role of lawyers in the claims process, and the economic effects on the legal profession produced by the statutory limitation on the right to assert tort claims. Information for the study was collected in a variety of ways, and the following chapters, which present and analyze the survey data, include descriptions of the techniques that were employed.

At the outset, it should be noted that the overall objective of the study was to examine the impact of no-fault personal injury insurance from as many vantage points as possible with a view to relating and integrating the results from different phases or segments of the study. For example, data about how accident victims were compensated under the no-fault system were developed 1) directly from the victims' perspective through personal interviews with persons reported to have been visibly injured in automobile accidents, 2) from interviews with attorneys who represent claimants, and 3) from an examination of insurance company claims files. The acquisition and analysis of data from several sources not only provided an overall view, but often served to corroborate information developed in a particular segment of the study. In addition, in several instances an opportunity was afforded for further investigation of a question that remained unclear or unanswered in some earlier phase of the investigation.

There were four principal segments in the Massachusetts study. First, information was sought from accident victims. Interviews were conducted with more than one thousand persons who were identified in reports filed with the Massachusetts Registry of Motor Vehicles as having been visibly injured in automobile accidents. These interviews were designed to acquire information both from persons who had

---

34. See especially, R. Bovbjerg, *The Impact of No-Fault Auto Insurance on Massachusetts Courts,* 11 NEW ENGLAND L. REV. 325, 343-353 (1976).

decided not to seek indemnification from the PIP insurer and from those who had pursued their PIP claims. In the pretests that were conducted for this phase of the study, we found that the interviewees had great difficulty providing accurate information on the amount of their claims or the amounts they were paid by insurance companies in response to claims. The inability of accident victims interviewed in the pretest to provide detailed claims information led to formulation of the plan for a separate segment of the study that would focus on data in insurance company claims files. The idea was that if the cooperation of a group of companies could be secured, it would be possible to develop precise and accurate data directly from insurance company files. This undertaking became the second major study segment.

One of the most intriguing questions in regard to the impact of the Massachusetts no-fault law was how the limitation on tort claims would affect the state's judicial system. Because the time from accident to trial in automobile tort cases is often several years, this portion of the CLRS study—the third of the four segments—was based on a survey of court filings in selected district and superior courts throughout the state.

The fourth segment was an investigation of how no-fault was affecting the professional lives of lawyers practicing in Massachusetts. In addition, information from lawyers was sought on how the PIP claims process worked, the role of the lawyers in making PIP claims, and the relationship between PIP claims and tort claims. A variety of techniques and approaches were employed in the course of developing information from lawyers—ranging from a mail survey that was sent to every third lawyer in the state to personal interviews with bar leaders.

Finally, it should be noted that discussions with lawyers, insurance industry executives, and government employees were essential in setting the course of the study. Although these discussions were not directly the basis for the findings presented in the following chapters, they were very important in the formulation of the survey design, and were often helpful in the course of analyzing the survey data.

CHAPTER 2
ACCIDENT VICTIMS UNDER
NO-FAULT AUTOMOBILE INSURANCE:
A MASSACHUSETTS SURVEY*

Alan I. Widiss**

I. INTRODUCTION

A. *Automobiles, Accidents, and Insurance Legislation*

It is well recognized that motor vehicles have contributed significantly to many of the vast economic and social changes that have occurred in the United States during the twentieth century. Among the principal societal problems accompanying the ever-expanding number of motor vehicles has been a concomitant increase in accidents resulting in personal injuries and deaths. The question of how to provide adequate compensation to persons injured or to relatives of those killed in motor vehicle accidents dates, of course, from the earliest use of automobiles. However, it was the advent of the mass-produced automobile, which placed the potential for causing substantial injuries literally in the hands of millions of people, that transformed the compensation question into a major social issue. Throughout the past 60 years, the availability of compensation for those injured as the result of motor vehicle accidents has turned primarily on an application of common law tort principles. Such

*This article reports on one segment of the Massachusetts No-Fault Study, a project of the Council on Law-Related Studies. The Council is a small private foundation created in 1969 by the Walter E. Meyer Research Institute of Law, Inc., which supported many of the studies of automobile accident compensation in the 1960's. For the Massachusetts study, the Council retained the author to serve as Director, and Mr. Randall R. Bovbjerg as Associate Director, of a broadly based empirical investigation of how the implementation of no-fault automobile insurance affected (1) the compensation system for persons involved in automobile accidents, (2) the number of automobile tort cases in the courts, and (3) members of the legal profession.

It goes without saying that a project of this type would have been virtually impossible without the cooperation of both public and private institutions and individuals. From the first contact in 1971, Governor Francis Sargent supported the idea of such a study and made his good offices available in a manner which helped secure the assistance of various government agencies. Similarly, the cooperation of the then Commissioner of Insurance, John Ryan, was invaluable, and Commissioner Ryan's staff was repeatedly generous in making relevant information available.

During the course of the study, many persons responded to requests for aid, counsel, or advice. At this point, it would be impossible to identify all of those who have made such contributions. However, a special note of acknowledgment is due Dr. Floyd J. Fowler, Director of the Survey Research Program (which did the interviewing for the study) and Mr. James R. Grifhorst who did the computer programming for the data analysis. In addition, I should like to acknowledge the efforts of several persons who worked on this phase of the study while they were law students of the University of Iowa: Ms. Marianne Baldridge, Ms. Jane Eikleberry, Mr. James E. Konsky, Mr. William P. Kovacs, Mr. Gary P. Malfeld, Mr. Donald F. Staas, and Mr. John C. Schupe.

Finally, drafts of this article have been sent to many persons, including insurance executives, lawyers, and professors of law or social science, who have provided extremely helpful comments and critiques. To each of these persons I am indebted.

** Professor of Law, University of Iowa; B.S. 1960, University of Southern California; LL.B. 1963, University of Southern California; LL.M. 1964, Harvard University.

Editor's Note: Reproduced from *Iowa Law Review*, Volume 61, October 1975, Number 1

principles predicate the right to be compensated on an allocation of fault among the parties to the accident.[1]

As the number of motor vehicles on the roads has increased, so too has the concern over the hazards they pose. Since 1925, state governments have enacted various forms of legislation designed to assure innocent accident victims that negligent operators or the owners of automobiles would be able to provide indemnification.[2] Most of the legislation adopted between 1925 and 1960 was directed at inducing motorists to acquire some minimum amount of liability insurance.[3] By the 1950's the majority of motorists throughout the United States, and almost all drivers in Massachusetts in accordance with the state's compulsory insurance law,[4] routinely purchased automobile liability coverage that distributed at least some portion of the economic risk of

---

1. There are many major works which examine the desirability of applying the fault system to motor vehicle accidents. For various approaches to the question, see W. BLUM & H. KALVEN. PUBLIC LAW PERSPECTIVES ON A PRIVATE LAW PROBLEM: AUTO COMPENSATION PLANS (1965); G. CALABRESI. THE COSTS OF ACCIDENTS (1970); A. CONARD. J. MORGAN. R. PRATT. C. VOLTZ & R. BOMBAUGH. AUTOMOBILE ACCIDENT COSTS AND PAYMENTS: STUDIES IN THE ECONOMICS OF INJURY REPARATION (1964); R. KEETON & J. O'CONNELL. BASIC PROTECTION FOR THE TRAFFIC VICTIM: A BLUEPRINT FOR REFORMING AUTOMOBILE INSURANCE (1965). *See also* DEPARTMENT OF TRANSPORTATION. AUTOMOBILE INSURANCE AND COMPENSATION STUDY: THE ORIGINS AND DEVELOPMENT OF THE NEGLIGENCE ACTION — STUDIES OF THE ROLE OF FAULT IN AUTOMOBILE ACCIDENT COMPENSATION LAW (1970).

2. *See* Murphy and Netherton, *Public Responsibility and the Uninsured Motorist* 47 GEO. L.J. 700, 701-10 (1959). For a discussion of the first financial responsibility laws, see Heyting, *Automobiles and Compulsory Liability Insurance,* 16 A.B.A. 362 (1930). *See also* Risjord and Austin, *The Problem of the Financially Irresponsible Motorist.* 24 U. KAN. CITY L. REV. 82 (1955). An interesting comparative analysis of various legislative enactments dealing with the problem of financial irresponsibility is found in Ward, *The Uninsured Motorist: National and International Protection Presently Available and Comparative Problems in Substantial Similarity,* 9 BUFFALO L. REV. 283 (1960).

3. *See generally* Murphy and Netherton, *Public Responsibility and the Uninsured Motorist,* 47 GEO. L. J. 700, 701-10 (1959).

4. MASS. GEN. LAWS ANN. 90 §§ 1A, 34A-I (1969) (Section 1A was originally enacted as Mass. Acts 1925, ch. 346, § 1 and became effective in 1927). See Murphy & Netherton, *Public Responsibility and the Uninsured Motorist,* 47 GEO. L. J. 700, 702-83 (1959) for a historical discussion of the Massachusetts compulsory insurance law. From 1927 to the late 1960's, only New York in 1956, N.Y. Veh. & Traf. Law § 312 (McKinney 1970), and North Carolina in 1957, N.C. Gen. Stat. §§ 20-309 through 20-311 (1975), enacted comparable compulsory insurance requirements. For a general discussion of these statutes see R. KEETON & J. O'CONNELL. BASIC PROTECTION FOR THE TRAFFIC VICTIM: A BLUEPRINT FOR REFORMING AUTOMOBILE INSURANCE 76-102 (1965). An interesting compilation of the proposals for and discussions of compulsory insurance up to 1936 may be found in Braun, *The Financial Responsibility Law,* 3 LAW & CONTEMPORARY PROBLEMS 505 (1936).

There has been considerable debate over the desirability of compulsory automobile liability insurance. For example, see W. BLUM & H KALVEN. PUBLIC LAW PERSPECTIVES ON A PRIVATE LAW PROBLEM: AUTO COMPENSATION PLANS (1965); G. CALABRESI. THE COSTS OF ACCIDENTS: A LEGAL AND ECONOMIC ANALYSIS. (1970), A. EHRENZWIEG. "FULL AID" INSURANCE FOR THE TRAFFIC VICTIM, 9-11 (1954); Marx, *Compensation Insurance for Automobile Accident Victims: The Case for Compulsory Automobile Compensation Insurance,* 15 OHIO ST. L. J. 134 (1954); McVAY. *The Case Against Compulsory Automobile Insurance,* 15 OHIO ST. L. J. 150 (1954); Risjord & Austin, *The Problem of the Financially Irresponsible Motorist,* 24 U. KAN. CITY L. REV. 82, 83-84 (1955); Comment, 10

liability for injuries.[5] Typically, drivers in Massachusetts and elsewhere acquired automobile insurance with liability limits that satisfied the minimum requirement of the applicable state financial responsibility law.

By the early 1960's, however, the existence of financial responsibility laws had not stopped the continuing increase in highway accidents, and the annual toll of injuries to persons and property had attained staggering proportions.[6] For example, in 1962 traffic deaths exceeded 40,000 for the first time and continued to climb in succeeding years.[7] The incidence of personal injuries which disabled the victim beyond the day of the accident ranged from 1.6 to 2.0 million per year during 1963 through 1970.[8] Moreover, the National Safety Council estimated that, in 1963, a typical year during this period, traffic accidents caused wage losses of $2 billion, medical expenses of $450 million, and property damage of $2.6 billion.[9] It is not surprising that these conditions led to several studies which examined the adequacy of the compensation system for automobile accident victims. In 1965, Professors Robert E. Keeton and Jeffrey O'Connell completed such a study and concluded that "the present automobile claims system . . . provides too little, too late . . ." and that the compensation paid is "unfairly allocated, at wasteful cost, and through means that promote dishonesty and disrespect for law."[10] Having made this appraisal of the then existing compensation system, Professors Keeton and O'Connell proposed the "development of a new form of compulsory automobile insurance (called basic protection insurance), which in its nature is an extension of the principle of medical payments coverage."[11] They envisioned an insurance that would compensate "all persons injured in automobile accidents without regard to fault for all types of out-of-pocket personal injury losses up to certain limits."[12]

VILL. L. REV. 545, 546-47 (1965); *Compulsory Automobile Insurance: The Massachusetts Experience,* 438 INS. L.J. 404 (1959).

5. *See* A. WIDISS. A GUIDE TO UNINSURED MOTORIST COVERAGE 1-12 (1969), and the authorities cited therein.

6. Statistical reports on the numbers and types of motor vehicle related injuries sustained in the United States are periodically published by many federal and state agencies. For a thorough exposition of such injuries incurred from 1968 to 1973, the period most relevant to the study described in this Article, see FEDERAL HIGHWAY ADMINISTRATION. U.S. DEPT. OF TRANSP., FATAL AND INJURY ACCIDENT RATES (1974).

7. *See* the annual editions of Accident Facts published by the National Safety Council. NATIONAL SAFETY COUNCIL. ACCIDENT FACTS (1963) at 40; (1965) at 40; (1966) at 40; (1968) at 40; (1969) at 40; (1970) at 40.

8. NATIONAL SAFETY COUNCIL. ACCIDENT FACTS (1964) at 40; (1965) at 40; (1966) at 40; (1967) at 40; (1968) at 40; (1969) at 40; (1970) at 40, (1971) at 40.

9. NATIONAL SAFETY COUNCIL. ACCIDENT FACTS 5 (1964).

10. R. KEETON & J. O'CONNELL. BASIC PROTECTION FOR THE TRAFFIC VICTIM: A BLUEPRINT FOR REFORMING AUTOMOBILE INSURANCE 3 (1965).

11. *Id.* at 5.

12. *Id.*

Professors Keeton and O'Connell further proposed "granting to basic protection insureds an exemption from tort liability. . . in those cases in which damages would not exceed the $10,000 limit of basic protection coverage."[13] These proposals renewed the debate over the desirability of no-fault compensation for persons injured in automobile accidents, which led to the enactment of the Massachusetts no-fault automobile insurance law in 1970, and subsequently to no-fault laws in other states.[14]

B. No-Fault Automobile Insurance in Massachusetts

On January 1, 1971, the Massachusetts no-fault law became operative. Its general objective is to provide indemnification on a no-fault basis for all drivers, passengers, and pedestrians injured in any automobile accident.[15] This statutorily required coverage, known as Personal Injury Protection (P.I.P.), provides first party insurance of up to $2,000 for loss of wages,[16] hospital and medical expenses incurred within two years of the accident, and the cost of replacement services occasioned by the injury.[17] The P.I.P. insurance provides coverage for the following individuals: the named insured, members of the insured's household, any authorized operator of the insured's vehicle, any authorized passenger in the insured's vehicle (including guests), and any pedestrian struck by the insured vehicle.[18] The coverage is thus keyed to both the individual and the insured vehicle. Persons injured while using an insured vehicle are covered unless they have no right to be in the vehicle. In addition, P.I.P. coverage is provided to innocent pedestrians, even when the auto which

---

13. *Id.*

14. *See generally* M. WOODROFF, J. FONSECA, & A. SQUILLANTE, AUTOMOBILE INSURANCE AND NO-FAULT LAW §§11:30-:33, at 329-32 (1974); W. ROKES, NO-FAULT INSURANCE (1971). The Council on Law-Related Studies provided grants for studies of the impact of no-fault automobile insurance in Florida and Delaware. The results of the Delaware study are reported in Clark & Waterson, "No-Fault" in Delaware, 6 Rutgers-Camden L. J. 225 (1974). A preliminary report on the Florida study appeared in Little, *How No-Fault Is Working In Florida*, 59 A.B.A. J. 1020 (1973).

A preliminary view of the results from other segments of the C.L.R.S. Massachusetts No-Fault Study is reported in Widiss & Bovbjerg, *No-Fault in Massachusetts: Its Impact on Courts and Lawyers*, 59 A.B.A. J. 487 (1973).

15. *See* Compulsory Motor Vehicle Liability Insurance, MASS. GEN. LAWS ANN. ch. 90, § 34A (Supp. 1975) (originally enacted August 13, 1970, Mass. Acts 1970, ch. 670 (Aug. 1970).

16. A 1971 enactment amended the no-fault law by allowing an injured person who receives benefits under a wage continuation plan to later reimburse the plan without loss of standing. By reimbursing the wage continuation plan, an insured's right to benefits are fully restored in regard to amounts and time previously accumulated under the plan. Mass. Acts 1971, ch. 794 (Sept. 1971). *See* MASS. GEN. LAWS ANN. ch. 90, §34A (Supp. 1975).

17. MASS. GEN. LAWS ANN. ch. 90, § 34A (Supp. 1975).

18. *Id.* Since the no-fault act in Massachusetts limits coverage for these individuals to injuries "while in or upon, or while entering into or alighting from or being struck as a pedestrian by [the insured vehicle]," *Id.* It appears that a person loading or unloading a vehicle may not be covered under this provision. *Id.*

strikes them is being used by an unauthorized driver.[19]

The Massachusetts legislation also creates a limited tort exemption in regard to accidents occurring within the state. Injured persons may recover for pain and suffering only if their medical expenses exceed $500, or if the accident causes death, involves a fracture, the loss of a body member, or permanent or serious disfigurement, or results in the loss of sight or hearing.[20] A tort action may be brought, however, for any actual losses not compensated by the P.I.P. coverage.[21]

The essence, then, of the Massachusetts no-fault law is, first, that persons are provided with up to $2,000 of no-fault insurance and, second, that injured persons may not sue for pain and suffering unless at least one of the possible conditions enumerated above is satisfied. The question of whether this system of no-fault insurance is a significant improvement over other forms of accident indemnification has been widely debated. The empirical study which is the subject of this Article was conducted with a view toward providing answers to some elements of this many-faceted question.[22]

C. The Accident Victim Survey: Scope and Objectives

Discussions on the merits of no-fault automobile insurance have involved a variety of issues, one of the most recurrent being whether such a modification of the tort compensation system will produce lower insurance premiums for the public.[23] The cost of no-fault insurance, of course, depends partially on what effect implementation of the coverage will have on the number of claims paid, since indemnification from automobile insurance companies under a no-fault system is available to all persons injured in automobile accidents, rather than being restricted to individuals whose injuries were caused by the negligence of insured drivers.[24] The essential question is whether payments to those persons

---

19. Mass. Gen Laws Ann. ch. 90, § 34A (Supp. 1975) (by inference).

20. *Id.* ch. 231, § 60 (Supp. 1975).

21. *See* M. Woodroof, J. Fonseca, & A. Squillante, Automobile Insurance and No-Fault Law § 15:15 at 450 (1974). *But cf.* Massachusetts Continuing Legal Education, Inc., The Massachusetts No-Fault Insurance Law 58 (1971). The claimant in such an action would not be entitled to recover damages for pain and suffering unless one of the specified thresholds were met.

If a Massachusetts driver is involved in an out-of-state accident and is sued, the tort exemption of the no-fault personal injury protection would not apply. Thus, Massachusetts drivers still need liability coverage for out-of-state accidents and for in-state accidents where the special damages exceed the $2,000 tort exemption, as well as for in-state accidents where one of the tort thresholds is satisfied thereby allowing an action for pain and suffering.

22. The no-fault law has been amended by Mass. Acts 1971, ch. 978 (Nov. 3, 1971) to include no-fault coverage for property damage. Mass. Gen. Laws Ann., ch. 90, § 34O (Supp. 1975). This study does not investigate the effects or relative merits of the no-fault property coverage.

23. For example, *see Sargent's Estimate of No-Fault 'Savings' Not Based on Insurance Department Evaluation*, The Weekly Underwriter, June 5, 1971, at 11.

24. *See* text accompanying notes 15-21 *supra*.

who could not have recovered under the fault system will exceed the projected economies produced both by limiting recoveries for pain and suffering and by reducing various other costs associated with the operation of the fault system. Some observers have predicted that, rather than lowering insurance premiums, no-fault automobile coverage would produce higher automobile insurance rates, since the new system would compensate many persons who formerly would not have been entitled to make claims.

Since Massachusetts was the first state to enact a no-fault law, the claims experience there has been, and continues to be, a subject of considerable interest. When reports on the first few months of no-fault insurance in Massachusetts indicated that the total number of automobile insurance claims was decreasing,[25] ascertaining what lay behind this claims trend, including the effect, if any, of no-fault insurance, became even more intriguing. Careful examination of this situation made it apparent that there was perhaps only one technique for obtaining the information needed to answer the questions raised. Interviewing persons who were actually involved in automobile accidents in Massachusetts seemed to be the most practical method of learning the extent to which persons who were injured in these accidents were choosing not to make claims under the available no-fault insurance coverage, and the reasons why such potential claimants (if there was an identifiable group) were not seeking indemnification. Once this basic approach was adopted, it became evident that several other interesting lines of inquiry could probably be best pursued in interviews with accident victims. After some experimentation with various questionnaires, four primary objectives for this study were established.

First, an attempt would be made to determine whether a significant number of persons injured in automobile accidents were deciding not to pursue a recovery under no-fault insurance. Second, if such a group was identified, the next objective of the survey would be to ascertain why these persons had chosen not to seek indemnification from the appropriate automobile insurer. Third, the questionnaire would be designed to secure information about the availability and use of other sources of indemnification by automobile accident victims for injuries that were covered by no-fault insurance. In other words, information would be sought on the actual use of collateral sources in order to ascertain the extent of duplication of coverage, and to determine whether the

---

25. *See, e.g.,* Insurance Claims in 'No-fault' Drop, NEW YORK TIMES. Apr. 24, 1971, at 58, col. 5,6; *Mass. Insurers Urge 'Guarded Optimisim' in Early Drop in 'No-Fault' Claims,* THE WEEKLY UNDERWRITER. March 20, 1971, at 8; *Farnam Ecstatic Over Early Result of Massachusetts No-Fault Program,* BUSINESS INSURANCE. Apr. 26, 1971, at 10.

availability of other sources of indemnification was a significant influence on the decisions accident victims were making about pursuing no-fault insurance (P.I.P.) claims. This information was deemed highly important, as the availability and use of collateral sources has been regarded as a significant factor in evaluating different compensation systems, and because relatively little information on the existence and utilization of collateral sources has been published to date.[26] In addition, data on the use of collateral sources were considered important because the receipt of indemnification from such sources constituted one of the most plausible explanations for the decrease in the Massachusetts automobile insurance claims rate. Fourth, the questionnaire would be designed to secure an evaluation from the accident victims' perspective of how well the no-fault insurance coverage was working.

The purposes of this Article are to acquaint the reader with the methodology used in the study, to present the results of the survey, and to consider the implications of the results as they relate to an evaluation of the no-fault insurance system. Part II of this Article provides an explanation of how the design for this portion of the no-fault study was conceived and implemented. Information is presented on how the survey approach was developed, the process employed for sampling the population of accident victims, and the interviewing methods used to collect the data. The final section of Part II discusses how representative the interviewees were of Masacusetts automobile accident victims generally.

The methodology section is followed by a summary of the data on the injuries sustained by the interviewees and the attendant consequences of these injuries. In Part III, the accident consequences for all of the respondents are described in order to provide the reader with a perspective that should prove helpful in considering the analysis in the succeeding sections that focus on the non-claimants and P.I.P. claimants as distinct groups. In Part IV, the analysis of the data provided by those respondents who chose not to make a no-fault claim explicates the factors which led potential claimants not to pursue indemnification from their no-fault insurer.[27] In Part V, consideration shifts to the information developed from those respondents who did make P.I.P. claims; this part

---

26. For an excellent study which has developed information and data on the availability and use of collateral sources, see A. CONARD. J. MORGAN. R. PRATT. JR.. C VOLTZ, & R. BOMBAUGH. AUTOMOBILE ACCIDENTS COSTS AND PAYMENTS: STUDIES IN THE ECONOMICS OF INJURY REPARATION (1964). The introduction to this study includes an extensive bibliography of the earlier field surveys of accident costs and reparation. *Id.* at 15-16. Since the publication of the above study, the Department of Transportation has completed its Automobile Insurance and Compensation Study which contributed several significant works to the literature. For example, see U.S. DEP'T. OF TRANS.. ECONOMIC CONSEQUENCES OF AUTO ACCIDENT INJURIES (1970).

27. *See* text accompanying notes 79-112 *infra.*

includes an analysis of whether the data indicate that the P.I.P. claimants differed in any significant respects from the non-claimants.[28] The Article then focuses on the data derived from those survey questions designed to illuminate claimants' relative degrees of satisfaction or dissatisfaction with the way in which their claims were processed and with the amount of indemnification received.[29]

In the sections which present the data gathered during the survey, the objective is primarily to report the results of the interviews with the persons selected for the study. Comments on the meaning of the data, including the author's observations and conclusions, are deferred until Part VI of this Article.

II. PROJECT DESIGN

A. The Pilot Study

Initially, the study was to include interviews with persons injured in accidents occurring both before and after the implementation of no-fault automobile insurance in Massachusetts. The plan was to acquire data from both groups on (1) the nature of their accident injury (if any) and the extent of the injury-related expenses; (2) whether a claim for indemnification had been made, and if not, why not; and, (3) if a claim had been made for indemnification from an automobile insurance company, how satisfied the insured was with the way the claim had been handled and the amount that had been paid.

In the spring of 1972, a pilot study was performed to evaluate the feasibility of this approach. This preliminary investigation revealed several problems. First, a substantial portion of the persons randomly selected for the pilot study could not be located. This problem was particularly acute in regard to those persons who had been involved in accidents that had occurred in the pre-no-fault period. For persons in this group, almost two years had intervened between the date of the accident and the time when the interviews were sought. The interviewers found that a large number of the potential respondents appeared to have moved in the interim, and that locating these persons was relatively difficult in most instances, and impossible in some. Second, many of the persons from the group whom interviewers were able to locate still had claims or lawsuits pending, and these persons frequently either did not feel free to, or had been instructed by their lawyers not to, discuss the accident or their subsequent experiences. Moreover, even when respondents were not reluctant to discuss their claims, generally they still could not provide the relevant information. For example, where lawsuits

---

28. *See* text accompanying notes 112-19 *infra.*
29. *See* text accompanying notes 119-40 *infra.*

were still pending, respondents obviously could not know how satisfied they would be with the final outcome. In addition, many of the persons who were located and who wanted to cooperate had great difficulty in providing an accurate report either of what their actual economic losses had been, or of the amount of money which had been paid by the insurance company in satisfaction of their claim. Often the interviewee could not supply the information because the insurer had paid hospitals and doctors directly, or the insurance benefits hadbeen sen to the claimant's attorney, who had then paid such bills for the client.

As a result of the experience with the pilot study, the project design was changed in several ways. First, it was decided that, rather than attempting to acquire information on the amounts of insurance paid from interviews with claimants, such data could be more accurately developed by a study which examined insurance company closed claim files.[30] Second, the effort to interview persons who had been injured prior to no-fault was abandoned. Third, the interview schedule was modified to focus directly on the objectives outlined in the introduction to this Article.[31] The decision to acquire certaîn elements of the claims data from the closed claim files of a representative group of insurance companies facilitated the creation of a survey instrument that was appropriate for use in both telephone and personal interviews. After some pre-testing of the revised survey instrument, the interviewing was begun in March, 1973. Although most of the interviewing was done during the succeeding three months, the last interviews were not completed until October, 1973.[32]

B. Selection of Persons to be Interviewed

The accident victims to be interviewed were randomly selected from reports that are filed with the Massachusetts Registry of Motor Vehicles following accidents.[33] Under state law, accident reports must be pre-

---

30. The character and scope of this undertaking, as well as certain advantages it afforded over attempting to acquire this information in other ways, will be reported in a separate article.

31. *See* text accompanying notes 23-27 *supra.*

32. The survey instruments used in the interviews for this study have been deposited at the University of Iowa College of Law. The data were placed on computer tapes, and those tapes are currently on file at the University of Iowa Computer Center. When all phases of the study are completed, all of the computer tapes and survey instruments will be deposited in the University of Iowa College of Law Library. A copy of the survey questionnaire is reproduced at APPENDIX A.

33. More precisely, the sample for this study was selected from among persons who were reported to have been visibly injured during August, 1972, in accident reports from the entire state submitted to the Massachusetts Registry of Motor Vehicles. The Registry accident report files for each year are organized by the city or town in which the accident occurred (*not* where the injured people live). Boston is subdivided into sections such as Roxbury and Dorchester. There are 39 cities and 312 towns in Massachusetts. The files for accidents in each location are kept in chronological order determined by the date of the accident. Reports on a single accident from all operators and Police are

pared and submitted by each operator of a motor vehicle involved in an automobile accident that results either in personal injuries or in property damages in excess of $200.[34] In some cases, a report is also completed by the police or sheriff's department when such officers have been on the scene or have made a subsequent accident investigation. The report form requests that information be provided on all persons who were injured in the accident, and that the severity of the injury be indicated.[35] The person preparing the report is directed to describe the gravity of the injury by checking one of the following four characterizations:

1. Killed
2. Visible signs of injury, as bleeding wound, or distorted member; or had to be carried from scene
3. Other visible injury, as bruises, abrasions, swelling, limping, etc.
4. No visible injury but complains of pain or momentary unconsciousness[36]

---

stapled together. Registry procedure calls for the Police report to be placed on top if there is one. If there is no police report, the form with the most information is placed at the top.

Accident reports from the entire state for August, 1972, formed the basis of the victim survey. Registry personnel searched the August files in December, 1972. Xerox copies were made of the front page of every top report which indicated that at least one person was injured. When more than three persons were injured, thereby exhausting the space on the top page, copies of the under pages were made.

The Registry, according to their count, supplied us with approximately 3936 reports, each of which identified one or more injured persons. However, the Registry figures show that there were about 4,700 injury accidents in August, 1972, so the survey was short some 700 accidents. There are several factors which may explain at least part of the discrepancy.

First, three clerks and a supervisor worked 28 hours overtime to do the search. This allows about 30 seconds per accident to locate, withdraw, examine, xerox if necessary, and replace the record. Thus, speed may have caused some errors. In addition, many of the reports were either very difficult to decipher or incomplete; therefore forms may have been skipped. For example, on some forms, injuries were checked but no names were given, and in one case a dog was identified as an injured person.

Second, the sampling at the Registry was done from transfer cartons, not from the permanent files, as the reports were en route between the Accident Records section of the Regsitry and the Computer Section. It seems possible that some subsets were passed over or had been mislaid, even though the Registry people were insistent that all records had been searched.

Third, more than half of the top accident reports show only property damage, and these files were passed over. Some injured persons were left out of the survey because their names were buried under a top report that showed only property damage. In addition, others may have been passed where the top report showed only one of two persons injured, but did not include someone who was identified on an under sheet. In such cases, the Registry personnel would not have checked the under sheet. However, this was probably not a problem of serious dimensions. A spot check was made of the entire file for 300 accidents in six towns. Among the 300 files, the top sheet showed the persons injured in all but five of the files. The reports underneath in these five files disclosed that persons were injured, but that such persons were not identified on the top sheet.

34. Mass. Gen. Laws Ann., ch. 90, § 26 (1969).

35. The Massachusetts Registry of Motor Vehicles' form for reporting a motor vehicle accident is on file at the University of Iowa, College of Law. Copies of the form may be obtained by writing to the Massachusetts Registry.

36. See id.

Since the person filing the report is specifically instructed to mark the first category that applies,[37] the indication on the report is, theoretically, of the most severe injury incurred.

For a variety of reasons, several distinct groups of reports were excluded when the sample was randomly selected from the Registry's accident files. First, no attempt was made to interview relatives of persons who were reported to have been killed in the accident. However, since relatively few persons, as compared to the total number of accident victims, are killed in automobile accidents during any time period, this decision had almost no impact on the sample drawn for the survey.[38]

The second group excluded were those persons who were described as having no visible injuries, but whose names had been included in accident reports because they had complained of pain or momentary unconsciousness. As explained above, the study was designed to focus on individuals who were potential claimants under P.I.P. coverage.[39] It was decided that individuals reported as having sustained no visible injury were not as likely to have injuries that would produce a P.I.P. claim. This category comprised over 41 percent of the persons reported to the Registry as having been injured in 1972.[40] Consequently, the decision to eliminate these persons represented a significant exclusion, at least in terms of numbers, but one which was viewed as essential to the execution of the study. To have done otherwise would have necessitated contacting great numbers of persons who had sustained no significant injuries. Moreover, there was no reason to suspect that the experiences of these individuals would be any different from those of the persons whose injuries were more "visible" at the time of the accident.[41]

The files which were elected for the study were limited to those in which there was an indication that one or more of the persons involved had been visibly injured. Following these guideline, several staff members of the Registry of Motor Vehicles copied the accident reports for August, 1972. The reports copied were then randomly sampled to

---

37. *See id.*

38. The Registry of Motor Vehicles reported that in August, 1972, there were 81 accidents that involved a death. This fatality level is comparable to those of other months in 1972. For example, in May there were 82 fatal accidents, in July there were 83, and in November there were 80 accidents involving a death. *See* COMMONWEALTH OF MASSACHUSETTS REGISTRY OF MOTOR VEHICLES, 1972 STATISTICAL FILES 2 (1973).

The Registry prepares annual editions of the statistical files which may be obtained by writing the Registry at 100 Nashua Street, Boston, Massachusetts 02114. Hereinafter, these files will be cited as REGISTRY STATISTICAL FILES.

39. *See* text accompanying notes 23-27 *supra*.

40. 1972 REGISTRY STATISTICAL FILES. *supra* note 38, at 17.

41. About one-half of the persons included in the group interviewed stated that they received no injuries or only minor injuries. In light of this finding, the decision to not interview persons who were not visibly injured appears even more reasonable.

produce a group of 1,425 persons who were reported to have been visibly injured in automobile accidents that occurred during August. From this sample, several additional small groups were subsequently excluded, including (1) persons who were not covered by the no-fault insurance because they had been riding motorcycles;[42] (2) persons whose residences were listed as being out-of-state; and (3) persons whose identity could not be sufficiently determined because of a garbled accident report. This process reduced the sample of 1,425 persons to approximately 1,350 potential interviewees.

C. The Interviewing Process

The interviewing, which was carried out by the field staff of the Survey Research Program (a facility of The University of Massachusetts at Boston, and the Joint Center for Urban Studies of Massachusetts Institute of Technology and Harvard University), was divided into two phases. In the first phase, the interviewing was conducted by telephone; the second phase consisted of in-person interviews with subjects who could not be contacted by telephone. Before beginning the interviewing, the 1,350 potential respondents were sent a letter which briefly described the study and indicated that an interviewer would telephone. In instances where the injured person was a child, the letter describing the study was sent to a parent of the child, and when the interviewer called, information was sought from an adult in the household who knew about the accident and its consequences. Usually this individual was one of the child's parents.

Following the mailing of the pre-interview letters, interviewers began trying to contact the 1,350 potential interviewees. During the first phase of the interviewing, a period of several weeks, 844 telephone interviews were successfully conducted. When this phase was completed, there remained some 506 persons in the sample with whom no interview had been obtained for a variety of reasons, including: (1) impossibility of finding their telephone number; (2) refusal by the respondent to be interviewed over the telephone; and (3) interviewers' lack of success in finding the respondent at home. The files for persons with whom no interview had been obtained were then reviewed to determine whether additional efforts to contact and interview were likely to be successful. In cases where the record in the file indicated that the refusal to be interviewed was absolute, or where the prsons were found to have died,

---

42. Rule 60 issued by the Massachusetts Commissioner of Insurance on December 4, 1970, excluded P.I.P. coverage for bodily injury sustained while operating or occupying a motorcycle. P.I.P. insurance, however, is provided under a motorcyclist's policy to a pedestrian who is struck by an insured motorcycle. *See* MASS. AUTO RATING AND ACCIDENT PREVENTION BUREAU, GENERAL NOTICE No. G-555 (Jan. 12, 1971).

and in a few other cases where the contact indicated that further interviewer effort would not be fruitful, the files were set aside. Almost 200 files were so characterized by the professional staff of the Survey Research Program, leaving a group of approximately 300 persons. Primarily, the remaining 300 individuals were persons who had no telephone or who repeatedly could not be reached when the interviewer called. In order to minimize any possible bias that might have been introduced by the failure to include data from such a group, it was decided that interviewers would try to contact half of this group in person. Therefore, 143 files were randomly selected for inclusion in this second phase of the interviewing.

Interviewers then went to the addresses given in the accident reports for the persons reported as injured. Where the respondent had moved, an effort was made to find out the new address, and follow-up attempts at interviewing were made if the individual still lived in Massachusetts. Whenever possible, the subjects were visited at their homes, and personal interviews were conducted. In a few instances, information was obtained in the course of visiting the residence that made it possible to contact the person and conduct an interview over the telephone. Of the 143 persons who were selected from the original sample to be included in this second phase of the survey, 106 were successfully interviewed. Because the selection process sought follow-ups from a random half of those who had not been successfully interviewed by phone, the information received from these personal interviews was double weighted in the analysis of the data.[43]

D. The Representativeness of the Sample

The persons interviewed for this study were identified in accident reports that were submitted to, and assembled into files by, the Massachusetts Registry of Motor Vehicles. It should be noted that enforcement of the reporting requirement in Massachusetts is such that there is good reason to believe that almost all accidents involving personal injuries are included in the Registry files.[44] The persons comprising the sample were randomly selected from the names in these files. Since the Registry uses these files to prepare a statistical analysis of

---

43. Information on the selection of persons to be interviewed for the second phase of the interviewing process and on the techniques that were used to contact these persons may be secured from Dr. Floyd J. Fowler, Director of Survey Research Program, 100 Arlington Street, Boston, Massachusetts 02116.

44. The Registry of Motor Vehicles has a comprehensive program designed to insure that all of the accidents that are covered by the statutory reporting requirement are reported. Among the special steps taken is a monitoring of all insurance claims arising from automobile accidents to ensure that every accident is reported to the Registry.

each year's accident experience for the state,[45] it is possible to compare certain data about the interviewees with comparable information compiled by the Registry from all the reports filed on persons injured in automobile accidents.

1. Classification of Injured by County

The Registry's statistical analysis includes a classification of accidents by the county in which they occurred. Although the location of accidents is not necessarily the same locale as where the injured persons live, there is at least a sufficient relationship to warrant comparing the Registry statistical analysis with the survey data on the respondent's county of residence. These statistics are set out in Table 1. Although there are some minor differences in the figures for individual counties, the similarity of the percentages in Table 1 is the more striking feature.

TABLE 1

Motor Vehicle Traffic Accidents Massachusetts:
Injured Persons By County in 1971

County	Registry Accident Site	Respondent's Residence
Barnstable Dukes Nantucket Plymouth	9.8%	9.7%
Berkshire	2.3%	1.8%
Bristol	9.9%	9.1%
Essex	11.6%	14.8%
Franklin Hampden	7.5%	5.9%
Hampshire	1.9%	1.8%
Middlesex	22.7%	25.5%
Norfolk	10.4%	11.4%
Suffolk	12.4%	8.6%
Worcester	11.6%	11.6%
Total:	100.1%	100.2%[46]
Base:	88,577[47]	1056

45. *See* note 38 *supra.*

46. The percentages in this and subsequent tables throughout the Article have been rounded to the nearest tenth of a percent. Therefore, when the percentages are added they will often total either slightly more, or slightly less than 100 percent.

47. The percentages in this column were computed from data reported in the 1972 REGISTRY STATISTICAL FILES, *supra* note 38, at 23.

Examining these variations from both a common sense and a statistical viewpoint, the differences appear to be within tolerable limits. However, since the precise degree of correlation between the location of the residences of accident victims and accident location was not determinable, it was also deemed necessary to test the representativeness of the sample by comparing the data in Table 1 with the 1970 United States census data for the Commonwealth's population.

TABLE 2
Massachussetts Motor Vehicle Accidents
By County

County	United States Census Data	Registry Accident Site	Respondent's Residence
Barnstable ⎫ Dukes ⎪ Nantucket ⎬ Plymouth ⎭	7.7%	9.8%	9.7%
Berkshire	2.6%	2.3%	1.8%
Bristol	7.8%	9.9%	9.1%
Essex	11.2%	11.6%	14.8%
Franklin ⎫ Hampden ⎬	9.1%	7.5%	5.9%
Hampshire	2.2%	1.9%	1.8%
Middlesex	24.6%	22.7%	25.5%
Norfolk	10.6%	10.4%	11.4%
Suffolk	12.9%	12.4%	8.6%
Worcester	11.2%	11.6%	11.6%
Total:	99.99%	100.1%	100.2%
Base:	5,689,170[48]	88,577	1056

The information set out in Table 2 indicates that while there are again some differences in the composition of the various samples, the similarities appear to be far more significant. Therefore, it can reasonably be inferred that the group of respondents surveyed is representative of the state's population viewed in relation both to the site of acci-

46. The percentages in this and subsequent tables throughout the Article have been rounded to the nearest tenth of a percent. Therefore, when the percentages are added they will often total either slightly more, or slightly less than 100 percent.

47. The percentages in this column were computed from data reported in the 1972 REGISTRY STATISTICAL FILES. *supra* note 38, at 23.

48. The computations of percentages for the Massachusetts counties are based on the United States Census Data for 1970 reported in U.S. BUREAU OF THE CENSUS. COUNTY AND CITY DATA BOOK. 1972—A STATISTICAL ABSTRACT SUPPLEMENT 222 (1973).

dents which occurred in 1972 and to the demographic information compiled by the United States census.

2. Classification of Injured by "Role"

The persons interviewed also appear to be representative of all accident victims with respect to their classification as an operator,
passenger, bicyclist, or pedestrian. For example, as shown in Table 3,
53.6 percent of all persons injured in 1972 were operators and operators
comprised 51 percent of the persons interviewed.

TABLE 3
Injured Persons: Classification By Role In Accident

Victim Status	Registry Data	Respondents Surveyed
Motor Vehicle Operator	53.6%	51.0%
Motor Vehicle Passenger	36.3%	30.2%
Pedestrian	6.5%	7.7%
Bicyclist	3.2%	10.8%
Other	0.1%	0.2%
Total:	99.7%	99.9%
Base:	81,086[49]	1053

The existence of a higher proportion of bicyclists and a somewhat
lower proportion of passengers among the persons interviewed than
among those reporting to the Registry is the most notable statistic in Table 3. These differences probably were produced, at least in part, by the
systematic preference for selecting those accident reports in which the
potential respondents were described as having been visibly injured.[50] In
other words, the process of excluding a number of less serious accident
injuries from the sample probably meant that a disproportionate number
of accidents in which the injury had been incurred as a passenger or
operator of an automobile were excluded, thereby producing a somewhat
lower proportion of operators and passengers among those surveyed. At
the same time, this selection process also resulted in a distinctly higher
proportion of bicyclists and a somewhat higher proportion of
pedestrians, those accident victims most likely to incur visible injuries.

Unfortunately, the Massachusetts Registry of Motor Vehicles does not

---

49. *See* 1972 REGISTRY STATISTICAL FILES at 17. The total population in the Registry's classification of the injured by status in the accident was 83,307. The base of 81,086 was arrived at by excluding the missing data (211), motorcycle operators (1,684), and motorcycle passengers (326).

50. *See* the text accompanying notes 33-42 *supra*.

publish statistics which indicate the accident severity for each of the role classifications, but statistics are published on the number of fatalities for such classifications. It is reasonable to assume that those role classifications which exhibit the highest fatality rates will also exhibit high rates of severe injury. Conversely, those classifications which exhibit low fatality rates can be expected to exhibit low rates of severe injury. To test the validity of this assumed correlation, the Registry fatality data were analyzed. The analysis disclosed several interesting points. First, the fatality rate for automobile passengers was the lowest of any classification (passengers, operators, pedestrians, and bicyclists) in both 1971 and 1972.[51] If the assumed correlation between the fatality rate and the accident severity in non-fatal personal injury accidents does exist, the lower fatality rate for passengers would lead to a prediction that there would be an underrepresentation of passengers in the sample drawn for this study. As stated previously, an underrepresentation of passengers in the survey data actually did occur. Second, the rate of fatalities in accidents involving pedestrians is several times that for accidents where an operator or a passenger is injured.[52] Again, the higher percentage of pedestrians actually found in the sample is consistent with the assumed correlation between fatality rates and accident severity. Thus, these fatality rate figures tend to confirm the explanation for the slightly greater representation in the sample of pedestrians and lower representation of automobile passengers among the respondents.

This analysis, however, does not explain the overrepresentation of bicyclists, since the fatality rates in 1971 and 1972 for accidents involving bicyclists were essentially the same as those for automobile drivers.[53] Even though the fatality rate for bicyclists does not correlate with the overrepresentation of this group in the sample, it still appears reasonable to expect that a person on a bicycle is usually going to be visibly injured as a result of a collision with an automobile. Therefore, on the basis of the apparent correlation between fatal and non-fatal accident rates for operators, passengers and pedestrians, as well as on the basis of what can reasonably be expected in regard to the likelihood of visible injury for accidents involving a collision between automobiles and bicyclists, it would be reasonable to anticipate that a sampling procedure that selected persons who were reported to have been visibly injured would produce a group with a somewhat greater representation of pedestrians and bicyclists than were present in the general population from which they were selected.

---

51. The fatality rates were computed from data reported in the 1971 REGISTRY STATISTICAL FILES, *supra* note 38, at 20-21 and the 1972 REGISTRY STATISTICAL FILES, *supra* note 38, at 18-19.

52. *Id.*

53. *Id.*

It is recognized, however, that the hypothesis set forth in the preceding paragraph does not completely explain the overrepresentation of bicyclists included in the group of respondents. Therefore, in order to ascertain whether the responses by the group of bicyclists prejudiced any of the data or analysis of this study, the basic tabulations and cross-tabulations discussed in this Article were recomputed excluding the responses by bicyclists. When this was done, there were no notable modifications in the results.[54] In fact, none of the percentage figures varied by more than one or two percent, and most variances were even less significant.[55]

3. Classification of Injured by Sex

The Registry also compiles information on injured persons according to sex. As can be seen from Table 4, the respondents interviewed in the study differed by about seven percent from the total population of accident victims.

TABLE 4
Injured Persons: Classification by Sex

Sex		Registry Data	Respondents Surveyed
Male		54.3%	61.7%
Female		45.7%	38.3%
	Total:	100.0%	100.0%
	Base:	80,667[56]	1,055

Although the selection process, which concentrated on persons with more serious injuries, may not be solely responsible for the somewhat higher proportion of males among the respondents, it probably was the primary factor.

If the hypothesis suggested above in regard to the over-selection of bicyclists and pedestrians is correct, it may also help to explain the higher proportion of males. In 1972, males constituted 73 percent of the bicyclists reported injured, 63 percent of the drivers reported injured,

---

54. The data upon which this statement are based is currently on file at the University of Iowa Computer Center. When all phases of the CLRS Massachusetts No-Fault Study are completed, the computer tape and related materials will be deposited in the University of Iowa Law Library. Hereinafter, when data supporting a statement are on file at the University of Iowa, the authority will be cited as CLRS NO-FAULT DATA.

55. Id.

56. The computations of the base figure and the percentages were based on data reported in the 1972 REGISTRY STATISTICAL FILES at 17-19. The base figure was arrived at by combining the data on motor vehicle operators, motor vehicle passengers, pedestrians and bicycle riders. Id.

and 62 percent of the pedestrians reported injured.[57] Thus, examining all accident victims, males predominate among drivers, pedestrians, and bicyclists. Females constitute 62 percent of all the passengers reported injured.[58] After the initial analysis, it appeared that whatever factor led to the under-selection of passengers also influenced the representativeness of subjects in regard to sex. To test this theory, the classification by role was broken down by sex as shown in Table 5.

TABLE 5

Injured Persons: Classification by Role and Sex

Classification by Role	Males in Registry Data	Males Among Respondents
Motor Vehicle Operator	63.0%	67.5%
Motor Vehicle Passenger	38.1%	45.6%
Pedestrian	62.7%	64.2%
Bicyclist	73.0%	76.3%
Base:	80,667[59]	650

From Table 5, it can be seen that the percentages of male respondents among motor vehicle operators, pedestrians, and bicyclists were only slightly higher than the percentages of males in these classifications in the Registry reports. In other words, when the sample is compared with the Registry census figures for 1972 on the basis of both role in the accident and sex, the respondents appear to be reasonably representative of the accident population from which they were selected, except for the still somewhat notable imbalance in the category of motor vehicle passengers. From this analysis, it appears that a slight bias was introduced by endeavoring to select potential respondents who were visibly injured.

The reasonableness of the overrepresentation of males appears to be confirmed by a further analysis of the number of fatalities compared to the number of injuries for each classification when considered according to sex. During 1971, 1972, and 1973, the number of fatalities in relation to the number of persons injured was notably higher for males than for females.[60] This was almost as true for the passenger classification as it

57. These computations are based on data reported in the 1972 REGISTRY STATISTICAL FILE, *supra* note 38, at 18-19.

58. *Id.*

59. This computation of the base figure and the percentages in this column are derived from data reported in 1972 REGISTRY STATISTICAL FILES, *supra* note 38, 17-19.

60. *See* 1971 REGISTRY STATISTICAL FILES. *supra* note 38, 20-21; 1972 REGISTRY STATISTICAL FILES, 18-19; and 1973 REGISTRY STATISTICAL FILES 18-19.

was for the operators, pedestrians and bicyclists. Accordingly, an assumed corrrelation between death rates and accident severity in non-fatal accidents would lead to the prediction of an overrepresentation of males in a group of accident victims selected on the basis on which the sample for this study was chosen.

The preceding data comparisons tabulated according to residence, accident role, and sex of the injured party support the conclusion that the persons interviewed constitute a representative cross-section of the population of persons injured in automobile accidents during 1972. Moreover, the sample is probably even more representative of the sub-group of accident victims — persons who were reported to have received visible injuries at the time of the accident — that was selected for the study.

4. Massachusetts: Then and Now

The interviews for this study were conducted primarily during the spring and summer of 1973, and the information sought related to accidents which occurred in August of 1972. Thus, an issue arises concerning the extent to which the survey results are representative of what is currently happening in Massachusetts. There appear to be sound reasons for believing that the findings herein would be replicated were a comparable survey to be conducted today.

First, the survey period was deliberately selected to avoid the effects of any special circumstances which may have prevailed during the transition from the fault to the no-fault system in 1971. Discussions with lawyers, claims adjusters, insurance company executives, and public officials in Massachusetts indicated that, by the spring of 1972, the no-fault system had become an established institution in Massachusetts and most, if not all, of the transitional phenomena had disappeared.

Second, the personal injury accident data compiled by the Massachusetts Registry of Motor Vehicles for 1972 and 1973 indicate that the accident experience for those two years was essentially the same.[61] During 1974, probably as a result of the energy crisis and the lowering of the maximum highway speed limits throughout the nation, there was a noticeable drop in the number of personal injury accidents reported.[62] In addition, data on personal injury accident claims compiled by the Massachusetts Rating Bureau indicate no significant changes in P.I.P. claims arising from accidents that occurred during 1972 and 1973.[63] Preliminary compilations of the 1974 claims data indicate that,

61. *See* 1972 REGISTRY STATISTICAL FILES; 1973 REGISTRY STATISTICAL FILES. *supra* note 38.

62. *See* 1974 REGISTRY STATISTICAL FILES *supra* note 38, and NATIONAL SAFETY COUNCIL. ACCIDENT FACTS (1975).

63. *See* MASS. AUTO. RATING AND ACCIDENT BUREAU. 1972 REVIEW OF EXPERIENCE: MEMORANDUM NO. 5—DEVELOPMENT OF COMPULSORY LOSSES (August, 1972); MASS. AUTO. RATING

consonant with the drop in the number of accidents reported to the Registry of Motor Vehicles in that year, fewer personal injury claims were filed.[64] Together, the accident data and the claims data indicate that aside from the reduction in the number of automobile accident injuries as a result of the energy crisis and the lowering of highway speed limits, there appear to have been no notable changes in the accident or claims experience in Massachusetts since these interviews were conducted in 1973.

III. THE ACCIDENT CONSEQUENCES
FOR ALL RESPONDENTS

In order to provide a basis for analyzing interviewees' answers to questions about their decision whether or not to make a claim, and about the nature of their claims experience, various inquiries were made concerning the consequences of their accident. These questions were designed to elicit information on the respondents' injuries, on whether the respondents had sought medical care, on whether they had lost any time from their jobs (if they were employed at the time of the accident), and on the extent to which they had been kept from carrying out other activities as a result of the accident. The discussion in this section analyzes the data provided by all of the respondents on injury severity and the accident consequences. The purpose of this section of the Article is to provide the reader with an overall perspective from which to consider the subsequent analysis of the data compiled on the non-claimants and claimants as distinct groups.

A. Accident Victims
1. The Uninjured "Injured"

One of the primary purposes of this study was to ascertain whether potential claimants were choosing not to make automobile insurance claims; therefore the survey interviews were focused on accident victims who had sustained injuries that were most likely to provide a basis for a claim under the P.I.P. insurance. Accordingly, the persons to be interviewed were selected from among those individuals who were described in accident reports filed by automobile owners and police officials with the Registry of Motor Vehicles as having been visibly injured in an automobile accident. Persons who were reported either as uninjured or as injured only to the extent that they complained of pain or were momentarily unconscious (that is, those who were not described in

---

AND ACCIDENT BUREAU. 1973 REVIEW OF EXPERIENCE: MEMORANDUM NO. 5—DEVELOPMENT OF EXPERIENCE (August, 1973).

64. This statement is based on informal discussion with persons responsible for the preliminary compilations. *See also* 1974 REGISTRY STATISTICAL FILES. *supra* note 38.

the accident reports as having sustained any *visible* injury) were excluded.[65] The basis for this exclusion was that although some of these persons would have P.I.P. claims,[66] on the whole, where the accident consequences were reported as only minor, such persons would be less likely to make insurance claims. Consequently, when the pilot study and the pre-test of the survey instrument disclosed that many of the individuals who had been selected on the basis of reported *visible* injuries stated that they had not been injured in any way, it was, to say the least, an unanticipated result.

Following the pilot study and subsequent pre-test of the final version of the survey instrument, the sampling technique was reviewed to determine whether the method of file selection had introduced any biases which would have produced a substantial group of persons whose "injuries" had not been appropriately described in the accident reports. Upon examination, the only answer which appears plausible is the obvious one: Accident reports, which are often prepared on the basis of observations at the scene of the accident, do not always provide an accurate characterization of the extent of injuries. Thus, it was not unexpected, in light of the pilot study and pre-test results, that 12 to 13 percent[67] of the group of "injured" persons interviewed stated that they had sustained no injury at all.[68] Although there were a few rather bizarre instances in which the characterization of the injury in the accident report was readily explainable (as in a case where the person had not been injured on impact, but subsequently had been cut in the course of bending a fender back into shape), in most of the cases there was no easily discernible explanation for the characterizations in the accident reports.

In general, answers by these "uninjured" persons to other inquiries in the survey instrument were consistent with the absence of any significant injury. For example, among those persons who indicated that they had received no injury *and* who also stated that they were employed, on-

---

65. *See* text accompanying notes 33-42 *supra.*

66. Undoubtedly, some persons who were reported to have had no visible injury, but who complained of ain or momentary unconsciousness, were, in actuality, seriously injured. However, as a group, the pilot study indicated that the injuries of such persons were ordinarily minor and did not lead to P.I.P. claims. Consequently, to have included persons who were so identified in the accident reports would only have resulted in a much larger group of uninjured "injured" among interviewees. As for those who were so described, but were actually seriously injured, there appears to be no reason to suspect that the accident consequences for these persons would be identifiably different than those who were identified as having been visibly injured in the accident report filed with the Registry.

67. It should be noted that in response to the direct query at the outset of the questionnaire as to whether they were injured in the accident, 12.3 percent of the respondents stated that they were not injured. However, when asked to describe any injuries, several of these persons indicated that they had sustained some type of injury, thereby reducing the percentage of respondents who described no injury at all.

68. CLRS No Fault Data, *supra* note 54.

ly 15 percent reported being absent from work for one or more days.[69] Similarly, about half of all the persons in this group reported that they had neither gone to a hospital nor sought any other type of medical attention following the accident.[70] The other half of the persons who reported no injury had sought medical attention of some type. For the vast majority of these persons, however, "medical attention" had consisted of an examination at a hospital, without the necessity of an overnight stay.[71] In other words, typically they had been sufficiently shaken up by the accident to desire a medical examination to confirm that there had been no injury. The interviews with these respondents, therefore, indicate that about one-eighth of the persons included in the survey sample who were described in accident reports as having been visibly injured had sustained either no injuries or injuries that were so minor that they were viewed in retrospect as non-existent.

2. The Slightly Injured

In addition to the respondents who reported no injuries, one-third of all the persons interviewed described relatively insignificant problems such as minor cuts, minor bruises, or some combination thereof. However, most of the individuals who reported such injuries (81 percent) had received medical attention.[72] A substantial majority of these persons had gone to a hospital, but almost always for only part of a day. Less than five percent of those who described such injuries to the interviewers had spent more than a single night in a hospital.

TABLE 6
Work Losses of the Slightly Injured

Number of Work Days Lost	The Slightly Injured	All Employed Respondents
0-No Work Loss	27.1%	19.3%
1 Day	6.0%	4.4%
2 to 3 Days	8.4%	8.0%
4 to 5 Days	5.7% 26.3%	7.1% 39.6%
6 to 10 Days	2.7%	5.4%
11 or More Days	3.5%	14.7%
Not Employed	46.6%	40.9%
Total:	100.0%	99.8%
Base:	369	1054

69. *Id.*
70. *Id.*
71. *Id.*
72. *Id.*

On the other hand, these persons reported fairly extensive periods of work loss as a result of the accident. Of the entire subgroup of respondents with minor injuries, slightly over half were employed, and about half of the employed persons (that is, one-quarter of the entire subgroup) reported that they had been absent from their jobs for at least one day. Although typically the amount of lost work time involved only a few days, some of the respondents who described only minor injuries indicated the type of work losses that would usually be associated with more serious injuries.

3. The Severely Injured

Slightly over half of the persons interviewed reported an injury of a relatively serious nature. In the course of the interviews, all persons who stated that they had been injured were asked to describe the character and extent of the injury sustained. Following the interviews, these responses were analyzed for the purpose of establishing several categories into which the injuries could be grouped. The responses of those who described fairly serious injuries were then divided into the five categories set out in Table 7. The respondents who reported severe injuries typically described more than one type of injury; consequently the subtotal in Table 7 exceeds 100 percent, reflecting the multiple injury descriptions by these respondents who in fact comprised only one-half of the interviewees.

TABLE 7
Types of Serious Injuries Sustained

Injury Description	All Respondents
Serious Bruises, Contusions or Sprains	25.6%
Serious Cuts, Torn Ligaments or Burns	33.2%
Whiplash, Sprained Neck, Separated Shoulder, Pinched Nerve, etc.	16.1%
Broken Bones, Dislocated Disc, Complicated Internal Injuries, Fractured Skull, etc.	29.2%
Lost or Broken Teeth, Injury to Jaw	8.5%
Subtotal:	112.6%
Non-Seriously Injured Respondents	
Minor Injuries	33.0%
No Injuries	12.0%
Total:	157.6%
Base:	1056

In order to minimize duplication of responses, and thereby provide a more precise characterization of the serious injuries sustained, the answers were reanalyzed to eliminate the double listing in Table 7 of those who reported "serious bruises, contusions or sprains," if they also reported other types of serious injuries. The results are set out in Table 8.

TABLE 8
Serious Injuries Eliminating Most Double Counting

Injury Description	All Respondents
Serious Bruises, Contusions or Sprains	25.0%
Serious Cuts, Torn Ligaments or Burns	18.0%
Whiplash, Sprained Neck, Separated Shoulder, Pinched Nerve, etc.	9.0%
Broken Bones, Dislocated Disc, Fractured Skull, and Other Types of Complicated Internal Injuries	16.0%
Lost or Broken Teeth; Injury to Jaw	5.0%
Subtotal:	73.0%
Non-Seriously Injured Respondents	
Minor Injuries	33.0%
No Injuries	12.0%
Total:	118.0%
Base:	1056

By eliminating most, but not all, of the double counting, it is possible to see more clearly in Table 8 the scope and character of the injuries sustained by the 54 percent of the repondents who reported what are characterized herein as serious injuries.

To recapitulate, the injury descriptions by the respondents seem to fall naturally into three classes. The smallest group, slightly over 12 percent, were those who stated that they had not been injured in the accident. When asked about other consequences of the accident, the answers of persons in this group of uninjured "injured" almost uniformly indicated the absence of any injury. The second group, about a third of all the persons surveyed, described relatively minor injuries. Again, analysis of the answers by these respondents to inquiries about periods of hospitalization or days missed from their employment were generally consistent with their characterizations of the injuries. However, some persons who described relatively minor injuries in the interviews reported substantial periods of work loss as a result of the accident. Taken together, nearly half of the persons who were reported as visibly injured had received at most minor injuries in the accident. On the other hand, the remainder of the respondents—constituting over half of the persons interviewed—described injuries that were relatively serious. Although these three classifications are obviously imprecise, they do provide a perspective on the nature and scope of injuries sustained by the respondents. Such a perspective is helpful in considering the data in the following discussion of the accident consequences.

B. Hospitalization and Other Medical Treatment

Seven of every eight persons interviewed in this study had sought some type of medical examination or treatment as a result of the accident, and for almost all of them that had involved some time at a hospital. In light of the data reported in the preceding section on varying degrees of accident severity, it is not suprising to find that approximately 60 percent of all the persons interviewed had remained in a hospital for only part of a day. However, the information presented in Table 9 also shows that for about one-fifth of the respondents the hospital stays had ranged from two days to more than two weeks.

TABLE 9
Hospitalization and Emergency Room Treatment

Hospitalization Period	All Respondents	
Part of a Day	59.8%	
Overnight	3.4%	
Two to Six Days	9.0%	⎫
One to Two Weeks	5.7%	⎬ 18.9%
Over Two Weeks	4.2%	⎭
No Hospitalization	17.9%	
Total:	100.0%	
Base:	1056	

Of course, a number of the respondents had undergone various other types of medical treatment. In fact, after the interviewers questioned the respondents about hospitalization or other care by a doctor, almost 45 percent of the persons interviewed stated in response to a separate question that they also had received other types of medical treatment or had incurred other medical expenses following the accident.[73] Only 13 percent of the persons interviewed stated that they had received no medical attention of any kind after the accident.[74] About half of these (six percent of the respondents) were persons who stated that they had not been injured in the accident.[75]

73. CLRS No-Fault Data. *supra* note 54.
74. *Id.*
75. *Id.*

C. Work Loss

Forty percent of the accident victims surveyed were not employed. Of the persons who were employed, about two-thirds (as shown in Table 10) had missed at least one day from their employment as a result of the accident.

TABLE 10
Employment and Work Loss

Work Loss	All Respondents	Employed Respondents
Absent from Job	39.4%	66.9%
No Work Loss	19.5%	33.1%
Not Employed	40.9%	—
Total:	99.8%	100.0%
Base:	1054	622

The number of days these persons reported that they had missed ranged from one to more than 250. About half of the employed persons had been absent from work for more than five days.

TABLE 11
Employed Persons: Number of Days Absent

Days Absent	Employed Respondent
One to Five Days	49.2%
Six to Ten Days	13.7%
Eleven to Fifteen Days	10.3%
Sixteen to Twenty Days	3.8%
More than Twenty Days	23.0%
Total:	100.0%
Base:	417

The respondents who reported that they had missed days on their jobs were asked whether they had lost any pay. Only 20 percent replied that no pay had been lost as a result of the days missed.[76]

D. Temporary Disabilities and Permanent Injuries

About half of the accident victims responded affirmatively when asked whether, as a result of the accident, they had been kept from carrying out some of their usual activities. As was true in the case of time lost

---

76. *Id.*

from work, the periods of disability ranged from one day to over 250 days.

TABLE 12
Temporary Disabilities

Length of Disability	All Respondents
Up to One Week	17.6%
One to Two Weeks	9.4%
Two to Three Weeks	3.5%
More than Three Weeks	21.7%
No Temporary Disability	47.7%
Total:	99.9%
Base:	1054

The interviewees were also asked whether the accident had resulted in any permanent injury or disfigurement. As indicated in Table 13, over one-third of all the persons interviewed responded affirmatively.

TABLE 13
Permanent Injury or Disfigurement

Injury Description	All Respondents		Seriously Injured Respondents	
Permanent Injury	6.3%	⎫	8.3%	⎫
Permanent Disfigurement	21.2%	⎬ 30.5%	27.4%	⎬ 39.7%
Permanent Injury and Disfigurement	3.0%	⎭	4.0%	⎭
No Permanent Injury or Disfigurement	68.6%		56.0%	
Respondent Did Not Know	0.8%		3.5%	
Total:	99.9%		99.2%	
Base:	1056		577	

It is interesting to note that while the percentage of the persons sustaining some type of permanent injury or disfigurement was somewhat greater among those who had suffered more serious injuries, it was not strikingly different from that prevailing among the total group of persons surveyed.

The interviewers were instructed to probe sufficiently to have the person describe with particularity the nature of the permanent injury or disfigurement. After the interviewing was completed, categories were established into which these descriptions could be grouped. These are set out in Table 14.

TABLE 14

Types of Permanent Injuries and Disfigurement of All Respondents

Injury Description	All Respondents	
Significant Scars	16.2%	
Need for Dental Work	4.5%	
Restricted Movement	5.6%	
Continued Pain	3.1%	33.2%
Headaches, Nausea, etc.	2.6%	
Internal Injury	1.0%	
Loss of Limb	0.2%	
Insignificant Scars	10.5%	
No Permanent Injuries or Disfigurements	63.7%	
Total:	107.4%	
Base:	1056	

The total percentage in Table 14 reflects the fact that slightly over seven percent of the interviewees described more than one type of permanent injury or disfigurement. The most significant fact to be discerned from the data is that over one-quarter of the persons surveyed reported some type of fairly significant long-term effect that existed at the time this study was made almost a year after the accident.[77]

E. Replacement Services

The Massachusetts P.I.P. coverage provides indemnification if an injured person hires someone to do things that he or she would have done had there been no accident.[78] Therefore, interviewees were asked whether they actually had hired people to provide replacement services; their responses appear in Table 15. Of the persons interviewed, fewer than three percent responded affirmatively to this inquiry. Consequently, it is logical to conclude that this aspect of the coverage was not significant for the great majority of the respondents.

---

77. The interviews for this study were conducted during the months of March through October, 1973, and sought information about the effects of accidents that occurred in August, 1972. *See* text accompanying notes 42-43, *supra.*

78. MASS. GEN. LAWS ANN. ch. 90, § 34A (Supp. 1975).

The foregoing discussion has provided a general view of survey data on the nature of both the injuries and the various consequences of the accident. The statistics presented were compiled for all of the persons who were interviewed. Generalizing from the data, it is fair to conclude that, for slightly over one-half of the respondents, the accident injuries were relatively serious, and that for the most part these were the respondents who reported the longer periods of hospitalization or lost work days.

TABLE 15
Replacement Services

Type of Service	All Respondents
Housework	0.8%
Yard and House Repair Work	0.6%
Babysitting	0.4%
Occupational Duties	0.9%
None	97.4%
Total:	100.1%
Base:	1056

The next portion of this Article, Part IV, analyzes the survey responses of those respondents who decided that they would not seek indemnification by filing a P.I.P. claim. Part V considers the data developed from the responses of the claimants. As would reasonably be expected, persons who reported that they had not been injured or that they had incurred relatively minor injuries represent a significant portion of the respondents who were non-claimants. However, by no means do they constitute all of the respondents who decided not to make a P.I.P. claim.

IV. NON-CLAIMANTS AND REASONS FOR
NOT SEEKING P.I.P. INDEMNIFICATION

Over 40 percent of the persons interviewed stated that they had not sought compensation from an automobile insurer for medical expenses, lost wages, or other losses resulting from personal injury in the accident. In order to learn why these persons did not seek indemnification, the interviews were structured so that those respondents who had not made a claim were asked to elaborate on the reasons for their decision. No attempt was made to anticipate what the responses to this question would be, and the answers were only subsequently analyzed to determine how they could be categorized. The question was "open-ended," and some of the respondents offered more than one reason, or made a statement that included several points, so that an average of slightly over 1.1 responses to this question were received for each of these interviews. Accordingly, when reported in terms of percentages, the responses by the non-claimants discussed in this section total approximately 113 percent, rather than 100 percent.

In addition to the "open-ended" question concerning the reasons for not seeking payments under P.I.P. coverage, several other inquiries were made which were deemed useful in ascertaining more completely the factors influencing the decision not to make a no-fault insurance claim. For example, non-claimants were specifically asked how much importance they had attached to the fact that any claim made would be against their own insurance company. Analysis of all these responses indicates that persons who decide against making no-fault insurance claims do so for a variety of reasons which can be divided into the five categories discussed in the following sections.

A. Non-Claimants: Their Injury Descriptions

The data on the injuries reported by all the respondents were discussed at the beginning of Part III. In Table 16, the information on the injuries reported by the non-claimants is presented. The interviewers did not limit the number of responses to the question about injuries, and many of the interviewees described more than one type of injury. Consequently, the total percentage in Table 16 exceeds 100 percent.

TABLE 16
Non-Claimants: Injury Descriptions

Injury Description	All Non-Claimants	
Minor Bruises	27.6%	
Serious Bruises	16.8%	
Minor Cuts	27.2%	
Serious Cuts	12.5%	
Whiplash	5.3%	
Knocked Unconscious	4.5%	31.5%
Broken Bones	7.5%	
Broken Teeth	1.7%	
No Injury	19.0%	
Total:	122.1%	
Base:	463	

The responses reflected by the percentages in Table 16 clearly show that while a significant portion of the non-claimants either stated that they had not been injured or described relatively minor injuries, this was not the case for over one-quarter of the non-claimants. Therefore, the discussion in the following sections focuses not only on the accident severity data, but also on other information compiled from the survey responses.

B. Non-Claimants: The ''Uninjured'' Injured

As stated previously, more than one-tenth of all the persons interviewed (that is, both claimants and non-claimants) and about one-fifth of the non-claimants indicated that they had not been injured in the accident.[79] Thus, it is not surprising that approximately 20 percent of the individuals who had not made a claim gave ''no injury'' as either the only reason or the primary reason for their decision.[80] About 60 percent of these non-claimants were employed, and only a few of these had missed a day at work as a result of the accident.[81] Accordingly, the great majority of these non-claimants did not lose any income as a result of the accident. However, almost 40 percent of these uninjured non-claimants stated that they had received some type of medical attention following the accident. Although typically this involved no more than a few hours at a hospital, usually only to confirm that there had been no injury, these uninjured non-claimants did incur some medical expenses as a result of the accident.[82]

No-fault coverage is limited to providing indemnification for costs actually incurred. Thus, it seems reasonable to subdivide the non-claimants who said they had not made a claim because they had not been injured into two groups based on whether they had incurred any out-of-pocket expenses. In those instances where no medical treatment had been sought, no time at work had been lost, and no replacement services had been secured, there was no basis for a claim. On the other hand, for those persons who reported some out-of-pocket costs — about 40 percent of the respondents who said they were not injured — a cross-tabulation was run to determine whether they were covered by collateral sources.[83] This analysis disclosed that of the non-claimants who reported that they had not been injured, about 20 percent stated that they had incurred some medical expenses that were not covered by any type of health insurance or that they had missed time at work which actually resulted in lost wages.[84] While very few of these persons gave any reason

79. *See* text accompanying note 65-71 *supra.*
80. CLRS No-Fault Study, *supra* note 54.
81. *Id.*
82. *Id.*
83. *Id.*
84. *Id.*

other than the absence of an injury for not having made a claim, the fair inference appears to be that either they had viewed the amount involved as too small or had felt that making a P.I.P. claim would have been too much trouble. In fact, these were reasons given by a substantial portion of the non-claimants whose responses are discussed in the following section.

C. Non-Claimants: The Slightly Injured

Over 40 percent of the non-claimants made statements to the effect that filing the claim would have been too much trouble, or that the amount involved had been too insubstantial to bother making a claim.[85] Typically, the non-claimants who gave these reasons described only minor injuries, such as cuts or bruises, and their responses to inquiries about medical attention and lost work time were also consistent with what would reasonably be expected to be the consequences of minor injuries. For example, while 66 percent of these persons had received medical attention,[86] only four percent had been in a hospital for more than part of a day.[87] Of those who were employed, only 25 percent reported the loss of more than a day of work.[88] Furthermore, the survey showed that nearly one-third of the non-claimants who, because of slight injuries, had missed work stated that they had suffered no wage loss or only a partial loss of wages since they had been able to take advantage of sick leave, workmen's compensation, or some other wage continuation plan.[89]

D. Non-Claimants and Collateral Sources

Among the other reasons given for not making claims, the most frequent was that the costs had been covered by some other source, such as medical insurance. Slightly more than one-fifth of all the non-claimants interviewed termed this a primary factor in their decision not to file a P.I.P. claim.[90] The responses of this group reflect the striking fact that many persons described a conscious decision not to seek duplicate recoveries. That is, they indicated that they had not made a claim under their P.I.P. coverage precisely because their costs had been covered by another source. This impression is further reinforced by analysis of the responses to questions which focused on the existence and use of medical insurance as a source of indemnification. The rele-

---

85. *Id.*
86. *Id.*
87. *Id.*
88. *Id.*
89. *Id.*
90. *Id.*

vant respondents were those who (1) had been injured, (2) had been covered by some type of health or medical insurance, and (3) had elected not to make claims under such coverage. When asked why they had not received any medical insurance benefits, about half of the group replied that their costs had been covered by a no-fault automobile insurer or, in a few instances, by a liability insurer.[91]

1. Non-Claimants: Medical Treatments and Collateral Sources

Additional perspective on the use of collateral sources to cover the costs of medical services is provided by analysis of the non-claimants' responses to several questions which specifically focused on this issue. The availability of collateral sources to provide coverage for medical expenses obviously was not an important factor for slightly over one-quarter of the non-claimants who had not sought any medical treatment after their accident.[92] Of the non-claimants who had sought some medical treatment following the accident, over half (58 percent) stated that they had secured indemnification from health insurance coverage.[93] As shown in Table 17, the individuals who had used their health insurance represent a significant segment of those non-claimants who had sought some medical attention; in addition, they constitute over 40 percent of all the persons who had chosen not to make P.I.P. claims.

TABLE 17
Non-Claimants: Medical Attention

Medical Attention	Non-Claimants Who Received Medical Attention	All Non-Claimants
No Medical Attention	—	27.5%
Medical Attention:		
Health Insurance Collected	58.0%	42.3%
No Health Insurance Collected	42.0%	30.6%
Total:	100.0%	100.4%
Base:	331	454

91. CLRS No-Fault Data. *supra* note 54.
92. *Id.*
93. *Id.*

As would be expected, the portion of the accident-related medical bills which the non-claimants reported as having been covered by health insurance varied from 100 percent to a very small amount. Responses to the inquiry as to what portion of the non-claimants' medical expenses had been covered are presented in Table 18. Examination of the data shows that over 75 percent of the non-claimants who had collected from their medical insurance had been reimbursed for either "all," (54.1 percent) or "almost all" (23.7 percent) of their medical expenses by the medical insurance.

TABLE 18
Non-Claimants: Health/Medical Insurance Payments

Medical Attention Portion of Expenses Paid by Health Insurer	Non-Claimants Who Collected Health Ins.	All Non-Claimants
All	54.1% ⎫ 77.8%	22.7% ⎫ 32.6%
Almost All	23.7% ⎭	9.9% ⎭
Some	11.3%	4.8%
A Small Part	4.1%	1.7%
Didn't Know	6.7%	2.8%
No Health Insurance Paid Medical Expenses	—	30.7%
No Medical Expenses	—	27.4%
Total:	99.9%	100.0%
Base:	194	463

The data presented in Table 18 indicate that most of the non-claimants who had received benefits from some type of health insurance reported that such insurance had covered almost all of their medical bills. On the other hand, the data also demonstrate that more than one-third of the non-claimants had incurred medical expenses that either wholly or in substantial measure had not been covered by such a collateral source. These were non-claimants who had received no health/medical insurance, or who had been only partially compensated for medical costs by such insurance. It is reasonable to assume that a person who has been reimbursed for medical expenses by his or her health insurance coverage would be less likely to also file a P.I.P. claim covering the same costs. This hypothesis was tested by running several cross-tabulations; the results, which are presented in Table 19, provide a vivid illustration of the interaction between a collateral source and the use of P.I.P. coverage.

TABLE 19

Health Insurance as an
Influence on P.I.P. Claims

Portion of Medical Expenses Paid by Health or Medical Insurance	Respondents Who also Made P.I.P. Claims	Respondents Who did not Make P.I.P. Claim	Respondent Uncertain Whether a P.I.P. Claim was Made
All	35.0%	64.4%	0.6%
Almost All	62.4%	36.8%	0.8%
Some	69.2%	28.2%	2.6%
A Small Part	72.4%	27.6%	0.0%

Base: 395

The data in Table 19 clearly indicate that as the proportion of the medical expenses covered by health insurance decreased, respondents turned to the P.I.P. coverage for indemnification. Thus, for example, of the respondents who stated that their health insurance had paid all of their medical expenses, slightly more than one-third also had made a P.I.P. claim. Of those who stated that medical insurance had covered only "a small part" of their medical bills, over 70 percent had made P.I.P. claims. Similarly in a separate cross-tabulation analysis of the respondents who reported that their health insurance had paid all their medical bills and that they had sustained no wage loss (either because they had been unemployed or they had suffered no wage loss), over 70 percent stated that no P.I.P. claim had been made.[94] This analysis of the data appears to lend further support to the conclusion that persons injured in automobile accidents do not generally exploit all sources of indemnification in order to maximize the amount of insurance benefits that might be collected.

2. Work Losses and Workmen's Compensation

Approximately one-quarter of the non-claimants stated that they had missed at least one day on the job. These persons were asked to estimate how much of their pay had been lost. The responses are set out below in Table 20.

---

94. CLRS NO-FAULT DATA. *supra* note 54.

TABLE 20
Employed Non-Claimants: Lost Pay

Portion of Wages Lost	Non-Claimants Who Missed Work		All Non-Claimants
All	59.6%		14.7%
Almost All	3.5%	78.9%	0.9%
Some	15.8%		3.9%
A Small Part	4.4%	18.4%	1.1%
None	14.0%		3.5%
Did Not Know	2.6%		0.6%
Total:	99.9%		24.7%
Base:	111		463

The data presented in Table 20 show that almost one-fifth of the employed non-claimants who had missed time at work had lost either no pay or only a small part of their pay as a result of the accident. On the other hand, approximately four-fifths of this group stated that a significant portion of their lost pay had not been made up by any collateral source, such as workmen's compensation or sick leave pay.

In order to provide a sense of the relative significance of the lost wages, a cross-tabulation was run to show how many days of work had been missed by those non-claimants who were employed and who reported that either "all" or "almost all" of their lost pay had not been made up by any collateral source. The results of this analysis appear in Table 21.

TABLE 21
Employed Non-Claimants: Days of Lost Wages

Days Lost			Employed Non-Claimants	
One Day		Group A	16.9%	33.8%
Two Days			16.9%	
Three Days			9.9%	
Four Days		Group B	4.2%	66.2%
Five Days			16.9%	
Six or More Days	Total:		35.2%	
			100.0%	
	Base:		71	

Although the number of non-claimants who had been employed and who reported that they had lost all their wages was a relatively small portion of the non-claimants interviewed, it was deemed worthwhile to pursue the analysis one step further to a consideration of the responses given by these persons to the question of why they had decided not to make a P.I.P. claim. For this purpose, these individuals were divided into two subgroups. Group A (24 persons) consisted of those who stated that they had missed one or two days of work; Group B (47 persons) comprised those who reported that they had missed three or more days. Since the number of persons who comprised these subgroups was small, the statistical significance of their responses is open to question. Nevertheless, the analysis is considered worthy of presentation because the responses offer some additional, albeit qualified, insight into the reasons why persons choose not to make P.I.P. claims.

As one would expect, the most frequent explanation given by those persons who had missed only a day or two (Group A) was that they had felt that the claim process was too much trouble or that the amount involved was too insignificant. This was true for more than 40 percent of Group A.[95] Among those persons with more time away from their jobs (Group B), about one-quarter stated that they had thought that making a claim would be too much trouble or that the amount involved was too insubstantial.[96] In other words, a much smaller portion of the persons in Group B than in Group A apparently had viewed the wage loss as insignificant. On the other hand, the proportion of persons in Group B who appeared either to be unaware of, or to misunderstand, the P.I.P. coverage was significantly larger than in Group A. Slightly over half of the persons in Group B made statements which indicated either ignorance of, or misconceptions about, the P.I.P. coverage; among those in Group A, only about a quarter of the responses were so characterized.[97]

In light of the number of respondents on which these observations are based, it obviously would be a mistake to attempt to generalize too much from this segment of the survey. Yet these responses do appear to be in accord with what might be hypothesized as the primary reasons why such persons would not make P.I.P. claims. Moreover, it is possible to carry the analysis further through an examination of the medical expenses incurred by these persons. Almost all of the respondents in Group B, the persons with the more significant wage losses, stated that they had received some medical attention after the accident.[98] About

---

95. CLRS NO-FAULT DATA. *supra* note 54.
96. *Id.*
97. *Id.*
98. *Id.*

half of the persons in Group B also reported that some type of medical or health insurance had covered "all" or "almost all" of their medical expenses.[99] Several more 'Group B members either had received at least some indemnification from health insurance or had been compensated from some other source for their medical expenses.[100] Consequently, the other principal out-of-pocket losses had been minimal for a significant portion of the non-claimants who reported uncompensated wage losses. This fact may explain in part why many of the persons in Group B had not pursued information about possible indemnification under the P.I.P. coverage.

3. Use of Collateral Sources in Compensation for Temporary Disability and Replacement Services

Approximately one-third of the non-claimants stated that they had been prevented by their injuries from performing some of their usual activities for a period of time following the accident.[101] As Table 22 indicates, for almost half of these persons, the period during which their activities had been curtailed or hindered had been a week or less. For a few, it had continued for several weeks.

TABLE 22
Periods of Temporary Disabilities

Days Temporarily Disabled	Non-Claimants Who Reported Some Temporary Disability	All Non-Claimants
None	—	65.8%
1 through 3 Days	27.8%	9.5%
4 through 7 Days	15.8%	5.3%
8 through 14 Days	21.5%	7.3%
15 through 21 Days	7.0%	2.4%
More than 21 Days	27.8%	9.2%
Total:	99.9%	99.5%
Base:	158	462

Although temporary disabilities were reported by many of the interviewees, including about one-third of the non-claimants, fewer than three percent of the respondents had hired someone to carry on activities that the accident had prevented them from performing.[102] Conse-

---

99. CLRS No-Fault Data, *supra* note 54.
100. *Id.*
101. *Id.*
102. *Id.*

quently, it appears that the possible use of collateral sources to cover the costs of replacement services was not a significant factor for the non-claimants as a group in their decision not to file a P.I.P. claim.

E. Non-Claimants: The Uninformed and Misinformed

The fourth category of responses by non-claimants as to why they had not sought a recovery under no-fault insurance includes a variety of answers which indicate either a misunderstanding of the P.I.P. coverage or even a total lack of awareness of its existence. About 21 percent of the non-claimants gave explanations which indicated either that they believed they were not covered by any relevant insurance or that they misunderstood the coverage provided by no-fault insurance.[103] The following statements are typical of the responses which have been placed in this category:

> I didn't think about it. My insurance agent handled everything for me. Could I have gotten paid for lost wages?

> I was under the impression that we couldn't.**** Isn't it like it has to be so much before you can receive anything? It was my $35 for the x-rays. Doesn't it have to be more than $50?

> Not that much of a medical expense except the x-rays. The operation came months later. How can I prove that?

> I don't think I would have collected. If we'd hit something—another car maybe—but I've been through all this with my father-in-law when he had an accident. Anyway the lawyer gets most of it.

> Because it was my car and I didn't think my insurance covered that.

> It was my sister's car, and I didn't know anything about it. I didn't know I could make a claim.

> Who would I file a claim with? If I could find who hit her (the respondent's daughter), then I would have found out the insurance company and sued (the driver of the car that struck the respondent's daughter).

> It's pretty complicated. I asked a lawyer and he said it wouldn't be worth it! He just said it wouldn't do any good.[104]

In addition, several respondents (one percent of all the non-claimants) stated that they were waiting for the insurance company to contact them.[105] While it is difficult to evaluate the significance of such comments in regard to particular situations, they also appear to manifest a certain misunderstanding of the operation of the P.I.P. system. Still another 3.5 percent of the non-claimants answered either that they had not considered making a P.I.P. claim, or that they did not know why they had failed to file a claim.[106] Both of these types of responses could

---

103. CLRS No-Fault Data. *supra* note 54.
104. *Id.*
105. *Id.*
106. *Id.*

reflect at least a degree of misunderstanding or lack of information. Alternatively, such responses might be interpreted as reflecting an attitude that not enough money had been involved to warrant making a claim. Finally, a few non-claimants stated that they had decided not to file a claim because they had felt that they had caused the accident.[107] Thus, overall, one-quarter of the non-claimants gave various types of answers which indicated some degree of misunderstanding of the no-fault system.[108]

F. Claimants Claiming Against Their Own Insurers

Some observers have suggested that many persons entitled to recover under the P.I.P. coverage would be deterred from doing so because the claim would be against their own insurer. Therefore, all non-claimants were specifically asked whether this fact had influenced their decision not to seek P.I.P. benefits. The results were striking: only slightly more than five percent of the total group of non-claimants stated that they had been influenced in any measure by this factor, and only half of these (two to three percent of the total) cited this as a dominant reason for their decision.[109] It may be concluded that for most Massachusetts accident victims, the fact that a claimant must apply for compensation to his or her own insurer is a relatively unimportant consideration.

This conclusion is further buttressed by the responses of non-claimants to inquiries about no-fault property claims, which are also made under first party coverage provided by the same insurance company. Of the total group of non-claimants, about one-third owned cars that had been damaged *and* that had been covered by unrestricted collision coverage.[110] Ninety-seven percent of the persons in this subgroup of non-claimants reported that they had filed a property claim against their own company.[111] Thus, their actions in regard to the property coverage were consistent with their answers that they had not been deterred by the fact that a P.I.P. claim would be made against their own insurer.

Furthermore, some of the respondents who indicated that their own insurance company's involvement had been a fairly important factor in their decisions not to seek indemnification under the P.I.P. coverage also

---

107. *Id.*

108. This level of misunderstanding among the non-claimants was also reflected in the separate analysis of the survey responses given by those non-claimants who reported they lost some, almost all, or all of their pay as a result of the accident. When these questionnaires were cross-tabulated with the reasons why these non-claimants did not make a P.I.P. claim, about 25 percent of the persos in this subgroup gave reasons which indicated they misunderstood the no-fault coverage. *See id.*

109. *Id.*

110. *Id.*

111. *Id.*

had suffered damage to their cars which had been covered by unrestrict-ed collision coverage, written, of course, by the same insurance com-pany. Although the number of respondents in this subgroup is small, and therefore the statistical significance of any analysis based on the sub-group is open to question, the fact remains that almost all of the persons in this subgroup *did* file property claims.[112]

V. THE CLAIMANTS

Nearly 55 percent of the persons interviewed in the survey stated that they had made a claim against an automobile insurance company as a re-sult of personal injuries sustained in the accident reported to the Registry of Motor Vehicles. There are no notable differences between the claimants and the non-claimants when the data on county of res-idence, sex, the respondent's role in the accident (operator, passenger, pedestrian, etc.), or the number of vehicles involved are compared. In fact, the striking feature of Table 23 below is the similarity of the percen-tages.

TABLE 23
Claimants, Non-Claimants and All Respondents
by County of Residence[113]

County	P.I.P.Claimants	All Respondents	Non-Claimants
Barnstable Dukes Nantucket Plymouth	9.2%	9.7%	10.2%
Berkshire	1.9%	1.8%	1.7%
Bristol	9.7%	9.1%	8.6%
Essex	14.7%	14.8%	15.1%
Franklin Hampden	6.4%	5.9%	5.4%
Hampshire	2.1%	1.8%	1.5%
Middlesex	24.8%	25.5%	25.9%
Norfolk	10.4%	11.4%	11.9%
Suffolk	8.5%	8.6%	8.6%
Worcester	12.3%	11.6%	11.1%
Total:	100.0%	100.2%	100.0%
Base:	577	1056	463

112. CLRS No-Fault Data, *supra* note 54.
113. The base figures for the claimants and non-claimants used in calculating these percentages do not equal the base figure for all respondents when added due to 16 uncodeable responses.

The same similarity exists in Table 24, which compares non-claimants with claimants on the basis of sex.

TABLE 24
Respondents by Sex

Sex	P.I.P. Claimants	Non-Claimants
Males	61.0%	63.2%
Females	39.0%	36.8%
Total:	100.0%	100.0%
Base:	577	462

The similarity is also present in Table 25, which is a comparison of claimants and non-claimants by their role in the accident.

TABLE 25
Respondents by Role in the Accident

Status	P.I.P. Claimants	Non-Claimants
Operator-Car	51.7%	51.7%
Passenger-Car	30.4%	29.2%
Passenger-Other	0.2%	0.2%
Pedestrian	6.9%	7.6%
Bicyclist	10.6%	10.8%
Total:	99.8%	99.5%
Base:	575	460

Finally, no significant differences between claimants and non-claimants are evidenced by the data compiled in Table 26.

TABLE 26
Respondents: Number of Vehicles Involved

Number of Automobiles	P.I.P. Claimants	Non-Claimants
Two Automobiles	57.2%	54.7%
Automobile-Bicycle	10.7%	12.0%
Automobile-Pedestrian	7.0%	7.6%
One Automobile	25.1%	25.8%
Total:	100.0%	100.1%
Base:	570	450

Having found that the P.I.P. claimants who were interviewed were sub-stantially similar to the non-claimants in regard to these general charac-

teristics, the question naturally follows as to whether the accident consequences for the claimants were also similar to those suffered by non-
claimants.

A. Claimants: The Accident and Its Consequences
1. The Nature of the Injuries

Ninety-seven percent of the persons who made claims reported that
they actually had been injured, and for most of these persons (69.3 percent of the claimants) the injuries had been fairly severe.[114] Although
Table 24 includes some reports of multiple injuries on the part of a given
respondent, much of the duplication has been eliminated by excluding
the reports of serious bruises where that respondent also described
another type of serious injury.

TABLE 27
Nature of Injuries Sustained by Respondents

Injury Description	Claimants		Non-Claimants	
Serious Bruises	15.6%		10.1%	
Serious Cuts	22.2%		13.2%	
Whiplash	11.8%	79.3%	4.8%	36.9%
Broken Bones	22.2%		7.6%	
Broken Teeth	7.5%		1.2%	
Minor Injuries Only	27.7%		44.7%	
No Injuries	3.0%		19.0%	
Total:	110.0%		100.6%	
Base:	577		463	

Almost half of the multiple injury descriptions that remain in Table 27
are the result of individual claimants' reports of both serious cuts and
broken bones. About 40 percent of the claimants interviewed reported
some type of permanent injury or disfigurement more extensive than a
slight scar. These descriptions provide additional information on the
nature and extent of the injuries sustained by the claimants and the non-
claimants.

The responses which produced the percentages in Tables 27 and 28
clearly indicate that serious injuries, permanent injuries, and disfigure-
ments were described more frequently by the claimants than by the non-
claimants. At the same time, it should be kept in mind that over a third
of the non-claimants described serious injuries, and that many of these
persons also described the same types of permanent injuries and dis-
figurements that were reported by the claimants.

---

114. CLRS No-Fault Data, *supra* note 54.

TABLE 28
Types of Permanent Injury or Disfigurement

Injury Description	Claimants		Non-Claimants	
Need for Dental Work	6.7%		1.8%	
Restricted Movement	8.1%		1.6%	
Continued Pain	3.1%	22.1%	2.6%	8.5%
Internal Injury	0.8%		0.6%	
Headaches, Nausea	3.4%		1.5%	
Loss of Limb	——		0.4%	
Significant Scars	21.3%		9.1%	
Insignificant Scars Only	9.7%		9.1%	
No Permanent Injury or Disfigurement	54.6%		76.9%	
Total:	107.7%		103.6%	
Base:	577		463	

2. Medical Treatment and Hospitalization

Nearly 99 percent of the persons who stated that they had made no-fault coverage claims had sought some type of medical assistance as a result of the accident. Similarly, over 90 percent of the persons who had filed P.I.P. claims had spent some time in a hospital following the accident. Typically, the claimants' hospitalization had been for only part of a day, but almost one-third of these persons had remained in the hospital at least overnight.

TABLE 29
Hospitalization or Emergency Room Treatment

Period	Claimants		Non-Claimants	
None	6.2%		33.0%	
Part of a Day	63.3%		55.7%	
Overnight	5.0%		1.5%	
2 to 6 Days	10.9%	30.4%	6.7%	11.2%
1 to 2 Weeks	8.3%		1.7%	
Over 2 Weeks	6.2%		1.3%	
Total:	99.9%		99.9%	
Base:	577		463	

The data in Table 29 indicate that one of the most apparent differences between the claimants and the non-claimants is with respect to the relative percentage of those who had remained in the hospital for more than part of one day. The data demonstrate that the portion of the claimants who had remained in a hospital for more than part of a day was almost three times that of the non-claimants.

3. Medical Insurance

Although almost all (98 percent) of the respondents who had made no-fault claims had obtained some form of medical assistance or treatment, as shown in Table 30, less than 40 percent of this group had received any payments from health insurance.[115]

TABLE 30
Medical Bills Paid By Health Insurance

Insurance Claim	Claimants	Non-Claimants Who Incurred Medical Costs
Health Insurance Paid	37.0%	56.5%
Health Insurance Did Not Pay	61.8%	40.9%
Didn't Know	1.2%	2.6%
Total:	100.0%	100.0%
Base:	576	340

The persons who had received payments from some type of health or medical insurance were asked to estimate what portion of the medical expenses had been covered by that insurance.

TABLE 31
Portion of Medical Expenses Paid by Health Insurance

Portion Paid	Claimants		Non-Claimants	
All	9.9%		22.7%	
Almost All	13.5%		9.9%	
Some	9.4%		4.8%	
A Small Part	3.6% }	65.4%	1.7% }	59.8%
None	61.8% }		58.1% }	
Didn't Know	1.8%		2.8%	
Total:	100.0%		100.0%	
Base:	577		463	

115. *Id.*

Only about 10 percent of the claimants had been reimbursed for "all" their medical expenses, and another 13.5 percent of all claimants stated that "almost all" of their medical bills had been covered by health insurance.[116] Conversely, as shown in Table 31, almost two-thirds of the claimants interviewed reported that none or almost none of their medical expenses had been covered by health or medical insurance benefits.

The respondents who stated that they had received no medical or health insurance payments were specifically asked why no payments had been received.

TABLE 32
Reasons for No Medical Insurance Benefits

Reasons Given	Claimants	Non-Claimants
Category I.		
No Health Insurance	40.3%	19.0%
Category II.		
Covered by Auto Insurance	34.6%	2.2%
Would Rather Auto Insurance Pay	1.6%	1.5%
Could not Get Both to Pay	3.3%	0.0%
Category III.		
Medical Plan Did Not Cover	2.5%	3.7%
Blue Cross Refused Payment	3.0%	1.5%
Under Deductible Amount	1.4%	1.1%
Category IV.		
Workmen's Compensation	0.5%	1.5%
Covered by Other Source	0.8%	3.0%
Category V.		
Don't Know	3.3%	2.6%
No Claim Made	5.1%	7.1%
Not Much Involved	1.6%	7.1%
No Injury	2.2%	49.8%
Total:	100.2%	100.1%
Base:	362	269

116. *Id.*

One of three explanations was given by more than 80 percent of the P.I.P. claimants. First, just over 40 percent stated that they had not been covered by any medical insurance. Second, slightly over one-third of the group stated that they had not made a medical insurance claim because the medical costs had been covered by automobile insurance. Third, seven percent indicated that, for some reason, their medical insurance had not provided coverage.[117] This data, along with the other explanations given by the respondents, is set out in Table 32.

One additional point should be made in regard to the percentages in Tables 31 and 32. In Table 31, the percentages for the claimants and non-claimants who stated that no portion of their medical expenses had been paid by health insurance are approximately the same (61.8 percent and 58.1 percent, respectively). For the non-claimants, however, this includes a substantial number of persons who had not sought such payments because they had not been injured; this is demonstrated by the "no injury" category in Table 32. By contrast, almost none of the P.I.P. claimants (only 2.2 percent) gave "no injury" as the reason for not having received health insurance payments.

4. Temporary Disabilities and Replacement Services

Almost two-thirds of the claimants stated that their injuries had prevented them from performing some of their usual activities.[118] The extent of their limitations ranged from inability to pursue sports or hobbies to total disability. While almost 20 percent of the claimants reported that their ability to move had been completely or significantly impaired, only four percent of the claimants reported that they had hired someone to do things that they would otherwise have done themselves.[119] Consequently, the fact that P.I.P. provides coverage for replacement services obviously played only a small part in the decisions by the respondents to seek or not to seek compensation from the no-fault insurance.

5. Employment and Work Loss

Of the persons who made claims, more than half had been employed at the time of the accident and had missed some time at work as a result of their injuries.

---

117. CLRS No-Fault Data, *supra* note 54.
118. *Id.*
119. *Id.*

TABLE 33
Work Loss

Work Loss	Claimants	Non-Claimants
Absent from Job	51.7%	24.4%
Not Absent	10.1%	32.0%
Not Employed	38.2%	43.4%
Total:	100.0%	99.8%
Base:	575	461

Each of these respondents was asked whether any of the pay lost because of absence from his or her job had been made up by regular salary, sick leave, workmen's compensation, or another source. Respondents were also questioned about the amount of pay they had lost. About one-quarter of the employed claimants responded that either little or no pay had been lost. On the other hand, two-thirds of the employed claimants reported that all or almost all of their pay had been lost.

TABLE 34
Portion of Pay Lost

Portion Lost	Employed Claimants		Employed Non-Claimants	
None	20.5%	} 25.2%	14.0%	} 18.4%
A Small Part	4.7%		4.4%	
Some	8.4%		15.8%	
Almost All	7.0%	} 65.4%	3.5%	} 63.1%
All	58.4%		59.6%	
Don't Know	1.0%		2.6%	
Total:	100.0%		99.9%	
Base:	298		111	

As shown in Table 34, when the groups which had lost most of their pay were combined, nearly two-thirds of the employed claimants who had missed time at work reported that they had lost "all" (58.4 percent) or "almost all" (7.0 percent) of their pay. The importance of the lost wages to these persons is underscored when viewed in relation to the amount of time lost. A cross-tabulation was run for those persons who reported that either none or almost none of their lost pay had been made up by any collateral source. The results of this analysis are presented in Table 35.

TABLE 35
Unrecompensed Claimant Period of Wage Loss

Period of Loss	P.I.P. Claimants	Non-Claimants
1 to 2 Days	24.2%	43.7%
3 to 4 Days	34.0%	33.8%
5 Days	24.2%	15.5%
6 or more Days	17.5%	7.0%
Total:	99.9%	100.0%
Base:	194	71

B. Claimant Satisfaction and Dissatisfaction with the P.I.P. System

Central to the evaluation of how well a compensation system works are questions of (1) the interval between the date on which injuries are sustained and the date when compensation is paid, (2) the adequacy of the amount provided to the injured person, and (3) the amount of difficulty involved in making a claim for compensation. Since these factors, either individually or in some combination, appear to be the primary determinants of whether most claimants are satisfied with any compensation system, the survey instrument for the study was designed to focus on them specifically. In addition, all respondents who had made claims (approximately 55 percent of the persons interviewed) were afforded an opportunity to offer comments or criticisms about anything which they regarded as relevant to the manner in which their claims had been handled.

1. Claimants Who Had Not Been Paid

At the time the interviews were conducted, in most instances some 17 to 19 months after the accident occurred,[120] approximately three-quarters of the persons who had made claims had received some payment.[121] When a respondent stated that the claim had not been paid, the interviewer was instructed to seek more information about the claim and to determine whether the respondent knew why the claim had not been paid. The data elicited by this question is set out in Table 36.

In half the interviews in which the claimant reported that no payment had been made, he or she also stated that the claim was being handled by an attorney.[122] In each case where the respondent so indicated, an attempt was made to acquire more information from the attorney concerning the status of the claim. In several instances, it was learned from the attorney that the no-fault claim had indeed been paid, but that either no disbursement had been made by the attorney because a tort action was

---

120. *See* text accompanying note 33 *supra,* for information concerning the interviewing process.
121. CLRS No-Fault Data, *supra* note 54.
122. *Id.*

still pending, or that the attorney had paid outstanding medical bills with the P.I.P. insurance. This pattern of responses was repeated sufficiently often by the lawyers with whom interviews were conducted that it appears reasonable to conclude that, in a significant number of these cases, the P.I.P. claim had been filed and paid even though the injured persons were not aware that payments had been received on their behalf.[123] Furthermore, this phase of the claims process was discussed in other interviews conducted with attorneys. The information derived from these conversations suggests that attorneys often file the P.I.P. claim and the tort claim more or less simultaneously and then either disburse the insurance payments to hospitals or physicians to pay the medical bills or hold them in trust until the tort claim is settled.[124]

TABLE 36
Status of Claims

Status of Claim	Claimants Who Had Not Been Paid		All Claimants	
Lawyer Handling Claim	51.9%		12.0%	
Amount Not Finalized	11.3%		2.7%	
Claim Only Recently Entered	2.3%	14.3%	0.5%	3.4%
Employer Did Not File Papers	0.7%		0.2%	
Insurer Denied Liability	6.0%		1.5%	
Didn't Know Why	27.8%		6.5%	
Claimants Paid	—		76.6%	
Total:	100.0%		100.0%	
Base:	133		577	

As Table 36 also indicates, in almost 15 percent of the cases in which compensation had not been paid, the claimant stated facts which in some way indicated that the delay had not been caused by the insurance company. For example, about one-tenth of these persons reported that the amount of their medical expenses had not been finalized. It is interesting to note in this regard that even though the P.I.P. coverage provides for

123. *Id.*
124. *Id.*

interim payments, most persons wait until all the medical costs are fixed before making a claim.[125]

It was not possible within the scope of this portion of the CLRS No-Fault study to investigate the reasons that lay behind the reports of respondents who stated that they did not know why they had not been paid.[126] However, it should be noted that, as shown by the right-hand column in Table 36, such respondents constituted only six percent of all claimants interviewed for this study.

2. *Claimants Who Were Paid: Satisfaction with Speed of Payment*

Slightly more than 80 percent of the persons who responded to the question of whether they were satisfied with the speed with which their claim had been paid indicated that they were either "very satisfied" or "fairly satisfied."

TABLE 37
Speed of Payment

Degree of Satisfaction	All Claimants	
Very Satisfied	58.3%	} 84.3%
Fairly Satisfied	26.0%	
Fairly Dissatisfied	8.1%	
Very Dissatisfied	7.6%	
Total:	100.0%	
Base:	446	

3. *Claimants Who Were Paid: Satisfaction*
with Amount of Payment

The great majority of the claimants who had received P.I.P. payments also expressed satisfaction with the amount that had been paid. In this regard, more than 80 percent of these persons also reported that the combined automobile insurance and health insurance had fully covered their medical expenses.[127]

---

125. Chapter 313 of the Acts of 1972 requires insurance companies, upon notification of disability of the insured from a licensed physician, to commence medical payments or provide notice of non-payment and reasons therefor within ten days. MASS. ACTS 1972, ch. 313 (May 25, 1972), *codified as* MASS. GEN. LAWS ANN. ch. 90 § 34M (Supp. 1975).

126. The reasons why insurance companies deny no-fault claims and the incidence of such denials is considered in another segment of the CLRS Massachusetts No-Fault Study that will be reported separately.

127. CLRS NO-FAULT DATA, *supra* note 54.

TABLE 38
Amount of Payment

Degree of Satisfaction	Claimants	
Very Satisfied	61.2%	87.7%
Fairly Satisfied	26.5%	
Fairly Dissatisfied	7.7%	
Very Dissatisfied	4.5%	
Total:	99.9%	
Base:	441	

4. General Claims Handling

A substantial majority of the respondents who had made claims were at least moderately pleased with the way in which their claims had been processed.[128] However, approximately one-third of the respondents indicated that they were "fairly dissatisfied" or "very dissatisfied" with either the amount received or the way in which their claim had been handled, or with both.[129] Consequently, some additional analysis of the views of these dissatisfied respondents was deemed both warranted and of interest.

In connection with the analysis of these responses, several things should be noted. First, after excluding individuals who reported that they had not been injured and those who expressed no dissatisfaction, the number of persons whose responses were analyzed was relatively small.[130] Consequently, the statistical significance of these figures is questionable. Second, analysis of the data suggests only slight correlations between dissatisfaction and other variables on which information was secured. It appears that the dissatisfied claimants were not significantly different from the satisfied claimants, and that their injuries likewise were not significantly different from those suffered by the total group of injured respondents.[131]

Several individuals offered more than one reason for their dissatisfaction with P.I.P.'s method of handling their claims. The total percentages in Table 39, which exceed 100 percent, reflect this fact.

---

128. *Id.*
129. *Id.*
130. *Id.*
131. *Id.*

TABLE 39
Types of Dissatisfaction

Nature of Dissatisfaction	Dissatisfied Claimants		All Claimants
I. Speed of Payment			
Claim Paid Too Slowly	27.8% ⎫		
Claim Paid Too Fast	4.0% ⎬ 53.8%		16.5%
Claim not yet Paid	21.0% ⎭		
II. Amount of Payment			
Medical Bills Claim not Paid	3.4% ⎫		
Wage Loss Claim not Paid	12.5% ⎪		
Amount Too Small	14.8% ⎬ 47.8%		14.7%
Pain not Compensated	17.1% ⎭		
III. Insurer's Attitude or Procedures			
Had to Argue with Insurer Over Amount of Payment	9.7% ⎫		
Insurer Did not Seem Concerned	6.3% ⎪		
Insurer Did not Provide Information About Progress on the Claim	8.0% ⎬ 24.6%		7.6%
Insurer Required a Release	0.6% ⎭		
IV. Miscellaneous Items			
Insurance Subsequently Cancelled	1.1% ⎫		
Not Dissatisfied with Company, but Dissatisfied with Someone Else	2.8% ⎬ 4.5%		1.5%
Bona Fide Claim not Paid	0.6% ⎭		
V. Not Dissatisfied			
Claim in Progress	—		13.6%
Claim Paid	—		54.9%
Total:	130.7%		108.8%
Base:	176[132]		565

5. *Extent and Intensity of Dissatisfaction*

An examination of the tables in the preceding sections raises the question of whether the responses represent a total dissatisfaction with the P.I.P. coverage system by these claimants. It is certainly conceivable that a respondent's dissatisfaction with one aspect of the relationship with the insurer could have been translated into expressions of displeasure with all aspects of the coverage and the claims process. If this were the case, the responses of such a claimant would, in some instances, be reflected in more than one of the above tables.[133] Therefore,

---

132. The percentages in this column are based on the interviews with 176 persons who provided at total of 229 codeable responses, an average of 1.3 responses per respondent.

133. *See* Tables 36-38 *supra.*

a cross-tabulation was run to determine whether persons who were dissatisfied with the speed with which their claims had been handled were
also dissatisfied with the amount they had been paid. Similarly, the converse cross-tabulation was also run to see if those who were dissatisfied
with the amount paid were also unhappy about the speed with which the
claims had been processed. This analysis indicates that while there was
considerable overlap, it was by no means pervasive nor even true of the
majority of the persons who were dissatisfied. For example, of those
persons who expressed dissatisfaction with the speed with which the
claim had been handled, over half indicated that they were satisfied with
the amount they had received.

TABLE 40
Of Those Dissatisfied with Speed:
Responses to Inquiry About Satisfaction with Amount

Very satisfied	32.4%	55.9%
Fairly Satisfied	23.5%	
Fairly Dissatisfied	16.2%	
Very Dissatisfied	22.1%	
Don't Know	5.9%	
Total:	100.1%	
Base:	68	

A similar result was achieved by the converse cross-tabulation, as
shown in Table 41.

TABLE 41
Of Those Dissatisfied with Amount:
Responses to Inquiry About Satisfaction with Speed of Payment

Very Satisfied	18.5%	50.0%
Fairly Satisfied	31.5%	
Fairly Dissatisfied	24.1%	
Very Dissatisfied	24.1%	
Don't Know/No Response	1.9%	
Total:	100.1%	
Base:	54	

As reflected in Table 41, more than half of the respondents who were
dissatisfied with the amount received indicated no displeasure with the
speed of payment. Only six percent of the persons who had made claims
and who responded to the survey inquiries regarding satisfaction with

the P.I.P. system reported displeasure with both the amount they had received and the time it had taken the claim to be handled.[134] The interviews also included a generalized inquiry about satisfaction with the manner in which the claim had been handled. Those respondents who reported that they were generally dissatisfied were asked to explain the reasons for their dissatisfaction. This inquiry generally elicited a repetition of the respondents' earlier answers to specific questions concerning their evaluation of either the speed of the claims process or the amount they had been paid.[135]

6. Attorney Involvement

In light of the relative simplicity of the P.I.P. claims process, it was interesting to find that fully one-quarter of the persons who had made claims indicated that they had received some assistance from an attorney.[136] While a majority of these respondents indicated that a tort claim also had been involved in their cases, many had filed only a P.I.P. claim.[137] In a few cases, even though no tort claim or action had been involved, attorneys had handled P.I.P. claims in a routine manner much as some attorneys are asked by clients to prepare relatively simple tax forms. Thus, from the interviews conducted with attorneys it appears that many lawyers file P.I.P. claims as an accommodation to their clients.[138]

Perhaps the most notable fact is that almost three-quarters of the claimants indicated that they had filed their claims without the assistance of an attorney. In a state where automobile accident victims had formerly gone to attorneys apparently as a matter of course,[139] this statistic suggests that the no-fault legislation may have substantially altered the claims behavior of accident victims. It should be noted that when cross-tabulations were run to ascertain whether representation by an attorney seemed to influence the relative degree of satisfaction or dissatisfaction with the P.I.P. coverage, no such correlation was found to exist. The percentages in Tables 37 ("Speed of Payment") and 38 ("Amount of Payment") showed essentially the same levels of satisfaction and dissatisfaction when the analysis was made separately for those who were represented by an attorney and those who were not.

---

134. CLRS NO-FAULT DATA, *supra* note 54.
135. *Id. See also* Table 39 *supra.*
136. CLRS NO-FAULT DATA, *supra* note 54.
137. *Id.*
138. *Id.*
139. *See* U.S. DEP'T TRANS., AUTOMOBILE INSURANCE AND COMPENSATION STUDY: AUTOMOBILE PERSONAL INJURY CLAIMS 78-80 (1970).

7. Claims Assistance from Other Persons

More than one-fifth of the claimants stated that they had received some assistance or guidance from other persons in connection with the filing of their P.I.P. claims, and about half of these (over 10 percent of the claimants) indicated that the person in question was their insurance agent.

TABLE 42

Claims Assistance from Other Persons

Person Assisting	All Claimants
Relatives	6.4%
Friends	1.9%
Insurance Agents	11.6%
Other	3.0%
Total:	22.9%
Base:	577

It was considered worthwhile to ascertain whether the participation of the insurance agent had affected the respondents' evaluations of the way in which their claims had been handled. Analysis indicates that the respondents who had received such assistance were slightly more satisfied with the amounts they had been paid and the speed with which their claims had been handled.[140] Since the absolute number of respondents who had sought assistance from their insurance agent was not large, and the difference in the levels of satisfaction was not markedly different, the statistical significance of this data is questionable.

VI. CONCLUSIONS AND OBSERVATIONS

The accident victim survey was designed to gather data which would provide answers to several specific questions basic to an evaluation of the Massachusetts no-fault system from the standpoint of those whom it was designed to compensate. As noted above, one set of inquiries was designed to determine whether potential claimants were choosing not to make P.I.P. claims, and the reasons for their decisions. Secondly, data was assembled on the receipt of benefits from collateral sources of indemnification to ascertain whether such sources were a significant factor in potential claimants' decisions in regard to filing P.I.P. claims. Finally, questions were asked of those who had pursued P.I.P. claims to gain the information necessary to evaluate their relative satisfaction or dissatisfaction with the no-fault claim system. The following discussion of

---

140. CLRS NO-FAULT DATA, *supra* note 54.

the effectiveness of the Massachusetts no-fault system presents conclusions and observations derived from an analysis of the data compiled
by this survey.

A. Non-Claimants

The first question this study was designed to answer was whether a
significant number of persons who had been injured in automobile accidents in Massachusetts had decided to pursue indemnification under
coverage provided by the no-fault insurance. To secure relevant data, it
was desirable to interview persons who had been injured, and who
therefore were likely to have sustained the type of economic loss that
would warrant making no-fault insurance claims. Consequently, the interviewees were randomly selected from among persons who were reported as having been visibly injured in an accident. The data compiled
in this study unequivocally indicate that many such persons do not file
P.I.P. insurance claims.[141] In addition, analysis of the data disclosed that
one or more of four reasons were generally given by the non-claimants in
response to the survey question inquiring about why they had chosen not
to pursue no-fault claims.

First, many of the persons who were reported as having been visibly
injured responded that they had not actually been injured. At least in the
retrospective view of these respondents, the characterizations in the accident reports were inaccurate. When the interviews were conducted,
about 20 percent of the respondents who had not filed P.I.P. claims stated that they had not been injured in the accident,[142] and about three-
quarters of these persons indicated that the absence of any injury was
the reason no claim had been made.[143] The remaining one-quarter of the
uninjured non-claimants typically had suffered some losses or had incurred some expenses, usually in connection with a medical examination
to confirm that they were indeed uninjured. Thus, these individuals'
prinicipal reasons for not filing a claim usually included statements
which led to grouping them with those respondents who stated that it
was not worth the inconvenience to apply for indemnification.

The responses of these uninjured non-claimants suggest that caution
should be exercised in relating personal injury data compiled from accident reports filed with the Registry of Motor Vehicles to the number of
personal injury claims made to insurance companies. This is not to suggest that the information compiled by the Registry is faulty. Rather, it indicates that drivers' accident reports, often based upon observations

---

141. *See* text accompanying notes 78-111 *supra.*
142. *See* Table 16 *supra.*
143. *See* text accompanying notes 80-84 *supra.*

made immediately following an accident, do not always furnish injury descriptions that will prove useful in conducting a census of the number of persons who sustain injuries of the type that would warrant P.I.P. claims.

Second, the survey confirmed that many persons who sustain minor injuries which involve little or nothing in the way of medical costs and only minimal loss of wages do not bother to seek indemnification from any source. Approximately 20 percent of the non-claimants made statements which were so characterized in the analysis of responses.[144] While it is difficult to estimate exactly the magnitude of losses or costs involved, it appears that many persons were prepared to absorb relatively modest medical costs or losses of up to $15 or $20, the amount typically expended to obtain a medical examination to confirm the absence of serious injury or to obtain treatment for minor injuries. Similarly, about one-quarter of the non-claimants who were employed stated that they had been absent from their jobs for some period of time as a result of the accident, and that the resultant lost income had not been made up by a collateral source.[145] Many of these individuals also viewed wage losses resulting from missing a day or two of work as amounts which were not substantial enough to warrant filing a P.I.P. claim.

Third, a significant number of the persons interviewed (almost one-quarter of the non-claimants) gave responses indicating that they had not sought indemnification because they had been uninformed or misinformed about the no-fault coverage.[146] Since their economic losses had been relatively small, many of these persons probably had not been sufficiently motivated to acquire additional information about the P.I.P. system, and thus had remained uninformed. Essentially, their actions are explicable on the same grounds as those of the interviewees who stated that making a claim simply was not worth the effort entailed. However, this was not the attitude of all uninformed or misinformed non-claimants. It seems reasonable, therefore, to anticipate that over time the class of persons who fail to assert claims involving more extensive economic losses because they are not adequately apprised of the coverage will become smaller as familiarity with the no-fault system increases.

In Massachusetts, a state whose population was considered especially claims-conscious in the pre-no-fault era,[147] it was at least moderately surprising to discover such a large group of persons who apparently

---

144. *See* text accompanying notes 85-89 *supra.*
145. *See* text accompanying Table 20 *supra..*
146. *See* text accompanying notes 103-108 *supra.*
147. *See* U.S. Dep't. of Trans., Automobile Insurance and Compensation Study: Automobile Personal Injury Claims 78-80 (1970).

were not aware of the possibility of recovery under the no-fault system. The lack of awareness manifested by these respondents indicates that the introduction of no-fault insurance in other states should be accompanied by an educational program to acquaint potential claimants with the coverage. In addition, consideration ought to be given to adopting procedures which would automatically provide all persons who are identified as having been injured with information about no-fault insurance.[148]

The fourth reason given by respondents for not making P.I.P. claims was that their expenses or losses had been either wholly or substantially covered by other sources. About 20 percent of the non-claimants indicated this as the primary reason for their election not to make a no-fault claim.[149] The statements and actions of these non-claimants appear to justify the generalization that a significant number of non-claimants fall into this category precisely because they do not wish to abuse the system. In fact, the interviews seem to indicate that the majority of respondents felt that the coverage was to be used only to compensate for substantial losses.[150] To the extent that these findings represent a continuing trend under the no-fault automobile insurance system. substantial savings could accrue to insurance companies and policy holders alike, especially since the administrative costs of handling small claims are often essentially the same as those involving large amounts.

Perhaps as important as the explanations of why indemnification was not sought from the P.I.P. coverage, are the data which indicate factors that were *not* significant. First, the propensity to make a claim was not influenced by geography. As shown by Table 38, there were no significant differences in the relative proportion of claimants and non-claimants in terms of their county of residence. In fact, the survey respondents from three of the most urban counties, Suffolk (which includes metropolitan Boston), Essex and Middlesex (which comprise much of the urban and suburban area around Boston), were actually slightly more likely to be non-claimants than claimants. These results are surprising in view of the fact that persons residing in heavily populated areas of the state might ordinarily be expected to be more claims-conscious than those living in rural districts.[151] If the data shown in Table 38, which in-

---

148. Information could be provided by automatically sending a brief description of the no-fault benefits to all persons identified as having been injured in the accident reports which motorists in most states are required to file following an accident that involves personal injuries. In Massachusetts, these reports are sent to the Massachusetts Registry of Motor Vehicles.

149. *See* text accompanying notes 90-100 *supra.*

150. *See* text accompanying notes 85-100 *supra.*

151. *See* U.S. Dep't. of Trans., Automobile Insurance and Compensation Study: Automobile Personal Injury Claims 45-46 (1970).

dicate that the claims level is substantially the same in urban and rural areas of the state, is validated by the insurers' claims experience, it will be a very significant trend.

Some observers have hypothesized that injured persons might be deterred from becoming claimants because they would be seeking indemnification from their own companies. In actuality, this was a dominant factor for less than three percent of the non-claimants, and a factor of "some importance" for only an additional three or four percent of the non-claimants.[152] A correlative conclusion to be derived from these statistics, of course, is that this factor was not significant for the vast majority of non-claimants. Moreover, many of these non-P.I.P. claimants did seek indemnification from the same insurer for property claims arising out of the same accident. Obviously, these persons were not totally deterred from filing all first party insurance claims. Nor did any respondent cite this factor as a deterrent to making a property claim. It therefore seems fair to conclude, that potential P.I.P. claimants are not significantly deterred by the fact that no-fault insurance is first-party coverage.

B. Collateral Sources: Their Use, Non-use, or Abuse by Claimants and Non-claimants

The economic consequences of an automobile accident that causes personal injuries usually include some type of medical expense, and, for the employed person, often a loss of income as a result of absence from work. As noted above in regard to such costs, analysis of the interviews disclosed that more than 20 percent of the non-claimants stated that they had not made P.I.P. claims because their expenses or losses had been covered by collateral sources.[153]

Of equal significance were the responses which indicated that many losses had not been covered by collateral sources. For example, nearly 60 percent of all respondents who were employed and had been absent from their jobs stated that none of their lost pay had been replaced by any type of wage replacement plan or sick leave pay. In addition, another 15 percent of the employed respondents stated that a significant portion of their pay had been lost even though they had received some compensation from a collateral source.[154]

In regard to health insurance, over 45 percent of the claimants and 25 percent of the non-claimants stated that the reason they had not received medical insurance benefits was either that they had not been covered by

---

152. *See* text accompanying notes 109-12 *supra.*
153. *See* text accompanying notes 90-91 *supra.*
154. CLRS No-Fault Data, *supra* note 54.

such insurance or that their insurance had not provided coverage for the medical costs they had incurred.[155]

Another perspective on the availability and use of collateral sources was provided by responses to the question which specifically asked whether indemnification had been provided by health or medical insurance. More than 20 percent of the P.I.P. claimants responded that they had not sought indemnification from their health insurer because the cost had been covered by their automobile insurance.[156] For these persons, the P.I.P. coverage served as an alternative source which they had preferred to use in lieu of their health insurance. Moreover, when this group of P.I.P. claimants is combined with the 20 percent of the non-claimants who reported that they had not made P.I.P. claims because their losses had been covered by collateral sources,[157] it becomes evident that a substantial segment of the respondents who had been injured chose not to seek duplicate recoveries.

In considering the existence and effect of multiple sources of compensation or indemnification, it is also relevant to examine the adequacy of the collateral coverage. It is clear from the interviews that many claimants were able to secure only partial indemnification from collateral sources, and that full indemnification was secured only by recoveries from both the P.I.P. coverage and the collateral source. For example, of the claimants who had received indemnification from their medical insurance, only 27 percent stated that the medical insurer had reimbursed them for all of their medically related costs.[158] Conversely, 35 percent of the P.I.P. claimants who had received medical payments from collateral sources stated that such payments had left most of their medically-related losses uncompensated.[159] Similarly, among the P.I.P. claimants who had been absent from their jobs as a result of the accident, nearly 75 percent reported the loss of "all," or "almost all," or "some" of their pay.[160] That is, only about 25 percent had had a collateral source, such as sick leave pay or workmen's compensation, which had made up the lost wages.[161]

---

155. *Id.* The explanation of one respondent as to why he had made no health insurance claim is illustrative of the way in which the insurance system can act in an idiosyncratic fashion to foreclose coverage. The respondent, who was 19 years old, had no longer been insured by his family's health plan at the time of his accident because it had not covered employed dependents over the age of 18, and he had not yet worked long enough to qualify for coverage under the health insurance furnished by his employer. While this is only one example, it is typical of many responses made in the course of these interviews.

156. *Id.*

157. *See* text accompanying notes 90-91 *supra.*

158. *Id.*

159. *Id.*

160. *Id.*

161. *Id.*

In summary, the results of the survey indicate that, on the whole, potential claimants in Massachusetts are not attempting to use the no-fault coverage as a means of securing duplicate recoveries for injuries sustained in automobile accidents. A clear majority of the claimants stated that they had filed P.I.P. claims in addition to utilizing collateral sources only because the collateral sources had not fully compensated them for their accident-related losses. Moreover, many other P.I.P. claimants reported that they had not sought indemnification from collateral sources at all because their losses had been covered completely by the no-fault insurance. Finally, a substantial number of non-claimants stated that they had not filed P.I.P. claims because collateral sources had fully indemnified them. Thus, it can be concluded that most automobile accident victims in Massachusetts are not abusing the compensation system by attempting to secure the maximum recovery possible from all available sources.

C. The Claimants

At the beginning of the discussion of the claimants in Part V of this Article, it was pointed out that the data on the claimants and non-claimants interviewed for this study showed that there were no significant differences between the two groups in regard to their county of residence, sex, role in the accident, or the number of vehicles involved in the accident. The two groups, however, are at least somewhat distinguishable when compared in terms of the severity of the injuries sustained and the attendant consequences suffered. This does not mean that this line of analysis provides a clear demarcation line between claimants and non-claimants. In fact, quite the opposite is true. For example, while none of the claimants reported loss of a limb, this type of permanent injury was described by two of the non-claimants.[162] Comparable observations about the nature of other accident consequences for the non-claimants and claimants are equally valid. For example, while proportionately the non-claimants had spent fewer days in hospitals and had lost fewer days at work,[163] many non-claimants also had experienced these accident consequences. Therefore, while on the whole the non-claimants described proportionately fewer serious injuries, many non-claimants had sustained significant injuries and had suffered accident consequences that were at least comparable to those described by the respondents who had filed P.I.P. claims.

D. Satisfaction and Dissatisfaction

Another major purpose of this study was to evaluate the claims process under the no-fault insurance system from the perspective of the

---

162. *Id.*
163. *Id.*

claimant. From an analysis of the survey questionnaires, both individually and collectively, it can be concluded that persons who had filed P.I.P. claims and had received P.I.P. payments felt that the system was working well. Seventy-five to 85 percent of these claimants indicated that they were either "fairly satisfied" or "very satisfied" with the manner in which their claims had been handled and with the amount they had received.[164] It is clear, however, that this general conclusion does not reflect the opinion of every person who was interviewed.

The comments of a number of respondents who had made P.I.P. claims indicate that they had encountered problems with the system. Undoubtedly, these comments, to some extent, reflect the type of bureaucratic inconveniences and complications which inevitably will result when large numbers of claims are being processed by any insurance compensation system. On the other hand, some of the criticisms were of such a nature that, in view of their incidence among the respondents, they warrant further investigation and possible remedial action. For example, many respondents stated that in the interim period between filing and payment they had not been kept apprised of the status of their claims. Thus, it would seem desirable for states which have enacted the no-fault insurance system to establish procedures whereby persons whose claims have been pending for some specified period, such as 45 or 60 days, would automatically be notified of the status of their claims.

Another disturbing result of the survey is that 15 percent of the respondents indicated dissatisfaction with the speed with which their P.I.P. claims had been processed.[165] Some of the problems which generated this dissatisfaction probably are easily overcome. For example, several respondents complained that they had been reimbursed prematurely while they were still incurring medical expenses. Had these claimants been fully informed of the operation of the no-fault insurance system, they would have realized that they were not precluded from filing additional claims for costs incurred after receipt of their initial P.I.P. payment. Thus, such complaints probably could be almost completely eliminated through a concerted effort on the part of insurers to increase claimants' understanding of the P.I.P. system.

A number of respondents also complained that their P.I.P. claims had remained unpaid for many months or had never been paid. In several instances, interviews with lawyers who represented these persons disclosed that, in fact, insurance payments had been sent to the attorney, who, in turn, had used them to pay the claimant's outstanding medical bills. In other cases, attorneys had held the payments in trust for their

---

164. *See* text accompanying notes 120-35 *supra*.
165. *See* text accompanying notes 126-27 *supra*.

clients, pending resolution of tort claims. In light of these facts, a relatively simple technique for alleviating claimant dissatisfaction would appear to be the establishment of a procedure whereby insurance companies would promptly notify a claimant when P.I.P. payments are mailed to his or her legal representative.

The survey data indicates that there also were many instances in which claimant dissatisfaction was not attributable to the factors discussed above. While an exhaustive analysis of these problems and their underlying reasons is beyond the scope of this Article, it should be noted that adverse comments were made both by respondents who were generally content with the P.I.P. system and by the approximately eight to 10 percent of the claimants who seemed to express total dissatisfaction with the no-fault coverage. These criticisms undoubtedly deserve careful consideration by the insurance industry in Massachusetts as well as by officials in other states which have adopted, or are planning to establish, a no-fault insurance system.

Of course, the unfavorable comments received from some respondents must be viewed in relation to the affirmative evaluations of the P.I.P. system offered by a substantial majority of the claimants who were interviewed for this study. While it is difficult to find benchmarks against which to measure the data compiled for the survey, it seems unlikely that many comparable systems exist in which the percentage of "fairly satisfied" and "very satisfied" consumers exceed 80 percent.[166]

E. A Final Assessment

The positive attitudes towards P.I.P. insurance expressed by the vast majority of the claimants interviewed for this portion of the CLRS No-Fault study are most encouraging. Moreover, in the course of the study numerous conversations that the author has conducted with both government and insurance industry officials suggest that these individuals also believe that the system is effectively serving the needs of most claimants. These discussions also disclosed that the industry sought to use the introduction of no-fault insurance as a means of substantially improving its relationships with consumers in Massachusetts. The survey data compiled this segment of the CLRS No-Fault study demonstrate that, from the perspective of the P.I.P. claimant, the industry has made significant progress towards attaining that goal.

---

166. *See* text accompanying note 123 *supra.*

APPENDIX

CLRS MASSACHUSETTS NO-FAULT STUDY
ACCIDENT VICTIM QUESTIONNAIRE

(DO Q.29 BEFORE INTERVIEW)

Interviewer's Name _____

Interview Number _____

am
Time Begun_____ pm

1. As a result of the accident, were you injured in any way?

   ☐ YES
   ☐ NO (SKIP TO Q.5)

2. Was it a broken bone or a fracture of any kind?

   ☐ YES
   ☐ NO

3. Did the accident leave you with any permanent injury or with any permanent disfigurement, such as a scar?

   ☐ YES, INJURY
   ☐ YES, DISFIGUREMENT
   ☐ YES, BOTH
   ☐ NO (SKIP TO Q.5)

4. Would you please describe the permanent injury/disfigurement?

   _____

   _____

5. As a result of the accident, did you miss any days on your job — not counting work around the house?

   ☐ YES
   ☐ NO (SKIP TO Q.9)
   ☐ NOT EMPLOYED (SKIP TO Q.9)

6. How many days did you miss? _____ (DAYS) (DON'T ACCEPT WEEKS OR MONTHS — ASK SPECIFICATION)

7. Was all or part of the pay for the time you missed made up:

	YES	NO	DON'T KNOW
by your salary?	☐	☐	☐
by sick leave?	☐	☐	☐
by an insurance plan where you work?	☐	☐	☐
by Workmen's Compensation?	☐	☐	☐
by any other source except auto insurance? (What was it?)_____	☐	☐	☐

8. All together, about how much pay did you actually lose from the days you missed: would you say *none, a small part, some, almost all,* or *all* of it?

   ☐ NONE
   ☐ A SMALL PART
   ☐ SOME
   ☐ ALMOST ALL
   ☐ ALL
   ☐ DON'T KNOW

9. Were you kept from carrying out any of your (other) usual activities for some period of time because of the accident?

   ☐ YES
   ☐ NO (SKIP TO Q.14)

10. About how long? _____

11. Would you please briefly tell me what you could not do?

    _____
    _____

12. Did you hire anyone to do things that you would have done yourself if you had not been involved in the accident?

    ☐ YES
    ☐ NO (SKIP TO Q.14)

13. Would you please tell me what kind of things:

    _____
    _____

14. As a result of the accident, did you do to a hospital?

    ☐ YES
    ☐ NO (SKIP TO Q.16)

15. For how long were you in the hospital?

    ☐ PART OF A DAY
    ☐ OVERNIGHT
    ☐ 2 to 6 DAYS
    ☐ 1 to 2 WEEKS
    ☐ OVER 2 WEEKS

16. As a result of the accident, (did you)/(then, you did) see a doctor?

    ☐ YES
    ☐ NO

17. Did you have any (other) kind of medical treatment or have any (other) medical expenses?

    ☐ YES
    ☐ NO

18. *INTERVIEWER CHECK:*

    ☐ R RECEIVED NO MEDICAL ATTENTION ("NO" ON EVERY QUESTION, 14, 16, AND 17) (SKIP TO Q.26)
    ☐ R RECEIVED SOME FORM OF MEDICAL ATTENTION

19. As a result of the accident, did any health insurance company, such as Blue Cross/Blue Shield, pay any of your medical expenses, either directly or by paying you back for expenses you had paid yourself? This includes the costs of a dentist, nurse, ambulance, medicines, and such items as crutches.

    ☐ YES
    ☐ NO (SKIP TO Q.21)

20. All together, about how much of your medical expenses did they pay — would you say, *all, almost all, some,* or *a small part*?

    ☐ ALL
    ☐ ALMOST ALL
    ☐ SOME   } (SKIP TO Q.22)
    ☐ A SMALL PART

21. Why didn't you receive any medical insurance benefits?
    ☐ R HAD NO HEALTH INSURANCE
    ☐ OTHER: _____
    _____

22. As a result of the accident, did Workmen's Compensation pa for any of your medical expenses?
    ☐ YES
    ☐ NO (SKIP TO Q.24)

23. About how much of your medical expenses did it pay — would you say *all, almost all, some,* or *a small part?*
    ☐ ALL
    ☐ ALMOST ALL
    ☐ SOME   (SKIP TO Q.25)
    ☐ A SMALL PART

24. Was that because Workmen's Compensation did not apply to you or for some other reason?
    ☐ NOT APPLICABLE
    ☐ OTHER: _____
    _____

25. Did your total medical expenses as a result of this accident, regardless of who paid them, come to over $500?
    ☐ YES
    ☐ NO

26. Now I would like to ask you a few questions about auto insurance claims. As a result of the accident, did you make a claim against any auto insurance company for any medical expenses, lost wages, or other losses, *not including property damage*? I am interested here only in any injury claim you may have made; we will discuss proerty damage in a few moments.
    ☐ YES
    ☐ NO

27. Against which company did you make a claim: was it your own or your family's auto insurance company, was it someone else's, or was it both?
    ☐ OWN (SKIP TO Q.39)
    ☐ SOMEONE ELSE'S
    ☐ BOTH (SKIP TO Q.37)

28. Did you make more than one claim?
    ☐ YES (SKIP TO Q.38)
    ☐ NO, ONLY ONE CLAIM
    ☐ DON'T KNOW

29. INTERVIEWER CHECK: (FROM ACCIDENT FORM)
    ☐ R WAS IN MOTOR VEHICLE
    ☐ R WAS NOT IN MOTOR VEHICLE (PEDESTRIAN, CYCLIST(— (SKIP TO Q.31)

30. Was your claim against the insurance for the car *you* were in, or against *another* car in the accident?
    ☐ R'S VEHICLE
    ☐ OTHER VEHICLE (SKIP TO Q.51)
    ☐ DON'T KNOW

31. I would like to get clear just what your claim was for:

	YES	NO	DON'T KNOW
a. Was it for medical expenses?	☐	☐	☐
b. Was it for wage losses?	☐	☐	☐
c. Was it for pain and suffering or any amount over and above your actual monetary losses?	☐	☐	☐

32. <u>INTERVIEWER CHECK:</u>
    ☐ R'S CLAIM WAS FOR MEDICAL OR WAGE LOSS ONLY (SKIP TO Q.39)
    ☐ R'S CLAIM INCLUDED PAIN AND SUFFERING (SKIP TO Q.51)
    ☐ R DIDN'T KNOW WHETHER HIS CLAIM INCLUDED PAIN AND SUFFERING (SKIP TO Q.39)

33. Do you think you could have gotten any medical expenses or wage losses from any auto insurance company if you had filed a claim?
    ☐ YES
    ☐ NO (SKIP TO Q.36)

34. Why didn't you make a claim?

    _____

    _____

    _____

    _____

35. How important were the following factors in your decision not to make a claim, *very important, fairly important,* or *not important at all?*

	VERY IMPT.	FAIRLY IMPT.	NOT IMPT. AT ALL	
The fact that —				
a. Only a small amount was involved:	☐	☐	☐	(SKIP TO
b. You didn't want to file a claim against your own company:	☐	☐	☐	Q.58)

36. Why not?

    _____

    _____

    (PROBE!!) _____

    _____ (SKIP TO Q.58)

37. First I would like to ask you a few questions about your claim against your own or your family's auto insurance. This is the so-called P.I.P. or "no-fault" claim. If you filled out the forms yourself, you may remember that the no-fault form is a very long yellow sheet. (SKIP TO Q.39)

38. First I would like to ask you a few questions about your claim for medical expenses and wage losses only. This does not include any additional claim for pain and suffering. The medical and wage claim is the so-called P.I.P. or "no-fault" claim. If you filled out the forms yourself, you may remember that the no-fault form is a very long yellow sheet.

39. Have you been paid anything yet?
    ☐ YES (SKIP TO Q.41)
    ☐ NO

40. Why haven't you been paid yet, do you know?

    _____

    _____ (SKIP TO Q.45)

41. How satisfied were you with the speed with which your claim for medical expenses and wage losses was paid? Were you *very satisfied, fairly satisfied, fairly dissatisfied,* or *very dissatisfied?*
    - ☐ VERY SATISFIED
    - ☐ FAIRLY SATISFIED
    - ☐ FAIRLY DISSATISFIED
    - ☐ VERY DISSATISFIED

42. How satisfied were you with the amount you were paid? Were you *very satisfied, fairly satisfied, fairly dissatisfied,* or *very dissatisfied?*
    - ☐ VERY SATISFIED ⎫ (SKIP TO Q.44)
    - ☐ FAIRLY SATISFIED ⎭
    - ☐ FAIRLY DISSATISFIED
    - ☐ VERY DISSATISFIED

43. Did the fact that you had a deductible cause any of your dissatisfaction?
    - ☐ YES
    - ☐ NO
    - ☐ NO DEDUCTIBLE

44. Did your auto insurance payment (and your health insurance payment together) cover all your medical expenses?
    - ☐ YES
    - ☐ NO

45. In general, how satisfied were you with the way your claim was handled? Were you *very satisfied, fairly satisfied, fairly dissatisfied,* or *very dissatisfied?*
    - ☐ VERY SATISFIED
    - ☐ FAIRLY SATISFIED
    - ☐ FAIRLY DISSATISFIED ⎫
    - ☐ VERY DISSATISFIED ⎭ (SKIP TO Q.47)

46. Were you dissatisfied in *any* (other) way?
    - ☐ YES
    - ☐ NO

47. <u>INTERVIEWER CHECK:</u>
    - ☐ R WAS NOT DISSATISFIED IN ANY WAY (QS. 41, 42, & 45 ALL AT LEAST "FAIRLY SATISFIED" & Q.46 IS "NO") — (SKIP TO Q.50)
    - ☐ R WAS FAIRLY DISSATISFIED OR VERY DISSATISFIED IN SOME WAY

48. Would you tell me (more about) why you were dissatisfied?
    _____
    _____

49. Was there anything else?
    _____
    _____
    _____

50. <u>INTERVIEWER CHECK:</u>
    - ☐ R CLAIMED *ONLY* AGAINST OWN COMPANY (Q.27 WAS "OWN") — (SKIP TO Q.54)
    - ☐ R CLAIMED *ONLY* FOR MEDICAL EXPENSES AND WAGE LOSS (Q.31c WAS "NO" PAIN AND SUFFERING) — (SKIP TO Q.54)
    - ☐ R MADE MORE THAN ONE CLAIM (Q.27 WAS "BOTH" OR Q.28 WAS "YES")

51. Now, concerning (your second claim/your claim for pain and suffering/your claim against the other car), have you been paid by the insurance company yet or is the claim still pending?
    ☐ PAID OR SETTLED
    ☐ PENDING

52. In general, how satisfied were you with the way your claim was handled? Were you *very satisfied, fairly satisfied, fairly dissatisfied,* or *very dissatisfied?*
    ☐ VERY SATISFIED ⎱
    ☐ FAIRLY SATISFIED ⎰   (SKIP TO Q.54)
    ☐ FAIRLY DISSATISFIED
    ☐ VERY DISSATISFIED

53. Would you tell me why you were dissatisfied?
    _____

54. Did you receive any help from a lawyer in making your claim(s)?
    ☐ YES
    ☐ NO

55. Did you receive any help from anyone else in making your claim(s)?
    ☐ YES
    ☐ NO (SKIP TO Q.57)

56. Who helped you make your claim(s)?
    ☐ RELATIVE
    ☐ FRIEND
    ☐ INSURANCE AGENT/BROKER
    ☐ OTHER: _____

57. (Has/Was) a lawsuit (been) filed in connection with your claim?
    ☐ YES
    ☐ NO

58. Now, about property damage — was your own car damaged in the accident?
    ☐ YES — OWN OR FAMILY'S CAR
    ☐ NO — TERMINATE INTERVIEW

59. What coverage did you have for property damage at the time of the accident? Was it:
    ☐ Option One — Collision Coverage,
    ☐ Option Two — Restricted Collision Coverage, or
    ☐ Option Three — No Collision Coverage?
    ☐ DON'T KNOW

60. When you took Option _____ (FILL IN NUMBER FROM Q.59) for 1972, was what it covered explained to you by someone from your insurance company or by a booklet or a brochure?
    ☐ YES
    ☐ NO
    ☐ NOT SURE/DON'T KNOW/CAN'T REMEMBER

61. Which Option do you have now? Is it now:
    ☐ Option One,
    ☐ Option Two, or
    ☐ Option Three?
    ☐ DON'T KNOW

62. Was a claim made against your own or your family's auto insurance company for the damage to your car?
    ☐ YES (SKIP TO Q.64)
    ☐ NO

63. Why was no claim made? (PROBE)

_____
_____   } (TERMINATE
_____   { INTERVIEW)
_____

64. How satisfied were you with the speed with which your claim was paid? Were you *very satisfied, fairly satisfied, fairly dissatisfied* or *very dissatisfied*?
   - ☐ VERY SATISFIED
   - ☐ FAIRLY SATISFIED
   - ☐ FAIRLY DISSATISFIED
   - ☐ VERY DISSATISFIED

65. How satisfied were you with the amount you were paid? Were you *very satisfied, fairly satisfied, fairly dissatisfied* or *very dissatisfied*?
   - ☐ VERY SATISFIED
   - ☐ FAIRLY SATISFIED
   - ☐ FAIRLY DISSATISFIED
   - ☐ VERY DISSATISFIED

66. In general, how satisfied were you with the way your claim was handled? Were you *very satisfied, fairly satisfied, fairly dissatisfied,* or *very dissatisfied*?
   - ☐ VERY SATISFIED
   - ☐ FAIRLY SATISFIED
   - ☐ FAIRLY DISSATISFIED }
   - ☐ VERY DISSATISFIED   }   (SKIP TO Q.68)

67. Were you dissatisfied in *any* (other) way?
   - ☐ YES
   - ☐ NO

68. <u>INTERVIEWER CHECK:</u>
   - ☐ R WAS NOT DISSATISFIED IN ANY WAY (Qs. 64-66 ALL AT LEAST "FAIRLY SATISFIED" & Q.67 "NO") — TERMINATE INTERVIEW
   - ☐ R WAS FAIRLY DISSATISFIED OR VERY DISSATISFIED IN SOME WAY

69. Would you tell me (more about) why you were dissatisfied?

_____
_____
_____

Thank you.
TERMINATE INTERVIEW

                                              am
TIME ENDED_____ pm

CHAPTER 3

MASSACHUSETTS NO-FAULT AUTOMOBILE INSURANCE: ITS IMPACT ON THE LEGAL PROFESSION

ALAN I. WIDISS*

INTRODUCTION

In the United States the rights of persons injured in automobile accidents to indemnification have rested primarily on an allocation of fault, and lawyers have been integrally involved in determining when, as well as to what extent, such persons have been entitled to compensation. Of course, not all claimants have been represented by lawyers, but the prospect of such representation undoubtedly constituted an implicit influence even in instances when no attorney was actually involved. It seems clear that the involvement of attorneys in the claims process became more frequent as the use of liability insurance by motorists increased. Although numerous factors contributed to this development, it is likely that one significant cause was the general perception that an injured person's recovery depended not only on the determination of fault, but also on the ability to negotiate successfully with insurance company representatives.

In 1925, Massachusetts became the first state to enact a compulsory insurance law which requires that all motorists secure liability insurance as a prerequisite to operating an automobile.[1] For over twenty-five years Massachusetts was the only state with such a legislative requirement [2]

---

* Professor of Law, University of Iowa. B.S., University of Southern California, 1960; LL.B., University of Southern California, 1963; LL.M., Harvard University, 1964. This article reports on one segment of the Massachusetts No-Fault Study, a project of the Council on Law-Related Studies. The Council is a small private foundation created in 1969 by the Walter E. Meyer Research Institute of Law, Inc., which supported many of the studies of automobile accident compensation in the 1960s. For the Massachusetts study, the Council retained the author to serve as Director, and Mr. Randall R. Bovbjerg as Associate Director, of a broadly based empirical investigation of how the implementation of no-fault automobile insurance affected (1) the compensation system for persons involved in automobile accidents, (2) the number of automobile tort cases in the courts, and (3) members of the legal profession.

The author would like to acknowledge the assistance of the many individuals who aided in the procurement and analysis of the data upon which this article is based. Although it would not be possible to identify everyone who contributed to the study, a few deserve special mention. Both the former Governor of Massachusetts, Francis Sargent, and the former Commissioner of Insurance, John Ryan, provided invaluable assistance in helping to make available necessary information. Also deserving of special note are the contributions of Dr. Floyd Fowler, who is Director of the Survey Research Program that did the interviewing for the accident victim survey, and Mr. James R. Grifhorst, who did the computer programming for the data analysis. In addition, I should like to acknowledge the efforts of several persons who worked on this phase of the study while they were law students at the University of Iowa: Ms. Marianne Baldridge, Ms. Jane Eikleberry, Ms. Nancy Hauserman, Mr. James E. Konsky, Mr. William P. Kovacs, Mr. Gary P. Malfeld, Mr. Donald F. Staas and Mr. John C. Schupe.

[1] Act of May 1, 1925, ch. 346, [1925] Mass. Acts & Resolves 426. The current version of the compulsory liability provision is Mass. Gen. Laws Ann. ch. 90, §§ 1A, 34A-I (1969).

[2] *See* Murphy & Netherton, Public Responsibility and the Uninsured Motorist, 47 Geo. L.J. 700, 702-03 (1959). From 1927 to the late 1960s, only New York in 1956, N.Y. Veh. &

Editor's Note: Reproduced from *Boston University Law Review*, Vol. 56, No. 2, 1976.

Accordingly, it was not surprising that the Department of Transportation Automobile Insurance and Compensation Study (DOT Study) disclosed that a substantial majority of claimants in Massachusetts who received payments from insurance companies as a result of injuries incurred in automobile accidents in Massachusetts were represented by attorneys,[3] and that Massachusetts ranked first among the nineteen states from which data were compiled in the percentage of accident victims represented by attorneys in those instances in which claims were paid.[4] The data for the DOT Study were compiled in 1969. Less than two years later Massachusetts became the first state to enact a no-fault insurance law requiring that compulsory liability insurance policies include an additional coverage that indemnifies all persons injured in automobile accidents without regard to fault.[5] This statutorily required no-fault coverage, known as Personal Injury Protection (PIP), provides injured persons with insurance of up to $2,000 for (1) loss of wages, (2) hospital and medical expenses incurred within two years of the accident, and (3) the cost of replacement services occasioned by the injury.[6]

The Massachusetts no-fault legislation also creates a limited tort exemption. The right to assert a tort claim for general damages is limited to those cases in which the accident consequences meet certain criteria.[7] Specifically, a claim for general damages, such as pain and suffering, may be brought in instances in which (1) the medical expenses exceed $500, (2) the accident causes death or involves a fracture, the loss of a body

---

Traf. Law § 312 (McKinney 1970), and North Carolina in 1957, N.C. Gen. Stat. §§ 20-309 to 20-311 (1975), enacted comparable compulsory insurance requirements. For a general discussion of these statutes see R. Keeton & J. O'Connell, Basic Protection for the Traffic Victim: A Blueprint for Reforming Automobile Insurance 76-102 (1965).

There has been considerable debate over the desirability of compulsory automobile liability insurance. *See, e.g.,* W. Blum & H. Kalven, Public Law Perspectives on a Private Law Problem: Auto Compensation Plans (1965); G. Calabresi, The Costs of Accidents: A Legal and Economic Analysis 1-16 (1970); Marx, Compensation Insurance for Automobile Accident Victims: The Case for Compulsory Automobile Compensation Insurance, 15 Ohio St. L. Rev. 134 (1954); McVay, The Case Against Compulsory Automobile Insurance, 15 Ohio St. L. Rev. 150 (1954); Risjord & Austin, The Problem of the Financially Irresponsible Motorist, 24 U. Kan. City L. Rev. 82, 83-84 (1955); Comment, 10 Vill. L. Rev. 545, 546-47 (1965).

[3] 1 Dep't of Transportation, Automobile Insurance and Compensation Study: Automobile Personal Injury Claims 78 (1970).

[4] *Id.*

[5] *See* Act of Aug. 13, 1970, ch. 670, [1970] Mass. Acts & Resolves 529; Mass. Gen. Laws Ann. ch. 90, § 34A (Supp. 1975). Several other states have since enacted no-fault laws of various types. The Council on Law-Related Studies provided grants for studies of the impact of no-fault automobile insurance in Florida and Delaware. The results of the Delaware study are reported in Clark & Waterson, "No-Fault" in Delaware, 6 Rutgers-Camden L.J. 225 (1974). A preliminary report on the Florida study appeared in Little, How No Fault Is Working in Florida, 59 A.B.A.J. 1020 (1973). The reports of the studies will appear in a forthcoming volume, A. Widiss, J. Little, R. Clark & R. Bovbjerg, No-Fault Automobile Insurance: The Massachusetts, Florida, and Delaware Experience (Oceana Publications, Inc.).

[6] Mass. Gen. Laws Ann. ch. 90. § 34A (Supp. 1975).

[7] *Id.* ch. 231, § 6D.

member, or permanent or serious disfigurement, or (3) the accident results in the loss of sight or hearing.[8] The essence, then, of the Massachusetts no-fault law is, first, that persons are provided with up to $2,000 of no-fault insurance to indemnify the losses arising from medical treatments, absences from employment, or the need to secure replacement services, and, second, that injured persons may not sue to recover general damages unless at least one of the several possible conditions is satisfied. Thus, the coverage is designed both to provide a minimum level of indemnification for all accident victims and to limit tort claims that would otherwise arise from the relatively minor injuries that are the result of most automobile accidents.[9]

There has been considerable interest in the effect that no-fault coverage and the limitation on tort actions have had on the legal profession. This article discusses both the impact of the no-fault coverage on the role of lawyers in the claims process and the related question of the economic effects on the legal profession of the statutory limitation on the right to assert tort claims. The article is based upon data compiled in a multi-faceted empirical investigation of the effect of no-fault automobile insurance on the automobile accident compensation system in Massachusetts.[10] The study is a project of the Council on Law-Related Studies, and this article presents a portion of the study results. Data collected in several segments of the Council on Law-Related Studies Massachusetts No-Fault Study (CLRS Study) have been relied upon in the preparation of this article, and, before proceeding to the analysis of the effects of the no-fault law, a brief description of the ways in which information was secured from lawyers, courts, accident victims and insurance companies will be given.

---

[8] A tort action may be brought, however, for any actual losses not compensated by the PIP coverage. *See* M. Woodroof, J. Fonesca & A. Squillante, Automobile Insurance and No-Fault Law § 15:15, at 450 (1974). *But cf.* Massachusetts Continuing Legal Education, Inc., The Massachusetts No-Fault Insurance Law 58 (1971). The claimant in such an action would nonetheless still be barred from recovering damages for pain and suffering unless one of the specified thresholds were met.

If a Massachusetts driver is involved in an out-of-state accident and is sued, the tort exemption of the no-fault personal injury protection does not apply. Thus, Massachusetts drivers still need liability coverage for out-of-state accidents and for in-state accidents when the special damages exceed the $2,000 tort exemption, as well as for in-state accidents that allow actions for pain and suffering because one of the tort thresholds is satisfied. *See* W. Rokes, No-Fault Insurance 39 (1971).

[9] The no-fault law was amended in 1971 to include mandatory no-fault coverage for property damage. Mass. Gen. Laws Ann. ch. 90, § 340 (Supp. 1975). This study did not investigate the effects or relative merits of the no-fault property coverage.

[10] The analysis of the information developed from interviews with accident victims is reported in Widiss, Accident Victims Under No-Fault Automobile Insurance: A Massachusetts Survey, 61 Iowa L. Rev. 1 (1975). A preliminary view of results from other segments of the CLRS Study is reported in Widiss & Bovbjerg, No Fault in Massachusetts: Its Impact on Courts and Lawyers, 59 A.B.A.J. 487 (1973). In addition, one further article analyzing the data derived from the examination of insurance company claims files is currently being prepared. *See* note 36 *infra*. All of the reports analyzing the import of no-fault in Massachusetts will be reprinted in A. Widiss *et al., supra* note 5.

I. The CLRS Massachusetts No-Fault Study

A. *Sources of Data Obtained Directly from Lawyers*

Information was sought from members of the legal profession in a variety of ways. First, questionnaires were sent to every third lawyer listed as having been admitted to the Massachusetts Bar. More than 1,700 responses to this questionnaire were returned during the period of May through August 1972. Second, questionnaires were sent to several hundred claimants' counsel and defense lawyers. Third, over seventy attorneys practicing primarily in the metropolitan Boston area were interviewed in depth about the impact of no-fault insurance upon their practice and about the operation of PIP coverage from their perspective. The scope and methodologies for these segments of the study are detailed below.

1. The General Survey of Massachusetts Lawyers

(a) *Survey Methodology.* The Massachusetts Bar Association attempts to maintain a comprehensive list of every living person admitted to practice in the Commonwealth. This list, which includes lawyers who no longer reside in Massachusetts and a number of lawyers who do not actively practice, is used for mailings to the Bar in general, not just to members of the Association. At the time this survey was conducted, the list included approximately 13,000 attorneys who had been admitted through April 1972.[11] The lawyers to be surveyed were identified by programming the computer in which the mailing list was maintained to select every third name from the master list. The list thereby created included a number of entries that could not be used, and these names were dropped.[12] This process created a survey list of 4,325 names. On May 18, 1972, an introductory letter explaining the survey was mailed to every person on this list.[13] This was followed by a second mailing which included the

---

[11] At the time of our use of the listing, the list was in the custody of Accelerated Business Services in Lowell, Massachusetts (headed by Mr. Wayne Peak). The "list" was on computer tape. All changes from the master list were made through the computer, and some errors occurred so that a number of addresses were not usable.

[12] The list produced by the computer included fifty-eight institutional names that were on the lawyer list in order to receive the MBA mailings, ninety-nine names of non-Massachusetts residents and sixty-one names incorrectly or incompletely printed-out by the computer so that they could not be used for mailings. This group of 218 names was excised, thereby reducing the survey list to 4,325 lawyers. It should be noted that thirty-nine of the sixty incorrectly printed-out names (sixty-five percent) were in Boston. Thus, Boston was slightly underrepresented in our mailing list.

[13] The survey instruments used in the mail surveys and interviews for this study have been deposited at the University of Iowa College of Law. The data derived from the questionnaires were placed on computer tapes, and those tapes are currently on file at the University of Iowa Computer Center. This data will be cited hereinafter as CLRS No-Fault Data—Bar Survey. When all phases of the study are completed, all of the computer tapes and survey instruments will be deposited in the University of Iowa College of Law Library. Unless otherwise indicated, all other data produced during the course of this study have been treated in the manner described above and will be deposited in the University of Iowa College of Law Library when all phases of the study are completed.

questionnaire together with a covering letter. The letter reiterated that the questionnaire responses would be anonymous. A postcard, to be returned separately, was enclosed with the questionnaire. Those attorneys from whom postcards had not been received after several weeks were sent follow-up mailings urging that they participate in the survey.[14] Questionnaires were eventually returned by 1,762 attorneys. This number of returns produced a response rate of about forty percent.[15]

(b) *Survey Accuracy.* In any large, general survey conducted by mail, there is always a concern whether the respondents are representative of the entire group because the responses come from a self-selected portion of those who are sent questionnaires. Accordingly, the responses were analyzed to ascertain whether they were representative of the Bar or whether there were discernible biases. There are several reasons for concluding that the respondents are a representative sample of the Massachusetts Bar. First, the response rate was uniform throughout the state. This means that the ratio of responses to the number of questionnaires sent was about the same for each of the counties in the state.[16] Second, the profiles of the respondents are comparable to the composition of the Bar indicated by the Massachusetts Bar Association surveys of 1970[17] and 1973.[18] For example, when the respondents to these surveys are com-

[14] On June 15, 1972, a postcard reminder was sent, and this was followed on July 6 by an explanatory letter designed to elicit participation from the 3,310 lawyers who had not responded as of about July 1. On July 7, 1972, a second wave of questionnaires was sent to the 3,211 Massachusetts lawyers who had not yet returned the postcard to indicate that they had responded to the first questionnaire.

[15] A response rate of forty percent would be produced if we assumed that a response was possible from each person on the survey list of 4,325 attorneys. However, there are several reasons why this number is not quite accurate for this purpose. For example, letters were received from the survivors of sixteen lawyers stating that the attorneys had died. Several lawyers returned their postcards saying that they had not answered the questionnaire because they were not actively in practice. Ten recipients wrote to say that they had received questionnaires both at home and at the office. And several questionnaires were returned by the Postal Service as undeliverable. It is impossible to ascertain how many other instances of this sort may have occurred. However, it is evident that the number of lawyers who actually received questionnaires was somewhat less than the 4,325 names that were on the final survey mailing list. Thus, the response rate is at least marginally higher than that reported above.

By way of comparison, the response rate for the Massachusetts Bar Association's 1970 survey of the Bar was characterized in the report as about thirty percent. *See* Massachusetts Bar Association, Economic Survey Conducted by the Massachusetts Bar Association 1 (1970) [hereinafter cited as 1970 MBA Survey]. And the response rate for the 1973 Massachusetts Bar Association survey apparently was 21.6 percent. This figure is based on the statement in the report of the survey that questionnaires were mailed out to the 9,000 members of the Massachusetts Bar Association and that 1,950 were returned. *See* Massachusetts Bar Association, Economic Survey Conducted by the Massachusetts Bar Association 2 (1973) [hereinafter cited as 1973 MBA Survey].

[16] CLRS No-Fault Data—Bar Survey.

[17] *See* 1970 MBA Survey 5-6.

[18] *See* 1973 MBA Survey 2, 3, 6, 12. The 1973 survey differed in one fundamental respect from the 1970 survey. The 1970 survey findings were based on 3,315 questionnaires returned as a result of a mailing to all of the 13,000 lawyers in Massachusetts. The 1973 survey findings were based on questionnaires that were sent only to the 9,000 members of the Massachusetts Bar Association. *See id.* at 2.

pared in regard to factors such as the county in which the respondent's principal office is located, it appears that very comparable responses were obtained. Comparisons of the nature of the respondents' professional positions support the same conclusion. Tables 1 and 2 contain tabulations of the data on these two criteria for the 1970 Massachusetts Bar Association Survey and the CLRS Study.

TABLE 1
Massachusetts Lawyers:
Location of Principal Office

County		MBA Survey—1970		CLRS Survey
Suffolk		53.6%		49.6%
Essex and Middlesex		20.2%		20.9%
Norfolk and Plymouth		7.3%		9.7%
Barnstable, Bristol, Dukes and Nantucket		5.1%		5.1%
Hampden and Worcester		11.3%		12.1%
Berkshire, Franklin and Hampshire		2.5%		2.4%
	Total:	100.0%	Total:	99.8%[19]
	Base:	3,265	Base:	1,696

TABLE 2
Massachusetts Lawyers:
Mode of Practice

		MBA Survey—1970		CLRS Survey
Sole practitioner		38.6%		40.1%
Partner in firm		23.8%		23.1%
Associate of sole practitioner or in firm		16.0%		17.8%
Government lawyer		5.2%		6.2%
Lawyer employee of business or institution (corporation attorney)		9.0%		6.3%
Other		7.4%		6.2%
	Total:	100.0%	Total:	99.7%
	Base:	3,315	Base:	1,733

The CLRS survey respondents are also similar to the Massachusetts Bar survey respondents in terms of the number of years in practice and the fields of law to which they allocate the most time.[20] In view of all these similarities, it seems clear that either the CLRS survey and the Massachusetts Bar Association survey are both representative of the state Bar or that comparable unrepresentative groups responded to both surveys. The first hypothesis seems the more likely.

[19] The percentages in this and subsequent tables throughout the article have been rounded to the nearest tenth of a percent. Therefore, when the percentages are added they will sometimes total either slightly more or slightly less than 100 percent.
[20] CLRS No-Fault Data—Bar Survey; 1973 MBA Survey 12.

2. Surveys of Claimants' and Defense Counsel

(a) *Claimants' Counsel.* The second portion of the attorney survey involved a mail questionnaire that was sent to attorneys who had represented substantial numbers of claimants who had been injured in automobile accidents. A list of such claimants' counsel was derived from data compiled by the Massachusetts Fraudulent Claims Board—a quasi-public agency that receives information on every insurance claim filed in the Commonwealth of Massachusetts. The Board's list included all attorneys who had represented clients who had had bodily injury claims under liability and/or no-fault coverages[21] as of September 1972 and indicated the number of claims each one had handled.[22] In order to identify lawyers who were most likely to have had significant automobile claims experience, only those attorneys who had represented at least fifty claimants were chosen for the survey. This process identified 590 attorneys. About thirty percent of this group had previously been sent a questionnaire as part of the general survey described earlier, and these names were set aside, as were the names of several individuals who had already been interviewed in person. This left a group of 391 attorneys to whom the claimants' counsel questionnaire was mailed on December 4, 1972.[23] Thereafter, several additional mailings were made to encourage participation in the survey.[24] About one third of the attorneys who received these mailings returned completed questionnaires.[25]

(b) *Defense Counsel.* The defense lawyer point of view was canvassed with a questionnaire similar to that sent to the claimants' counsel. The names of defense attorneys were obtained by examining the membership list for the Defense Research Institute and the listing of defense attorneys in the *Insurance Bar, Best's List of Insurance Counsel* and the *Diary.* In instances in which statements in a list indicated that a particular attorney's practice did not include automobile insurance cases, the name was dropped from the combined list. Names of those attorneys who had previously been contacted in connection with other phases of the study, such as the survey of every third lawyer admitted to Massachusetts practice, were also

---

[21] Claims under the Medical Payments Coverage included in most automobile insurance policies apparently were not used by the Board to identify the names of attorneys, if any, associated with the assertion of such claims.

[22] The Associate Director of the CLRS Study was unable to obtain information on when the attorneys on the list had made the insurance claims. Thus, it was not possible to distinguish attorneys who had a continuing insurance claims practice.

[23] The mailing included the questionnaire, a covering letter, a return envelope and a separate return postcard for a respondent to notify us that he had returned the questionnaire.

[24] A reminder postcard was mailed a week later, on December 12, and a second questionnaire with accompanying materials and a different covering letter was sent on December 16, 1972, to 328 lawyers who had not yet indicated by return postcard that they had completed the first questionnaire. On January 12, 1973, a second postcard reminder was mailed to the 273 lawyers who had still not responded.

[25] The data derived from this survey will be cited hereinafter as CLRS No-Fault Data—Claimants' Counsel Survey.

set aside. This culling produced a group of seventy-six lawyers, and in February 1973 these lawyers were sent a questionnaire with an explanatory covering letter, a return envelope, and a postcard to notify us that they had returned the questionnaire. Several subsequent mailings were made to those attorneys whose failure to return the postcard indicated that they had not participated in the survey.[26] The response rate again was about one in three.[27]

3. Personal Interviews

As a supplement to the various mail surveys, over seventy attorneys were interviewed in depth about PIP's impact on their practice and about the working of the PIP claims process. Those interviewed included attorneys whose practices were both plaintiff- and defense-oriented. Although most of the interviews were in the Boston area, several were conducted with attorneys practicing in smaller towns. Among the interviewees were several attorneys who were employed in the litigation departments of insurance companies. In general, these interviews served to provide a more complete understanding of how the no-fault compensation system was operating. However, because these attorneys were not scientifically selected, use of the information acquired in the interviews with them was limited to providing a perspective from which to analyze the statistical data developed in other segments of the study.[28]

B. *Other Surveys That Provided Relevant Data*

1. Surveys of Court Filings

As part of the study of the effects of no-fault insurance on the judicial system, an extensive survey of the motor vehicle tort action filings in five of Massachusetts' fourteen counties was undertaken.[29] The five counties surveyed include about sixty percent of the state's population and were chosen so as to include both the population centers and a representative cross section of the other counties in the state. In each county, the filings in the single superior court and in one or more of the district courts were surveyed. The resulting data indirectly indicates the effect of no-fault insurance on practicing lawyers.[30]

---

[26] On March 5, 1973, five days after the original mailings, all seventy-six lawyers were sent a reminder postcard requesting the questionnaire's return. On March 13, 1973, a second copy of the questionnaire with accompanying materials was mailed to the lawyers who had not yet mailed in their postcards to indicate that they had responded to the survey.

[27] The data derived from this survey will be cited hereinafter as CLRS No-Fault Data—Defense Attorney Survey.

[28] The data derived from these interviews will be cited hereinafter as CLRS No-Fault Data—Attorney Interviews.

[29] A preliminary analysis of some of this data may be found in Widiss & Bovbjerg, *supra* note 10. A complete report of the scope, methodology and results of this segment of the CLRS Study may be found in Bovbjerg, The Impact of No-Fault Auto Insurance on Massachusetts Courts, 11 New Eng. L. Rev. 325 (1976).

[30] The data derived from this study will be cited hereinafter as CLRS No-Fault Data—Court Study.

2. Interviews with Accident Victims

Interviews with persons who were involved in automobile accidents in Massachusetts and who were reported to have been injured in those accidents are another important source of information reported in this article. The interviewees were randomly selected from reports that are filed with the Massachusetts Registry of Motor Vehicles following accidents. Under state law, these accident reports must be prepared and submitted by each operator of a motor vehicle involved in an automobile accident that results either in personal injuries or in property damages in excess of $200.[31] The scope, methodology and principal results of this portion of the study are reported in a separate article.[32]

3. Survey of Insurance Company Claim Files

The other primary source of data for this study was an examination of insurance company claim files. This aspect of the study was patterned on the Department of Transportation Study of Automobile Personal Injury Claims. The DOT Study included "the 15 largest (by volume) auto insurance carriers in the United States, plus another smaller company."[33] Thirteen of these companies sell insurance in Massachusetts, and twelve of these agreed to participate in the CLRS Study.[34] Two additional insurers also accepted invitations to participate in the CLRS Study, thereby both replacing the companies that did not do business in the state and giving somewhat more balance between the stock companies and the mutual companies.[35] The study involved an examination of several thousand claim files that were closed by the participating companies during the survey period in 1973.[36]

---

[31] Mass. Gen. Laws Ann. ch. 90, § 26 (1969). The files that were selected for the study were limited to those in which there was an indication that at least one person had been visibly injured. *See* Widiss, *supra* note 10, at 11-14.

[32] *See* Widiss, *supra* note 10. The data derived from this study will be cited hereinafter as CLRS No-Fault Data—Accident Victim Survey.

[33] 1 Dep't of Transportation, *supra* note 3, at 4.

[34] The companies that participated in both the DOT Study and the CLRS Study were Aetna Life and Casualty Company, Allstate Insurance Company, Continental Insurance Companies, Fireman's Fund American Insurance Companies, Government Employees Insurance Company, Hartford Accident and Indemnity Company, Insurance Company of North America, Kemper Insurance Group, Liberty Mutual Insurance Company, Nationwide Mutual Insurance Company, State Farm Mutual Automobile Insurance Company, and The Travelers Insurance Companies. The authors of the DOT study noted that:

The 15 largest (by volume) auto insurance carriers in the United States, plus another smaller company, accepted the invitation to participate in the [DOT] survey. Together, these carriers represent more than half of the nation's auto bodily injury liability insurance business.

1 Dep't of Transportation, *supra* note 3, at 4.

[35] The two companies that participated in the CLRS Closed Claim Study are American Mutual Insurance Company and Commercial Union Insurance Company. Both of these were among the twenty largest automobile liability insurance companies in Massachusetts as of 1970. This information was derived from the 1970 Massachusetts Automobile Liability Premium Annual Statements prepared by the Massachusetts Automobile Rating and Accident Bureau, 89 Broad Street, Boston, Massachusetts 02110.

[36] The scope, methodology and principal results of this portion of the CLRS Study will be reported in a separate article. The data derived from this study will be cited hereinafter as

II. The Utilization of Lawyers After the Adoption of No-Fault

Prior to the introduction of no-fault insurance, as noted above,[37] persons injured in automobile accidents in Massachusetts typically retained attorneys to represent them in connection with claims arising as a result of such accidents. This was clearly shown by the 1969 Department of Transportation Personal Injury Claims Study which indicated that in Massachusetts over seventy-five percent of those asserting claims under the then-existing compulsory liability coverage were represented by lawyers,[38] and that a higher proportion of the claimants in Massachusetts were represented by attorneys than were the claimants in any other of the states surveyed.[39] This section examines the effect that the enactment of the no-fault law has had on the participation of attorneys in the claims process and the functions attorneys now perform in connection with PIP claims.

A. *Representation by Attorneys*

In analyzing the extent to which the advent of no-fault insurance has affected the frequency of attorney use for liability claims, it is useful to distinguish between those cases involving only a PIP claim and those in which a tort claim is involved. The relevance of this distinction was confirmed by interviews with attorneys conducted in the fall of 1971, about eleven months after no-fault became operative. The attorneys interviewed typically stated that they were advising both clients and potential clients to file their own PIP claims. In some instances attorneys stated that they provided advice to the claimant on how to file a PIP claim and then suggested that the individual proceed to take the necessary steps. Although these interviews were not the basis of any statistical data for the study, the impression gained from the conversations was that unless a PIP claim posed unusual problems or the accident also involved a tort claim, clients who were potential PIP claimants were generally being advised by attorneys to file claims without retaining a lawyer to represent them. As a result, several portions of the CLRS Study were designed to test the impression that the involvement of attorneys differed depending on whether the case was limited to a PIP claim.

CLRS No-Fault Study—Insurance Claims Survey. This data has also been filed at the State Farm Mutual Automobile Insurance Company Computer Center in Bloomington, Illinois.

[37] *See* text accompanying notes 3-4 *supra.*

[38] 1 Dep't of Transportation, *supra* note 3, at 78. This survey of automobile personal injury liability claims closings was made by sixteen automobile insurance companies, including the fifteen largest (by volume) companies, at the request of the Department of Transportation in 1969. The survey "encompassed claims being settled in nineteen states, chosen partially to offer a broad, nationally representative sample of claims and settlement experience." *Id.* at 4.

[39] The states included in the DOT study were: California, Colorado, Connecticut, Florida, Georgia, Illinois, Indiana, Massachusetts, Michigan, Minnesota, Missouri, New Jersey, New York, North Carolina, Ohio, Pennsylvania, Texas, Washington and Wisconsin. *Id.* at 4.

1. PIP Claims

The observations derived from the attorney interviews seem to be confirmed by the responses to the general survey of Massachusetts lawyers. The survey data show that most attorneys either were not handling PIP claims at all or were representing very few clients with such claims.[40] As Table 3 indicates, almost half of the respondents stated that they had handled no PIP claims, and another third stated that they had handled between one and five claims. Only about seven percent of the attorneys reported that they had handled more than ten PIP claims up to the time they responded to the survey questionnaire, which was at least eighteen months after no-fault went into effect.

TABLE 3
Estimate of PIP Claims Handled

None		48.7%
1 to 5		36.2%
6 to 10		8.2%
More than 10		6.9%
	Total:	100.0%
	Base:	1,642

Another indication of lawyers' attitudes toward representing PIP claimants was provided by a survey question that inquired whether the respondent's office had any policy with respect to handling PIP claims. Forty-five percent of the attorneys indicated that their office policy was that they preferred not to handle PIP claims.[41] Another twenty percent responded that they would handle PIP claims only if there were also a possible tort claim.[42] However, twenty-eight percent of the respondents stated that their offices would handle PIP claims without regard to whether a tort claim was involved.[43] Since over one quarter of the attorneys indicated that their offices would handle PIP claims,[44] an unwillingness on the part of the lawyers to represent such clients does seem to constitute, in and of itself, a significant factor in the changed pattern of attorney representation occasioned by the enactment of the no-fault law.

The general survey of Bar members produced some information about the patterns of attorney use. However, it did not provide any measure of the actual extent to which lawyers are in fact involved in the PIP claims process. Such information was provided by the surveys of accident victims and insurance company claim files.

Data compiled in the interviews with persons who were reported to have been visibly injured in automobile accidents clearly verify the im-

---

[40] CLRS No-Fault Data—Bar Survey.
[41] *Id.*
[42] *Id.*
[43] *Id.*
[44] *See* Table 3 *supra.*

pression that the great majority of persons who were only making PIP claims were not represented by attorneys. Only about one quarter of the persons interviewed who stated that they had filed a PIP claim reported that they had received some assistance from an attorney.[45] Even if these data were interpreted to mean that one quarter of all PIP claimants were represented by attorneys, it would of course support the conclusion that most PIP claimants were not represented by lawyers. However, there are two reasons why the percentage of PIP claimants represented by attorneys is undoubtedly much lower. First, these responses were from accident victims who were selected for interviews because the accident reports filed with the Massachusetts Registry of Motor Vehicles indicated that they received fairly serious injuries.[46] Accordingly, these interviewees represent only a portion of the possible PIP claimants among persons injured in automobile accidents, and they comprised a group of accident victims who were very likely to have also had a possible tort claim that would have warranted assistance from or representation by an attorney.[47] Second, this question inquired as to whether the claimants had been "assisted" by an attorney, and the responses do not warrant an interpretation that all of these PIP claimants were "represented" by attorneys. In light of these factors, and viewing the answers in relation to other information recorded in the interviews with these claimants, it seems likely that substantially less than one quarter of all the persons who *only* make PIP claims are actually represented by lawyers.

The data compiled from the survey of insurance company claim files further corroborate the impression that the vast majority of PIP claims were filed by the claimants themselves and not by attorneys. Of the some 1,500 PIP claim files examined, just over fifteen percent indicated that the claimant was represented by an attorney.[48] Again, however, this figure should be viewed as including a number of claimants whose injuries were serious enough to meet the requirements for bringing a tort action and whose purposes in retaining an attorney, therefore, were primarily to aid in asserting the tort claim. Analysis of the data from these claim files indicates that a majority of the PIP claimants who were represented by attorneys also had possible tort claims. For example, of the claim files that indicated an attorney had been involved, about half showed medical expenses in excess of $500.[49] A third of the files indicated that the injury sustained in the accident included a fracture.[50] And there were also a number of files that indicated injuries that would satisfy one of the other tort thresholds.[51] Taken together, and allowing for files in which more

---

[45] *See* Widiss, *supra* note 10, at 56.
[46] *See* text accompanying notes 31-32 *supra*.
[47] CLRS No-Fault Data—Accident Victim Survey.
[48] CLRS No-Fault Data—Insurance Claims Survey.
[49] *Id.*
[50] *Id.*
[51] *Id.*

than one of the criteria for a tort suit were satisfied, about three quarters of the PIP claimants who had been represented by an attorney had sustained some type of injury that would have allowed them to assert a tort claim as well as the no-fault claim. Although there was no way to ascertain from the information in a PIP claim file whether such a tort claim had been made, it seems likely that the involvement of an attorney in these PIP claims was usually attributable to the possibility of a tort claim. If so, these data also indicate that only a small percentage of those asserting only a PIP claim were represented by attorneys.

2. Tort Claims

The Massachusetts no-fault legislation provides that, if at least one of several possible criteria is met, a person injured in an automobile accident in Massachusetts may still assert a tort claim.[52] Accordingly, the CLRS Study focused on the retention of lawyers by claimants with tort claims as well as on the use of lawyers in connection with PIP claims. The compulsory liability insurance requirement was retained when no-fault was adopted, and, as a result, almost all tort claims involve third-party automobile liability insurance coverages that are applicable to the accidents in addition to the first-party no-fault insurance coverage.

In addition to examining the PIP claim files, the CLRS Study included an examination of insurance company liability claim files as part of the insurance claims survey. The CLRS claims survey was designed to track the pre-no-fault Department of Transportation Claims Study,[53] thus making possible a comparison of the involvement of attorneys in Massachusetts before and after no-fault went into effect. In the pre-no-fault period, the Department of Transportation Study indicates that about seventy-eight percent of the persons asserting claims in Massachusetts were represented by attorneys.[54] The CLRS survey data from these same companies show that attorneys represented only about fifty percent of the liability claimants injured in accidents after no-fault became effective.[55] Thus, the information compiled from these files indicates that after the introduction of no-fault insurance proportionately fewer claimants in Massachusetts were retaining attorneys in connection with tort claims. The shift downward was not an anticipated result. In fact, it seemed reasonable to predict exactly the opposite trend, because under no-fault only accidents causing more serious injuries can be the basis for a tort claim. The hypothesis is that cases involving serious accident injuries are more likely to warrant retention of a lawyer, and consequently the percentage of tort claimants being represented by attorneys would increase. The decline in attorney involvement is therefore surprising. None of the information derived in this study gives any indication of the causes for

---

[52] See text accompanying notes 4-9 supra.
[53] See text accompanying notes 33-36 supra.
[54] 1 Dep't of Transportation, supra note 3, at 78.
[55] CLRS No-Fault Data—Insurance Claims Survey.

this decline, and there has been no subsequent research to indicate whether this is a stable trend.

B. *The Functions Performed by Attorneys*

The CLRS surveys showed that often PIP claimants still look to attorneys for assistance, but that only a fairly small percentage are actually represented by lawyers.[56] There appear to be several different functions that attorneys continue to perform in connection with PIP claims. Although there is no precise way to classify claimants who choose to be represented by lawyers, it seems reasonable to differentiate among them for the purpose of discussing the functions performed by their attorneys according to whether a tort claim is also involved, and whether a PIP claim, which does not also involve a tort claim, is disputed or undisputed.

1. Undisputed PIP Claims

Insurers writing automobile policies in Massachusetts have developed standard forms for use by injured persons claiming PIP benefits. The three forms are: an accident report, an authorization for the insurance company to get medical information from the claimant's doctor, and a similar authorization to get wage information from the claimant's employer. A claimant normally is also required to submit itemized bills for out-of-pocket expenses, such as medical costs, that the insurer is to pay. The forms are usually mailed by insurance companies directly to the claimant after the insurer receives notification of an accident.

A majority of the claimants' and defense attorneys surveyed felt that the average PIP claimant did not require legal assistance because the forms were not complicated.[57] Typical of this group was the response of one attorney who observed: "It's just like Blue Cross or any health or accident claim."[58] Others felt that the problems that did arise could be handled by other types of assistance, such as the claimant's insurance broker.[59] A number of attorneys commented that such assistance was preferable because it was usually provided without charge. However, it seems evident that some persons find even relatively simple forms incomprehensible or at least distasteful. For these individuals an attorney can provide a service comparable to that requested by many persons who have uncomplicated tax returns prepared by lawyers.

A considerable number of attorneys did not share the opinion that most PIP claimants could prosecute their claims without assistance. In fact, among several hundred claimants' counsel surveyed by interviews and mail questionnaires, over a quarter of the respondents felt that an attor-

---

[56] *Id.*
[57] CLRS No-Fault Data—Claimants' Counsel Survey; CLRS No-Fault Data—Defense Attorney Survey.
[58] CLRS No-Fault Data—Attorney Interviews.
[59] CLRS No-Fault Data—Claimants' Counsel Survey; CLRS No-Fault Data—Attorney Interviews.

ney should be retained by many PIP claimants.[60] These attorneys offered a number of illustrations of the types of situations that they felt warranted the use of an attorney. The two categories most frequently cited were (1) those in which the injuries were such that consideration of a tort claim in addition to the PIP indemnification was warranted, and (2) those in which the existence or extent of the PIP coverage was disputed.[61] These two categories are discussed in the following two parts of this section. The discussion here is limited to the attorney's role when the PIP claim is not disputed.

A significant number of claimants' attorneys counseled, as one lawyer put it, that "you always need an attorney when an insurance company is involved."[62] However, this attorney, as well as several others, also pointed out that, even if the attorney is able to do a better job of presenting the client's claim, the amount involved in a PIP claim is usually not sufficient to justify hiring a lawyer.[63] Many lawyers felt this was true even though they also felt that some insurance companies were unjustifiably disputing medical bills, especially those for hospitalization and X rays. One attorney, who suggested that some claims departments were paying only a percentage of the amounts claimed, summarized the situation by observing that because "claimants don't stand to gain enough from suing the insurer to make it worthwhile, they are at the mercy of the insurer, and the insurer takes advantage."[64]

Several attorneys also noted that although the forms are simple enough for an educated adult they could be difficult for persons with little formal education. One Boston attorney, for example, explained that many of his clients were only "semi-literate and could never understand the forms or procedures."[65] Similarly, for non-English speaking claimants, attorneys often fill the role of interpreter as well as that of legal counsel.

In summary, these survey responses indicate that most attorneys felt that functionally literate persons are able to assert successfully undisputed PIP claims, but that for a variety of reasons there are still a substantial number of instances in which some claimants may need assistance. Of equal importance, however, is the observation that absent the existence of a tort claim, retention of an attorney probably is not economically justifiable because the attorney's fees would typically exceed the amount being disputed. When attorneys are consulted in regard to PIP claims or disputes over the no-fault coverage, the surveys indicate that attorneys will often provide claimants some guidance and then suggest that individuals either file their own claims or seek further assistance from their insurance broker or agent.

---

[60] CLRS No-Fault Data—Claimants' Counsel Survey.
[61] *Id.*
[62] CLRS No-Fault Data—Attorney Interviews.
[63] *Id.*
[64] *Id.*
[65] *Id.*

2. Disputed PIP Claims

No-fault insurance claims are usually paid without disputes over either the existence of coverage or the amount due the claimant. This conclusion is primarily derived from the interviews with accident victims[66] and is generally corroborated by data developed for other segments of the CLRS Study[67] and by the observations of both private and public officials concerned with the operation of the no-fault coverage system in Massachusetts. Yet numerous responses by both claimants' attorneys and accident victims indicate that a variety of problems were encountered by a significant portion of the claimants. Table 4 presents data on the types of problems encountered and the frequency with which they were mentioned by the claimants' attorneys who were surveyed.[68]

TABLE 4
Portion of Claimants' Attorneys Describing Recurring
Difficulties in Connection with PIP Claims

Disputes over amount due		43.5%
Disputes over coverage		5.3%
Delays in payment		5.3%
Other problems		3.8%
More than one of the above		13.0%
No difficulties		29.0%
	Total:	99.9%
	Base:	125

Although the vast majority of the difficulties reported by the attorneys involved disputes over the amount due, there were also a variety of other problems. The types of problems some claimants encounter with securing payments under the PIP coverage is corroborated by data compiled in the survey of accident victims who described why they were dissatisfied with the PIP coverage.[69]

In theory an aggrieved claimant has several possible ways in which to challenge an insurance company that disputes a PIP claim. First, a claimant can sue the insurer for failure to carry out its duties under the insurance policy. In fact, this is not a very practical approach because the amounts at issue are small—never in excess of $2,000. Furthermore, even if a company's conduct is flagrant enough to justify the awarding of punitive damages, the amount will still not be large because the amount of

---

[66] CLRS No-Fault Data—Accident Victim Survey.

[67] CLRS No-Fault Data—Insurance Claims Survey; CLRS No-Fault Data—Claimants' Counsel Survey; CLRS No-Fault Data—Attorney Interviews.

[68] CLRS No-Fault Data—Claimants' Counsel Survey.

[69] Although a substantial majority of the respondents indicated satisfaction with the claims process, approximately one third stated that they were "fairly dissatisfied" or "very dissatisfied" with either the amount received or the handling of their claim or both. Further analysis of the views of this group was undertaken to ascertain the sources of their displeasure. The results of this analysis are contained in the following table:

the punitive damages cannot exceed one quarter of the amount of the claim.[70] The attorneys interviewed observed that such suits, even if warranted, were simply not worth an attorney's time for the small amounts involved.[71] The lawyers surveyed anticipated that suits would be filed rarely, and only if a claimant or the attorney got angry enough to fight for the principle involved rather than the money. On the other hand, a few attorneys believed that suing a PIP insurer was a useful means of resolving PIP disputes.[72] Accordingly, even though litigation arising out of PIP disputes has been relatively rare, it seems that attorneys may occasionally institute suits when there are disagreements about the existence or extent of PIP coverage.

Types of Dissatisfaction Described by PIP Claimants

Nature of Dissatisfaction	Dissatisfied Claimants	All Claimants
I. Speed of Payment	53.8%	16.5%
Claim paid too slowly		
Claim paid too fast		
Claim not yet paid		
II. Amount of Payment	47.8%	14.7%
Medical bills claim not paid		
Wage loss claim not paid		
Amount too small		
Pain not compensated		
III. Insurer's Attitude or Procedures	24.6%	7.6%
Had to argue with insurer over amount of payment		
Insurer did not seem concerned		
Insurer did not provide information about progress on the claim		
Insurer required a release		
IV. Miscellaneous Items	4.5%	1.5%
Insurance subsequently cancelled		
Not dissatisfied with company but dissatisfied with someone else		
Bona fide claim not paid		
V. Not Dissatisfied		
Claim in progress	—	13.6%
Claim paid	—	54.9%
Total:	130.7%	108.8%
Base:	176	565

For a number of reasons, these responses should be analyzed cautiously. First, the number of persons whose responses were analyzed was relatively small. Consequently, the statistical significance of these figures is questionable. Second, analysis of the data suggests only slight correlations between dissatisfaction and other variables on which information was secured. It appears that the dissatisfied claimants were not significantly different from the satisfied claimants and that their injuries likewise were not significantly different from those suffered by the total group of injured respondents. Finally, in some cases the percentages total more than 100 percent because several individuals offered more than one reason for their dissatisfaction with the insurers' method of handling their claims.

[70] *See* Mass. Gen. Laws Ann. ch. 176D, § 7 (Supp. 1975).
[71] CLRS No-Fault Data—Attorney Interviews.
[72] *Id.*

A second possible method of seeking redress in connection with disputes over PIP claims is to make a complaint to the Commissioner of Insurance. The Commissioner's office gives advisory interpretations when questions of law arise under the PIP policies,[73] and in some instances will try to resolve disputes between a claimant and an insurance company. Moreover, the Unfair Claims Settlement Practices Act of 1971[74] enlarged the Insurance Commissioner's powers to regulate insurers by giving him the power to assess fines of up to $10,000 and to suspend an insurer's license. The attorneys who were interviewed were divided on the utility of referring PIP claims problems to the Commissioner. For example, one attorney with a large automobile tort practice stated that he made frequent use of the Insurance Commission's help. However, other attorneys said that their experience was that complaints were usually "filed and forgotten." In addition, one attorney pointed out that there was little incentive for either a lawyer or a claimant to bring a formal complaint because, even if an insurer has been found to have engaged in unfair claims settlement practices, any fine assessed is paid to the Commonwealth of Massachusetts and not to the policy holder who filed the complaint.[75]

Finally, it may be possible in some cases to secure a judicial resolution of a disputed PIP claim by filing an action in the Small Claims Court. Several attorneys noted that when the sum in dispute is less than $400 the claimant may file his own suit in Small Claims Court, and that by using the Small Claims Court a claimant can avoid long delays as well as attorney fees.[76] However, these attorneys also noted that there are several reasons why the Small Claims Court may not always be a satisfactory approach. First, the insurer will often be represented by an attorney or other person who is experienced in dealing with such disputes, even if the claimant is not. Second, the insurer may rely on relatively technical defenses, such as noncooperation or failure to notify the insurer, which the average claimant might not understand well enough to overcome. Third, the insurer can request that the case be transferred to a higher court, where a delay of several years can be expected. One attorney explained that the tactic of transferring to delay was used routinely by some insurance companies in response to suits under property damage coverage, and he anticipated that insurers would employ the same technique in personal injury cases.[77]

In conclusion, all three of these methods of redress for the claimant who is dissatisfied with an insurer's treatment of a PIP claim suffer from severe practical limitations which undoubtedly account for the minimal use that the interviewed attorneys indicated the methods were given.

---

[73] 4 Mass. Admin. Reg. § 8, at 376 (1969).
[74] Mass. Gen. Laws Ann. ch. 176D, §§ 3, 10 (Supp. 1975).
[75] CLRS No-Fault Data—Attorney Interviews.
[76] *Id.*
[77] *Id.*

3. Tort Claims and PIP Claims

The dominant factor leading to the use of an attorney in connection with a PIP claim is that injuries sustained in the accident also warrant a tort claim. Typically, an attorney is retained to prosecute a tort claim by one or more of the persons who were injured, and the entire matter—including the no-fault claim or claims—is handled by the attorney. In this situation, the attorney's role is no different from that which is present in any tort case, except to the extent that the lawyer pursues the PIP claim for a portion of the reparation. The surveys of both accident victims and lawyers indicate that well over half of the cases in which PIP claimants are represented by attorneys are situations in which a tort claim is involved.[78]

III. The Economic Impact of No-Fault on the Legal Profession

The advent of no-fault insurance in Massachusetts appears to have substantially reduced the role of attorneys in the claims process because most PIP claimants are not represented by lawyers. This suggests that lawyers may have sustained adverse economic consequences as a result of the PIP coverage. The survey data on the use of lawyers in connection with no-fault claims, reported in the preceding section, only provide an indirect indication of the possible economic impact on practicing attorneys. This section considers the survey data on the economic impact and the professional consequences for some of the lawyers who reported that they were most adversely affected.

A. Direct Measurements of the Effects of No-Fault

The CLRS survey of Massachusetts Bar Association members included several different inquiries designed to elicit information about the effect of no-fault insurance on the respondents' practices. Two questions were designed to identify those lawyers whose pre-no-fault practice would be most susceptible to the effects of no-fault. First, the attorneys were asked to state the portion of their income in 1970 (the last pre-no-fault year) that was derived from personal injury claims arising from automobile accidents. As Table 5 shows, over seventy percent of the respondents derived less than twenty-five percent of their income from automobile personal injury claims work. Accordingly, in 1970 tort claims work arising out of automobile accidents was a relatively unimportant source of income for a substantial majority of the lawyers in Massachusetts. However, at the other end of the spectrum, almost thirteen percent of the respondents indicated that at least one half of their income was earned by representing

---

[78] *Id.*; CLRS No-Fault Data—Accident Victim Survey. *See also* Widiss, *supra* note 10, at 56-57.

TABLE 5
Portion of 1970 Income from Automobile
Personal Injury Claims

None	36.1%	
Under 25%	36.5%	72.6%
25% to 50%	14.8%	
50% to 75%	7.7%	
Over 75%	4.8%	12.5%
Total.	99.9%	
Base:	1,655	

clients with such personal injury claims, and obviously for these attorneys this type of personal injury work was the most important source of income.

Second, insight into the portion of the bar that would be directly affected was provided by responses to an inquiry concerning the field of law to which each attorney allocated the greatest amount of time in 1970. The 1970 survey by the Massachusetts Bar Association[79] included a similar question,[80] and, as shown in Table 6, both surveys indicated that just over twenty percent of the respondents spent most of their time on personal injury work.

TABLE 6
Field of Law to Which the Greatest Amount
of Time Was Allocated in 1970

	CLRS Survey	MBA Survey
Personal Injury—Predominantly Plaintiff (CLRS)[81] Civil—Primarily Plaintiff (MBA)	14.4%	16.7%
Personal Injury—Predominantly Defendant (CLRS) Civil—Primarily Defendant (MBA)	6.7%	7.0%
	21.1%	23.7%

Base CLRS Survey: 1,517
Base MBA Survey: 2,098

In light of the fact that over one third of the respondents to the CLRS survey indicated that they handled no personal injury cases, it was not surprising to find that over one third of the respondents indicated that no-fault had not had any effect on their practices, or that another twenty-five percent indicated that the effect of no-fault on their practices

[79] 1970 MBA Survey 22.

[80] The terminology used in the two surveys differed slightly. In the Massachusetts Bar Association Survey, the terms used to describe the types of litigation with which this study is concerned were "civil—primarily defendant" and "civil—primarily plaintiff." The terms used in the CLRS Survey were "personal injury, predominantly plaintiff" and "personal injury, predominantly defendant."

[81] 1970 MBA Survey 22.

had been small. As shown in Table 6, when these groups are combined, nearly two thirds of the respondents stated that up to the time of the survey no-fault insurance had had at most a small effect on their practices.

TABLE 7
Impact of No-Fault on Respondents' Practice

None	39.8%	
Small	25.9%	65.7%
Moderate	17.5%	
Substantial	16.7%	
Total:	99.9%	
Base:	1,704	

Furthermore, these respondents anticipated that the future impact would be about the same as that which they had experienced during the first eighteen months of no-fault.[82] Most respondents—over eighty percent of all the attorneys surveyed (regardless of whether they reported that they had been significantly affected)—indicated that their offices had not taken any measures to offset the impact of no-fault insurance.[83] And almost ninety percent of the attorneys surveyed stated that in the foreseeable future they anticipated that their offices would not take any measures (such as reducing the number of attorneys already employed, declining to hire any additional attorneys, reducing the nonlawyer staff, or reducing the amount of office space) to mitigate the effects of no-fault.[84]

The effects described by those attorneys whose pre-no-fault practices involved significant amounts of automobile personal injury cases were distinctly different. As noted above,[85] almost thirteen percent of the attorneys responded that over half of their income from the practice of law prior to the adoption of no-fault was derived from this type of personal injury claims work. These attorneys predominated among the nearly one sixth of all the attorneys surveyed who reported that no-fault had had a substantial impact on their practice.[86] The responses of the attorneys who reported that no-fault insurance had had a substantial impact on their practices were analyzed separately to discern whether as a group they differed notably from the attorneys who stated that no-fault had either "no" impact or only a "small" impact on their practices. Although in most respects the profiles of the groups are similar, there are a few notable differences. These same differences were also generally present when the answers of those attorneys who reported a "moderate impact"[87] were separately analyzed. The most apparent differences that

[82] CLRS No-Fault Data—Bar Survey.
[83] *Id.*
[84] *Id.*
[85] *See* Table 6 *supra.*
[86] CLRS No-Fault Data—Bar Survey.
[87] *See* Table 10 *infra.*

these tabulations revealed involved the time in practice, the location of the respondent's office, and the mode of practice.

First, the comparisons showed that the attorneys who had been in practice from ten to twenty years were overrepresented among those lawyers who reported a significant effect on their practice. This group constituted over thirty percent of the attorneys who reported a substantial impact, and less than twenty percent of the respondents who indicated little or no impact on their practices. As shown in Table 8, this was offset by the underrepresentation of lawyers who had been practicing less than five years. In other words, lawyers who had been in practice from ten to twenty years were most likely to have had a significant reduction in their practice, while lawyers who had been in practice less than five years were least likely to have sustained a significant impact.

TABLE 8
Length of Time in Practice

		Substantial Impact		Small or No Impact
0 to 5 years		14.8%		27.6%
5 to 10 years		14.1%		14.4%
10 to 20 years		32.7%		19.2%
20 to 30 years		17.8%		15.4%
Over 30 years		20.5%		23.4%
	Total:	99.9%	Total:	100.0%
	Base:	297	Base:	1,218

Second, attorneys from Essex, Norfolk and Worcester—the middle-sized counties in the state according to population—were overrepresented among the attorneys who reported that no-fault had had a substantial impact on their practices. On the other hand, attorneys whose main

TABLE 9
Location of Principal Office

		Substantial Impact		Small or No Impact
Barnstable		—		5.0%
Berkshire		0.7%		1.4%
Bristol		3.4%		3.8%
Dukes or Nantucket		—		0.3%
Essex		10.2%		5.3%
Franklin		—		0.8%
Hampden		2.0%		5.3%
Hampshire		—		0.7%
Middlesex		16.7%		14.6%
Norfolk		8.2%		5.3%
Plymouth		2.7%		2.5%
Suffolk		44.7%		53.7%
Worcester		11.3%		5.1%
	Total:	99.9%	Total:	100.1%
	Base.	293	Base:	1,199

TABLE 10
Mode of Practice

	Substantial Impact	Moderate Impact	Small or No Impact
Individual Practitioner			
With no employees (or associates) who are attorneys.	31.8% } 56.5%	28.5% } 52.5%	25.6% } 34.2%
With employees who are attorneys	24.7%	24.0%	8.6%
Partner in a Firm			
With three or fewer attorneys (including associates)	12.2%	16.0%	6.4%
With four or more attorneys (including associates)	5.1%	6.7%	18.3%
Associate in a Firm			
With three or fewer attorneys	5.4%	5.8%	2.6%
With four or more attorneys	7.4%	7.0%	13.0%
Other	13.5%	11.8%	25.6%
Total:	100.1%	99.8%	100.1%
Base:	296	312	1,226

offices were in Suffolk County (Boston) were slightly underrepresented. Attorneys practicing in the state's least populous counties were generally, although not invariably, underrepresented among those who reported a substantial impact on their practices. These responses are set out in Table 9 on page 344.

Finally, as Table 10 on page 345 shows, the lawyers who were most likely to have reported a substantial impact on their practice were those who were sole practitioners or who practiced in a firm of three or fewer lawyers. This is not surprising; automobile tort litigation is not typically a significant portion of the case load for larger law firms.

Another indication of the impact of no-fault is provided by the survey answers to the inquiry concerning how the respondents' income in 1971, the first year of no-fault coverage, compared with their 1970 income, the last pre-no-fault year. When the responses of all the attorneys were tabulated, slightly over half stated that their income was greater in 1971 than it was in 1970.[88] However, when the responses are examined in subgroups the survey data are more informative. As shown in Table 12, among the respondents reporting that no-fault had had a substantial impact, only about one fourth of the attorneys indicated an increased income in 1971.[89] And proportionately greater numbers of the attorneys who reported that no-fault had had a substantial impact on their practices stated that their incomes were less in 1971 than in 1970. These responses are particularly striking when compared to the estimates of the attorneys who reported that no-fault had had either a small impact or no impact, and these figures are set out in Table 11.

TABLE 11
Comparative Income Estimates for 1970 and 1971
by Respondents Who Reported Differing
Impacts of No-Fault

	Substantial Impact	Moderate Impact	Small or No Impact
More in 1971 than in 1970	25.1%	45.3%	66.0%
About the same in 1971 and 1970	26.9%	36.0%	26.5%
Less in 1971 than in 1970	48.1%	18.7%	7.6%
Total:	100.1%	100.0%	100.0%
Base:	283	300	1,084

[88] The following table sets out the Comparative Income Estimates for 1970 and 1971 of all the respondents to the survey.

Comparative Income Estimates for
1970 and 1971 by All Respondents

More in 1971 than in 1970	55.1%
About the same in 1971 and 1970	28.2%
Less in 1971 than in 1970	16.7%
Total:	100.0%
Base:	1,557

[89] CLRS No-Fault Data—Bar Survey

The survey questionnaire also included a number of inquiries concerning the ways in which the attorneys affected by no-fault were altering their professional lives[90] in response to either the actual or prospective impact. As Table 12 indicates, about one third of all the respondents stated that they were engaging in other fields of practice to offset the actual or prospective impact of no-fault.

TABLE 12
Portion of Attorneys Reporting Increasing
Work in Other Fields of Practice

	All Respondents		Respondents Who Reported Modifying Their Practices
To a small extent	9.0%		24.3%
To a moderate extent	15.2% } 36.9%		41.3%
To a substantial extent	12.7%		34.3%
No change in practice	63.1%		—
Total:	100.0%	Total:	99.9%
Base:	1,627	Base:	600

The types of work to which these lawyers reported shifting are listed in Table 13. Since most of these lawyers identified more than one new area of practice, the percentages in this table are only indicative of the fact that the field was identified by that portion of the attorneys who were engaged in new fields of activity.

TABLE 13
Fields of Practice to Which Attorneys
Reported Allocating More Time

Field of Practice	Attorneys Mentioning
Real Estate Law	52.3%
Estate Planning, Wills, or Probate	50.8%
Business, Commercial, Corporate, or Tax Law	46.5%
Civil Litigation (Other Than Auto)	34.8%
Criminal Law	31.8%
Base:	600

There are several indications that the attorneys who reported modifying their practices as a result of no-fault were successful in this endeavor. First, about forty-eight percent of these attorneys stated that their income in 1971 exceeded their 1970 income. Another twenty-four percent estimated that their income was about the same in both years.[91]

Second, about half of the attorneys who reported that they were modifying their practices also indicated that they had not changed nor were

---

[90] As used here, an "alteration in professional life" means a change in the type of legal work normally done. A "change in professional position," on the other hand, means a change in jobs from one employer to another (or to no job). *See* text accompanying notes 95-100 *infra*.

[91] CLRS No-Fault Data—Bar Survey.

TABLE 14
Comparative Income for 1970 and 1971
of Attorneys Who Were Engaging in
Other Fields to a Substantial Extent

1971 Income greater than 1970	48.1%
1971 Income about the same as 1970	24.3%
1971 Income less than 1970	27.6%
Total:	100.0%
Base:	216

they considering changing their professional positions as a result of no-fault. Another eighteen percent of this subgroup had already changed their positions or formed a new professional association. As shown in Table 15, at the time the survey was taken, only about a quarter of the attorneys who stated that they already had substantially altered their practice were considering changing their professional position as a result of no-fault.

TABLE 15
Responses to Question Whether Attorneys Had
Changed or Were Considering Changing Their
Professional Positions by Those Who Reported
Having Already Substantially Modified Their Practices

No. No-fault insurance has not caused me to change or consider changing my position	50.5%
Yes. I am considering changing my position as a result of no-fault insurance	26.4%
Yes. I have formed a new partnership or association with other attorneys as a result of no-fault insurance	10.4%
Yes. I have discontinued private practice and now	
am a government attorney	5.2%
am a corporation attorney	1.9%
have left law practice	1.9%
cannot find a job	0.5%
Other	3.3%
Total:	100.1%
Base:	212

From these responses the inference seems justified that a significant portion of the attorneys who had most radically modified their practices—including those who had already taken a new position or formed a new partnership—had made a satisfactory adjustment in their professional lives.

This conclusion also seems to be supported by an examination of the data on the portion of the Bar that engages in predominantly claimant-oriented personal injury work. In the CLRS survey, about fourteen percent of all the respondents stated that such personal injury work was the

field to which they allocated the most time in 1970.[92] The first Economic
Survey of the Massachusetts Bar Association was also based on data for
1970, the last year before no-fault automobile insurance went into effect.
In this survey, 16.3 percent of the respondents identified "civil—primarily
plaintiff" as the field of law that produced the greatest amount of gross
income for them in 1970.[93] Thus, the CLRS survey and the 1970 MBA
Survey had similar proportions of respondents who were engaged in such
practices. In the 1973 Economic Survey of the Bar, 12.7 percent of the
respondents stated that they devote the greatest amount of their fee-
producing time to "civil cases—primarily plaintiff."[94] Although there was
a decrease from about sixteen percent to 12.7 percent from 1970 to 1973,
this category continues to constitute the principal income producing practice for a significant portion of the Massachusetts Bar. This continuing
importance of plaintiff's civil cases is probably at least in part due to a
successful effort on the part of many of these attorneys to increase the
amount of time they were allocating to other types of civil litigation.

A somewhat different perspective on the effect of no-fault insurance is
provided by the answers to an inquiry in the CLRS Study about whether
the respondents had changed or had considered changing their professional position or mode of practice as a result of no-fault insurance.
Slightly over eighty-two percent of all the attorneys responded that no-
fault had not caused them either to change or even to consider changing
their positions.[95] On the other hand, eighteen percent answered this
question in the affirmative, and over two thirds of this subgroup were
considering changing, but had not yet actually changed, their positions.[96]

At the time of the survey, about eighteen months after no-fault became
effective, 2.5 percent of the attorneys stated they had already discontinued private practice as a result of no-fault insurance.[97] Almost three
fifths of these attorneys stated that they had left private practice to take
positions with the government.[98] Although this was a small group, several
cross tabulations were developed to provide some additional biographical
information on these persons. Nine of these attorneys, about half the
group, were practicing in Suffolk County.[99] The others were practicing in
Middlesex, Norfolk and Worcester counties. And more than half of these
attorneys (57.1 percent) reported that their incomes in 1971 exceeded
their 1970 income.[100]

A few of the respondents, less than one percent of all those who
replied, stated either that they had left law practice completely or that

---

[92] *Id.*
[93] 1970 MBA Survey 22.
[94] 1973 MBA Survey 11.
[95] CLRS No-Fault Data—Bar Survey.
[96] *Id.*
[97] *Id.*
[98] *Id.*
[99] *Id.*
[100] *See id.*

they were unsuccessfully seeking a new position. This group was far too small to be the basis of any statistical analysis.

B. *Indirect Indications of the Effects of No-Fault*

    1.   Analysis of Classified Listings for Attorneys in the Metropolitan Boston Area

In the course of the discussions with leaders of the Bar in Massachusetts and the personal interviews with attorneys practicing largely in the Boston metropolitan area, there were repeated statements that substantial numbers of attorneys practicing in the metropolitan Boston area had been forced to cease their law practices as a result of the Massachusetts no-fault coverage. However, the attorneys being interviewed either did not know or were reluctant to provide the names of lawyers who had been so affected. Therefore, much thought was given to finding some method of determining whether there were indeed a substantial number of attorneys in the metropolitan Boston area who had been forced to abandon their practices during the two years following the introduction of the no-fault coverage. It was finally postulated that a year-by-year comparison of the classified telephone book listings might yield some additional insight into this question beyond that provided by the interviews and the general survey of attorneys in Massachusetts. Although no attempt was made to verify whether all attorneys are included in the classified listings, comparisons with the *Martindale-Hubbell Law Directory* and the membership lists of several professional organizations composed of lawyers showed that the classified listings represented a very comprehensive list of the attorneys practicing in Boston.[101]

The classified listings of attorneys were compared to ascertain the number of address changes and listing terminations from year to year for the Boston metropolitan area during the period from 1968 through 1974. The three year-to-year periods from 1968 through the issuance of the 1971 directory provide a basis with which to compare the three year-to-year periods after the 1971 directory, which was issued before the attorneys would have been responding to the effects of no-fault. Any alteration in the address listed was counted as an address change. Any name that did not appear in classified listings for the following year was counted as a termination. In each year, only the first eight pages of listings were compared. This resulted in a total of approximately 2,848 names examined for each year, which was about half the number of attorneys in the classified listings. The results of this examination are set out in Table 16.

---

[101] It is also probably fair to conclude that attorneys practicing as individuals or in small groups are very likely to have their names included in the classified listing. Thus, to the extent that the classified listings do not represent a comprehensive list, it would err most in regard to lawyers in large firm practices. Because the attorneys who reportedly had left the practice were attorneys engaged in individual or small group practices, the "yellow page" listings seemed most appropriate to the task.

TABLE 16
Alterations in the Lawyer Listings in the
Metropolitan Boston Telephone Book

Years	Address Changes		Listings Terminated		Total Changes	
1968 to 1969	4.9%		6.4%		11.3%	
1969 to 1970	7.8%	Average Rate = 6.5%	5.7%	Average Rate = 6.7%	13.5%	Average Rate = 13.1%
1970 to 1971	6.7%		7.9%		14.6%	
1971 to 1972	5.9%		7.7%		13.6%	
1972 to 1973	5.7%	Average Rate = 5.7%	7.2%	Average Rate = 8.3%	13.0%	Average Rate = 14.0%
1973 to 1974	5.5%		10.0%		15.5%	

Base: 2,848

PIP went into effect January 1, 1971.

In the three years prior to no-fault the average rate of address changes
was 6.5 percent. In the three years subsequent to the enactment of
no-fault, the rate of address changes dropped to 5.7 percent. Obviously,
lawyers relocate their offices for a variety of reasons. As a result, the only
significance of these figures is that they indicate that there certainly was
no massive change in the rate of office relocations in the years following
the introduction of no-fault coverage.

The analysis of listing terminations showed that in the three years prior
to no-fault an average of 6.6 percent of the lawyers dropped their listings
from year to year. In the three years following the introduction of no-
fault, the average rate increased 1.6 percent to an annual rate of 8.3
percent. These figures seem consistent with the responses to the general
survey of the Massachusetts Bar, which indicated that approximately 1.7
percent of the attorneys had terminated their practices as a consequence
of no-fault.[102] Therefore, both the general survey of the bar and the
analysis of the classified telephone listings indicate that the percentage of
attorneys who gave up their practices in the Boston metropolitan area
after the introduction of no-fault was at most one to two percent a
year greater than the percentage that would have done so had no-fault
insurance not gone into effect.[103] These results appear to refute the
assertions that no-fault had caused a rather substantial number of attorneys to abandon their practices.

2. Automobile Accident Litigation

Another indirect indication of the economic impact on lawyers is provided by an examination of the number of automobile accident claims
being litigated in Massachusetts courts. The no-fault legislation was designed to eliminate tort claims except when an automobile accident causes
relatively serious injuries. This limitation on tort actions has led to a very
significant drop in the number of automobile civil litigations being filed in
the courts. In fact, this has been one of the most notable effects of
no-fault insurance to date.

The CLRS survey of court filings consisted of an examination of court
records in five of Massachusetts' fourteen counties. The records of the
various district courts revealed that, after no-fault went into effect on
January 1, 1971, bodily injury suits from accidents occurring after that

---

[102] See text accompanying notes 95-100 supra.
[103] Professor Robert Keeton suggested an alternative interpretation of this data after
having read the analysis put forth in the text:
  There is an alternative hypothesis that is at least as plausible, and maybe even more so.
  The 1968-71 data show a trend of increased changes from 11.33 to 14.57 percent.
  Projection of that trend would have brought the figure to a percentage in excess of
  15.57 by 1974. Three years is too short a period to establish a credible trend, but this
  perspective suggests at least that there is real doubt about whether the data "indicate"
  that the number who gave up practice was "probably about 1 or 2 percent a year
  greater" than it would have been if no-fault had not been adopted.
Letter from Professor Robert Keeton of the Harvard Law School to author, December 22,
1975 (on file at Boston University Law Review).

date virtually disappeared from the dockets of Massachusetts district courts.[104] Illustrative of the data collected from this segment of the study are the results from Middlesex County. Middlesex, which extends from Boston to the New Hampshire border, is the state's most populous county, with nearly a fourth of the state's population. As would be expected, in the pre-no-fault years about one quarter of the motor vehicle tort suits commenced in Massachusetts were filed in the Middlesex district courts and the Middlesex Superior Court.[105] The examination of the court dockets for the three largest Middlesex district courts showed a post-no-fault drop in the number of bodily injury motor vehicle tort suits of 92.9 percent.[106] In fact, the survey sample for the Third District Court of Eastern Middlesex County did not turn up any bodily injury suits arising out of accidents occurring after no-fault went into effect.[107] Although the reductions of motor vehicle tort case filings in the district courts elsewhere in the state were not quite that dramatic, they were very substantial.

The impact in the state's superior courts has also been significant. For example, in the Middlesex Superior Court, the number of personal injury entries arising from automobile accidents occurring after no-fault went into effect appears to have been at least halved.[108] Unpublished official data on the total number of motor vehicle actions being filed in the state's superior court system indicate that the survey conducted in Middlesex is representative of the state as a whole.[109] As shown in Table 17 on page 354, by 1974 the total number of motor vehicle tort suits in the superior courts had been reduced to about one third of the pre-no-fault level.[110]

There are several reasons why the reduction in motor vehicle tort case filings is probably not fully attributable to the no-fault personal injury coverage. First, no-fault property insurance, which went into effect a year after no-fault personal injury insurance,[111] undoubtedly is a significant factor in reducing the amount of litigation after January 1, 1972. Second, the fuel crisis, which led to lower highway speeds and to a concomitant reduction in both the number and severity of automobile

---

[104] CLRS No-Fault Data—Court Survey.

[105] Id.

[106] Id.

[107] Id.

[108] Id.

[109] Each fiscal year, the Executive Secretary of the Supreme Judicial Court reports on the operation of the Massachusetts judicial system in the *Annual Report to the Justices of the Supreme Judicial Court*. Some data compiled by the court clerks in the course of preparing these reports are not published, and this study refers to such information as official unpublished data.

[110] This tabulation of cases in the Massachusetts superior courts includes both those originally filed in the courts and those that were removed to the superior courts. A more comprehensive breakdown of the source of these filings is contained in Bovbjerg, *supra* note 29. The gradual nature of the year-to-year reduction is due to the existence of the two-year statute of limitations that would allow suits based on pre-no-fault accidents to be filed in the two years following the enactment of no-fault.

[111] *See* Mass. Gen. Laws Ann. ch. 90, § 340 (1975).

TABLE 17
Civil Cases and Motor Vehicle Tort Cases
Either Filed in or Transferred to the
Massachusetts Superior Courts*

Year	All Civil Cases	Motor Vehicle Tort Cases	
1961	36,005	23,705	
1962	33,832	20,999	
1963	35,908	23,103	
1964	38,518	25,729	
1965	37,442	25,216	
1966	34,826	23,305	
1967	33,570	23,006	
1968	33,849	22,931	
1969	33,784	23,024	
1970	35,726	23,006	
—	—	—	PIP went into effect January 1, 1971.
1971	34,442	21,194	
—	—	—	No-Fault Property Insurance (PPI) went into effect January 1, 1972.
1972	27,649	14,507	
1973	23,587	9,308	
1974	24,829	7,616	
1975 (est.)	26,613	6,708	

* This does not include a small number of equity cases which were also filed as civil matters.

accident injuries,[112] presumably is also partially responsible for the reduction in court cases. Third, it is also conceivable that ongoing attempts to improve automobile and highway design may have further reduced the number of automobile accidents that caused bodily injuries in Massachusetts during this same period. Finally, January 1, 1971 was also the date when the legislature opted to have the doctrine of comparative negligence replace the contributory negligence rule in Massachusetts.[113] In theory, comparative negligence should make possible some claims that are foreclosed by applications of the contributory negligence doctrine. If this theory is accurate, then the results of changing to comparative negligence would have countered the impact of no-fault in Massachusetts, which appears to have substantially reduced litigation. However, what effect comparative negligence has had in Massachusetts remains a matter of speculation. In any case, it is impossible to separate the effects produced by these factors from those that resulted from the PIP coverage. Although no-fault is therefore not the singular cause of these results, it no doubt was the most significant factor in the reduction of motor vehicle tort filings.

[112] See National Safety Council, Accident Facts 1974, at 40.
[113] See Mass. Gen. Laws Ann. ch. 231, § 85 (Supp. 1975).

Conclusion

The implementation of no-fault automobile insurance in Massachusetts appears to have had a significant effect on the role of attorneys in the claims process. This is most evident in the substantial reduction in the use of attorneys by accident victims. In addition, most no-fault claimants now make their insurance claims themselves. The use of attorneys by claimants in connection with liability claims also appears to have lessened. The survey results indicate that only about half of the liability claims are now being settled with claimants who have been represented by attorneys. These changes are particularly notable because in the pre-no-fault years in Massachusetts almost three quarters of the claimants were represented by legal counsel in connection with claims arising from automobile accidents.

Although the reduction in the retention of attorneys had no overwhelming effects on a majority of the lawyers in Massachusetts, no-fault insurance has had a marked economic impact on the trial bar and on at least a portion of the lawyers in general practice. Many of the attorneys whose practices were substantially affected appear to have offset the economic effects by increasingly engaging in other fields of practice. And, in view of the responses of these attorneys to inquiries of how their 1971 incomes compared with their 1970 incomes, it appears that a substantial portion of these attorneys were able to avoid major disruptions in their professional lives.

It is, of course, hazardous to attempt to extrapolate too much from such survey information. No definitive statements can be made about those attorneys who either changed their professional affiliations or were considering possible changes. Nonetheless, it seems reasonable to predict that ultimately no more than ten to fifteen percent of the attorneys in Massachusetts will have had to make significant changes in their professional lives as a result of no-fault insurance. How many of these career modifications will prove to be advantageous and professionally rewarding to those attorneys is of course impossible to predict. However, the adaptability of Massachusetts lawyers, as demonstrated by the data on those who have already either modified their practices or altered their professional lives as a consequence of no-fault insurance, leads to the observation that many of these transitions will indeed be successful.

The following questionnaire was used for the general survey of every third lawyer in Massachusetts. This survey provided most of the data considered in the preceding chapter. Similar inquiries were used in the somewhat shorter questionnaires that were sent to lawyers who were specifically identified as having been involved in tort litigation on behalf of claimants or insurance companies.

COUNCIL ON LAW-RELATED STUDIES
THE MASSACHUSETTS NO-FAULT AUTO INSURANCE STUDY
1563 MASSACHUSETTS AVENUE
CAMBRIDGE, MASS. 02138

ALAN I. WIDISS
Study Director

RANDALL R. BOVBJERG
Associate Study Director

May 25, 1972

Attached to this letter is the questionnaire I wrote you about several days ago. As I explained in that letter, the Council on Law-Related Studies is an independent non-profit foundation. However, we have sought advice from leaders of the organized bar in the preparation of the questionnaire, and the objectives of this study have been approved by:

James P. Allen, Jr., Massachusetts Chairman
Defense Research Institute

Thomas E. Cargill, Jr., Chairman
Boston Bar Association Section on Insurance
and Injury to Persons and Property

Kathleen Ryan Dacey, President
Massachusetts Trial Lawyers Association

Richard K. Donahue, President
Massachusetts Bar Association

They join me in urging you to cooperate with this survey, since your answers are important to the success of the study regardless of whether your practice has included automobile accident claims.

The questionnaire is easy to fill out, and takes only a short time to complete. I will appreciate it if you would take a few minutes to answer it today, and then return the form in the enclosed prepaid envelope.

Thank you for your assistance.

Cordially yours,

Alan I. Widiss
Study Director

ALL RESPONSES WILL BE ANONYMOUS, SO THAT
CONFIDENTIALITY IS GUARANTEED.

PLEASE CHECK ONE ANSWER FOR EACH QUESTION.

PART I

. If you were a member of the Massachusetts legislature and had the opportunity to vote on the continuation of <u>personal injury</u> no-fault automobile insurance, how would you vote?

[ ] To continue   [ ] To discontinue

2. If you were a member of the Massachusetts legislature and had the opportunity to vote on the continuation of <u>property damage</u> no-fault automobile insurance, how would you vote?

[ ] To continue   [ ] To discontinue

3. Assuming the continuation of the present Massachusetts no-fault plan, if you were a legislator how would you vote on a bill to increase the no-fault coverage from $2,000 to $5,000?*

[ ] In favor of the bill   [ ] Against the bill

4. Assuming the continuation of the present Massachusetts no-fault plan, if you were a legislator how would you vote on a bill to increase the level of medical costs necessary for the recovery of damages for pain and suffering from $500 to $1,000?†

[ ] In favor of the bill   [ ] Against the bill

5. Assuming the continuation of the present Massachusetts no-fault plan, if you were a legislator how would you vote on a bill to decrease the level of medical costs necessary for the recovery of damages for pain and suffering from $500 to $250?

[ ] In favor of the bill   [ ] Against the bill

6. Assuming the continuation of <u>some</u> form of no-fault automobile insurance in Massachusetts, which of the following would you prefer?

[ ] Mandatory no-fault automobile insurance paying all special damages (medical costs, rehabilitation expenses, wage losses, disability compensation) and eliminating all auto tort actions;

[ ] Mandatory no-fault automobile insurance paying special damages up to $2,000 and permitting tort suit for general damages only in defined cases (that is, the present system in Massachusetts); or

[ ] Mandatory automobile insurance paying special damages up to $5,000 and permitting tort suits for special damages above $5,000 and for general damages in all cases.

---

* This question is based on the Florida statute, which requires no-fault coverage of $5,000.
† The Florida statute allows suit for general damages when medical bills exceed $1,000.

7.   If you were a Massachusetts legislator, what modifications (if any) of the no-fault
      insurance system would you favor?

PART II

1.   How would you characterize the impact of personal injury no-fault auto insurance (P.I.P.)
      on your practice since January, 1971?

               | | None | | Small | | Moderate | | Substantial

2.   Assuming no major changes in the law, what do you expect P.I.P.'s impact will be on your
      practice during the next three years?

               | | None | | Small | | Moderate | | Substantial

3.   Approximately what proportion of your income from the practice of law in 1970 and
      1971 was derived from personal injury claims arising from automobile accidents?

              <u>1970</u>   <u>1971</u>

               | | None | | None
      | | Under 1/4 | | 1/2 to 3/4 | | Under 1/4 | | 1/2 to 3/4
      | | 1/4 to 1/2 | | Over 3/4 | | 1/4 to 1/2 | | Over 3/4

4.   Are you now increasingly engaging in other fields of practice (or in other lines of eco-
      nomic activity) to offset the actual or prospective impact of no-fault insurance?

               | | Yes | | No | Skip to Question #7 |

      5. | | To a small extent
            | | To a moderate extent
            | | To a substantial extent

      6.   Since January, 1971, as a consequence of no-fault insurance I have increased
            the amount of time I worked on:

                         | Please check as many as are applicable |

            | | Business, commercial, corporate, | | Estate planning, wills,
                 or tax law   or probate
            | | Civil litigation (other than auto) | | Real estate law
            | | Criminal law | | Other:

7. Do you anticipate that <u>in the future</u> you will engage to an increasing extent in other fields of professional practice (or in other lines of economic activity) to offset the impact of no-fault insurance?

[   ] Yes, to a small extent   [   ] No
[   ] Yes, to a moderate extent
[   ] Yes, to a substantial extent

8. Has your law office already taken any measures to offset the impact of no-fault automobile insurance?

[Please check as many as are applicable]

[   ] No measures taken
[   ] Reduced the number of attorneys already in the office
[   ] Decided not to hire additional attorney(s)
[   ] Other: _____

_____

9. Do you anticipate that your office will take any measures (like the ones suggested in the preceding question) during the next two years?

[   ] No
[   ] Yes, we plan to _____

_____

0. Have you changed or are you considering changing your professional position (or mode of practice) <u>as a result</u> of no-fault automobile insurance?

[   ] No. No-fault insurance has not caused me to change or to consider changing my position.

[   ] Yes, I am <u>considering</u> changing my position as a result of no-fault insurance.

[   ] Yes, I have formed a new partnership or association with other attorneys as a result of no-fault insurance.

[   ] Yes, I have _____ and now am
             (e.g., discontinued private practice)

_____ as a result of no-fault insurance.
   (e.g., a government attorney)

PART III

1. How long have you been admitted to practice?

    [   ] 0 - 5 years   [   ] 20 - 30 years
    [   ] 5 - 10 years   [   ] Over 30 years
    [   ] 10 - 20 years

2. In which county is your <u>principal</u> office located?

    [   ] Barnstable   [   ] Hampshire
    [   ] Berkshire   [   ] Middlesex
    [   ] Bristol   [   ] Norfolk
    [   ] Dukes or Nantucket [   ] Plymouth
    [   ] Essex   [   ] Suffolk
    [   ] Franklin   [   ] Worcester
    [   ] Hampden

3. Please indicate your <u>present</u> mode of practice:

    Individual Practitioner
    [   ] With no employees (or associates) who are lawyers
    [   ] With employees (or associates) who are lawyers

    Employee (or associate) of an Individual Practitioner
    [   ]

    Partner in Firm
    [   ] With three or fewer attorneys (including associate)
    [   ] With four, five or six attorneys (including associates)
    [   ] With seven or more attorneys (including associates)

    Associate in Firm
    [   ] With three or fewer attorneys (including associate)
    [   ] With four, five or six attorneys (including associates)
    [   ] With seven or more attorneys (including associates)

    Government Attorney
    [   ]

    Corporation Attorney
    [   ]

    Other: _____

    Not in practice
    [   ]   [Please skip to Part IV.]

4. In 1971, was at least three-quarters of your income derived from the practice of law?

    [   ] Yes, at least 75%   [   ] No, less than 75%

6.   To which two fields of law did you allocate the greatest amounts of time during 1970 and 1971?   [Please enter the appropriate number from the list below.]

<table>
<tr><td>5.</td><td>1970</td><td>1.</td><td>Business, corporation, or tax law</td></tr>
<tr><td></td><td>[   ] Most time</td><td>2.</td><td>Criminal law</td></tr>
<tr><td></td><td>[   ] Next most time</td><td>3.</td><td>Personal injury, predominantly plaintiff</td></tr>
<tr><td></td><td></td><td>4.</td><td>Personal injury, predominantly defendant</td></tr>
<tr><td>6.</td><td>1971</td><td>5.</td><td>Other civil litigation</td></tr>
<tr><td></td><td>[   ] Most time</td><td>6.</td><td>Real estate law</td></tr>
<tr><td></td><td>[   ] Next most time</td><td>7.</td><td>Wills, estate planning, probate</td></tr>
<tr><td></td><td></td><td>8.</td><td>Other: _____</td></tr>
</table>

7.   Approximately how many claims for personal injury no-fault (P.I.P.) benefits have you handled since January 1, 1971?

    [   ] None
    [   ] 1 to 5
    [   ] 6 to 10
    [   ] More than 10

8.   What is your office policy with respect to handling a client's claim for personal injury no-fault (P.I.P.) benefits?

    [   ] We handle P.I.P. claims.
    [   ] We handle P.I.P. claims if there is also a possible tort claim.
    [   ] In general, we prefer not to handle P.I.P. claims.
    [   ] Other: _____

_____

9.   We would very much appreciate an approximation of your annual income from the practice of law.

    [   ] Less than $20,000   [   ] $20,000-$30,000   [   ] Over $30,000

10.   How did your income from the practice of law in 1971 compare with your income from practice in 1970?

    [   ] My income from practice in 1971 was greater than in 1970.
    [   ] My income from practice in 1971 was about the same as in 1970.
    [   ] My income from practice in 1971 was less than in 1970.

PART IV

ADDITIONAL COMMENTS

We invite your comments both on matters dealt with in this
questionnaire and on other aspects of no-fault insurance.

(1) Please return the questionnaire in
the enclosed prepaid envelope to:

Professor Alan I. Widiss
College of Law
University of Iowa
Iowa City, Iowa 52240

THANK YOU VERY MUCH
FOR
COOPERATING WITH THIS STUDY

(2) Please mail the enclosed prepaid
post card separately from the
completed questionnaire.

CHAPTER 4

The Impact of No-Fault Auto Insurance on Massachusetts Courts*

By
RANDALL BOVBJERG**

I. INTRODUCTION

Massachusetts was the first state to require no-fault auto insurance. Compulsory Personal Injury Protection, commonly known as PIP, insurance became effective on January 1, 1971;[1] the companion Property Protection Insurance, or PPI, took effect a year later.[2] Together, the two statutes wrought a tremendous change in the law of motor vehicle torts. Within the limits of no-fault coverage, a motorist's accident claim runs against his own insurance company in contract, rather than against another motorist in tort, and his injured passengers and pedestrian victims claim as beneficiaries of his insurance policy.

Under Personal Injury Protection insurance, a person injured in an auto accident will collect the first $2000 of his wage loss and

* This study is part of a project of the Council on Law-Related Studies, of Cambridge, Massachusetts, under the direction of Professor Alan I. Widiss, College of Law, University of Iowa. The Council is a small private foundation created in 1969 by the Walter E. Meyer Research Institute of Law. For references to other studies in the project, see note 8 infra.

** Research Attorney, Program on Legal Issues in Health Care, Duke Law School; from 1971-73, Associate Director, Massachusetts No-Fault Auto Insurance Study; A.B., 1968, University of Chicago; J.D., 1971, Harvard Law School. The author is indebted to Professor David F. Cavers for editorial advice and suggestions. The author also wishes to acknowledge the capable assistance of the many student researchers who helped collect and compile data for this article and to cite, in particular, the special contributions of Mark Pomerantz, A.B. 1972, Harvard University.

[1] MASS. GEN. LAWS ANN. ch. 90, §§34A, D, M, N; ch. 175, §§22E-H, 113B-C; ch. 231, §6D (1971). No effort will be made in this article to provide a complete analysis of the no-fault laws' provisions.

[2] MASS. GEN. LAWS ANN. ch. 90, §34O (1972).

Editor's Note: Reproduced from *New England Law Review,* Volume 11, Spring 1976, Number 2.

medical bills on a first-party basis from the motorist's insurer;[3] additional amounts may be sought in tort on a third-party basis.[4] General damages for pain and suffering may be sought only if: (1) medical expenses exceed $500; (2) the injury consists of a fracture, loss of a body member, or permanent and serious disfigurement; or (3) the injury results in loss of sight or hearing or in death.[5] These restrictions on the collection of general damages, commonly called the "tort threshold," were widely expected to ease the burden of motor tort suits on the state's courts. Although suit was still allowed for many elements of damages,[6] the elimination of pain and suffering recovery from most cases was thought to make such suits much less attractive.

The Property Protection Insurance statute exempts Massachusetts motorists from tort liability for property damage to other PPI-insured vehicles, while providing for first-party and self-insurance options.[7] No tort threshold enables claimants to breach the PPI barrier. However, PPI requires insurance to cover tort liability up to $5000 for damage to a vehicle not under PPI or to non-vehicular property.

No-fault's effects on the number of tort entries was the principal focus of the court study component of the Massachusetts No-Fault Auto Insurance Study;[8] the goal was to determine

---

[3] Mass. Gen. Laws Ann. ch.90, §34A (1971). Wage losses are reimbursed only to 75% of the injured claimant's average weekly wage; and, further, any wage continuation plan payments must be offset against the PIP payment. Payments in lieu of wage loss are available to unemployed people, and replacement services (e.g., a person hired to replace an injured housewife) are also covered.

[4] PIP's tort liability exemption, 90 Mass. Gen. Laws Ann. ch. 90, §34M (1971), is exactly tailored to the PIP benefits received by the claimant. Thus, any special damages not covered by PIP may be sought in tort.

[5] Mass. Gen. Laws Ann. ch. 231, §6D (1971).

[6] Many elements of automobile injury damages survived PIP. Detailed lists of plaintiffs' civil remedies are contained in Rafalowicz, *The Massachusetts "No-Fault" Automobile Insurance Law: An Analysis and Proposed Revision*, 8 Harv. J. Legis. 455, 488 (1971); Kenny & McCarthy, *"No-Fault" in Massachusetts Chapter 670, Acts of 1970—A Synopsis and Analysis*, 55 Mass. L.Q. 23, 51 (1970). *See also* note 4, *supra*.

[7] Mass. Gen. Laws Ann. ch. 90, § 34O (1971).

[8] The Massachusetts No-Fault Auto Insurance Study also investigated the effects of no-fault on lawyers and auto accident victims, as well as on claims settlement by insurers. For a preliminary report on this court segment of the Study and on the lawyer inquiry, *see* Widiss & Bovbjerg, *No-Fault in Massachusetts: Its Impact on Courts and Lawyers*, 59 Am. Bar Assn. J. 487 (1973); Other reports include: Widiss, *Massachusetts No-Fault Automobile Insurance: Its Impact on the Legal Profession*, 56 Bos. U.L. Rev. No. 2 (1976);

whether the decrease in recourse to litigation anticipated by no-fault proponents[9] was actually achieved. Though in retrospect it may seem obvious that litigation would decline, at the time not all observers agreed. In the immediate aftermath of the PIP legislation, for example, some observers emphasized that numerous tort rights survived PIP,[10] while others noted that the early experience would be misleading, since many fault cases would not be filed until the constitutionality of the no-fault regime was established and lawyers and claimants learned the new claims process. The constitutional challenge to PIP's limitation on tort recovery, especially pain and suffering damages, was not settled until the decision in *Pinnick v. Cleary*[11] on June 29, 1971.

A preliminary report on the findings of the court study's survey of judicial entries was made in early in 1973,[12] before the statute of limitations had run on all pre-no-fault accidents. That report predicted that no-fault would ultimately reduce personal injury motor vehicle tort cases by about 80 percent in the lower-level District Courts and by about 50 percent in the higher-level Superior Courts, which generally handle the larger cases and

---

Widiss, *Accident Victims Under No-Fault Automobile Insurance: A Massachusetts Survey*, 61 IOWA L. REV. 1 (1975); Widiss, *Automobile Accident Personal Injury Insurance Claims: An Examination of Insurers' Massachusetts Experience* (not yet published). These and studies of the Florida and Delaware no-fault experiences, supported by the Council on Law-Related Studies, are to be collected in a book to be published this summer under the Council's auspices. The Florida study has not yet appeared; for the Delaware study, *see* Clark & Waterson, *'No-Fault' in Delaware*, 6 RUTGERS-CAMDEN L.J. 225 (1974).

[9] *See, e.g.*, R. KEETON & J. O'CONNELL, BASIC PROTECTION FOR THE TRAFFIC VICTIM: A BLUEPRINT FOR REFORMING AUTOMOBILE INSURANCE 13-15 (1965). The PIP statute evolved from the Keeton-O'Connell plan, introduced in the legislature by then-State Representative, now-Governor Michael S. Dukakis. *See, e.g.*, Dukakis & Kinzer, "If Your House Burns, You're Covered, No Matter Whose Fault it Was. And If Your Car Crashes—?" N.Y. Times Magazine 32, 32 & 74-75 (Apr. 9, 1972).

[10] *See, e.g.*, note 6 *supra*.

[11] 360 Mass. 1, 271 N.E.2d 592 (1971). One theory then commonly advanced was that many lawyers had held back on both PIP claims and tort claims pending the test case's resolution. This "cases in a drawer" hypothesis is not borne out by the few available statistics. While this Study's court survey was not begun until October, 1971, precisely to avoid PIP's "shakedown" period, official statistics for the state's Superior Courts, compiled monthly by the Courts' statistician, show no sharp drop in MVT entries before *Pinnick* and no upsurge afterwards. Official but unpublished statistics were supplied by Eleanor J. Flynn, statistician; *see* note 19, *infra*.

[12] Widiss & Bovbjerg, *supra* note 8.

where trial by jury is available.[13] Those predictions have since been borne out by a continued survey in two representative courts and by the official records of Massachusetts' Clerks of Courts. If anything, the early predictions were overly conservative, and the full impact of the two no-fault laws on property damage motor vehicle torts can now be seen to be even greater than that on personal injury cases.

A decline in the number of cases entered on the dockets of a court system may not seem of much significance if the number of trials has not similarly decreased. As to this, as a later section notes, post-no-fault causes of their drop are still unclear, at least in the Superior Courts.[14] However, cases that do not reach trial are not inconsequential in assessing the load on a court system. Thus, in his opinion in *Pinnick v. Cleary*[15] holding the no-fault law constitutional, Mr. Justice Reardon declared, after calling attention to the "avalanche" of motions and other papers which a court must handle after entry:

> The time of the court consumed in this preliminary war of nerves between counsel, or between claimant and insurer, is almost impossible to estimate, but probably far exceeds that spent in the trial of the small proportion of all entries which must be tried.[16]

The diminution in entries found in this court study also suggest that the number of persons asserting claims of bodily injury has fallen. A study survey found over 40 percent non-claimants among "visibly injured" persons filing official reports of bodily injuries in motor accidents.[17] Moreover, resort to claims against

---

[13] *Id.* at 488-89. Superior Courts remand their small cases to appropriate District Courts for trial, and a defendant may remove a large case from the District to the Superior Court level. During the time covered by the no-fault surveys, the dividing line was $2,000 (only by coincidence equal to the PIP coverage limit); MASS. GEN. LAWS ANN. ch. 231, §102C (1974): Superior Courts could, on their own or a party's motion, transfer a case to a District Court if "there is no reasonable likelihood that recovery will exceed" $2,000 (since 1974, $4,000). An amendment, *Id.* §104 (1965), has since July, 1965, allowed defendants to remove cases to Superior Court (subject to transfer) if the *ad damnum* exceeds $2,000 (since 1974, $4,000). As jury trial is ordinarily not available in a District Court, a small case tried there may be heard *de novo* in Superior Court, either as a retransfer by a plaintiff earlier transferred or as a removal by a defendant. *Id.* §§102C & 104 (1974).

[14] *See* Section IV, *infra*.

[15] *See* note 11 *supra*.

[16] 360 Mass. at 18, 271 N.E.2d at 603.

[17] *See* Widiss, *supra* note 8.

a motorist's own insurer in lieu of recourse to the courts seems likely to produce a more expeditious and economical settlement of claims. The handling of claims was examined in a project survey of post no-fault claims closings by a group of Massachusetts automobile insurers.[18]

II. The Overall Downward Trends: Official Docket Census Data

The official tabulations of civil entries and motor vehicle torts (MVTs) for the entire state are presented in Tables 1 and 2.[19] Though not as yet definitive,[20] the data clearly show the strong downturn in cases that followed PIP and PPI—both in total civil entries (equity suits excepted) and in MVTs. (In the Tables and Figures that follow, the term "civil cases" will be used without taking note of the equity exception.)

All District Court MVTs now number fewer than 4300 annually, as against about 33,000 a year just prior to no-fault—an enormous decline of 87 percent. (Table 1) The large drop in District Court MVTs is all the more striking when considered in the light of the long-term pre-no-fault upward trend. For nearly a decade before PIP, a steadily rising number of MVTs was almost as certain as death and taxes, whereas total civil litigation[21] rose

---

[18] See, Widiss, supra note 8. This survey was designed to permit comparison with the Massachusetts findings in a 19-state 1969 survey by the U.S. Dept. of Transportation. See 1 & 2 U.S. DEPT. OF TRANSPORTATION, AUTOMOBILE PERSONAL INJURY CLAIMS (July 1970).

[19] Official judicial data are published for each fiscal year. See COMMONWEALTH OF MASSACHUSETTS, [Nth] ANNUAL REPORT TO THE JUSTICES OF THE SUPREME JUDICIAL COURT BY THE EXECUTIVE SECRETARY (as of June 30, [year]) (Mass. Pub. Document No. 166) [hereinafter cited as SJC REPORT] (The Report as of June 20, 1974, has a new, enlarged format and does not carry the familiar Document No. 166.) The published data, being in many respects incomplete, have been supplemented by official, but unpublished, data. Ms. Eleanor J. Flynn, Statistician, New Court Bldg., Pemberton Sq., Boston, MA 02108, supplied many years' Superior Court data [hereinafter cited as Flynn Data]; and Mr. Jerome S. Berg, Director, Office of Administration for the Chief Justice of the District Courts, 1309 Washington St., West Newton, MA 02165, made similar District Court data available [hereinafter cited as Berg Data].

[20] Because the statute of limitations did not bar most pre-PPI accident cases until 1974, see notes 42 and 88 infra, only subsequent periods truly reflect the full impact of both no-fault statutes, namely, District Court data beginning with fiscal 1976 and Superior Court data beginning with calendar year 1975; but complete data for these periods are not yet available.

[21] For equity cases in the Superior Courts, which are excluded from Table 2, see notes 71 & 72, infra. In District Courts, Table 1 excludes cases entered in small claims courts.

TABLE 1

MASSACHUSETTS DISTRICT COURT* CASES: TOTAL CIVIL CASES
ENTERED AND MOTOR VEHICLE TORT ENTRIES

fiscal year	all civil cases**	motor veh. torts***
1964	97,278	26,631
1965	95,709	28,644
1966	93,829	29,212
1967	95,518	30,807
1968	93,827	29,770
1969	94,242	32,962
1970	97,994	33,861
+1971	101,068	32,856
+1972	92,331	24,225
1973	76,155	12,934
1974	67,817	6,485
1975	73,551	4,277

  * Not including Boston Municipal Court.
 ** From SJC Reports.
*** *Berg Data*, note 19 *supra*.
  + Effective date, PIP, Jan. 1, 1971; PPI, Jan. 1, 1972.

TABLE 2

MASSACHUSETTS SUPERIOR COURT CIVIL CASES: MOTOR VEHICLE
TORT AND OTHER CASES, ORIGINAL WRIT AND REMOVED CASES*

calendar year	all civil cases	all MVTs	original MVT writs	MVT removals***
1964	38,518	25,729	17,412	8,317
1965	37,442	25,216	17,173	8,043
1966	34,826	23,297	16,310	6,987
1967	33,570	23,006	15,376	7,630
1968	33,849	22,931	14,674	8,257
1969	33,784	23,022	14,446	8,576
1970	35,726	23,597	14,309	9,288
+1971	34,422	21,194	12,991	8,203
+1972	27,649	14,507	9,400	5,107
1973	23,587	9,308	6,515	2,793
1974	24,829	7,616	5,569	2,047
1975**	26,586	6,706	4,956	1,750

  * *Flynn Data*, note 19 *supra*.
 ** Extrapolated by doubling first six months' experience.
*** "Removals" are cases removed from District Court to Superior Court. See note 13, *supra*.
  + Effective date, PIP, Jan. 1, 1971; PPI, Jan. 1, 1972.

only unevenly. (Table 1) The decline after PIP was immediate and sharp—both in MVTs and in total civil cases.

Before no-fault, Massachusetts District Courts handled almost 100,000 civil entries per year; the post-no-fault decline "bottomed out" at 68,000 cases in fiscal 1974 and only began to rise once more in 1975, though MVTs continued to decline. (Table 1) Before 1971, about a third of the District Court[22] civil caseload was motor vehicle torts; the latest available data show MVTs as fewer than six percent (Table 1). The proportion is still dropping from the combined effect of rising total cases and declining MVTs.

In Superior Courts, about two-thirds of all pre-no-fault civil cases were MVTs. But MVTs have declined in every year since PIP, and the figure projected for 1975 shows that MVTs probably now account for only about one quarter of all civil cases. Since PIP, MVTs have dropped 70 percent—from about 23,000 annually to fewer than 7,000 in 1975. The Superior Court post-no-fault trend did not, however, reverse a past pattern of steadily rising litigation—both total MVTs and total civil cases were more or less constant for many years before no-fault—nor were the declines so precipitous as at the District Court level. (Compare Table 1 with Table 2)

Superior Court dockets now bear a considerably larger share of the total MVT caseload. In 1975 half again as many more MVT cases were entered there than in the District Courts; before 1971, the reverse was true. Moreover, the proportion of the Superior Court MVT caseload composed of removals from District Courts has dropped considerably since 1971,[23] seeming to confirm that the lower-level court entries were more affected by no-fault than the higher.

---

[22] Data presented here cover the 72 District Courts administered by the Chief Justice of the District Courts, *see* note 19, *supra*; The largest District Court, Boston Municipal Court, is administered separately. No official records from that court are presented because clerks there do not keep a tally of MVTs entered as clerks do in the other 72 courts; MVTs are instead estimated as a percentage of all tort entries.

[23] Whereas about 40% of pre-no-fault MVTs were removals (in 1970, 9,288 of 23,597), since PIP the proportion has fallen considerably (in 1974, about 27%, or 2,047 of 7,616). Meanwhile, the proportion of removals among other Superior Court civil cases (omitted from Table 2) has stayed relatively constant—and at a much lower figure (17% in 1970; 21% in 1974).

The decline in total civil cases ceased in calendar year 1973, about the same number of reporting periods after PIP as the comparable upturn in the District Courts. (Compare Table 1 with Table 2) But the number of MVTs is still falling, though at a declining rate. In contrast, the volume of criminal cases—over 38,000 in fiscal 1971—imposes a heavy burden despite a decline to 34,239 in fiscal 1974.[24]

III. THE PRECIPITOUS DECLINE ANALYZED: THE COURT SURVEY

Detailed understanding of the post-no-fault decline in Massachusetts motor vehicle accident litigation requires examination of the in-depth court survey. While the complete official census statistics are the best evidence of the statewide decline, they do not show the dynamics of the falling-off of cases, and, since the observed decline has not yet halted, they do not indicate how far it will ultimately go.

Official records do not distinguish between MVTs involving only bodily injury (BI), only property damage (PD), or both (BI/PD), and therefore do not clarify differences in impact between PIP and PPI. Nor do they clarify the situation in the transition years between a wholly fault-based compensation system and a predominantly no-fault one.[25] For insights into these phenomena, we must turn to the study's survey of Massachusetts courts.

A. Survey Methodology

The study compared MVTs entered after no-fault with corresponding cases entered before no-fault. Analysis of PIP's judicial impact centers on cases entered *after* PIP's effective date that also arise from *post*-PIP accidents. It is these cases that were directly affected by the law's barriers to third-party bodily injury

---

[24] *See* notes 70 and 71, *infra*.

[25] There is no way for official statistics to distinguish between cases based upon pre-no-fault accidents and those from post-no-fault ones, both because of the continuing entry of pre-PIP fault cases after no-fault and because the official data are published by fiscal year (July-June), whereas PIP and PPI took effect on January 1. The exact reductions finally achieved by PIP and PPI together thus can only be seen after the two-year statute of limitations has barred substantially all pre-no-fault accidents suits. *See also* note 42, *infra*.

claims and lawsuits. The method of comparing these post-PIP MVTs with their pre-PIP counterparts will be described in Subsection B of this Section. The method of comparing PPI effects is similar.

The principal survey—made in the winter and spring of 1972—undertook to examine court entries before and after the January 1, 1971, implementation of PIP. A broad territorial sample was selected, comprising five representative counties of the state's fourteen: Hampden, Middlesex, Plymouth, Suffolk, and Worcester. Together they have 62.7 percent of the state's population, 66.5 percent of pre-no-fault auto injury accidents, 79.6 percent of District Court MVTs, and 75.8 percent of Superior Court MVTs.[26] Although these counties are not a perfect microcosm of the entire state, they do include some very disparate areas, much as the state does.

In each county its single Superior Court (for a total of five) and one or more of its District Courts (for a total of eight) were surveyed. Severe data collection problems discouraged extending the survey to the Federal District Court in Boston.[27] Table 3 shows that the eight District Courts surveyed contained very important proportions of the counties' population, auto injury accidents, and MVT entries.[28]

A two-year base-line period was canvassed to provide a picture of the court system before PIP; a single year's sample represented the early post-PIP experience. The first post-PIP sample period began October 1, 1971—a date late enough to have given a good picture of the post-no-fault era, since it allowed nine months "shakedown" time for the new system to stabilize, including three months after the Supreme Judicial Court had upheld PIP's constitutionality.[29]

---

[26] For the data on population, *see* U.S. DEPT. OF COMMERCE, 1970 CENSUS OF POPULATION: NUMBER OF INHABITANTS—MASSACHUSETTS, Table 9 (Pub. No. PC(1)-A23, June, 1971); on pre-no-fault auto injury accidents, *see* MASSACHUSETTS REGISTRY OF MOTOR VEHICLES, 1970 MOTOR VEHICLE TRAFFIC ACCIDENT EXPERIENCE (July, 1971) [hereinafter cited as REGISTRY REPORT]; on MVTs in the District and Superior Courts (two-year average, fiscal 1970-71), *see* SJC REPORTS, *supra* note 19.

[27] Decision reached after discussion with the then Clerk of Court, Russell H. Peck.

[28] Sources: SJC REPORTS, REGISTRY REPORTS, U.S. DEPT. OF COMMERCE, 1970 CENSUS, all *supra*, note 26.

[29] *Pinnick* v. *Cleary*, *supra* note 11.

TABLE 3

CHARACTERISTICS OF DISTRICTS SELECTED FOR SURVEY
(as percentages of County Totals)

	population (1970)	auto acc. (1970)	MVTs (1970-71)
Hampden County			
Springfield Dist. Ct.	52.9	54.5	78.4
Middlesex County			
First Dist. Ct. of Eastern Middlesex	15.9	15.2	21.0
Third Dist. Ct. of Eastern Middlesex	13.0	14.8	16.9
Lowell Dist. Ct.	14.5	15.1	13.1
Plymouth County			
Brockton Dist. Ct.	36.0	41.0	57.8
Third Dist. Ct. of Plymouth	18.0	17.1	9.6
Suffolk County			
Boston Municipal Ct.*	100.0	100.0	unavail.
Worcester County			
Central Dist. Ct. of Worcester	38.7	47.7	58.2

* Boston Municipal Court does not separately tally MVTs; see note 21 *supra*. It shares jurisdiction with eight separately administered District Courts.

No seasonal fluctuations having been discovered,[30] only half of each year was sampled. The sample period for each "year" ran from the fourth quarter of one year through the first quarter of the next. The post-no-fault sample covered entries from October, 1971 through March, 1972. Two corresponding sample periods in 1969-70 and 1970-71 formed the two-year pre-no-fault baseline against which the post-no-fault experience was measured. (Data derived from these two pre-PIP periods have been presented below as averages of the two periods in order to facilitate comparison with the single post-no-fault period.)

This method of sampling treats October, 1970 through March, 1971 as one of the two pre-PIP sample "years". It may

---

[30] Official unpublished Superior Court statistics did not disclose any differences between totals of October-March and April-September entries. *Flynn Data, supra,* note 19. Month-by-month statistics for District Courts were not available, but there was no reason to suspect them to differ from the Superior Courts'.

seem odd that the first three months of 1971 should serve as part of the pre-no-fault baseline, since PIP took effect on January 1, 1971. However, cases from this period are actually representative of the pre-PIP rather than post-PIP experience because almost no 1971 accident cases were entered quickly enough to appear in the January-March 1971 sample.[31]

The sample proportion of cases surveyed was quite high, one case in three in two Superior and four District Courts; one case in six in three Superior and four District Courts. In all, more than 7100 cases were analyzed in this survey—about 3700 in the Superior Courts and 3400 in the District Courts. In presenting survey findings, however, data on cases from the one-case-in-six courts have been doubled to give them a weight equal to that of cases from one-case-in-three courts. Otherwise, one-in-three cases would have been overrepresented in the survey results, since each of them had had twice the chance of being included than had each one-in-six case. Thus, for example, Figure 1 *infra* shows a weighted total of 4750 Superior Court cases for three sample periods rather than the 3700 actual survey cases just mentioned.[32]

The population surveyed comprised all MVTs entered in the sample periods that had not been transferred—i.e., cases whose papers remained in the court being surveyed. A case that had been removed or remanded was ignored; without its papers, the crucial information of the date of accident and type of damage could not be determined. This sampling method also avoided the problem of double counting cases, once in Superior and again in District Court, since papers could only be in one court.

The sample cases were chosen at regular intervals (every nth MVT) from haphazard starts, though sometimes more than one start per sample period was made, so that strict intervals were not maintained. There is no reason to believe that any periodicity in the docketing of motor torts diminished the randomness of the interval sampling; clerks in every court were questioned, but no significant departure from random listings was discovered.[33]

---

[31] Section IV, Subsection C, *infra* considers speed of entry.

[32] The doubling of some sample data frustrates the calculation of statistical tests of significance where the tests are sensitive to the number of cases analyzed. However, such tests were run on the raw data, and only significant results are presented in this article.

[33] One source of potential sample error should be mentioned—misclassification of

B. Bodily Injury Cases after PIP

The most striking survey finding mirrors the official census data: entries of cases involving bodily injury (BI & BI/PD cases) from post-PIP accidents were precipitously lowered in the wake of no-fault. Thus, PIP's limitation on tort recovery of damages for bodily injury (including pain and suffering) seems to have accomplished the objective of reducing BI & BI/PD lawsuits,[34] in both Superior and District Courts.

Superior Courts generally entertain larger bodily injury cases than do District Courts; only in the former is a jury trial available,[35] and suits entered there claiming damages under $2000 are automatically remanded to District Court for trial.[36] One would thus expect the impact of PIP to be less severe in the Superior Courts, whose more seriously injured plaintiffs should more easily surpass the tort threshold or exhaust PIP's $2000 coverage. This is indeed what happened in the survey courts, but the reduction of Superior Court bodily injury entries was nonetheless remarkable.

"Over-Threshold" Cases

To establish the exact extent of the decline in BI & BI/PD cases that followed the introduction of personal injury no-fault, it is necessary to focus first on cases both *entered* after PIP and based on accidents *occurring* after PIP. These post-PIP accident BI & BI/PD entries, it should be remembered, had to meet or exceed the PIP tort threshold[37] and are hereafter termed "over-threshold" cases.

---

cases by court clerks in their own docket books. Knowing that official statistics reflect their classifications, clerks are normally careful, and the sample drawn from their listing should be a good one of all MVTs. In only one instance did the survey find a significant error: a substitute docket clerk's error in recording MVTs as simple torts for several weeks—a lapse the survey quickly discovered and corrected.

[34] Of course, factors other than PIP may have affected the entry of MVTs after January 1, 1971, but none seems to have been a significant influence. *See* Subsection F, *infra*.

[35] Hence the provision for removal of cases from District Courts, *see* note 13, *supra*. Two special statutes allow six-person juries in the Central District Court of Worcester and the Central District Court of Northern Essex: MASS. GEN. LAWS ANN. ch. 218, § 19A & B (1967). The former was one of the courts surveyed.

[36] *See* note 13, *supra* .

[37] The PIP tort threshold was described in Section I *supra*. As used in the analysis of

"Analogous" Cases

In order to set a baseline for comparison, one must next identify an analogous group of entries from the two pre-PIP sample periods. The over-threshold cases from the October 1971-March 1972 sample are, of course, identified by reference to the effective date of PIP, January 1, 1971: their accidents occurred on or after that date. Pre-PIP MVTs can therefore be identified as analogous if they arose from accidents on or after the corresponding January 1 date for their sample periods—for 1969-70 entries, January 1, 1969, and for 1970-71 entries, January 1, 1970. Cases meeting these specifications will hereafter be termed "analogous" cases.

"Held-Over" Cases

MVTs entered in 1971-72 based on accidents occurring before January 1, 1971 were held over from the fault system despite their appearance in the post-PIP sample. These entries are termed "held-over" cases, as are pre-PIP MVTs based on accidents occurring before the corresponding January 1 date for their sample periods. Held-over cases are discussed in Subsection C below.

Figure 1, which follows, presents both pre-PIP and post-PIP survey data. In addition to the over-threshold and analogous cases described above, Figure 1 presents two other categories: cases claiming property damage only and held-over cases noted above, to be discussed in the two subsections following.

As Figure 1A shows, there were only 353 over-threshold BI & BI/PD cases after PIP, compared with 786 analogous MVT entries before PIP—a remarkable 55.1 percent drop.[38] Over-threshold

---

the court data, however, "over-threshold" MVTs are not strictly restricted to cases exceeding the pain-and-suffering threshold but include *all* tort suits for BI or BI/PD from accidents on or after PIP's effective date. For example, suits by people not entitled to PIP benefits are considered "over-threshold" cases even though they may claim for all damages and need not surpass the PIP tort threshold.

[38] If the 899 held-over cases entered in the two pre-PIP sample periods had not been distinguished from the 785 analogous cases, the drop in over-threshold cases in the post-PIP period would, of course, have appeared still greater. But these held-over cases, unlike the analogous cases, were based on accidents arising over a considerably longer period of time than was true of the over-threshold cases. To have added these held-over cases to the analogous cases would have inflated the pre-PIP sample and distorted comparison with over-threshold cases.

FIG. 1: MVT Entries in 5 Mass. Superior Courts
—PIP's Effect on Bodily Injury Cases

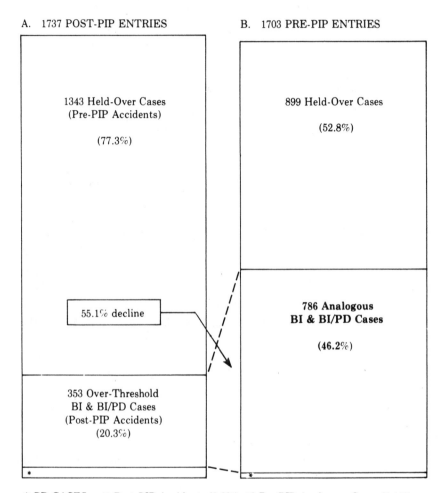

A.   1737 POST-PIP ENTRIES   B.   1703 PRE-PIP ENTRIES

1343 Held-Over Cases
(Pre-PIP Accidents)

(77.3%)

899 Held-Over Cases

(52.8%)

55.1% decline

786 Analogous
BI & BI/PD Cases

(46.2%)

353 Over-Threshold
BI & BI/PD Cases
(Post-PIP Accidents)
(20.3%)

* PD CASES: 41 Post-PIP Accidents (2.3%); 18 Pre-PIP Analogous Cases (1.1%).

(Case numbers reflect averaging and
weighting as explained in text.)

cases thus constituted only 20.3% of the entire sample caseload of 1737 MVTs in the post-PIP period, whereas analogous cases before PIP amounted to fully 46.2 percent of the pre-PIP total of 1703 MVTs.

Almost equally remarkable was the finding that the decline in MVTs involving bodily injuries was much the same in all five Superior Courts, ranging from 42.1 percent in Hampden County to 65.8 percent in Worcester. Surprisingly, neither supposedly super-litigious Boston (Suffolk County) nor its suburbs (composing much of Middlesex County) led in the number of bodily injury suits apparently averted by no-fault. Rather, Worcester County, well west of metropolitan Boston and far less urbanized, showed the greatest decline.[39]

The corresponding drop at the District Court level in post-PIP BI & BI/PD entries based on post-PIP accidents was little short of incredible. (The computation of the difference in post-PIP and pre-PIP District entries was made in the same way as the Superior Court comparison explained above.)

As Figure 2 shows, over-threshold BI & BI/PD cases were only 11 percent as frequent after PIP as analogous cases had been before. This astonishing decline, averaging 89.0 percent, ranged from 71.4 to 100.0 percent in the eight District Courts surveyed.[40] Amazingly, in the Third District Court of Eastern Middlesex, with jurisdiction over Boston's innermost northern suburbs, the post-PIP sample found not a single case alleging bodily injury from a post-PIP accident; the court had had about 50 analogous cases in each of the two sample periods prior to no-fault.

C. A Transitional Phenomenon: More Fault Cases after No-Fault

Perhaps the next most striking observation to be made from Figures 1 & 2 is how little changed total MVT dockets were, given

---

[39] This decline does not seem due to greater use of the District Courts; the post-PIP decline in over-threshold BI & BI/PD cases in the Central District Court of Worcester was 81.8%—about the same as in the other District Courts surveyed.

[40] The 71.4% drop found in the Third District Court of Plymouth was considerably less than the drop found for any other District Court and is not statistically significant because the post-PIP sample was so small. A statistical test showed a 9% probability that the post-PIP changes could have been due to chance.

FIG. 2:   MVT Entries in 8 Mass. District Courts
—PIP's Effect on Bodily Injury Cases

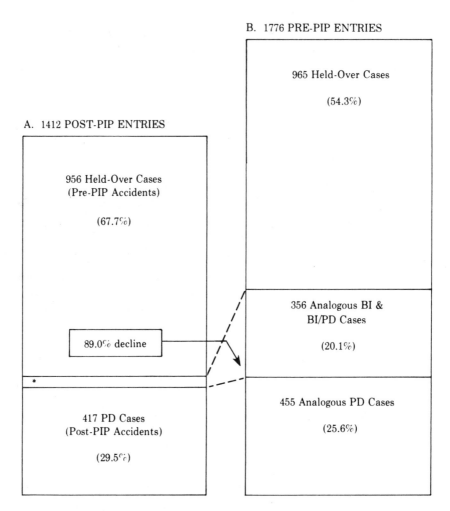

B. 1776 PRE-PIP ENTRIES

965 Held-Over Cases

(54.3%)

A. 1412 POST-PIP ENTRIES

956 Held-Over Cases
(Pre-PIP Accidents)

(67.7%)

356 Analogous BI &
BI/PD Cases

(20.1%)

89.0% decline

*

455 Analogous PD Cases

(25.6%)

417 PD Cases
(Post-PIP Accidents)

(29.5%)

* 39 Over-Threshold BI & BI/PD Cases from Post-PIP
Accidents (2.8%)

(Case numbers reflect averaging and
weighting as explained in text.)

the tremendous declines in suits involving bodily injury (BI & BI/PD) from post-PIP accidents.[41] The heights of the Figures' bar graphs, scaled to represent post- and pre-PIP survey period caseloads, are almost identical for the Superior Courts and not much different for the District Courts. The reason for this is that much of the decline in over-threshold cases just noted was obscured by the continuing entry after PIP of MVTs unaffected by PIP: either PD cases or held-over BI & BI/PD cases based on pre-PIP accidents. This effect was expected—because PIP was not aimed at PD and because the two-year statute of limitations had not run on pre-no-fault BI & BI/PD suits at the time of the survey.[42] It was the magnitude of the effect, at least in Superior Court, that was surprising.

In the District Courts, the astonishing post-PIP drop in over-threshold BI & BI/PD suits based on post-PIP accidents (from 356 sample cases to only 39) was fully visible in the total caseload's drop (from 1776 to 1412). No change in the entry of other cases offset the drop in post-PIP over-threshold cases, since post-PIP accident cases alleging only property damage dropped slightly from corresponding pre-PIP levels (from 455 to 417), as did entries of all MVT held-over cases (from 964 to 956).

The effect of held-over cases in the Superior Courts, however, was striking, completely counter-acting PIP's influence. There, the survey found that the total MVT caseload actually *increased* slightly, despite the large drop in over-threshold BI & BI/PD cases based on accidents occurring after PIP. As Figure 1 shows, the number of held-over cases in the post-PIP sample rose sharply above held-over entries in the pre-PIP samples (from 899 to 1343). This more than offset the drop in over-threshold cases after PIP from the level of analogous entries in the pre-PIP samples (from

---

[41] This seeming lack of change after PIP was mirrored in the official statistics for fiscal 1971, the first to be published after PIP's effective date. It led the SJC REPORT to note the lack of evidence of PIP's reducing litigation. FIFTEENTH ANNUAL SJC REPORT, *supra*, note 19, at 6, ¶17. The low visibility of PIP's early influence seemed to belie trial lawyers' contemporary claims that PIP had eroded 90% of their caseload. *See, e.g.*, "No-Fault: Trial Lawyers Ask Repeal; Claim Business Off 90%," Boston *Globe*, Feb. 2, 1972, p.1. The trial lawyers were correct about PIP's impact at the District Court level.

[42] The statute's obscuring effect was one reason for making a survey rather than relying on published data. *See* note 25, *supra*. As to the operation of the statute, *see also* notes 88 & 89, *infra*.

786 to 353). Superior Courts handle predominantly cases involving some bodily injury, and it was entries of held-over BI & BI/PD cases from pre-PIP accidents that showed the largest rise after no-fault, a 51.0 percent jump over the pre-PIP sample period level. PD cases from post-PIP accidents also increased, but these had less effect on caseload, since PD cases are far less important than BI & BI/PD cases in Superior Court dockets.

This rise in every category of Superior Court MVT lawsuit not affected by PIP may be explained by any or all of four hypotheses about post-no-fault behavior: (1) Plaintiffs' attorneys may have brought more lawsuits after PIP either because the lack of new cases after PIP allowed them to concentrate on older ones, bargaining harder and instituting more suits, or because the prospect of a reduction in new fees led them to seek to augment their old ones by bringing suit.[43] (2) Injured victims may have sought to wring the last dollar out of pre-PIP accidents, insisting upon more lawsuits as a kind of "last-hurrah" of the notoriously claims-conscious Massachusetts motorist. (3) Insurers may have adopted a settlement strategy of increased resistance to 1968-70 claims arising from pre-PIP accidents, perhaps because of their well-publicized conviction that the then (unconstitutionally) frozen auto liability insurance rates would not cover losses under a business-as-usual approach,[44] or perhaps because of their suspicion that claimants' attorneys, in a bind for new business, would have to settle on better terms rather than hold out for trial. (4) Individual claims adjusters may have adopted a hard-line stance, forcing more litigation, either because having fewer new bodily injury claims allowed them to pay more attention to old ones or because increased activity on old claims improved their job security in an uncertain period of reduced settlement activity.[45] Fi-

---

[43] Traditionally, plaintiffs' lawyers have charged a higher contingency fee for bringing suit than for merely handling an insurance claim. For data suggesting that lawyers did not claim higher damages in held-over fault cases after no-fault, see Section IV, subsection B, infra.

[44] Insurers in Massachusetts had contended for years that their rates were too low. After the auto liability rates were frozen in 1968 pending resolution of whether no-fault should be enacted, a number of insurers sued the Insurance Commissioner. On Dec. 14, 1970, the Supreme Judicial Court held the freeze unconstitutionally confiscatory, Travelers Indemnity Co. v. Comm'r Insurance, 358 Mass. 387, 265 N.E.2d 90 (1970).

[45] A number of insurance executives told No-Fault Study interviewers that some

nally, the introduction of comparative negligence may also have played a role.[46]

All of these possible explanations are speculative from the point of view of the court survey; judicial data cannot in themselves explain the underlying motivations for their existence. In any case, this increase in older cases in the immediate aftermath of PIP is, by definition, of limited importance, since it is eliminated in the transition to a no-fault regime as the statute of limitations runs on more and more fault cases. Indeed, continuation of the decline revealed by the initial survey is evident in official statewide census data and in the continuing court survey results.[47]

D. The Unexpected Decline in Property Damage Cases after PIP

PIP quite surprisingly seems to have had almost as great an effect upon lawsuits for property damage—not directly addressed by the PIP statute—as upon those claiming bodily injury, at which PIP was aimed. To ascertain PIP's influence on PD litigation, one must examine cases claiming any property damage (either PD or BI/PD)—as contrasted with cases involving only BI.

After January 1, 1971, Superior Court PD & BI/PD entries arising from post-PIP accidents dropped by 60.6 percent over the pre-PIP average for analogous cases. (Figure 3) The cause of this unexpected decline was a very large drop in BI/PD cases, which more than offset a small rise in PD cases. (Table 4) Apparently, before PIP, an additional claim for property damage was often brought as a "rider" to the basic Superior Court bodily injury lawsuit, often the vehicle for inflated claims for pain and suffering. Thus, when the BI claim was rendered infeasible after PIP, the PD rider, though legally independent, was usually dropped altogether rather than entered by itself. (A few cases claiming only property damage were evidently brought in Superior

---

other companies were laying off insurance adjusters in 1971, since PIP claims were easier to handle than liability claims.

[46] Unlike PIP, however, the comparative negligence statute should have helped to stimulate litigation. *See* Subsection F *infra.*

[47] For the official whole-state census data, *see* Tables 1 & 2, *supra*; for the continuing court survey results, *see* Figs. 5 & 6 *infra.*

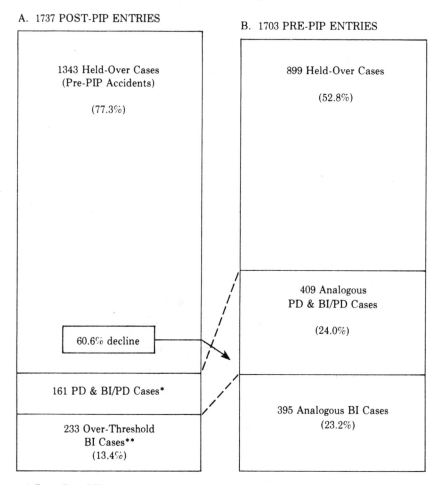

Fig. 3: MVT Entries in 5 Mass. Superior Courts
—PIP's Effect on Property Damage Cases

A. 1737 POST-PIP ENTRIES

B. 1703 PRE-PIP ENTRIES

1343 Held-Over Cases
(Pre-PIP Accidents)

(77.3%)

899 Held-Over Cases

(52.8%)

60.6% decline

409 Analogous
PD & BI/PD Cases

(24.0%)

161 PD & BI/PD Cases*

233 Over-Threshold
BI Cases**
(13.4%)

395 Analogous BI Cases
(23.2%)

* From Post-PIP Accidents (9.3%)
** From Post-PIP Accidents

(Case numbers reflect averaging and
weighting as explained in text.)

TABLE 4. 5 MASSACHUSETTS SUPERIOR COURTS
Changes in MVT Entries after PIP

type of case	Post-PIP Accident Cases (after 1/1/71) & Analogous Cases			MVTs Held over from Pre-PIP Accidents			Total
entry period	BI	BI/PD	PD	BI	BI/PD	PD	
	(over-threshold cases)						
Entries after PIP	233	120	41	541	687	115	1737
	(analogous cases)						
Entries before PIP	395*	391*	18*	425†	388†	86†	1703
% change	41.0 down	69.3 down	127.8 up	27.3 up	77.1 up	33.7 up	2.0 up

* Cases from accidents *on or after* January 1 preceding sample period of entry.

† Cases from accidents *before* January 1 preceding sample period of entry.

(Case numbers reflect averaging and weighting as explained in text.)

Court—at least, Table 4 shows a small increase in the number of such cases after PIP.) One might be tempted to speculate that other such PD cases might have been brought in District Court after no-fault,[48] but post-PIP PD suits actually declined in District Courts. (Figure 4 and Table 5)

The PD "rider" hypothesis is also consistent with the pattern of rises of Superior Court held-over cases entered after PIP over those entered before PIP. (Table 4) The post-PIP increase in these held-over cases was more pronounced among BI/PD cases than in the BI category. It would seem that once a held-over plaintiff had decided to sue for personal injury, (s)he was more likely than not to add a PD count. (Pedestrians and non-car-owning passengers would, of course, be exceptions to this supposition.)[49] After PIP, far more BI plaintiffs still under the fault system in held-over cases had an additional PD count than their counterparts had had before no-fault. (Table 4)

PD litigation at the District Court level was also lowered in the aftermath of PIP, but the 35.5 percent decline found there is well short of the Superior Court reduction just discussed. (Compare Figure 4 with Figure 3)

This analysis of property damage litigation in the interim between PIP and PPI would seem to show that, among the policy justifications underlying the latter statute, the need to reduce the volume of such litigation must in retrospect be ranked quite low in importance, given the reduction already achieved. This was of course not known at the time of PPI's enactment, and PPI did in fact later act to reduce caseloads still further.[50]

---

[48] Without an accompanying BI claim, a PD suit is quite apt to be worth under $2000. This would require entry in or remand to a District Court. *See* note 13, *supra*.

[49] One phenomenon visible in both Superior and District Court data (see Tables 4 and 5) is not explained by the "rider" hypothesis. After PIP, BI/PD cases declined more than BI cases. If PD counts had been merely tacked onto BI entries—as the "rider" hypothesis suggests—the decline should have been the same in each category. This phenomenon is hard to explain. The only systematic difference between BI/PD claimants and BI claimants is that fewer of the latter own one of the accident vehicles; passengers and pedestrians typically do not sue for PD.

[50] *See* Subsection E, *infra*.

Fig. 4: MVT Entries in 8 Mass. District Courts
—PIP's Effect on Property Damage Cases

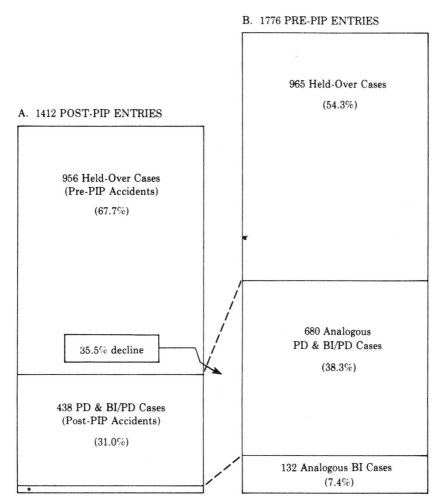

B. 1776 PRE-PIP ENTRIES

965 Held-Over Cases

(54.3%)

A. 1412 POST-PIP ENTRIES

956 Held-Over Cases
(Pre-PIP Accidents)

(67.7%)

35.5% decline

680 Analogous
PD & BI/PD Cases

(38.3%)

438 PD & BI/PD Cases
(Post-PIP Accidents)

(31.0%)

132 Analogous BI Cases
(7.4%)

* 18 Over-Threshold BI Cases (Post-PIP Accidents) (1.3%)

(Case numbers reflect averaging and
weighting as explained in text.)

TABLE 5: 8 MASSACHUSETTS DISTRICT COURTS
Changes in MVT Entries after PIP

type of case / entry period	Post--PIP Accident Cases (after 1/1/71) & Analogous Cases			MVTs Held over from Pre-PIP Accidents			Total
	BI	BI/PD	PD	BI	BI/PD	PD	
Post-PIP Entries	(over-threshold cases) 18	21	417	215	322	419	1412
Pre-PIP Entries	(analogous cases) 132*	225*	455*	202†	329†	435†	1776
% change	86.3 down	90.6 down	8.4 down	6.7 up	1.9 down	3.6 down	20.5 down

* Cases from accidents *on or after*
   January 1 preceding sample period
   of entry.

† Cases from accidents *before*
   January 1 preceding sample period
   of entry.

(Case numbers reflect averaging and weighting as explained in text.)

E.   The Impact of PPI: The Continuing Court Survey

Property Protection Insurance, or PPI, did not take effect until January 1, 1972. Its impact on Massachusetts motor vehicle tort filings was therefore not felt until after the dates sampled in the main court survey. A continuation of the survey, however, clearly shows a sharp drop in PD & BI/PD cases in the two years after PPI became effective. The extended survey covered MVTs entered from October through March in 1972-73 and 1973-74 in Middlesex Superior Court and the Third District Court of Eastern Middlesex. This survey was not limited to property damage cases after PPI but sampled every third entry of all MVTs.

The method of analysis used to compare MVTs before and after PPI was very similar to that used to examine post-PIP trends, though the PPI survey benefited from a longer post-no-fault experience. As in the earlier analysis, the focus is upon MVTs *entered* after PPI and claiming property damage from an accident *occurring* after PPI. It is these cases whose entry might have been affected by PPI, and they are thus similar to the "over-threshold" cases entered after PIP. However, the term "over-threshold" cannot be aptly applied to post-PIP cases because PPI had no pain-and-suffering threshold as such, but instead barred tort actions for property damage to vehicles to which PPI was applicable. A tort action for property damage based on a post-PPI accident may be maintained only where the plaintiff was not covered by the compulsory PPI (e.g., an out-of-state vehicle or non-vehicular damage). PPI compulsory coverage for such cars is limited to $5,000.

Cases termed "analogous" in comparisons with post-PPI entries based on post-PPI accidents (on or after January 1, 1972) are PD & BI/PD MVTs entered in the two years before PPI and based on accidents on or after the corresponding January 1 date in 1970. "Held-over" cases are all those MVTs (1) entered after PPI based on pre-PPI accidents or (2) entered before PPI based on accidents occurring before January 1, 1970.

PPI's thoroughgoing restriction of tort actions for property damages would lead one to predict that its effect on judicial PD caseload would be even greater than PIP's effect had been on BI cases. And, in fact, the continuing survey showed that in the two years after PPI became effective, District Court PD & BI/PD cases from post-PPI accidents were 91.8 percent fewer than analogous cases had been in the two years before PPI. (Table 6) Cases involving only property damage showed a similar pattern; they declined by 92.6 percent after PPI. (Table 6)

As with District Court BI & BI/PD cases after PIP, there was no surge in held-over PD & BI/PD cases after PPI took effect to offset the post-PPI decline in cases from post-PPI accidents. Instead, there was a considerable drop in held-over PD cases, whereas, after PIP, held-over BI cases were more or less unchanged over the pre-PIP levels. (Compare Table 6 with Table 5) After PPI, held-over PD & BI/PD cases declined by 24.1 percent, while those involving only PD dropped 7.5 percent. (Table 6) The

TABLE 6: CHANGES IN DISTRICT COURT MVT ENTRIES AFTER PPI
(3d District, Eastern Middlesex)

type of case	Post-PPI Accidents (after 1/1/72) & Analogous Cases			MVTs Held-over from Pre-PIP Accidents			Total
entry period	PD	BI/PD	BI	PD	BI/PD	BI	
Entries after PPI-2 Periods	13	6	0	74	11	5	109
Entries before PPI-2 Periods	(Analogous Cases) 176*	57*	13*	80†	32†	24†	382
Post-PPI % Change	92.6 down	89.5 down	100.0 down	7.5 down	65.9 down	79.2 down	71.5 down

cases alleging
PD down 91.8%

cases alleging
PD down 24.1%

* Cases from accidents
 on or after 1/1/70

† Cases from accidents
 before 1/1/70

(Case numbers reflect weighting as explained in text.)

continuing impact of PIP on suits for property damage[51] may account for these drops among cases held over from the pre-PIP era.

In Middlesex Superior Court, the MVT property damage pattern was very similar. Among cases alleging some property damage, with or without additional BI claims, those based upon post-PPI accidents were down 88.5 percent as compared with comparable pre-PPI entries. (Table 7) The drop was almost the same for cases involving only PD—89.8 percent. (Table 7) As in the District Court, held-over cases from pre-PPI accidents showed no off-setting rise—unlike held-over entries in Superior Courts after PIP.[52] Superior Court PD cases were down 11.1 percent in the wake of PPI, and PD & PD/BI cases dropped 45.2 percent. (Table 7)

---

[51] *See* Subsection D, *supra.*
[52] *See* Subsection C, *supra.*

TABLE 7: CHANGES IN SUPERIOR COURT MVT ENTRIES AFTER PPI
(Middlesex County Superior Court)

type of case	Post-PPI Accidents (after 1/1/72) & Analogous Cases			MVTs Held over from pre-PIP Accidents			Total
entry period	PD	BI/PD	BI	PD	BI/PD	BI	
Entries after PPI-2 Periods	5	45	275	47	125	185	682
Entries before PPI-2	(Analogous Cases) 49*	386*	396*	54†	260†	209†	1354
Post-PPI % Change	89.8 down	88.3 down	30.6 down	13.0 down	51.9 down	11.5 down	49.6 down

cases alleging   cases alleging
PD down 88.5%   PD down 45.2%

  * Cases from accidents   † Cases from accidents
     on or after 1/1/70   *before* 1/1/70

(Case numbers reflect weighting as explained in text.)

The continuing court survey also shows the continuing effect of PIP. Figures 5 and 6 show the trends in the two courts in the sample periods over the five years surveyed. In the Superior Court, cases involving bodily injuries (BI & BI/PD) continued to drop slightly in the second and third years after PIP. Both the total MVT caseload and the BI & BI/PD categories each came to only about a third of their pre-PIP levels,[53] while cases involving property damage (PD & BI/PD) were only one tenth as numerous as analogous cases had been before PIP. (Figure 5)

In the District Court, MVTs have almost ceased to be a factor in the caseload; only a handful of BI, BI/PD, or PD cases persists.[54] (Figure 6) If the no-fault laws remain unchanged, there

---

[53] This drop accords nicely with the one-third drop for all Superior Courts by calendar 1974, showing how representative Middlesex Superior Court is. *See* Table 2 *supra.*

[54] Even several years after PIP and PPI, some of these cases antedate no-fault, having tolled the statute of limitations. *See also* notes 88 & 89 *infra.*

Fig. 5:   MVT Entries in Middlesex Superior Court
The Continuing Effect of No-Fault

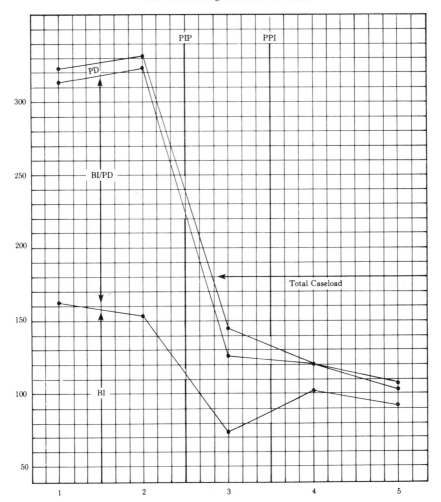

Sample period numbered on baseline run from Oct. 1-Mar. 31 in following years: #1. 69-70; #2, 70-71; #3, 71-72; #4, 72-73, #5, 73-74.

will almost certainly always remain some MVTs—predominantly those involving property damage—at the District Court level, but very few.[55] In future years, MVT litigation is likely to be confined

---

[55] Survey researchers noted that many post-PPI entries involved nonvehicular damage—often to bicycles—and that a few were really not MVTs, sounding more properly as

almost exclusively to Superior Courts, where more serious cases—those exceeding the tort threshold—will be brought.

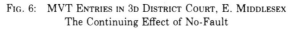

FIG. 6: MVT ENTRIES IN 3D DISTRICT COURT, E. MIDDLESEX
The Continuing Effect of No-Fault

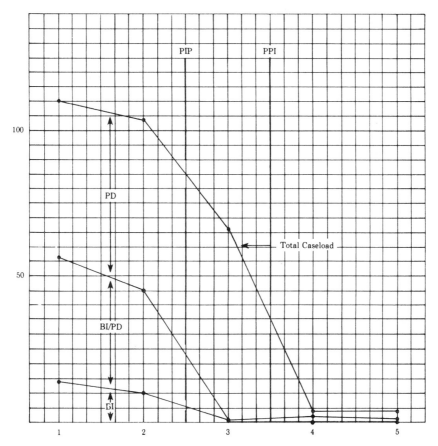

Sample periods numbered on baseline run from Oct. 1-March 31 in following years: #1, 69-70; #2, 70-71; #3, 71-72; #4, 72-73; #5, 73-74.

F. *Potentially Confounding Variables*

Factors other than the changes in tort law wrought by the no-fault statutes must also be considered in attempting to explain

conversions. Thus, the persistence of "MVTs" is partly due to court clerks' categorization. Since the court survey was completed, Massachusetts procedure has changed. District Courts now handle cases up to $4,000. *See* note 13 *supra*. However, since so few small cases remain, this change is unlikely to recreate a substantial District Court MVT caseload.

changes in Massachusetts court dockets since 1971. There is little reason to believe, however, that other influences than PIP and PPI are responsible for the drastic curbing of motor tort cases observed in the wake of no-fault.

First are the legal considerations: Massachusetts adopted the comparative negligence[56] rule at the same time as PIP. The effects of the two reforms are therefore not separable by a simple docket survey or census. However, the expected impact of the comparative negligence rule is distinguishable from that of PIP and PPI, since its effect on lawsuits, if any,[57] seems likely to have been the reverse of no-fault—increasing motor (and other) tort cases by allowing plaintiffs to bring suit who were previously barred by their own negligence.[58] An automobile guest statute[59] became effective on January 1, 1972, allowing passengers injured in Massachusetts to recover in tort upon a showing of ordinary rather than gross negligence. This change should also have encouraged lawsuits, so that, while its effects are intermingled with no-fault's, their expected directions are opposed, and any reduction actually observed indicates that no-fault's impact was all the more noteworthy.

Second, changes in rates of motor vehicle accidents and injuries merit consideration. If causes other than no-fault reduced accidents and injuries, they might have been responsible for reduced claims and lawsuits instead of, or in addition to, PIP and PPI. For example, the amount of driving—and thus the number of accidents—might have been reduced by the recession economies of 1971 or 1974-75 or by the oil embargo and its aftermath in 1973-74. Unusually mild winters might have reduced accidents, as might have better law enforcement or safer design of highways or cars. In fact, it was not unusual in the early no-fault years for detractors to point informally to the probable impact of such non-no-fault factors.

---

[56] Mass. Gen. Laws ch. 231, §85 (1974), as amended.

[57] Many believe the former contributory negligence rule had long been paid only lip service.

[58] A survey in Arkansas (a very different state from Massachusetts) indicated that most lawyers there accepted clients after the change to comparative negligence that they would previously have turned away, though the new rule also tended to promote settlements before trial. Rosenberg, *Comparative Negligence in Arkansas: A "Before and After" Survey*, 13 Ark. L. Rev. 89 (1959).

[59] Mass. Gen. Laws ch. 231, §85L (1971).

However, although all these considerations are theoretically relevant, they are unsupported by the motor vehicle statistics now available for the post-no-fault period. (1) Massachusetts motorists drove just as many miles after no-fault as before, at least until well after the observed drop in litigation. Not until 1973 and 1974 was there a leveling off, then reversal of the historical upward trend in mileage.[60] (Figure 7) (2) The number of re-

FIG. 7: REPORTED INJURIES AND MILES DRIVEN

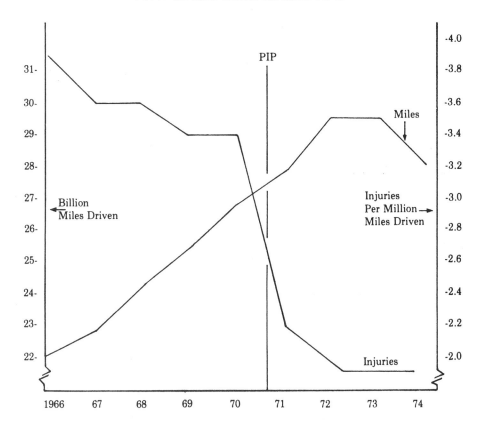

Source: REGISTRY REPORTS, 1966-74, *supra* note 27.

[60] The reduction was presumably caused by higher fuel prices or lower speed limits, but may be partly a statistical artifact. The Registry bases mileage on the amount of fuel sold in the state and on the average mpg of Massachusetts vehicles. The latter figure used remained almost constant in the 1970s, despite the national trend to much more frugal cars. *See* REGISTRY REPORTS 1970-74, *supra* note 26.

ported injuries per million miles driven has indeed declined over the years, consistent with the hypotheses of improved safety and law enforcement. But the decline in reports of injuries was enormous in 1971, as PIP took effect, and seems more likely due to PIP-induced changes in motorists' reporting than to sudden and dramatic safety or law-enforcement improvements.

(3) The long-term trend in auto accidents is up, not down. (Figure 8) Total accidents reported to the Massachusetts Registry of Motor Vehicles (as required by law when there is a bodily injury or property damage to one vehicle of at least $200[61]) did drop after PIP, compared with the very high levels reached in 1969 and 1970. But the rate of increase of reported post-no-fault accidents is not greatly different from the longer-run trend (dotted line) and is still high and rising.[62] It is also true that reported injuries have dropped drastically since no-fault. Whereas half of all accidents were formerly reported to involve bodily injury, after no-fault this proportion dropped rapidly and has continued to decline somewhat even as the total number of reported accidents has increased. (Figure 8) It seems very likely, however, that reporting changes are due chiefly to motorists' changed characterizations of their accidents and injuries. If so, fewer injuries have not caused lessened litigation; rather, lessened opportunities for liability claims and lawsuits after PIP have caused fewer motorists to claim injuries in their reports.

This reading of the decline in reported injuries is supported by close inspection of Figure 9. The more discretion motorists had in deciding whether there was an injury, the greater was the post-no-fault change in reported injuries; conversely, the more objectively verifiable the injury, the lesser the change. At one end of the spectrum is fatality, always reported by police, and deaths continued to rise after no-fault.[63] Next, "severe visible injury" (in the words of the report form), also objectively apparent, has also

---

[61] Mass. Gen. Laws ch. 90, §26 (1971), as amended.

[62] Inflation in repair costs is probably a major reason for the continued rise. As more and more minor accidents can lead to $200 worth of repairs, the number of reported accidents should continue to rise.

[63] After PIP, Massachusetts motor vehicle deaths rose for the first time to more than

Fig. 8: Reported Accidents Involving Bodily
Injuries or Only Property Damage

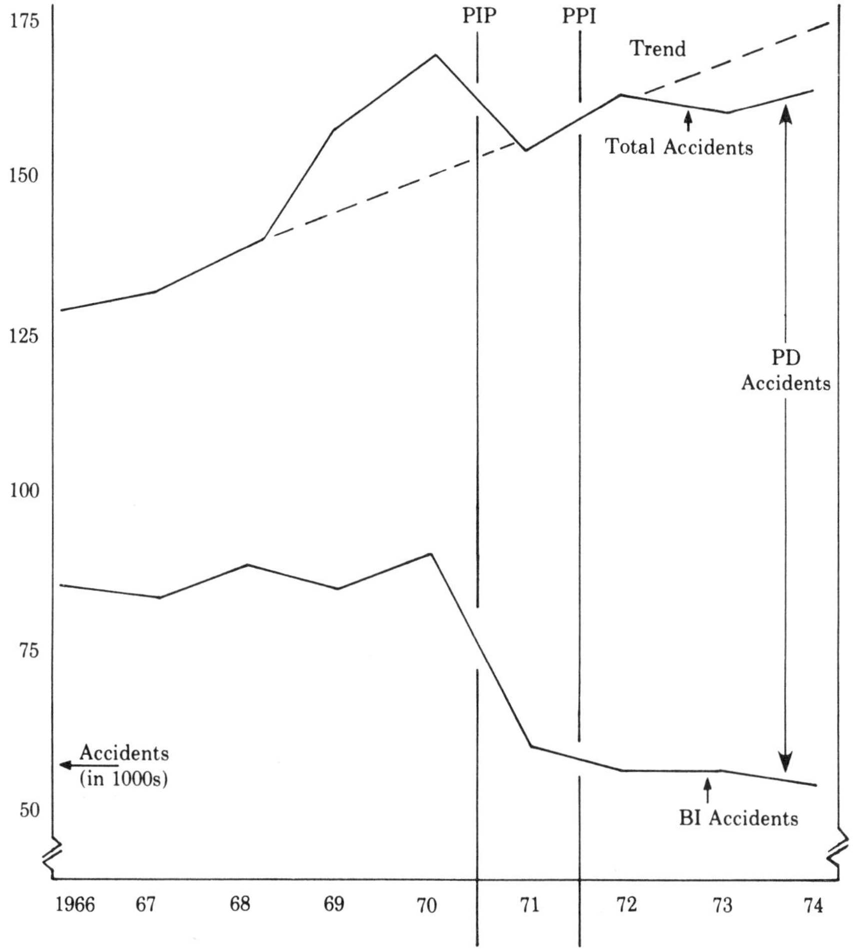

Source: Registry Reports, 1966-74, *supra* note 27.

1,000 per year—despite any reduction in driving, good weather, safety improvements, and the like.

Pre-PIP Deaths		Post-PIP Deaths	
1967	867	1971	908
1968	897	1972	991
1969	898	1973	1,010
1970	904	1974	961

Source: Registry Reports, *supra* note 26, for each year.

FIG. 9: CHARACTERIZATION OF BODILY INJURIES IN REPORTS

Source: unpublished data from Registry of Motor Vehicles, supplied by Registry Statistician, Ms. Evelyn F. Trefry.

risen steadily over the years, with little change in or after 1971. "Minor visible injury" allows more reporting discretion. After a marked fall in 1971, this category has fallen slightly, accelerating a downward trend apparent even before PIP. Finally, the big drop in reported injuries, over one-third, has come in the "no visible injury" category, formerly called "shaken up"—those with no objective signs of injury who subjectively feel injured.[64]

This reporting decline is thus concentrated among the less serious cases—exactly those at which PIP was aimed. But, though PIP bars many tort suits for minor injuries, it has no direct effect on reporting of accidents to the Registry. People in similar accidents before and after 1971—in the absence of a no-fault effect—should be expected to report the same levels of injury.[65] That they do not and that the changes in reporting follow the motorists' discretion provide strong support for the hypothesis that PIP has significantly changed the way people think about auto injuries. Before no-fault, personal injury claims were almost routine in the aftermath of an accident—filed to put pressure on the third-party insurer to settle a PD claim, if for no other reason. This was perhaps the major reason that Massachusetts led the nation in claims frequency.[66] Now, however, the accident injury report no longer seems an integral part of the typical Massachusetts claims procedure.

IV. No-Fault, Court Congestion, and Speedy Trials

A major one of no-fault's potential virtues was reduction in court congestion and, indirectly, in the exceedingly long wait for trial faced by pre-no-fault Massachusetts motor vehicle tort plaintiffs—up to 40 months or even more for a jury trial.[67] That

---

[64] It is claims arising from this category of injuries—whiplash, for example—that one would expect to be most affected by PIP's bar on pain-and-suffering recovery (below the "tort threshold").

[65] Since motorists must report their accidents anyway, to show property damage, they could easily check the box on the form to show an injury if they felt one had occurred, or might manifest itself later on. There is still no disincentive to report injuries to the Registry, though the positive incentive to report a possible tort claim has disappeared in most cases.

[66] See "How Meaningful is Massachusetts Experience to No-Fault Operations Elsewhere?" Nat. Underwriter, Apr. 21, 1972, p. 11, cols. 1-4, pointing out that the state's bodily injury claims frequency has been three times the national average.

[67] SJC Report, supra note 19, at 7-8, ¶¶27-35 (fiscal 1971).

PIP and PPI have significantly reduced the courts' civil caseload is completely clear. Whether no-fault has as yet actually reduced court congestion in terms of judicial time spent on trials and pretrial proceedings and thus speeded resolution of MVT cases is not at all clear, at least in the Superior Courts. Official court census data on trials shed some light on this subject; and, though the court surveys could not directly assess no-fault's impact on judge's time or speed of disposition,[68] their data on size of bodily injury damages claimed and on the speed of MVTs' entry are relevant.

A. Motor Vehicle Tort Trials

One would not expect no-fault to make a significant contribution to reducing trials in Superior Courts, where relatively large bodily injury suits predominate (Tables 9 A & B, *infra*) since the intent and effect of the two no-fault statutes were to weed out the small cases. Moreover any reduction actually achieved might easily be offset by other factors. Most notably, court congestion and the length of time between entry and trial are much more sensitive to criminal caseload than to civil—including MVTs.[69] Criminal cases obviously take priority because of the constitutional guarantee of a speedy trial and have in recent years become not only far more numerous[70] but also more complex and time-consuming, as procedural requirements have multiplied. Since mid-1971 there have been more criminal cases entered in Massachusetts Superior Courts than civil suits,[71]

---

[68] Far too few post-PIP MVTs had been resolved by the time of the surveys for disposition to be analyzed, and disposition data were not sought after the first few courts' experience had shown this.

[69] Interview in 1971 with Richard D. Gerould, then Executive Secretary of the Supreme Judicial Court.

[70] Criminal caseload has grown enormously in the past decade, from only 21,556 Superior Court entries in fiscal 1967 to 41,201 in fiscal 1972, and then dropping to 34,239 in fiscal 1974. However, even after that drop, cases "on hand at end of year" stood at 34,336, still above the 1972 level of 33,194, SJC REPORTS, *supra* note 19, at App. II (fiscal year 1972 & 1974).

[71] In fiscal 1971, for example, there were 38,353 criminal entries and 42,894 civil (including 6,441 equity cases); in fiscal 1972, 41, 201 criminal versus only 38,692 (7,121 equity)—as the post-PIP reduction in civil entries began, SJC REPORTS, *supra* note 19, at App. II (1971 & 1972). In fiscal 1974, though criminal entries had fallen to 34,239, civil entries were down to 31,908 (including 8,754 equity), *Id.* at 68 (1974).

and, if equity cases—now no longer a separate category—are excluded, substantially more criminal trials.[72]

Quick disposition of civil cases has also long been hampered by a shortage of judges,[73] compounded by a recent Massachusetts constitutional amendment mandating judges' retirement at age seventy.[74] Moreover, any decline in the pretrial wait for civil cases might well prompt a higher proportion of MVT cases to hold out for trial. This would offset the original decline, so that little change in speed of disposition would be achieved by reducing the total MVT caseload. Indeed, Professors Keeton and O'Connell expressed this reservation about the ability of no-fault reform to lessen court congestion.[75]

Official data however show that from the last fiscal year which escaped any substantial impact from no-fault—fiscal 1971 —to the end of the second year under no-fault—fiscal 1973— the drop in MVT trials in the Superior Courts was substantial (41.1 percent). It seems unrelated to the drop in MVT entries (46.1 percent).[76] Given the long delay before trial in many courts, a time lag was to be expected. Several more years' experience is necessary before a definitive judgment will be possible. Many courts are doubtless still trying many pre-no-fault cases. Not only did the two-year statute of limitations permit some pre-PIP cases to be entered as late as the end of 1972 but, thanks

---

[72] Fiscal 1971 saw 3,634 criminal trials and 3,150 civil (698 equity); 1972, 4,040 criminal and 2,577 civil (729 equity). *Id.* at App. II (1971 & 1972). For fiscal 1974 (including equity), the levels were 2,006 criminal, 2,248 civil but the totals exclude trials by District Court Judges in Superior Court criminal and MVT cases, both included in the 1971 and 1972 totals. *Id.* at 68 (1974).

[73] *E.g., Id.* at 9, ¶40 (fiscal 1971); p.10, ¶30 (fiscal 1972); p.40 (fiscal 1974).

[74] MASS. CONST., Pt. 2, Ch. 3, Art. 1 [§82], ratified Nov. 7, 1972.

[75] They liken the judicial backlog of litigation to an iceberg because so few cases survive the lengthy claims settlement and judicial process to reach trial. They note further:

> The analogy to an iceberg may also be valid in another way. That is, it may be that when the top of the iceberg has been melted away by [reforms]. . . , the underlying body of potential cases rises to expose substantially as great a backlog of cases waiting for trial as existed before.

R. KEETON & J. O'CONNELL, BASIC PROTECTION FOR THE TRAFFIC VICTIM 15 (1965). *But see* H. ZEISEL, H. KALVEN, & B. BUCHHOLZ, DELAY IN COURT 111-19 (1959): "We conclude therefore that it is improbable that a reduction or removal of the delay in the New York Court would increase the number of cases that will reach trial." *Id.* at 119.

[76] SJC REPORTS *supra* note 19. The 1974 format provides no separate data for MVTs. In the old format a large fold-out table headed "Civil Business Statistics—Superior Court

mainly to tolling, quite a few even later. Moreover, to the statutory period must be added an additional average waiting period, in the most congested court (as of fiscal 1971) of up to three and a half years from entry to trial.[77]

The situation at the District Court level is quite different. There, despite a large volume of criminal cases,[78] the pretrial wait for civil cases was, historically, much shorter than in the congested Superior Courts,[79] where jury trial is available. Moreover, in District Courts, the effect of no-fault on the MVT caseload was so drastic that it would necessarily have been accompanied by a lessening of MVT trials.

TABLE 8

MASSACHUSETTS DISTRICT COURT CASES: ENTRIES AND TRIALS*

Fiscal Year	MVT Cases†	MVT trials††	per-cent	nonMVT cases†	nonMVT trials†	per-cent
1970	33,861	7,598	22.4	64,133	9,589	15.0
1971	32,856	7,894	24.0	68,212	9,411	13.8
1972	24,225	7,278	30.0	?68,106	10,095	14.8
1973	12,934	4,334	33.5	63,221	9,852	15.6
1974	6,485	2,609	40.2	61,332	10,538	17.2
1975††	4,277	1,720	40.2	69,274	11,068	16.0

* Excluding Boston Municipal Court, no reliable MVT data being available.

† Source: SJC REPORTS, *supra* note 19, App.II (fiscal years 1970-1974).

†† Source: *Berg Data, supra* note 19.

---

for the Year-Ending June 30, [year], as Reported by Clerks of said Court" gives the numbers of MVTs entered for the year and tried by Superior Court and District Court judges in that year but does so on a county-by-county basis. Therefore, tabulation was required to obtain the following statewide data: MVTs entered in fiscal 1971: 22,739, in fiscal 1973: 12,140; MVT trials in fiscal 1971: 1,483, in fiscal 1973: 874. *Id. supra* note 19, at App. II (fiscal 1971 & 1973).

A factor influencing the drop in the number of civil trials in the Superior Court has been assignment of more judges to criminal cases. *See id.* at 40 (fiscal 1974).

[77] *See* SJC REPORTS, *supra* note 19, at 11 (fiscal 1972). The same report shows an increase for Middlesex County (Cambridge) of from 41 months to 51, a level that rose to 64 months in fiscal 1973 and dropped 7% to 60 months in fiscal 1974. *Id.* at 10 (fiscal 1973), at 70 (fiscal 1974). For provisions in the statute of limitations enlarging the gap between accident and entry, *see* notes 88 and 89 *infra.*

[78] Criminal cases, of which the largest single category is minor traffic offenses, are far more numerous than civil actions at the District Court level, totaling over 700,000 a year at the time no-fault was introduced. SJC REPORTS, *supra* note 19 (fiscal 1970 & 1971).

[79] All court personnel interviewed during the survey agreed that in District Court the parties could get an expeditious trial if both wanted it.

The expected drastic diminution of District Court MVT trials has indeed occurred. From a pre-PIP level of over 7000 per year, the number of MVT trials fell to under 2000 in fiscal 1975. (Table 8) MVT trials may well decline still further since MVT entries are still dropping.

Table 8 also supports the Keeton-O'Connell hypothesis of an increasing proportion of trials. The ratio of each year's MVT entries to MVT trials (expressed in Table 8 as a percentage) has risen as the number of entries has fallen. In 1970, there were 22.4 percent as many trials as entries. By 1975, the figure had almost doubled, to 40.2 percent.[80] This change somewhat overstates the true proportion of suits being prosecuted to trial rather than dropped or settled, since not all of a year's trials are of that year's entries. Because MVT entries have been declining sharply, the true proportion of cases entered that are tried in that year is probably somewhat lower than 40 percent. Nonetheless this rise in proportion, far exceeding that of other civil cases, clearly demonstrates trial dockets' resistance to reduction in caseload.

B. *Amounts of Damages Sought by BI Plaintiffs*

If, as anticipated, PIP eliminated proportionately more small than large lawsuits one might expect the number of trials to decline much less than the number of entries. The main court survey investigated the amounts of damages sought (the *ad damnums*)[81] by MVT bodily injury plaintiffs before and after PIP took effect.[82] Because the PIP coverage was intended to substitute for the previous third-party claim and possible lawsuit and because PIP eliminated suits for pain and suffering below the tort threshold,

---

[80] The MVT trial percentage had not risen in the few years immediately before PIP, indicating that the post-1971 rise was not part of a longer trend. *Berg Data, supra* note 19, not included in Table 8.

[81] The *ad damnum* sought in an MVT case is not a reliable measure of damages actually incurred. A better indicator is probably the settlement received. However, the *ad damnum* is the sole usable indicator obtainable from court records, since settlements are typically recorded as one dollar. The exact recovery is recorded after a trial judgment, but few cases from post-PIP accidents had gone to trial at the time of the no-fault survey. The *ad damnum* figures are presented here as relevant to lawyers' and plaintiffs' behavior. For an analysis of actual compensation paid, *see generally* Widiss, *supra* note 8.

[82] The continuing court study (after PPI) found far too few cases of property damage after PPI for an *ad damnum* analysis.

one might expect the number of cases claiming small amounts of damages to have dropped after PIP. Large suits, on the other hand, would be expected to clear the tort threshold or exceed the $2000 PIP coverage more readily, so that their numbers after no-fault should have been comparatively little affected. Cynical observers might also expect higher *ad damnums* to predominate after PIP because lawyers might compensate for fewer cases with larger claims in each; the *ad damnum* amount is completely within the discretion of the plaintiff.

In the Superior Courts, over-threshold cases—based on post-PIP accidents—moved toward a larger percentage of cases with sizable *ad damnums*. Before PIP, the typical case involving BI sought between $10,000 and $25,000 in damages;[83] for accidents after PIP, the typical case sought about $50,000, (Table 9 A) and the smaller cases almost disappeared. There were only 20 bodily injury cases seeking under $10,000 among post-PIP accident cases in contrast to an average of some 204 analogous cases before PIP; this is a drop of 90.2 percent. Though total BI cases after PIP dropped 55.2 percent, from a 786 average to 352, yet the number of very large cases—those seeking over $50,000—dropped only 23.5 percent, from a 228 average to 174.

The change in *ad damnums* can perhaps be better appreciated from the distribution of cases among *ad damnum* brackets; the proportion of post-PIP accident cases in the lower three *ad damnum* brackets (expressed in Table 9 A as a percentage) has uniformly fallen, while those in the higher brackets (over $25,000) had risen sharply. Thus, whereas cases of over $25,000 constituted only 42.2% of the pre-PIP *ad damnum* sample, they made up fully 68.7% of the post-PIP cases.

This change in size distribution seems due to PIP's virtual elimination of the small case, not to greed on the part of post-PIP attorneys or plaintiffs. This conclusion follows from a comparison of the post-PIP held-over cases (entered after PIP but based on pre-PIP accidents) with comparable held-over cases entered before PIP. If no-fault had led claimants or their attorneys to inflate

---

[83] Many of these cases are BI/PD; some portion of their *ad damnum* is for property damage, but the exact amount cannot be determined from court documents, which give merely a lump sum for both. The PD share is probably significant only among cases with very small *ad damnums*.

TABLE 9: *Ad Damnums* IN MVT BODILY INJURY CASES IN 5 SUPERIOR COURTS

A. Post-PIP Accident Cases and Analogous Pre-PIP Accident Cases*

entry period 000s		under $5	$5-10	$10-25	$25-50	over $50	Total
Post-PIP Entries:	No.	9	11	90	68	174	352
	%	2.5	3.1	25.6	19.3	49.4	100
Analogous Pre-PIP Entries:	No.	57	147	251	104	228	786
	%	7.3	18.7	31.9	13.2	29.0	100
% change		84.2 down	92.5 down	64.1 down	34.3 down	23.5 down	55.2 down

B. Held-over Cases From Pre-PIP Accidents†

entry period 000s		under $5	$5-10	$10-25	$25-50	over $50	Total
Post-PIP Entries:	No.	90	194	449	165	326	1224
	%	7.4	15.9	36.7	13.5	26.6	100
Pre-PIP Entries:	No.	76	122	262	112	239	810
	%	9.3	15.0	32.4	13.8	29.5	100
% change		19.2 up	59.7 up	71.4 up	47.3 up	36.4 up	51.1 up

* Cases from accidents *on or after* January 1 preceding sample period of entry.

† Cases from accidents *before* January 1 preceding sample period of entry (2 yr. ave.).

(Case numbers reflect averaging and weighting as explained in text.)

the *ad damnums* of surviving fault cases, one would expect the inflation among held-over MVTs from pre-PIP accidents entered after PIP to equal the inflation among post-PIP entries for post-PIP accidents that surpassed PIP's tort threshold. But this is not what the figures in Tables 9 A and 9 B show. To the contrary, the amounts sought in held-over accident cases were little changed before and after PIP: In both cases, $10,000-$25,000 cases were most numerous. To be sure, there were more post-PIP entries in all *ad damnum* brackets, but this merely reflects the general post-no-fault increase in fault cases discussed earlier, not a shift toward relatively higher *ad damnums*. In fact, the post-PIP increase among these pre-PIP accident cases was not greatest among the largest *ad damnums*, but rather in the middle range—the $10,000-$25,000 cases.

In the District Courts, smaller cases have traditionally predominated,[84] and too few over-threshold survived PIP to permit analysis of PIP's effect on *ad damnums*.[85] However, analysis of District Court MVTs from pre-PIP accidents showed held-over BI and BI/PD cases after no-fault almost identical in *ad damnum* distribution to held-over cases entered before no-fault. Both before and after PIP, the typical bodily injury *ad damnum* was about $10,000. It would seem that PIP itself did not increase District Court *ad damnums* but merely eliminated small cases, thereby boosting the proportion of larger cases.

C. *Speed of Entry of MVT Bodily Injury Cases*

The post-no-fault drop in the number of over-threshold BI & BI/PD cases did not result in faster entry of these cases. Though it is too soon to predict whether the wait from entry to ultimate judicial disposition of MVTs will be reduced in the wake of no-fault, the preliminary indication is that PIP at least did not prompt a speedier start to bodily injury litigation.[86]

Before PIP, the median time elapsed between accident and entry[87] of MVTs alleging bodily injury was 14 months in District Court (where many cases are on remand) and 11.5 months in Superior Court, while the post-PIP medians rose sharply to 22.5 and 18 months, respectively. However, the simple reason for this

---

[84] In the two sample periods before PIP, *ad damnums* of fully 538 cases of the 728 surveyed (73.9%) were under $10,000.

[85] In the post-PIP survey sample, only 36 of 569 BI and BI/PD cases arose from post-PIP accidents.

[86] Not surprisingly, PIP had no effect on the pattern of entry speeds for cases claiming only property damage. Both before and after no-fault, the District Court median was about 12 months for these cases; the Superior Court figure was about 20 months. Although the total number of PD cases increased after PIP, the increase was evenly spread over all ages of entries.

[87] In making speed-of-entry calculations, zero months are by convention considered to elapse between accident and entry if the case is docketed in the same month as its accident occurred, one month if docketing occurs the first month after an accident and so on, regardless of the day of the month the accident and entry occurred.

seemingly startling rise is that PIP eliminated so many "young" BI & BI/PD cases—those arising from post-PIP accidents. Thus, a better way of viewing post-PIP developments is to chart the pattern of entries by length of time after their accidents.

Table 10 presents speed-of-entry data in this way. Before PIP there was a large bulge of cases entered from three to eleven months after their accidents. Another bulge occurred at 24 to 26 months, or just before the statute of limitations would have cut off suit.[88]

TABLE 10: FIVE MASSACHUSETTS SUPERIOR COURTS

Speed of Entry of Bodily Injury* Cases Before and After PIP

Months between Accident & Entry	Post-PIP Entries** (Post-PIP Accidents)	Analogous Pre-PIP Entries	Post-PIP Entries† (Pre-PIP Accidents)	Other Pre-PIP Entries
0-2	18	29		
3-5	124	239		
6-8	108	268		
9-11	74	194	51	43
12-14	35	67	175	133
15-17			157	126
18-20			123	108
21-23			152	103
24-26			473	234
27-29			36	28
30-32			11	6
33-35			8	2
36+			34	25

* Includes both BI & BI/PD cases.

** These are "over-threshold" cases; see p. 336, *supra*.

† These are "held-over" cases; see p. 337, *supra*.

(Case numbers reflect averaging and
weighting as explained in text.)

[88] The statute of limitations for MVTs is two years, MASS. GEN. LAWS ch. 260, §2A (1971), but for technical reasons, a case may be entered up to three months after the two-year period, *see* note 89 *infra*, even without tolling the statute of limitations. There are other reasons for entries after two years. In District Court, some of these entries are

The judicial surveys found that over-threshold cases were entered in much the same pattern as their pre-PIP predecessors, though in substantially smaller numbers, both in Superior and District Courts. The most striking observation about speed of entry, however, is confined to the older accident cases, the held-over cases from pre-PIP accidents. In Superior Court, there was a very large increase among very old BI & BI/PD cases (24 to 26 months old).[89] Whereas the pre-no-fault average was only 234 cases in this age group, the post-no-fault survey found 473 cases—an increase of 102.6 percent. This dramatic rise accounts for much of the observed increase in fault cases after no-fault and seems to indicate that the increase in cases held over after PIP was not a systematic attempt by any of the participants in the settlement process to try more cases, a tactic which would have caused a more uniform rise.

In the District Courts, there was no great post-PIP influx of held-over cases. They were entered in about the same pattern as before no-fault—with some exceptions in individual categories. For example, the survey disclosed that post-PIP cases entered 24 months after their accidents increased by two-thirds, and cases entered after 36 or more months increased by one-half, over the levels of their pre-PIP counterparts.

V. Conclusion

Though no-fault's ultimate effects on judicial business cannot as yet be completely determined, obviously major changes in motor vehicle tort litigation have already occurred. The Massachusetts No-Fault Auto Insurance Study's extensive before-and-

---

remanded or transferred cases, entered on District Court dockets well after their original entry elsewhere. Other cases have doubtless tolled the statute, which does not run under many circumstances, among them the plaintiff's disability and the defendant's absence from the state. Mass. Gen. Law ch. 260, §7-9. One District Court case found in the survey was not entered until 138 months after the accident.

[89] MVTs docketed 24-26 months after their accidents avoid the two-year limitation because the action is considered to commence with the plaintiff's issuance of a *writ* (formal notice of general nature of suit served on defendant) and not with the formal *entry* date, when the case is docketed. Mass. Gen. Laws Ann. ch. 223, §§16, 20; *Rosenblatt* v. *Foley*, 252 Mass. 188, 147 N.E. 558 (1925); *Parker* v. *Rich*, 297 Mass. 111, 8 N.E.2d 345 (1937). A case may be entered in Superior Court as long as three months after the date of its writ, 60 days in District Court. Mass. Gen. Laws Ann. ch. 223, §§ 22, 23 (1971) (since July 1, 1974, Superior Courts governed by Mass. R.Civ.P. 4,5).

after court survey found bodily injury MVT's virtually eliminated from District Court dockets (down 89 percent) and drastically reduced (down 55 percent) in Superior Courts as well. These findings were based on careful surveys of five Superior and eight District Courts' dockets in three six-months sample periods, two before, and one after, the first no-fault insurance (PIP) went into effect. Reinforcement for the findings of the initial survey came from its continuation in a survey of the Superior Court and the 3rd District Court in populous Middlesex County for two more six-months sample periods (in 1972-73 and 1973-74) after the effective date of the second no-fault law providing for property damage insurance (PPI). Property damage litigation fell considerably after PPI became effective.

Official judicial census data for the entire state (both published and unpublished), though less detailed than the Study's, confirm the drastic post-no-fault decline which the surveys disclosed. That decline is not to be explained by factors other than the influence of the Commonwealth's two no-fault statutes such as other changes in tort law or changes in the ratios of reported injuries to miles driven or of reported accidents to bodily injuries, or in the reported severity of the bodily injuries sustained. There is no reason, moreover, to believe that no-fault has led to the replacement of MVTs with a comparable burden of contract litigation between insureds and insurers or of arbitration among insurers over subrogation rights.[90]

As expected, no-fault seems to have disproportionately reduced smaller bodily injury suits, especially in Superior Courts, where the more serious cases are handled. Surprisingly, personal injury no-fault seems to have significantly reduced the number of suits for property damage even before property damage no-fault took effect. Another transitional phenomenon was a marked increase in pre-no-fault injury cases entered after no-fault, ini-

---

[90] Contract suits brought against an insured's own PIP insurer did not, of course, appear in the survey sample of motor vehicle torts; as a small proportion of all contract cases, they would be difficult to sample in a docket-based survey. Anecdotal evidence from interviews with lawyers and insurers indicated that few such suits were being brought. Disputes among PIP and PPI insurers under the legislation's fault-based subrogation provisions, MASS. GEN. LAWS ch. 90, §34(M), (O) (1972), are generally settled by arbitration, not by lawsuit.

tially almost offsetting the large drop in post-no-fault accident
suits.

Given the huge overhang of pre-no-fault MVT cases and the
protracted delay between the entry of a case and its trial in the
principal Superior Courts, the rate at which MVT trials have
declined is understandably somewhat less than the drop in new
MVT cases entered, leaving no-fault's ultimate effect on the rate
of bodily injury trials as yet uncertain. It does seem clear that
post-no-fault bodily injury suits, despite the reduction in their
numbers, were not entered sooner after the accidents that caused
them than were their pre-no-fault counterparts.

Current complaints against the complex Massachusetts no-
fault provisions governing property damage insurance do not
challenge no-fault's effectiveness in reducing property damage
tort litigation in the Commonwealth's courts. And now that delay
in those courts has reached crisis proportions, the role of no-fault
automobile insurance law in reducing bodily injury litigation has
achieved special importance.

CHAPTER 5

A SURVEY OF THE
NO-FAULT PERSONAL INJURY CLAIMS EXPERIENCE
IN MASSACHUSETTS

Alan I. Widiss*

INTRODUCTION

In 1925, Massachusetts was the first state to establish a legislative requirement that all motorists carry personal injury liability insurance. Almost a half-century later, in 1970, Massachusetts became the first state to require that no-fault personal injury insurance be included as an additional coverage in all automobile liability insurance policies. Thus, since January 1, 1971, Massachusetts motorists have been required to have both automobile liability and no-fault personal injury insurance.

In 1972, the Council on Law Related Studies (the CLRS) initiated a project to examine how the no-fault insurance compensation system was working in Massachusetts. The CLRS study employed several different approaches to gathering relevant data including interviews with accident victims, attorneys, and claims adjusters.[1] Although these interviews provided considerable insight into how the no-fault coverage was functioning, they did not provide any quantifiable data on questions such as the nature of the injuries that gave rise to no-fault claims, how much indemnification claimants were receiving in relation to the amounts claimed, or how quickly claims were being paid. The most reasonable means of securing such information seemed to be a survey of insurance company claim files comparable to the study conducted several years earlier as one portion of the Department of Transportation study of the consequences of automobile accidents.

In 1969, the Department of Transportation cooperated with a group of insurers in a multi-company, nationwide study of automobile insurance claims under the tort liability system. This project, the DOT Automobile Personal Injury Claims Study,[2] surveyed automobile personal injury liability claim files of sixteen insurance companies.[3]

---

*Professor of Law, University of Iowa; B.S. 1960, University of Southern California; LL.B. 1963, University of Southern California; LL.M. 1964, Harvard University.

1. See A. Widiss, *Accident Victims Under No-Fault Automobile Insurance: A Massachusetts Survey,* 61 IOWA LAW REVIEW 1-72 (1975), and A. Widiss, *Massachusetts No-Fault Automobile Insurance: Its Impact on the Legal Profession,* 56 BOSTON UNIVERSITY LAW REVIEW 323-355 (1976). These articles are reprinted as Chapter 2 and Chapter 3 in this book.

2. Department of Transportation, AUTOMOBILE INSURANCE AND COMPENSATION STUDY: AUTOMOBILE PERSONAL INJURY CLAIMS (July, 1970).

Since Massachusetts was among the nineteen states in which information was collected for the DOT study, there was already a body of data on a representative sample of claims and settlement experience from the Commonwealth's pre-no-fault period. In order to take advantage of this existing survey data and the expertise developed in the course of conducting the DOT study, a series of informal discussions were conducted with executives of the thirteen companies that participated in the DOT study and who also do business in Massachusetts. The primary purpose of these discussions was to ascertain whether these companies would cooperate in the execution of a comparable post-no-fault survey of the claims experience in Massachusetts that would parallel the DOT study. Of the thirteen companies, twelve agreed to participate in the CLRS survey.[4] In addition to these twelve companies, two other companies with significant shares of the Massachusetts market—American Mutual Insurance Company and Commercial

3. *Id.* at p. iii of Volume 1. The companies that particpated in the DOT study included:

        Aetna Life And Casualty Company
        Allstate Insurance Company
        American Family Mutual Insurance Company
        Continental Insurance Companies
        Detroit Automobile Inter-Insurance Exchange
        Farmers Insurance Exchange
        Fireman's Fund American Insurance Company
        Government Employees Insurance Company
        Hartford Accident And Indemnity Company
        Insurance Company of North America
        Kemper Insurance Group
        Liberty Mutual Insurance Company
        Nationwide Mutual Insurance Company
        State Farm Mutual Insurance Company
        The Travelers Insurance Companies
        United States Fidelity And Guaranty Company

4. The companies that participated in both the DOT and CLRS Surveys were:

        Aetna Life And Casualty Company
        Allstate Insurance Company
        Continental Insurance Companies
        Fireman's Fund American Insurance Companies
        Government Employees Insurance Company
        Hartford Accident And Indemnity Company
        Insurance Company of North America
        Kemper Insurance Group
        Liberty Mutual Insurance Company
        Nationwide Mutual Insurance Company
        State Farm Mutual Insurance Company
        The Travelers Insurance Companies

Union Insurance Company—accepted invitations to participate in the study.[5] Although several of the companies that participated in the DOT study—which included the ten largest automobile insurance company groups in the United States—did not have shares of the Massachusetts market comparable to their market positions nationally, the CLRS survey did include seven of the eight insurance carriers with the largest segments of the Massachusetts automobile liability insurance coverage business as measured by premium dollars.[6] And taken as a group, the carriers who participated in the CLRS study provided almost half of the state's automobile bodily injury liability insurance coverage—again based on the Massachusetts automobile liability premiums.[7]

As was true in the DOT survey, the participation of these companies represented a significant commitment, since each company provided the personnel for identifying the relevant files, gathering them together at some central location where they could be examined, and transferring the requested information from each file to the survey instruments. These activities involved considerable effort and the contribution of their employee's time by the participating companies was as important to making the study possible as was their decision to participate in the survey.

I. SCOPE AND METHODOLOGY OF THE SURVEY

A. Design of the Survey Instruments

In designing the CLRS claim files study the objective was to develop a survey instrument that would retain the basic approach and format of the DOT study, but that would also if possible be improved as a result of the experience gained in the DOT study. Several of the persons who participated in the DOT study suggested a number of modifications in the DOT form. Primarily, they recommended deletion of survey items which their experiences with the DOT study showed to be relatively unworkable because the relevant information was not generally ascertainable from the claim files so that such items were either left blank or "guessed at" in the DOT study. Their suggestion that such items be deleted was accepted. In addition, since the CLRS study included both bodily injury liability claims and no-fault claims, the single form developed for the DOT survey was not completely suitable. After considerable discussion and some experimentation, it seemed preferable to develop a separate survey instrument for the no-fault claims.

During the summer and fall of 1972, the preliminary design for the survey

5. Data on Massachusetts automobile premium writings are compiled by the Massachusetts Automobile Rating and Accident Prevention Bureau. The characterization in the text is based upon the information on Massachusetts automobile liability insurance premiums compiled for the period July 1, 1970 to June 30, 1971.

6. *Ibid.*

7. *Ibid.*

instruments was completed. Early in the spring of 1973, a pre-test was conducted, and this was followed by a full-scale pilot survey to evaluate both the survey instruments and the instructions. The evaluation of the pre-test and pilot study results indicated that the survey instruments were essentially sound, although a few minor modifications were subsequently made in both the forms and the instructions.

Definition of a Claim File

No uniform practice is followed by insurance companies for defining who is a claimant, what is a claim file, or when a claim file has been "opened."[8] In the Department of Transportation study, a "claim" was defined as one which met all three of the following requirements:

     (a) A claim file was established;

     (b) A statistical reserve was established;

     (c) Notice of claim was received from or on behalf of a third party claimant or an investigation of the accident was undertaken and a contact was made with the claimant or his representative by correspondence, telephone, or in person.[9]

Conversations with representatives of several companies that participated in the DOT study in the course of formulating the survey instructions and pre-testing the forms for the CLRS study indicated that the DOT definition had not always proved workable and that companies had not uniformly interpreted and applied the definitions. Consequently, the definition of the claim files to be surveyed was slightly modified for this survey. In essence, the participating companies were asked to include all files or subfiles closed in October of 1972 on any person who had reported an accident injury to the company. For most companies, this meant that they had established both a file number and a reserve. However, some insurers do not formally establish a file or create a reserve until claim papers are submitted. Since we were interested in acquiring data on the accidents that did not mature into claims, special procedures were worked out so that all of the participating companies were providing information on all accidents for which they had received any report of personal injuries. However, if a file was erroneously created—as for example, when a person was not acturally insured by the participating company— the closing of such a file during the survey period would not lead to its inclusion in the CLRS study.

---

8. This conclusion is based on discussions that occurred in the course of a meeting in Cambridge, Massachusetts. This meeting was attended by representatives of most of the companies who had agreed to participate in the CLRS claims study.

9. Department of Transportation, AUTOMOBILE INSURANCE AND COMPENSATION STUDY: AUTOMOBILE PERSONAL INJURY CLAIMS—VOLUME 1 (July, 1970), p. 6. Hereinafter, this study publication be cited as the DOT CLAIMS STUDY.

Definition of Economic Loss

Both the DOT and the CLRS claim surveys sought to identify the economic losses sustained by each of the claimants. The definition of "economic loss" used for the DOT study was adopted for the CLRS study. Economic loss was defined to include all "objectively measurable expenses [sustained as a result of the accident] which would be recoverable in a lawsuit, sometimes referred to as court specials.' "[10] These damages were classified into the following categories for both surveys:

> (1) Medical: including doctor bills, hospital bills, drugs, prosthetic devices, treatment, ambulance service, etc.;
>
> (2) Wages /Income: including gross wages, salary, commission and self-employment income before taxes. . .; and
>
> (3) Other Economic Loss: including all expenses other than medical and wage/income loss directly related to bodily injury sustained.[11]

Claim Files That Were Surveyed

The types of claim data surveyed included any information in the files related to no-fault personal injury insurance (PIP), no-fault subrogation payments (PIP Sub), bodily injury liability insurance (BI), uninsured motorist coverage (UM), and medical payments coverage (Med Pay). Information was collected from all files that involved PIP claims regardless of where the accidents occurred.

The CLRS survey encompassed all files closed by the participating companies during October, 1972. The October period was selected for the CLRS survey in order to parallel the DOT study. October had been selected for the DOT study as a period that would minimize as much as possible any extremes which might result from seasonal or cyclical variations such as those resulting from weather, holiday weekends, vacations, court activity, and end of month reporting.[12] If an insurance company's "month" for internal purposes did not coincide exactly with the calendar month of October, the period most closely corresponding to the calendar month of October was used for the CLRS survey. In one or two instances, a company was unable to use its October files for the survey and an essentially equivalent period was substituted.

Each company was asked to uniformly apply its own definition as to when a file was closed. For those companies that maintain an individual file for each claimant, the survey included all files closed in October. Where a company's file system was based on the accident—so that a single file might include several claimants—all

10. *Id.* at p. 27.
11. *Ibid.*
12. *Id.* at p. 5.

claimants that were in any such file closed in October were surveyed, even though some of the claims might have been resolved earlier. Every person identified in such a claim file was treated as a separate claimant, and a form was completed for each individual.

Survey Instruments

Two survey instruments were developed for the study, and they were designated Form A and Form B/C.

Form A was used for the PIP claims, Med Pay claims, and any PIP Subrogation (Applicant) claims by the company that had paid PIP benefits and was asserting the subrogation claim. One form was filled out for each claim.[13]

Form B was used for the Bodily Injury, Uninsured Motorist, or PIP Subrogation (Respondent) claims from the vantage point of the respondent company. The first page of Form B was used to record information about the accident, and the following pages were used to record information about the claimant and the claim. If the company file included information on more than one claim, information on the additional claimants injured in the same accident was recorded on Form C, which was identical to the second and third pages of Form B. All Form C's for a given accident were inserted into the Form B folder and clipped into place. When the survey information was transferred to computer cards, the accident information for all claims recorded on Form C's was coded from the first page of Form B.

B. Conduct of the Survey

Each of the participating insurers appointed "company coordinators" who supervised the conduct of the survey by their own claims offices. The companies were sent copies of the survey forms together with instructions about how to complete them. In order to maximize the uniformity, in each case where the survey of company files was conducted in Massachusetts or Connecticut, a CLRS coordinator was present at the beginning of the survey to resolve ambiguities, and in general to try to assure that comparable approaches to the interpretation both of information in company files and of the guidelines for transferring that information to the survey instruments were employed. In a few cases, the information transfer was not done in the New England area. Each of these insurers cooperated fully by way of telephone conferences, and there is no reason to suspect any substantial departures from the procedures or interpretations that were used when there was a CLRS representative present. In any case, in each of the instances where the survey was conducted without the direct assistance of a CLRS coordinator, the survey involved a relatively small number of claim files. Consequently, even if there were substantial variations in the way claim files data were interpreted, the impact on the survey generally would be minimal.

---

13. The Forms used for the Study are included in the Appendices following this Chapter.

The completed survey instruments were sent to the University of Iowa where the forms were checked and the information was transferred from the survey forms to two sets of computer cards.[14] A complete set of computer cards was then sent to both the University of Iowa Computer Center and the State Farm Insurance Companies Computer Center in Bloomington, Illinois, where the data were transferred to computer tapes for analysis.[15]

C. The Survey Data

The analysis of no-fault claims in the CLRS study is based on information from 2,340 PIP claims that were closed by the participating companies during the survey period.[16] About two-thirds of these claim files showed that some payment had been made. The data analysis in this article is primarily based on the 1,528 claims where some payment was made by the insurance company involved.[17] The remaining one-third of the claim files surveyed were almost all files which had been opened by the insurance company claim departments upon receiving some notice of an accident, and were subsequently closed when no claim was made.[18]

II. THE P.I.P. CLAIMANTS

The CLRS survey compiled basic biographical data for each claimant. Although the following discussion is primarily designed to provide the reader with a profile of the PIP claimants as a group, some comparisons and contrasts between the PIP claimants and the claimants surveyed by the DOT study are also considered.

14. The survey was conducted by the participating companies over a period of several months. Almost all the forms were received at the University of Iowa within the four-month period following the commencement of the survey. After the forms were received, they were scanned to assure that the entries were clearly marked and the information was then coded to facilitate transfer to computer cards.

15. One of the computer tapes resulting from this survey will be retained by the State Farm Insurance Companies Computer Center in Bloomington, Illinois. The other tape will be deposited in the University of Iowa Law Library.

16. The data upon which this statement is based are currently on file at the University of Iowa Computer Center and the State Farm Insurance Companies Computer Center. When all phases of the CLRS Massachusetts No-Fault Study are completed, the computer tape used at the Iowa Computer Center will be desposited in the University of Iowa Law Library. Hereinafter, when claim files data supporting a statement are on file at the University of Iowa or the State Farm Insurance Companies Computer Center, the authority will be cited as CLRS NO-FAULT STUDY–INSURANCE CLAIMS SURVEY DATA.

17. CLRS NO-FAULT STUDY–INSURANCE CLAIMS SURVEY DATA.

18. *Id.* The PIP files that were closed without payments are discussed in Part G of this chapter.

A. Classification of Claim Files by County of Residence

The counties of residence of the persons for whom the surveyed claim files were opened are generally consistent with the population distribution in the state.[19] This conclusion is based on a comparison of the survey data with the United States Census information, and these statistics are set out in Table 1, along with some data compiled by the Massachusetts Registry of Motor Vehicles.[20]

TABLE 1
County of Residence

County	CLRS Claim File Survey	United States Census Data	Registry Accident Site Data
Barnstable)			
Dukes)			
Nantucket)			
Plymouth)	7.8%	7.7%	9.8%
Berkshire	2.6%	2.6%	2.3%
Bristol	6.6%	7.8%	9.9%
Essex	12.2%	11.2%	11.6%
Franklin)			
Hampden)	8.5%	9.1%	7.5%
Hampshire	1.6%	2.2%	1.9%
Middlesex	25.5%	24.6%	22.7%
Norfolk	9.6%	10.6%	10.4%
Suffolk	12.2%	12.9%	12.4%
Worcester	13.3%	11.2%	11.6%
TOTAL:	99.9%[21]	99.9%	100.0%
Base:	2,340[22]	5,689,170[23]	88,577[24]

19. Also see A. Widiss, *Accident Victims Under No-Fault Automobile Insurance: A Massachusetts Survey,* 61 IOWA LAW REVIEW 1 at pp. 14-16 (1975), which is reprinted as Chapter 2 of this volume.

20. The Massachusetts Registry of Motor Vehicles prepares annual editions of accident statistics for the Commonwealth. The annual editions may be obtained by writing to the Registry at 100 Nashua Street, Boston, Massachusetts, 02114.

21. The percentages in this and subsequent tables have been rounded to the nearest tenth of a percent. Therefore, when the percentages are added they will often total either slightly more or slightly less than 100 percent.

22. CLRS NO-FAULT STUDY—INSURANCE CLAIMS SURVEY DATA.

23. The computations of percentages for the Massachusetts counties are based on the United States Census Data for 1970 reported in U.S. BUREAU OF THE CENSUS, COUNTY AND CITY DATA BOOK 1972—A STATISTICAL ABSTRACT SUPPLEMENT 22 (1973).

The Massachusetts Registry of Motor Vehicles maintains statistics on the locations where accidents occur. Although accidents obviously do not always occur in the county of residence, the sites of accidents do correspond to the distribution of population. The figures on Table 1 also indicate that the claimants' residences in the files surveyed were reasonably representative of the population of accident victims as reflected in the Registry's statistics on accident sites.

B. Age of Claimants

An analysis of the PIP claimants by age indicates that they were on the whole generally comparable to the group of Massachusetts accident claimants surveyed in the DOT study. The data on claimants' ages among the files analyzed for the two surveys are presented in Table 2.

TABLE 2

Percentage Distribution of Claimants by Age

	CLRS PIP CLAIMANTS		MASSACHUSETTS POPULATION	DOT: MASSACHUSETTS B.I. CLAIMANTS[25]	
	CWP*	CNP**		CWP*	CNP**
0 - 15 yrs.	14.5%	17.2%	29.4%	17.0%	19.3%
16 - 20 yrs.	21.2%	19.2%	8.9%	13.2%	17.3%
21 - 24 yrs.	11.7%	9.9%	6.4%	11.2%	8.9%
25 - 44 yrs.	25.1%	29.7%	22.7%	33.6%	31.8%
45 - 64 yrs.	20.1%	17.9%	21.3%	19.6%	17.0%
65 and over	7.4%	5.6%	11.2%	5.0%	4.0%
TOTAL:	100.0%	100.0%	99.9%	99.9%	98.3%
Base:	1497				

*CWP = Closed With Payment
**CNP = Closed Without Payment

There are some differences between the claimants in Massachusetts and in the DOT survey generally, yet as shown on Table 3, overall the profiles are quite similar. Accordingly, the comments in the DOT Report that addressed the data on the claimants' ages are applicable to Massachusetts claimants. When the

24. The percentages in this column were derived from data reported in the 1972 REGISTRY STATISTICAL FILES for the calendar year 1972. See note 20, *supra.* Hereinafter, these files will be cited as REGISTRY STATISTICAL FILES.

25. The data from the Department of Transportation Automobile Personal Injury Claim Study is stored at the State Farm Insurance Companies Computer Center in Bloomington, Illinois. The DOT data from Massachusetts was separately analyzed for the CLRS study. Hereinafter, this material is cited as DOT CLAIMS STUDY—MASSACHUSETTS.

data from the DOT survey in general are compared with the DOT data for Massachusetts, the most noticeable difference appears to be with respect to the under-sixteen age group. The persons in the 0-15 years age group comprised a notably greater portion of the claimants in Massachusetts than among the DOT claimants generally.[26] This difference was not accounted for by the demographic makeup of the state, since this age group comprised just under 29.5 percent of the Massachusetts population and they constituted slightly over 30 percent of the U.S. population.

TABLE 3

**DOT Study: Percentage Distribution of Claimants
by Age and Claim Status**

	DOT: MASSACHUSETTS		DOT: SIXTEEN STATES[27]		U.S. POPULATION[27]
	CWP*	CNP**	CWP*	CNP**	
0-15 years	17.0%	19.3%	14.7%	15.5%	31.1%
16-20 years	13.2%	17.3%	14.7%	19.3%	9.0%
21-24 years	11.2%	8.9%	11.2%	10.7%	6.4%
25-44 years	33.6%	31.8%	32.9%	28.9%	23.6%
45-64 years	19.6%	17.0%	20.5%	16.6%	20.4%
65 and over	5.0%	4.0%	6.0%	9.0%	9.6%
TOTAL:	99.6%	98.3%	100.0%	100.0%	100,0%

* CWP = Closed With Payment
** CNP = Closed Without Payment

There are two additional points in regard to the ages of the claimants surveyed that are worth noting. In the report of the DOT study, the authors pointed out that although the age group 16-24 years comprised about 15 percent of the population, that group accounted for 26 percent of the claimants who received payments in the national survey sample.[28] The DOT report speculated that this age group's "exposure to the automobile is also disproportionate to their share of the total population with their exposure to accidental injury even more disproportionate."[29] Although the authors of the DOT study report did not draw attention to it, there was another notable difference in regard to a portion of the claimants in

26. The data from the Department of Transportation Automobile Personal Injury Claims Study is stored at the State Farm Insurance Companies Computer Center in Bloomington, Illinois. Hereinafter, this material will be cited as DOT CLAIMS STUDY: SIXTEEN STATES.

27. The DOT data and the United States Census Data on Table 3 is taken from the DOT AUTOMOBILE CLAIMS STUDY—VOLUME 1, p. 12, Table II-2.

28. DOT PERSONAL INJURY CLAIMS STUDY--VOLUME 1, p. 12.

29. *Ibid.*

the 16-24 years age group—specifically those in the 16-20 years age group. As shown in Table 3, persons in the 16-20 years age group comprised only 14.7 percent of the claims closed with payment (CWP), but they represented 19.3 percent of the claims closed without payments (CNP) in the DOT survey. This was the only age group where on the average a claim file was more likely to be closed without a payment being made. These data from the DOT study are set out in Table 4.

TABLE 4

DOT Study: Percentage Distribution of Massachusetts Claimants by Claim Status and Age[30]

CLAIMANT'S AGE	CLOSED WITH PAYMENT	CLOSED WITHOUT PAYMENT
0 - 15 yrs.	17.0%	19.3%
16 - 20 yrs.	13.2%	17.3%
21 - 24 yrs.	11.1%	8.9%
25 - 44 yrs.	33.6%	31.8%
45 - 64 yrs.	19.6%	17.0%
65 yrs. and over	5.0%	4.0%
not stated	0.3%	1.6%
TOTAL:	99.8%	99.9%

When the DOT data for Massachusetts are separately analyzed, the percentages are slightly different but the same contours exist.[31] In addition, among the Massachusetts claimants, this was also true of the persons in the 0-15 years age group, since they constituted 19.3 percent of the claims closed without payments and only 17.0 percent of the claim files that were closed after a payment was made.

C. Occupations of Claimants

About half of the PIP claimants were employed. As in the DOT study, information was compiled on the occupations of the claimants. The occupational information both for the Massachusetts claimants included in the DOT survey and for those in the CLRS study is presented on Table 5.

30. DOT CLAIMS STUDY—MASSACHUSETTS DATA, *supra* note 25.

31. *Ibid.*

TABLE 5

Percentage Distribution of Claimants
By Claim Status and Occupation

OCCUPATION	PIP CWP	DOT: MASSACHUSETTS[32] CWP	DOT: SIXTEEN STATES[33] CWP
Professional	5.8%	4.3%	5.3%
Farm owners & managers	0.07%	0.03%	0.2%
Managers & officials	3.0%	3.1%	3.6%
Clerical	9.0%	9.2%	10.0%
Sales workers	2.5%	3.5%	3.6%
Craftsmen	5.8%)	9.6%)	7.2%)
Operating workers	6.1%) 11.9%	9.7%) 19.3%	8.5%) 15.7%
Service workers	8.7%	7.2%	6.5%
Farm workers	0.2%	0.1%	0.4%
Non-farm laborers	3.4%	3.6%	3.7%
Unemployed	6.3%	4.0%	2.8%
Housewives	11.6%	15.7%	14.8%
Students	21.2%	17.0%	18.6%
Preschool children	4.3%	5.9%	4.9%
Retired	5.1%	2.1%	2.6%
Military	0.4%	0.7%	1.1%
Others	6.5%	4.0%	6.0%
TOTAL:	100.0%	99.7%	99.8%
Base:	1433		

32. DOT CLAIMS STUDY—MASSACHUSETTS DATA, *supra* note 25.
33. DOT PERSONAL INJURY CLAIMS STUDY—VOLUME 1, p. 13.

The authors of the DOT study pointed out that "occupational status is an important determinant of total loss," since lost wages account for more than half of the economic losses sustained by accident victims.[34] However, beyond that observation, the authors of the DOT Report did not consider whether the data on the claimants' occupations provided any other insights.

When the composition of the claimants from Massachusetts surveyed in the DOT study is compared with the claimants who received PIP insurance compensation, the most notable feature is undoubtedly the similarity of the profiles of the two groups. There are only a few occupational categories where there are differences that seem worth noting, and where speculation about the causes of the differences may be fruitful.

First, "craftsmen" and "operating workers" both constituted larger percentages of the DOT claimants than the PIP claimants in the files surveyed. If these two groups are combined, they comprise over 19 percent of the claimants in the DOT survey of Massachusetts' files that were closed with payments, while they represented about only 12 percent of the PIP claimants who received compensation.[35] One possible explanation may be that these two occupation groups are employed in jobs that generally provide better wage continuation and medical insurance than other employee groups, and therefore more of the accident victims with these jobs were provided with other sources of indemnification. In other words, the hypothesis is that the collateral benefits provided many persons in these occupations with sufficient indemnification so that they opted not to pursue the possibility of additional compensation under the PIP coverage. Although the data compiled in the interviews with accident victims do not directly validate this hypothesis about these occupations, the interviews with accident victims did disclose that many persons who are injured in automobile accidents in fact do not elect to pursue PIP claims because they receive compensation from other sources.[36] However, since the survey of accident victims did not compile information on occupations, it is not possible to use data from that portion of the study to verify the hypothesis in regard to craftsmen and operating workers.

The second difference which seems worth considering is that "housewives" comprised only 11.6 percent of the PIP claimants that were paid,[37] while they constituted almost 16 percent of the DOT claims that were closed with payments.[38] In other words, there were about half again as many housewives among the DOT claimants. Housewives do not sustain income losses, and accordingly would normally not have the basis for wage claims. However, the PIP coverage was designed

---

34. *Id.* at p. 12.

35. CLRS NO-FAULT STUDY—INSURANCE CLAIMS SURVEY DATA, *supra* note 16.

36. A. Widiss, *Accident Victims Under No-Fault Automobile Insurance*, 61 IOWA LAW REVIEW 1 at pp. 33-40 (1975), reprinted as Chapter 2 in this book.

37. CLRS NO-FAULT STUDY—INSURANCE CLAIMS SURVEY DATA, *supra* note 16.

38. DOT PERSONAL INJURY CLAIMS STUDY—VOLUME 1, p. 13.

to afford non-wage earners the possibility of seeking indemnification for replacement services -such as child care or house maintenance—necessitated by personal injuries caused by automobile accidents. The interviews with accident victims,[39] as well as the claim files survey data discussed below, indicate that the number of claims for replacement services by housewives has been negligible. Therefore, the difference between the composition of the PIP and DOT claimant groups with respect to housewives is probably a function of the fact that typically under the PIP coverage only indemnification for medical costs was involved. In this context it seems reasonable to theorize that housewives are less likely to make PIP claims that only involve reimbursement for medical costs than they are to make liability claims which include medical costs as well as damages for pain and suffering. In addition, it also seems plausible that, as a subgroup among PIP claimants, housewives whose only compensable damages are medical expenses are less likely to make claims than persons who sustain both medical costs and lost wages. However, an exception to this observation probably is warranted for the subgroups discussed in the following paragraph.

"Retired persons" and the "unemployed" both constituted a greater percentage of the PIP claimants than they did of the liability claimants among the files surveyed in the DOT study. Retired persons constituted 4.7 percent of the PIP claimants,[40] whereas they represented only 2.1 percent of the Massachusetts claimants in the DOT study [41] and 2.6 percent of the claimants in all sixteen states surveyed in the DOT study.[42] The unemployed constituted more than 6 percent of the PIP claimants,[43] and only 4 percent of Massachusetts claimants whose claims were closed after a payment in the DOT survey.[44] Persons in both of these groups were not employed and therefore they did not sustain wage losses. In regard to the retired persons, it appears that even though Medicare was available to most, if not all, of these persons, the additional compensation for medical costs is sufficiently significant to retired persons as a group to lead them to take advantage of the available sources of indemnification. And, although Medicare would not be available to the unemployed, a similar observation in regard to the incentive to take advantage of the PIP coverage also seems to be applicable to the unemployed. It seems unwarranted to try to carry the analysis of these statistics any further, and the data produced thus far probably should be viewed merely as being sufficiently intriguing to warrant further investigation.

---

39. A. Widiss, *Accident Victims Under No-Fault Automobile Insurance,* 61 IOWA LAW REVIEW 1 at p. 48 (1975), reprinted as Chapter 2 in this book.

40. CLRS NO-FAULT STUDY- INSURANCE CLAIMS SURVEY DATA, *supra* note 16.

41. DOT CLAIMS STUDY—MASSACHUSETTS, *supra* note 25.

42. DOT CLAIMS STUDY, at p. 13, *supra* note 9 at p. 25.

43. CLRS NO-FAULT STUDY- INSURANCE CLAIMS SURVEY DATA, *supra* note 16.

44. DOT CLAIMS STUDY—VOLUME 1 at p. 13, *supra* note 9.

D. Family Status of Claimants

The profile of the family status of the claimants in the CLRS survey was generally comparable to the profile developed in the DOT study of the liability insurance claimants. In the DOT study, the most notable feature in regard to the family status data was that it indicated that claims by "sons" were at least somewhat more likely to result in files that were closed without payment than those by members of any other class among the family status groups.[45] This observation was true for both the DOT survey generally and the DOT survey data for Massachusetts.[46]

TABLE 6

Percentage Distribution of Claimants by Claim Type, Payment Status and Claimants' Family Status

CLAIMANTS' FAMILY STATUS	PIP CLAIMANTS		DOT: SIXTEEN STATES B.I. LIABILITY CLAIMANTS[47]	
	CWP	CNP	CWP	CNP
Husband	21.6%	25.0%	28.5%	28.3%
Wife	25.1%	22.9%	25.6%	21.0%
Son	22.9%	24.2%	16.8%	21.5%
Daughter	16.9%	15.4%	13.5%	14.9%
Single Male Head of Household	5.3%	4.3%	5.9%	5.9%
Single Female Head of Household	5.4%	4.6%	7.8%	6.4%
Other Male Relative	1.0%	2.2%	0.8%	0.8%
Other Female Relative	1.7%	1.8%	0.8%	1.2%
TOTAL:	100.0%	100.0%	100.0%	100.0%
Base:	1,417	813		

The hypothesis suggested in regard to persons in the age group 16-20 years seems equally reasonable in regard to sons—that is, a larger percentage of these liability claims was closed without payment as a result of fault determinations. In other words, as a group sons were relatively less successful in securing compensation for injuries because their claims were denied on the basis of fault determinations. The under-representation of "sons" among the closed with payment files in the DOT survey was compensated for by a comparably larger portion of "wives" among the

45. DOT CLAIMS STUDY—VOLUME 1 at pp. 14-15, *supra* note 9.
46. DOT CLAIMS STUDY—MASSACHUSETTS DATA, *supra* note 25.
47. DOT CLAIM STUDY—VOLUME 1 at pp. 14-15, *supra* note 9.

claim files closed with payment. Among the PIP claimants, wives also constitute a larger percentage of the claimants among the files closed with payment. Among the PIP claimants, the under-represented claimants from the point of view of house-hold status were husbands. One plausible explanation for this situation may be that this is another effect of payments from collateral sources.[48] However, again the data are at best sparse, and therefore the most justifiable observation seems to be that this is an aspect of the CLRS survey findings which bears further investigation.

E. Other Indications of Representativeness of the CLRS Survey of Claim Files

The Massachusetts Registry of Motor Vehicles compiles data and prepares an annual analysis of accidents and accident victims based upon accident reports that are filed with the Registry.[49] The group of persons included in the PIP files surveyed for the CLRS claim study appears to be representative of the total population of accident victims identified in the reports filed with the Registry of Motor Vehicles. For example, when the profiles of the accident victims whose claim files were surveyed are compared with the Registry's data on classifications such as "role in the accident" and "sex," the overwhelming similarities in the two groups are very evident. These statistics are presented in Tables 7 and 8.

TABLE 7

Classification by Role in Accident

	REGISTRY DATA[50]	PIP CLAIMANTS
Operator	53.6%	54.5%
Passenger	36.3%	35.7%
Pedestrian	6.5%	5.1%
Bicyclist	3.2%	3.7%
Other	0.4%	0.9%
TOTAL:	100.0%	99.9%
Base:	81,086	2,317

48. See text accompanying notes 35-36, *supra.* Also see A. Widiss, *Accident Victims Under No-Fault Insurance,* 61 IOWA LAW REVIEW 1 at pp. 33-40 (1975), reprinted as Chapter 2 in this book.

49. See note 20, *supra.* Also see the discussion of the Registry's data in A. Widiss, *Accident Victims Under No-Fault Insurance,* 61 IOWA LAW REVIEW 1 at pp. 9-12 (1975), reprinted as Chapter 2 in this book.

50. 1072 REGISTRY STATISTICAL FILES at p. 17, *supra* note 20.

TABLE 8

Classification by Sex

	REGISTRY DATA	*PIP FILES SURVEYED*
Male	54.3%	52.6%
Female	45.7%	47.4%
TOTAL:	100.0%	100.0%
Base:	80,667[51]	2,158

F. An Observation on PIP Claimants

Comparisons between the data compilations for the DOT study and the CLRS study showed that overall the profiles of the two groups are very similar. There are a few instances when a noticeable difference exists. For example, there are several instances when claimants in a subgroup—such as the age group 16-20 years—were compensated under the PIP coverage in about the proportions that they were represented among the DOT liability claim files that were closed without payment. This result seems to validate what would be reasonably expected of a no-fault coverage—specifically that no-fault coverage provides compensation for claimants who were or would have been precluded from receiving reparation under the fault system.

G. The Non-Claimants:
The PIP Files That Were Closed Without Payments

Of the files examined for the CLRS survey, approximately one-third were closed without any payment.[52] Among the files closed without payments, the vast majority were files which had been routinely opened by insurers upon receiving a report of an accident, and were closed when no claim was filed. This pattern exists because, following notification of an accident, insurance companies typically establish a file and then send the insured an "Application for Benefits"—usually referred to as a PIP No. 1 form. This form is designed to provide the insurance company with the essential information on the claimant, a brief accident description, and a statement specifying the economic losses sustained as a result of the accident if known at the time when the form is filed. The form also includes authorizations which allow the company to secure information from a doctor, hospital or employer to verify the amounts claimed.

---

51. The computations of the base figure and the percentages were based on data reported in the 1972 REGISTRY STATISTICAL FILES at pp. 17-19. The base figure was arrived at by combining the data on motor vehicle operators, motor vehicle passengers, pedestrians, and bicycle riders.

52. CLRS NO-FAULT STUDY—INSURANCE CLAIMS SURVEY DATA, *supra* note 16.

Almost half of the files surveyed where no payment was made—one-third of all the claim files—were closed when the PIP No. 1 form was never returned. An approximately equal number—again constituting almost half of these files—was closed because although a PIP No. 1 form was returned, no claim for medical costs, income losses or other expenses resulting from the accident was subsequently asserted. As shown in Table 9, in over 97 percent of the files surveyed,[53] either payments were made to a claimant or no payment was made because indemnification was not sought—that is, less than 3 percent of the PIP files surveyed involved a denial of a claim by an insurance company.

TABLE 9

How PIP Claim File Was Closed

STATUS OF FILE	*PERCENTAGE OF ALL FILES SURVEYED*
Closed Without Payment Because. . .	
PIP No. 1 Form Never Returned. . . .16.0%)	
Claim Not Pressed. . . . . .16.5%)	34.8%
Claim Was Denied. . . . . 2.3%)	
Closed After Payments Were Made	65.2%
TOTAL:	100.0%
Base:	2,336

The data for those files which were closed without any payments having been made because no compensation was sought were analyzed,[54] and the frequency distributions were compared with those for the claimants whose files were closed after PIP claims were paid. While there were some differences in the profiles of the two groups, almost all of them were minor and there is no statistical significance to even the most apparent differential.[55]

53. *Ibid.*

54. In the event a person elects not to pursue a PIP claim, the information in the claim file is often incomplete. This usually means that the file does contain some biographical information on the insured, but that no information on the nature and extent of the accident injuries or economic losses can be ascertained by an examination of the insurance company files. To overcome this problem, one segment of the CLRS study sought to acquire information directly from persons who were injured in automobile accidents and who elected not to pursue PIP claims. The results of these interviews are reported and analyzed in the article reprinted as Chapter 2 of this book.

55. CLRS NO-FAULT STUDY—INSURANCE CLAIMS SURVEY DATA, *supra* note 16.

In slightly over 2 percent of the files surveyed, the PIP claims were denied.[56] As shown in Table 10, there were a variety of reasons for these claim denials, including most of the grounds upon which denials can be made under the Massachusetts no-fault law. There were, however, no denials on the grounds that the accident occurred in the course of committing a felony, that the injuries resulted from an intentional act, or that the insured failed to cooperate.

TABLE 10

Reasons PIP Claims Were Denied

Claim Was Denied Payment Because. . .

No Injury	1.0%	)
No Policy Coverage	0.5%	)
Loss Was Under the Deductible	0.3%	)
Non-Cooperation	——	)
		) 2.3%
Workmen's Compensation Exclusion	0.3%	)
Alcohol or Drug Exclusion	0.2%	)
Felony Exclusion	——	)
Intentional Injury	——	)

Claim Paid or Claim Not Pressed   97.7%

TOTAL: 100.0%

Base: 2,336

Given the very small number of cases in which the insurance companies denied liability, further analysis of these files did not seem warranted.

III. THE ACCIDENTS

The DOT and CLRS claim surveys both included several items designed to provide information about the type of accident that led to the creation of each claim file. When the data on the types of accidents that give rise to PIP claims are compared with the relevant data from the DOT survey of liability claims, some interesting differences are revealed. These contrasts are considered in this section.

The references to the DOT data in the following discussion are primarily based on the portion of the data derived from Massachusetts, rather than on the body of claims information developed in all sixteen states included in the DOT study. However, there are some instances when the Massachusetts statistics are not comparable to the DOT data generally. In situations where such differences seemed interesting

56. *Ibid.*

and where they might influence the conclusions or observations that could be derived from those data, both the DOT Massachusetts and DOT national survey results are included.

When the reports of the accidents that led to PIP claims are analyzed, it is evident that several types of accidents predominated. Rear-end collisions produced the most no-fault automobile insurance claims: nearly one-quarter of all the claims made.[57] Almost as many claims—over 20 percent of the PIP claims—were paid as a result of one-car accidents.[58] Taken together, these two categories accounted for almost half of the accidents that produced PIP coverage claims. The percentage figures for the various accident types that led to no-fault payments are set out in Table 11.

TABLE 11

Percentage Distribution of Claimants by Type of Accident [59]

Type of Accident	Percentage of PIP Claimants Paid
Rear-End Collisions	24.7%
One-Car Accidents	22.2%
Wrong Side of Road or Wrong Way on One-Way Street Accidents	11.4%
Traffic Signal Violation Accidents	9.2%
Pedestrian and Automobile Collisions	9.2%
Accidents Occurring During Turns	7.3%
Accidents Occurring During Lane Changes	3.3%
Accidents on Parking Lots and Private Property	1.3%
Other Types and Unknown Causes	11.2%
TOTAL:	100.0%
Base:	1525

Among the claimants that were paid in the DOT study only 2.9 percent of the claims resulted from accidents involving a single vehicle.[60] This is obviously in

57.   CLRS NO-FAULT STUDY—INSURANCE CLAIMS SURVEY DATA, *supra* note 16.

58.   *Ibid.*

59.   The accident classifications used in the DOT study were also employed for the CLRS survey, and a number of these classifications were combined in order to present the data in Table 11. The classifications are included in the Appendices to this Chapter

60.   DOT PERSONAL INJURY CLAIMS STUDY—VOLUME 1, p. 17.

marked contrast with the some 22 percent of PIP claims that were paid as a result of injuries that were incurred in such accidents. Likewise, noticeably larger percentages of PIP claimants than liability insurance claimants were provided compensation as a result of accidents which resulted when cars were on the wrong side of the road or headed the wrong way on a one-way street, and as a result of collisions between automobiles and pedestrians.[61]

The differences between the type of accidents that led to no-fault claims and the accidents that led to liability claims is almost certainly attributable to the essential difference between the two insurance coverages—specifically, that the PIP coverage provides a source of indemnification for accident victims in situations where "fault" would have foreclosed a recovery by the injured person under the tort liability system. In other words, the hypothesis is that the accident patterns that produced the claims in the two surveys are different as a result of the fact that many persons who were injured could not have recovered under the fault system, but could secure compensation under a no-fault coverage.

This theory is perhaps most clearly illustrated by analyzing the data on the number of vehicles involved in the accidents. The information from both the CLRS and the DOT studies is set out in Table 12. Slightly over one-third of the PIP claimants were injured in accidents involving one vehicle. This is in marked contrast to the percentage of the claimants who were compensated in the DOT survey as a result of an accident involving only one vehicle. Such accidents were the cause of the injuries for 12 percent of the claimants whose file closed with payment in the DOT study generally,[62] and for only slightly more than 6 percent of the Massachusetts claimants who received payments.

TABLE 12

Percentage Distribution of Claimants by Number of Vehicles Involved in Accidents

NUMBER OF VEHICLES	CLRS SURVEY		DOT: MASSACHUSETTS		DOT: SIXTEEN STATES	
	CWP	*CNP*	*CWP*	*CNP*	*CWP*	*CNP*
1	35.2%	29.8%	6.7%	12.6%	12.0%	16.7%
2	57.1%	62.3%	85.4%	76.3%	74.7%	69.5%
3 or more	7.5%	7.6%	7.8%	11.3%	12.9%	13.7%
TOTAL:	99.8%	99.7%	99.9%	100.2%	99.6%	99.9%
Base:	1,525	548				

61. *Ibid.*
62. *Ibid.*
63. DOT CLAIMS STUDY—MASSACHUSETTS DATA, *supra* note 25.

If the hypothesis is correct, the percentage of PIP claimants injured in one-car accidents ought to be similar to the percentage of one-car accidents that occur in the state. One measure of the number of one-car accidents is provided by the Massachusetts Registry of Motor Vehicles statistics which show that over one-fifth of the reported accidents involved only one vehicle.[64] The number of one-vehicle accidents reported to the Registry of Motor Vehicles—almost 22 percent of the collisions in the state—is substantially greater than the portion of Massachusetts claimants—just under 7 percent—who were compensated as a result of such accidents among the files surveyed for the DOT study.

TABLE 13

Number of Vehicles Involved in Massachusetts Accidents

NUMBER OF VEHICLES	PIP CLAIMANTS	DOT: MASSACHUSETTS CWP	MASSACHUSETTS REGISTRY OF MOTOR VEHICLES [65]
1	33.3%	7.7%	21.8%
2 or more	58.9%	92.2%	78.9%
TOTAL:	99.9%	99.9%	100.0%
Base:	2,334	3,248	

One-third of the PIP claimants were injured in accidents that involved only one vehicle. The Registry's data, based on reports filed by drivers following accidents, may understate the relative percentage of injuries sustained in such accidents. In any case, it appears that the PIP claimants injured in one-car accidents do correspond more closely with the population of accident victims than did Massachusetts tort claimants surveyed in the DOT study. Moreover, other comparisons of the accident description data produced by the CLRS survey with the statistics compiled by the Registry indicate that the PIP claimants surveyed do reflect the accident population. For example, the Registry's accident analysis for accidents occurring in 1972 indicated that 29 percent of the accidents that resulted in personal injuries or death involved rear end collisions [66]—which is quite comparable to the some 25 percent of the PIP claimants who were injured in such accidents.

Almost 90 percent of the PIP claimants were injured while they were occupying an automobile. This is almost precisely the same proportion of accident claimants who received payments in the DOT survey in Massachusetts liability claim-

64. See notes 20 and 49, *supra.*
65. 1972 REGISTRY STATISTICAL FILES at p. 13.
66. 1972 REGISTRY STATISTICAL FILES at p. 13, *supra* note 20

ants.[67] However, when the remaining 10 percent of the claimants in the CLRS and DOT studies are compared, some interesting differences are disclosed. It should be noted at the outset that the full measure of the significance of these differences is difficult to assess because only 1 percent of the PIP claimants were injured in accidents involving commercial vehicles.[68] Although this is not unexpected in light of the objectives of the Massachusetts no-fault coverage, it does make the assessment of the differences identified in the following discussion somewhat more uncertain.

TABLE 14

**Percentage Distribution by
Type of Vehicle Claimant Was Occupying**

VEHICLE	PIP CLAIMANT CWP	DOT: MASSACHUSETTS B.I. LIABILITY		DOT: SIXTEEN STATES B.I. LIABILITY	
		CWP	CNP	CWP	CNP
Private Passenger	89.5%	89.3%	87.2%	84.2%	79.9%
Commercial	1.0%	8.0%	9.1%	2.7%	3.1%
Public	1.1%	1.2%	1.8%	1.2%	1.5%
Motorcycle	—	—	—	4.3%	1.8%
Bicycle	3.6%	0.03%	—	1.7%	2.6%
Other	0.0%	0.1%	0.2%	0.2%	0.3%
Pedestrian	4.7%	1.0%	1.4%	8.0%	10.7%
TOTAL:	99.9%	99.6%	99.7%	102.3%[69]	99.9%
Base:	1525	2705			

First, as shown on Table 14, bicycle riders comprised a far more significant portion of the no-fault claimants. Fault considerations again may be significant in regard to such claims, since bicyclists had filed a somewhat larger portion of the bodily injury liability claim files that were closed without payments in the DOT survey. In other words, bicyclists may also constitute a group of persons who, when injured in automobile accidents, were often precluded from recovering and who now are afforded compensation under the PIP coverage. A comparison of the PIP claimants surveyed with the Registry data on Classification by Role in the

67. DOT CLAIMS STUDY—MASSACHUSETTS DATA, *supra* note 25.
68. CLRS NO-FAULT STUDY—INSURANCE CLAIMS SURVEY DATA, *supra* note 16.
69. DOT PERSONAL INJURY CLAIMS STUDY—VOLUME 1, p. 15. The percentages on Table II-6 in the DOT study total 102.3%.

Accident seems to support the theory since the portion of bicyclists among the PIP claimants corresponds with their involvement in automobile accidents in Massachusetts as reported to the Registry of Motor Vehicles. The profile of the PIP claimants when they are classified by their role in the accident is almost identical to the profile of accident victims produced from the data compiled by the Registry of Motor Vehicles. The percentage distributions for these classifications is set out in Table 15.[70]

TABLE 15

Percentage Distribution of Injured Persons by Role in Accident

	PIP CLAIMANTS	MASSACHUSETTS REGISTRY DATA
Motor Vehicle Operator	54.2%	53.7%
Motor Vehicle Passenger	35.5%	36.4%
Pedestrian	6.6%	6.8%
Bicyclist	3.7%	3.2%
TOTAL:	100.0%	100.1%
Base:	2,330	81,822[71]

70. The comparable data from the DOT survey seems to indicate that both bicyclists and pedestrians were at least somewhat less likely to be successful in securing reparation payments under the bodily injury liability coverage. Although the data indicate that this situation was slightly less pronounced for pedestrians than bicyclists, it appears to be shown in the analysis of the distribution of claimants both by "Status in Accident" (Table II-4) and by "Type of Vehicle" (Table II-6). The entries for pedestrians and bicyclists have been changed to italics on the following tables from Chapter II of the DOT Claims Study.

TABLE II-4

Percentage Distribution of Claimants by Claim Type, Payment Status and Claimants' Status in Accident

CLAIMANT ACCIDENT STATUS	BODILY INJURY LIABILITY	
	CWP	CNP
Driver Other Car	49.6%	45.7%
Driver Insured Car	0.5%	0.8%
Passenger Other Car	33.6%	25.0%
Passenger Insured Car	7.2%	17.4%
Pedestrian	*5.5%*	*6.2%*
Motorcyclist	1.6%	1.6%
Bicyclist	*1.7%*	*2.6%*
Other	0.3%	0.8%
TOTAL:*	100.0%	100.0%

* Detail may not add to totals due to rounding.

IV. THE CLAIMANTS' INJURIES AND ECONOMIC LOSSES CLAIMED

The consequences of the automobile accidents for the PIP claimants were, as would be anticipated, quite varied. Personal injuries typically resulted in both quantifiable consequences (such as medical costs) and various non-quantifiable effects. This section of the report is designed to provide the reader with information on the nature of the injuries sustained by the persons who made PIP claims, and on the economic consequences of those injuries as reflected in the amounts claimed principally as the result of wage losses and medical expenses.

A. Type of Injuries

The survey included several items which provide information on the nature and extent of the injuries sustained by the PIP claimant. As shown on Table 16 and Table 17, most of the PIP claimants did not incur serious injuries. Over 85 percent of the claimants had injuries which were not classified as serious by the insurance company employees who examined the files and transferred the data to the survey forms. Among the PIP claimants, only about 13 percent sustained what seemed to warrant being classified as "serious injuries". In regard to the characterizations of the injuries in the classifications on Table 16, the survey personnel were requested to mark each of the categories that were applicable. Thus, for example, a person

70. (continued)

TABLE II-6

**Percentage Distribution of Claimants by Claim Type,
Payment Status and by Type of Vehicle**

CLAIMANT VEHICLE	BODILY INJURY LIABILITY	
	CWP	*CNP*
Private Passenger	84.2%	79.9%
Commercial	2.7%	3.1%
Public	1.2%	1.5%
Motorcycle	4.3%	1.8%
Bicycle	*1.7%*	*3.6%*
Other	0.2%	0.3%
None	8.0%	10.7%
TOTAL:*	100.0%	100.0%

* Detail may not add to totals due to rounding.

71. The base figure and percentages in this column were derived from data reported in the 1972 REGISTRY STATISTICAL FILES at p. 17. The base figure was arrived at by combining the data on motor vehicle operators, motor vehicle passengers, pedestrians and bicyclists.

might well have sustained both medical costs in excess of $500 *and* a permanent injury. Accordingly, the total percentage on Table 16 is slightly in excess of 100 percent.

TABLE 16

Percentage Distribution of PIP Claimants
by Accident Consequences

ACCIDENT CONSEQUENCES	PIP CLAIMANTS
No Serious Injury or Death	86.5%
Medical costs over $500	8.2%
Fracture	7.0%
Loss of Body Member	–––
Permanent and Serious Disfigurement	0.3%
Loss of Sight or Hearing	––
Death	1.2%
TOTAL:	103.6%[72]
Base:	1,466

TABLE 17

Percentage Distribution of PIP Claimants
by Non-Fatal Injury Descriptions

	COSMETIC	BRUISE	STRAIN	FRACTURE
NONE	86.5%	38.2%	62.7%	86.9%
MULT	2.5%	20.3%	7.9%	1.1%
HEAD	3.0%	11.6%	–––	0.7%
FACE	5.5%	4.5%	–––	2.8%
NECK	0.1%	0.9%	12.8%	0.1%
BODY	0.3%	10.6%	2.4%	2.2%
BACK	0.1%	1.8%	8.7%	0.5%
LIMB	1.8%	11.7%	4.5%	3.8%
OTHER	0.3%	0.5%	1.4%	1.9%
TOTAL:	100.1%	100.1%	100.4%	100.0%
	Base:	1,524		

72. The percentages in this column add to more than 100 percent because the persons who examined the claim files were instructed to circle as many of the classifications as were applicable among those accident consequences enumerated in Item 34 on Form A. Form A is reprinted in the Appendices to this Chapter.

B. Permanent Injury and Death

Only a small portion of automobile accidents occurring during any period cause permanent injury or death. This conclusion is particularly true when an examination is made of all accidents, which of course include very minor ones that often go unreported and typically do not involve any insurance claim. However, even among the population of accidents that produce liability claims, the DOT survey indicated that less than 8 percent involve serious or fatal injuries. The percentage distributions from the DOT study on permanent injuries sustained by the paid claimants are set out in Table 18.

TABLE 18

Percentage Distribution of Paid Claimants by Type of Permanent Injury or Fatality

TYPE OF PERMANENT INJURY	DOT: SIXTEEN STATES[73]	DOT: MASSACHUSETTS[74]
Permanent Total Disability	0.2%	——
Permanent Partial Disability	4.0%	1.0%
Permanent Disfigurement	2.5%	2.0%
Death	1.0%	0.6%
None	92.4%	96.4%
TOTAL:	100.1%	100.0%
Base:		2,667

Among the PIP claimants, the CLRS survey also confirms that most of the accidents did not result in either permanent injuries, permanent disfigurement or death. More than 93 percent of the PIP files surveyed indicated that there had been no permanent accident consequences.[75] Slightly over 1 percent of the PIP claims involved a death,[76] about the same as in the DOT survey. About 0.7 percent of the PIP files indicated that the claimants had sustained permanent and serious disfigurement.[77] This was somewhat less than 2.5 percent of the paid claimants in the DOT survey.[78] No PIP claims showed the loss of a body member, sight or hearing[79]—so that any permanent disabilities among the PIP claimants in this survey involved impairment of function rather than loss.

73. DOT PERSONAL INJURY CLAIMS STUDY—VOLUME 1, p. 19, *supra* note 9.

74. DOT CLAIMS STUDY--MASSACHUSETTS DATA, *supra* note 25.

75. CLRS NO-FAULT STUDY –INSURANCE CLAIMS SURVEY DATA, *supra* note 16.

76. *Id.*

77. *Id.*

78. DOT PERSONAL INJURY CLAIMS STUDY--VOLUME 1, p. 19, *supra* note 9.

79. CLRS NO-FAULT STUDY—INSURANCE CLAIMS SURVEY DATA, *supra* note 16.

C. Hospitalization

The fact that most of the PIP claimants were not seriously injured is reflected in the data on hospitalization. As shown on Table 18, over 85 percent did not spend so much as a day in a hospital.

TABLE 19

Percentage Distribution of PIP Claimants by Number of Days Hospitalized

NUMBER OF DAYS	PERCENTAGE OF PIP CLAIMANTS
0	86.8%
1 - 7 days	6.9%
8 -14 days	3.3%
15 days and over	3.1%
TOTAL:	100.0%
Base:	1,409

On the other hand, it should be noted that among those files which showed a hospitalization, the persons spent an average of over 11 days.[80]

D. Medical Expenses

Almost all PIP claimants had some medical expenses for which they sought indemnification under the no-fault coverage. However, the great majority of claimants sustained only relatively small medical expenses that were consistent with relatively modest injuries. For example, only about 10 percent of the PIP claimants had expenses in excess of $500[81] (which is one of the thresholds that permits an injured party to assert a tort claim under the Massachusetts no-fault law),[82] and less than 5 percent of the claims for medical expenses exceeded $1500.[83] The average medical expense claimed in the files surveyed was about $250.[84] These findings are presented in Table 20.

80. *Id.*
81. *Id.*
82. See the discussion of the Massachusetts statutory thresholds in Chapter 1, *supra* at p. 10.
83. CLRS NO-FAULT STUDY—INSURANCE CLAIMS SURVEY DATA, *supra* note 16.
84. *Id.*

TABLE 20

Percentage Distribution of PIP Claimants
by Medical Expenses Claimed

AMOUNT OF EXPENSES CLAIMED	PERCENTAGE OF PIP CLAIMANTS	CUMULATIVE PERCENTAGE
$ 1 - $25	24.9%	24.9%
$26 - $50	19.1%	44.0%
$51 - $100	23.2%	67.2%
$101 - $250	16.6%	83.8%
$251 - $500	5.8%	89.6%
$501 - $1,500	5.7%	95.3%
$1,501 - $1,999	1.4%	96.7%
More than $1,999	3.3%	100.0%

TOTAL: 100.0%
Base: 1,463

E. Wage Losses of PIP Claimants

Almost one-half of the PIP claimants were employed at the time they made their claim.[85] The data on employment status are presented in Table 21.

TABLE 21

Percentage Distribution of PIP Claimants
by Employment Status

EMPLOYMENT STATUS	PERCENTAGE
Employee	47.5%
Self-Employed	2.9%
Unemployed	42.9%
Unknown	6.8%

TOTAL: 100.1%
Base: 1,427

85. CLRS NO-FAULT STUDY—INSURANCE CLAIMS SURVEY DATA, *supra* note 16. Representatives of each of the insurance companies that participated in this survey were invited to review the manuscript for this chapter. After reading the text, several of the companies observed that a portion of the data from the survey was not consonant with their current experience. These insurers stated that they felt that the proportion of the PIP claimants who were employed had risen and that "approximately 75 percent of the PIP claimants are (now)

Among those who were employed, almost two-thirds missed time from their jobs.[86] Not all of those persons who missed time from their jobs sought compensation from the PIP coverage for lost wages. About 15 percent were covered by wage continuation plans of some type,[87] and thus did not press any claim for lost wages under the PIP insurance—although they did seek reimbursement for their medical expenses, and in a few instances for other expenses resulting from the accidents.

The number of days lost as reflected in the claim files ranged from one day to several months.

TABLE 22

**Percentage Distribution of Employed PIP Claimants
Who Made Claims For Lost Wages
by Number of Work Days Lost**

NUMBER OF WORK DAYS LOST	PERCENTAGE OF EMPLOYED PIP CLAIMANTS MAKING CLAIMS FOR LOST WAGES
1 - 2 days	16.3%
3 - 5 days	21.9%
6 - 10 days	18.2%
More than 10 days	43.7%
TOTAL:	100.0%
Base:	357

Among those employed claimants who missed time from their employment and were not covered by a wage continuation plan, the average amount of time lost was almost 18 days.[88] As would be expected, the salary range for these persons was

85. (continued)
employed at the time of the accident." Letter to the author dated September 22, 1976. Hereinafter this letter will be cited as *Insurance Research Department Letter,* dated September 22, 1976.

86. CLRS NO-FAULT STUDY—INSURANCE CLAIMS SURVEY DATA, *supra* note 16.

87. *Id.* Also see A. Widiss, *Accident Victims Under No-Fault: A Massachusetts Survey,* 61 IOWA LAW REVIEW 1 at pp. 33-34, pp. 36-39, and pp. 48-49 (1976).

88. CLRS NO-FAULT STUDY—INSURANCE CLAIMS SURVEY DATA, *supra* note 16.

substantial—with a low of $9 per week and a high of $900 per week.[89] Viewed as a group, the average wage or income loss reported by these claimants was $129 per week,[90] A more precise picture of these income losses is provided by Table 23.

TABLE 23

**Percentage Distribution of PIP Claimants
by Amounts Paid for Lost Wages**

AMOUNTS PAID	PERCENTAGE OF PIP CLAIMANTS COMPENSATED FOR LOST WAGES	CUMULATIVE PERCENTAGE
$ 1 - $25	12.9%	12.9%
$26 - $50	16.1%	29.0%
$51 - $100	17.7%	46.7%
$101 - $250	26.7%	73.4%
$251 - $500	11.9%	85.3%
$501 - $1,000	6.1%	91.4%
$1,001 - $1,500	3.5%	94.9%
$1,501 - $1,999	2.9%	97.8%
$2,000	1.9%	99.7%

TOTAL: 99.7%

Base: 311

V. Adequacy of the PIP Insurance Coverage

The PIP insurance provides indemnification for economic losses sustained as a consequence of an automobile accident. Most of the PIP claims in the files surveyed involved medical expenses or income losses. The PIP insurance benefits may also be claimed if replacement services are required—as in the case where it is necessary to employ a housekeeper or to pay for child care because a parent is incapacitated. And the PIP insurance may be used to cover funeral expenses in the event the accident caused the death of an insured. The CLRS survey compiled data on the amounts claimed and the amounts paid in each of these categories.

Analysis of the claim files data produces considerable insight into the economic consequences of automobile accidents for persons who sustain injuries, but translating the payment data into an accurate appraisal or evaluation of the adequacy of the PIP insurance coverage is a somewhat elusive goal. However, since the question of the adequacy of the compensation system is central to any judgment of how

89. *Id.*
90. *Id.*

well the no-fault coverage is working, several approaches were employed in the analysis of the survey information to provide the basis for such an evaluation.

A complete appraisal of the adequacy of the PIP coverage system in Massachusetts is complicated by the fact that recourse to the tort system is still possible for those accident victims who sustain relatively serious injuries. The data compiled from the PIP claim files do not reveal to what extent claimants who sustained the more serious injuries also pursued tort claims which produced additional compensation. In addition, this survey does not provide information on the adequacy of the PIP coverage for persons who were seriously injured, but who for some reason chose not to assert a PIP claim.[91] It may eventually be possible to analyze the automobile tort claims to ascertain what portion of these claimants have not sought PIP benefits, but such an analysis is beyond the scope of this study and the size of such a group—if one does exist—remains unknown.

A. Total Economic Losses and the PIP Limits

There are a variety of approaches which might be employed to consider the relative adequacy of the $2,000 of PIP coverage afforded to every person injured in an automobile accident in Massachusetts. The most direct survey information on the relation between the economic losses and the PIP coverage was theoretically provided by an item on the survey form which specifically sought an evaluation by the person examining the file on whether the loss was more than the PIP coverage. The persons who transferred the information from each claim file to the survey forms were asked to indicate whether the economic loss claimed exceeded the total available PIP coverage. Of the 1,523 claim files where payments were made, only 1.5 percent of the files were so characterized.[92] In other words, the appraisals of

91. In theory, accident victims who received injuries that were sufficiently serious to warrant or allow a tort action would seek the PIP benefits as well. However, in interviews with attorneys during 1972 and 1973, it was repeatedly suggested that some lawyers handling automobile tort claims did not always counsel their clients to claim their PIP benefits. It seems reasonable to anticipate that lawyers will advise all clients to take full advantage of the coverage benefits under the PIP insurance. The experience of several of the insurance companies that participated in the claims study indicates that by 1976 this had occurred so that lawyers "in Massachusetts, as well as in other no-fault states,. . .are now extremely active in counseling their clients on utilizing PIP benefits. *"Insurance Research Department Letter"*, dated September 22, 1976, *supra* note 85.

92. CLRS NO-FAULT STUDY—INSURANCE CLAIMS SURVEY DATA, *supra* note 16.

93. *Id.* In considering the data on the amounts of insurance benefits paid to the PIP claimants, it should be remembered that there has been considerable inflation during the period since the accidents that gave rise to the claims occurred and the economic losses were sustained. Undoubtedly, an appropriately larger portion of the no-fault claims now involve economic losses that approach or exceed the $2,000 of coverage provided under the Massachusetts no-fault insurance.

the information in the files indicated that less than 2 percent of the claimants who sought indemnification under the PIP insurance sustained economic losses beyond the $2,000 provided by the Massachusetts no-fault coverage.[93]

TABLE 24

Percentage Distribution of PIP Claimants by Economic Loss in Relation to PIP Coverage

PIP Coverage Exceeded Economic Loss	98.4%
Economic Loss Exceeded PIP Coverage	1.5%
TOTAL:	99.9%
Base:	1,523

There is some reason, however, for suspecting that this figure of less than 2 percent probably understates the number of instances in which accident victims' economic losses are not fully indemnified by the PIP coverage.

Among the files surveyed where there were claims, 4.4 percent of the PIP files showed the payments totaled $2,000.[94] And as shown on Table 25, another 2 percent of the files showed payments in excess of $1,500.[95]

TABLE 25

Percentage Distribution of Claimants by the Total Amount of PIP Payments

AMOUNT OF PIP PAYMENTS	PERCENTAGE OF CLAIMANTS	CUMULATIVE PERCENTAGE
$ 1 - $10	6.4%	6.4%
$11 - $25	14.7%	21.1%
$26 - $50	17.0%	38.1%
$51 - $75	14.1%	52.2%
$76 - $100	7.6%	59.8%
$101 - $200	14.0%	73.8%
$201 - $500	12.0%	85.8%
$501 - $1,000	5.2%	91.0%
$1,001 - $1,500	2.5%	93.5%
$1,501 - $1,999	2.0%	95.5%
$2,000	4.4%	99.9%
TOTAL:	99.9%	
Base:	1,452	

Whenever the amounts paid approach the limits of the coverage, it seems reasonable to question whether the PIP insurance was adequate to fully compensate the claimants. In order to secure a more complete evaluation, the survey data of all files which showed payments in excess of $1,500 were further analyzed.

The files of those PIP claimants who received total payments of at least $1,500 were examined to identify what types of economic losses had produced the claims that led to the payments. As shown on Table 26, less than 5 percent of the files showed a payment of medical expenses of more than $1,500.[96]

TABLE 26

Percentage Distribution of PIP Claimants
by Amount Paid for Medical Expenses

AMOUNT PAID FOR MEDICAL EXPENSES	CUMULATIVE PERCENTAGE
$ 1 - $25	25.0%
$ 26 - $50	44.0%
$ 51 - $100	67.5%
$ 101 - $250	84.2%
$ 251 - $500	89.8%
$ 501 - $1,000	93.9%
$1,001 - $1,500	95.4%
$1,501 - $1,999	96.9%
$2,000	99.9%

Base: 94

The files where the medical expenses were at least $1,500 were then analyzed to ascertain what other economic losses were claimed. The analysis of the other economic losses for these claims files showed that the amount claimed by almost all of these insureds for other economic losses was less than the amount of PIP coverage remaining after the amount claimed for medical expenses was paid. A similar analysis was made for the files that showed the PIP payment for wage losses was in excess of $1,000. Again, in the great majority of cases, this analysis showed that the amounts claimed for economic losses other than wages had not exceeded the remaining PIP coverage. Viewing these files as a group, this analysis indicates

94. CLRS NO-FAULT STUDY—INSURANCE CLAIMS SURVEY DATA, *supra* note 16.

95. *Id.*

96. *Id.*

that between 3 and 4 percent—and certainly no more than 5 percent—of the PIP claimants had incurred economic losses in excess of the PIP coverage.[97]

B. Amounts Claimed in Relation to PIP Payments

The analysis of the adequacy of the PIP coverage in the preceding section was based on an examination of the amounts paid to the claimants. As an adjunct to this approach, it seemed reasonable to examine how the amounts claimed related to the amounts paid for medical expenses, wage losses, and other expenses.

1. *Medical Expenses.* Payments were made by the insurers in 1,457 of the files that were surveyed, and all of these files showed that claims for medical expenses were paid.[98] Each of these files was analyzed to ascertain how the amount claimed for the medical loss compared to the amount allowed by the insurance company. In over 98 percent of the cases, the amounts claimed by the insured were allowed and were paid by the insurer—that is, no differential existed between the amount claimed and the amount paid for medical expenses.[99]

2. *Wage Losses.* When the wage loss claims were compared to the amounts allowed, the analysis disclosed that over 90 percent received exactly what they claimed.[100] Of the some 10 percent of the claimants who lost wages and were compensated in some amount that was less than what had been claimed, the difference was less than $50 for over half of these claimants. In other words, less than 5 percent of the claimants who sought reimbursement for wage losses made claims that exceeded the PIP payments for wage losses by more than $50.[101] These findings are set out in Table 27.

TABLE 27

Percentage Distribution of PIP Claimants by Difference Between the Amount Claimed and the Amount Paid for Wage Losses

AMOUNT OF DIFFERENCE	PERCENTAGE OF CLAIMANTS WITH WAGE LOSSES	CUMULATIVE PERCENTAGE
No Difference[102]	91.3%	91.3%
$ 1 - $50	4.5%	95.8%
$ 51 - $100	2.3%	98.1%
$100 or more	1.9%	100.0%
TOTAL:	100.0%	
Base:	311	

97. *Id.* Also see the comment on inflation during the period since the survey in note 93, *supra.*

98. CLRS NO-FAULT STUDY—INSURANCE CLAIMS SURVEY DATA, *supra* note 16.

99. *Id.*

100. *Id.*

101. *Id.*

3. *Funeral Expenses.* When an examination was made of funeral expenses to determine the differences between the amount claimed and the amount paid, the analysis showed that all of the funeral expenses were allowed in the amounts claimed.[103]

VI. Timeliness of PIP Payments

One of the primary goals generally set for the PIP system was to assure that indemnification would be speedily available to injured persons. Therefore, the CLRS survey sought rather detailed information about the dates when various events occurred for each of the PIP claims.

Conversations with insurance industry executives in the course of preparing the survey forms indicated that frequently, and perhaps in most instances, an insurance company receives notice of the accident from the insured sometime prior to the receipt of the requisite supporting documents such as medical bills, hospital bills, or wage loss statements. In fact, these conversations indicated that in most cases the dates on which medical information or wage loss information is sufficient to make the first payment occur several weeks after the insured has reported the accident and submitted the required claim forms—usually the PIP No. 1 form. Accordingly, the survey sought to identify when the following events occurred:

1. Accident date.
2. Date the accident was reported to the insurance company.
3. Date the PIP No. 1 form was received by the insurance company.
4. Date medical information was sufficient to make a PIP payment.
5. Date wage loss information was sufficient to make a PIP payment.
6. Date of first PIP payment.
7. Dates of subsequent PIP payments.

Obviously, the data on these dates in each of the files could be analyzed in many ways. However, the following discussion focuses on the time periods which seem to be the most relevant to an evaluation of the timeliness of the payments:

> First, the elapsed time from the accident date to the date of the first PIP payment.

> Second, the elapsed time from the accident date to the date the PIP No. 1 form was received by the insurance company.

> Third, the elapsed time from the date information was sufficient for a payment to the date of the first PIP payment.

---

102. In a few of these cases, the amount paid was greater than the sum claimed, and these were included in the "no difference" group.

103. *Id.*

The average elapsed time from the date of the accident to the date of the first PIP payment was 69 days.[104] However, as shown by the data set out in Table 28, the periods range from a few days to over a year.

TABLE 28

Percentage Distribution of PIP Claimants by Elapsed Time from Accident to First PIP Payment

NUMBER OF DAYS	PERCENTAGE OF PIP CLAIMANTS PAID	CUMULATIVE PERCENTAGE
1 - 6 days	0.3%	0.3%
7 - 30 days	16.1%	16.4%
31 - 60 days	27.3%	43.7%
61 - 90 days	19.6%	63.3%
91 - 120 days	9.9%	73.2%
121 - 180 days	11.6%	84.8%
181 - 240 days	5.5%	90.3%
241 - 365 days	4.2%	94.5%
More than 365 days	5.5%	100.0%
TOTAL:	100.0%	
Base:	1,498	

Ascertaining the elapsed time from when the accidents occurred to when the first PIP payments were made provides no indication of whether the longer time periods are appropriately attributed to the claimants or the insurance companies.

An insurance company is not, of course, in a position to make PIP insurance payments until the insured provides information on the nature and extent of the economic losses. Upon being notified of personal injuries in an automobile accident, insurance companies in Massachusetts provide the injured persons with a PIP No. 1 Claim Form, and the return of this form to the insurance company is the initial step in the PIP claims process. The completed PIP No. 1 form provides the insurance company with general information about the accident and the injuries sustained. The form also includes authorization statements by the insured which allow the insurance company to secure appropriate confirmations of the amount claimed for wage losses from employers and of the amounts claimed for medical expenses from doctors or hospitals.

The median elapsed time between the accident and the date the PIP No. 1 form was received by the insurance companies was more than a month, and some forms were not received by the insurance companies until more than a year had passed.[105]

104. CLRS NO-FAULT STUDY—INSURANCE CLAIMS SURVEY DATA, *supra* note 16.
105. *Id.*

The data on the amount of time that passed before the PIP No. 1 forms were returned to the insurance companies is presented in Table 29.

TABLE 29

Percentage Distribution of PIP Claimants by Elapsed Time from Accident Date to Receipt by the Insurer of the PIP No. 1 Form

NUMBER OF DAYS	PERCENTAGE OF PIP CLAIMANTS	CUMULATIVE PERCENTAGE
1 - 6 days	3.9%	3.9%
7 - 30 days	43.9%	47.8%
31 - 60 days	22.5%	70.3%
61 - 90 days	11.1%	81.4%
91 - 120 days	4.5%	85.9%
121 - 180 days	5.3%	91.2%
181 - 240 days	1.9%	93.1%
241 - 365 days	2.9%	96.0%
More than 365 days	4.0%	100.0%
TOTAL:	100.0%	
Base:	1,342	

The time periods between when the accidents occurred and the commencement of the claim process by the insureds through the return of the PIP No. 1 form indicate that in many instances the extended time periods that preceded the first PIP payments involved delays that probably are not appropriately attributed to the insurance companies. Rather, they seem to represent decisions by the insureds to defer the filing of their claims. Moreover, claimants often submit the PIP No. 1 form without providing the insurance company with bills or wage statements that document the losses that were sustained as a result of the accidents. In some instances this involves no more than a request by the insurance company that then results in the insured sending the company some papers such as medical bills. Often, however, the insureds do not have the requested materials. For example, frequently, the insureds do not have records of their medical expenses and copies of the bills must be secured from a doctor or hospital. Similarly, where the accident injury leads to wage losses, statements from the employer are usually needed to establish the exact wage loss before any PIP payment is made. Therefore, the data on the time periods between the accident dates and the dates the PIP No. 1 forms were received by the insurance companies provide only a partial picture of the reasons for the time intervals that preceded the first PIP payments in the claim files surveyed. Additional perspective on the speed with which the insurance companies respond to the PIP claims is afforded by examining how much time elapsed from when the insurance companies received the necessary supporting information on the amounts claimed to when the first PIP payments were made by the insurance companies.

Almost every PIP claim file surveyed showed that payments were made to compensate the insureds for medical expenses.[106] Among these files, in 85 percent of the cases the initial PIP payments were exclusively to provide significant indemnification for medical expenses.[107] Therefore, one of the most significant measures of the promptness of payments by the insurance companies are the time periods between the dates on which the medical information was sufficient for payment of medical expenses, and the dates on which the first payments were made to these insureds. Table 30 summarizes the survey results of this analysis.

TABLE 30

Percentage Distribution of PIP Claimants by Time Period From Receipt of Supporting Documents to First PIP Payment for Medical Expenses

TIME PERIOD	PERCENTAGE OF PIP CLAIMANTS PAID	CUMULATIVE PERCENTAGE
1 - 3 days	29.4%	29.4%
4 - 7 days	21.5%	50.9%
8 - 14 days	11.5%	62.4%
15 - 30 days	17.9%	80.3%
31 - 60 days	9.6%	89.9%
61 - 90 days	3.1%	93.0%
91 -180 days	4.9%	97.9%
More than 180 days	2.1%	100.0%

TOTAL: 100.0%
Base: 1,271

About half of these PIP claimants received a payment to reimburse them for their medical expenses within 7 days after the insurance companies had received the necessary supporting documents.[108] Equally significant, over 80 percent had received payments within the 30 days following the submission of such documents.[109] These elapsed time data indicate that generally PIP claims for medical expenses were handled very expeditiously by the insurance companies following receipt of the supporting documents.

106. CLRS NO-FAULT STUDY—INSURANCE CLAIMS SURVEY DATA, *supra* note 16.
107. *Id.*
108. *Id.*
109. *Id.*

The same analysis was employed for the files where the first payment was to provide indemnification for wage losses. Although there are some variations in the percentages, the analysis of the time periods between the receipt of supporting documents for wage losses and the date of the first PIP payments to indemnify for wage losses seems to support the conclusion that most wage claims were also promptly handled by the insurance companies. These data are presented in Table 31.

TABLE 31

Percentage Distribution of PIP Claimants by Time Period from Receipt of Supporting Documents to First PIP Payment for Wage Loss

TIME PERIOD	*PERCENTAGE OF PIP CLAIMANTS WHERE FIRST PAYMENT WAS FOR WAGE LOSS*	*CUMULATIVE PERCENTAGE*
1 - 3 days	24.6%	24.6%
4 - 7 days	14.6%	39.2%
8 - 14 days	12.8%	52.0%
14 - 30 days	17.6%	69.6%
31 - 60 days	15.2%	84.8%
61 - 90 days	4.7%	89.5%
91 - 180 days	7.6%	97.1%
More than 180 days	2.9%	100.0%
TOTAL:	100.0%	
Base:	72	

The data on the elapsed time periods presented in the preceding paragraphs are generally corroborated by the survey findings from the interviews with accident victims who made insurance claims.[110] The vast majority of the PIP claimants who were interviewed—more than 80 percent—stated that they were either "very satisfied" or "fairly satisfied" with the speed which their claims had been paid.[111] The interview survey results are set out in Table 32.

110. See A. Widiss, *Accident Victims Under No-Fault Automobile Insurance: A Massachusetts Survey,* 61 IOWA LAW REVIEW 1 at p. 52 (1975), which is reprinted at Chapter 2 of this book.
111. *Ibid.*

TABLE 32

**Percentage Distribution of PIP Claimants by
Degree of Satisfaction With Speed of Payment**

DEGREE OF SATISFACTION	PERCENTAGE OF CLAIMANTS INTERVIEWED	
Very Satisfied	48.3%	)
		) 84.3%
Fairly Satisfied	26.0%	)
Fairly Dissatisfied	8.1%	)
		) 15.1%
Very Dissatisfied	7.6%	)
TOTAL:	100.0%	
Base:	446	

As the data in Table 32 illustrate, almost 8 percent of the accident victims who filed PIP claims stated they were "very dissatisfied" with the time it took their insurance companies to handle the claims.[112] In addition, another 8 percent responded that they were "fairly dissatisfied" with the amount of time that preceded the payment of their PIP claims.[113] In light of these responses, considerable importance was attached to designing the survey of claim files so as to ensure that information would be collected that would provide a body of data against which the opinions of these accident victims could be weighed.

The claim files survey showed that about 70 percent of the claimants had received payments within the 60-day period following the accidents.[114] However, the survey also showed that about 10 percent of the claims remained unpaid more than two months after the relevant documents or information supporting the PIP claims were received by the insurance companies.[115] The data from the claim files surveyed are not only disturbing, but lend credence to the complaints made by some accident victims about delays in the claims process. There is a striking correlation between the dissatisfaction voiced by some 10 to 15 percent of the accident victims and the claims survey data which show that approximately 10 percent of the PIP claimants had not received any payments more than 120 days after the insurers had received adequate information in support of the claims. The claim

112. See A. Widiss, *Accident Victims Under No-Fault Automobile Insurance: A Massachusetts Survey,* 61 IOWA LAW REVIEW 1 at p. 52 (1975), which is reprinted as Chapter 2 in this book.

113. *Ibid.*

114. See Table 29, *supra.*

115. CLRS NO-FAULT STUDY—INSURANCE CLAIMS SURVEY DATA, *supra* note 16.

survey findings on the elapsed time between the receipt of the required supporting information and the first PIP payments for both medical expenses and wage losses are presented in Table 33.

TABLE 33

Percentage Distribution of PIP Claimants by Time Period From Receipt of Supporting Documents to First PIP Payment

TIME PERIOD	WHERE FIRST PIP PAYMENT WAS FOR MEDICAL EXPENSES	WHERE FIRST PIP PAYMENT WAS FOR WAGE LOSS
	Cumulative Percentage	Cumulative Percentage
1 - 3 days	29.4%	24.6%
4 - 7 days	50.9%	39.2%
7 - 14 days	62.4%	52.0%
15 - 30 days	80.3%	69.6%
31 - 60 days	89.9%	84.8%
61 - 90 days	93.0%	89.5%
91 - 180 days	97.9%	97.1%
More than 180 days	100.0%	100.0%
	Base: 1,271	Base: 72

In the interviews with accident victims, many of the respondents indicated they were not only distressed by the amount of time which passed before they were paid, but also by the failure of the insurers to keep them apprised of where their claim stood. When PIP payments are made within a few days after the insurer receives the appropriate supporting documents from the claimants, keeping the insureds informed on the status of their claims is irrelevant. When claims go unpaid for not only some months after they have been filed, but then for several more months after the insured has supplied the supporting information requested by the insurance company, the need to keep the claimants informed is clear.

Some delays in the claims process are undoubtedly justifiable. Which of the claims among the files surveyed—where the records in the files indicated the claims went unpaid for several months after the insurance companies received sufficient information to make the first payment—involved special problems that justified delays in the payments is a matter that goes beyond the scope of this study.

Yet, taken together, the data from the claim files survey and the victim interviews certainly suggest that the payment patterns should be scrutinized from time to time to ascertain whether the goal of prompt payment is being realized for all claimants.[116]

Multiple PIP Payments

Another feature of the PIP insurance—designed to facilitate prompt compensation for economic losses—allows the injured persons to seek a series of payments rather than either requiring or encouraging claimants to wait until all expenses are incurred before presenting their insurance claims. In order to analyze how this aspect of the coverage was operating, the survey recorded the numbers of payments, what type of economic losses were being compensated by each payment, and to whom the payments were made. Among the files surveyed, only one-third of the PIP claimants received more than one payment, and only slightly more than one-tenth of the claimants received three or more payments.[117] The data on the number of payments received by PIP claimants are set out in Table 34.

TABLE 34

Percentage Distribution of PIP Claimants
by Number of Payments

NUMBER OF PAYMENTS	PERCENTAGE OF CLAIMANTS WHO RECEIVED PIP PAYMENTS
1	100.0%
2	34.2%
3	12.2%
4	4.9%
5 or more	2.4%

Base: 1,416

116. Representatives of each of the insurance companies that participated in this survey were invited to review the manuscript for this chapter. After reading the text, several of the company representatives observed that the experience of their companies was "that very few claims remain unpaid over 30 days which are the result of unjustified delay." They further commented that "those which do remain unpaid are those which involve unreasonable or unnecessary treatment, inflated medical bills, or questions of causal relationship." *Insurance Research Department Letter,* dated September 22, 1976, *supra* note 85. These comments are not necessarily inconsistent with the data compiled in the survey of the claim files. It may well be that claims which remain unpaid for extended periods involve special situations that warrant such treatment. On the other hand, it is also conceivable that the critical responses made by the accident victims in reply to inquiries about their relative satisfaction with the speed of payment are not groundless. The answers cannot be found in data compiled in this study since the surveys were designed with a view to describing the payment patterns, and unfortunately did not include provisions for the investigation of what lay behind these facts.

117. CLRS NO-FAULT STUDY—INSURANCE CLAIMS SURVEY DATA, *supra* note 16.

The fact that two-thirds of the PIP files showed only one payment could be a result of decisions by these insureds to hold off making claims until all the bills were received. However, the same payment pattern would exist if the insurance companies delayed payment until a claim was asserted in its entirety. If insurers pursued this latter course, it would clearly be contrary to the purpose of the PIP statute. There are several reasons for concluding that in most instances where only one payment was made it was the result of the way the insured opted to seek compensation.

First, as pointed out above in the text, the survey data showed that over 75 percent of the claims were paid within the 30-day period following the dates when the insurers received information sufficient to make the first payments.[118] This suggests that the claim procedures used by the companies were designed to process PIP claims without any undue delays.

Second, the data on the time periods between the accidents and submission of the PIP No. 1 forms seem to indicate that many insureds chose to defer initiating their claims for relatively long periods of time following the accidents.[119] Only about 4 percent of the insureds filed claims in the week following the accidents.[120] And even though half of the claimants filed PIP No. 1 forms sometime over the month following the accident, nearly 30 percent delayed filing a claim for periods of at least eight weeks.[121] In other words, the time periods between the accident dates and claim dates are certainly consistent with decisions by the insureds to not seek interim payments from the insurance companies. These patterns are perhaps most understandable if it is borne in mind that a substantial majority of the insureds sustained injuries which only caused relatively small economic losses. As shown on Table 35, over one-third of the PIP claimants received less than $50, and almost three-quarters of the claims involved payments of no more than $200.

118. *Id.*
119. *Id.* Also see Table 29, and the discussion in the associated text.
120. *Id.*
121. *Id.*

TABLE 35

Percentage Distribution of PIP Claimants
by Total Amount of Payments

AMOUNT OF PAYMENTS	PERCENTAGE OF ALL CLAIMANTS	CUMULATIVE PERCENTAGE
$ 1 - $ 50	39.2%	39.2%
$ 51 - $ 100	22.0%	61.2%
$ 101 - $ 200	12.8%	74.0%
$ 201 - $ 500	11.7%	85.7%
$ 501 - $1,000	5.3%	91.0%
$1,001 - $1,500	2.3%	93.3%
$1,501 - $2,000	6.7%	100.0%

TOTAL: 100.0%
Base: 1,482

Thus, it really does not seem too surprising that about two-thirds of the claimants apparently waited until all the medical bills and wage losses were known before making their claims.

The data compiled on the types of economic losses sustained by the claimants that were being compensated by each of the PIP payments and the recipients of the payments did not provide any particular insight into the reasons why most of the claims involved only a single payment. However, two aspects of this survey data are interesting.

First, approximately 90 percent of the initial PIP payments were made to provide indemnification for medical expenses.[122] Only about 5 percent of the first PIP payments were made to provide compensation for wage losses.[123] However, among the PIP claimants who received more than one payment, about 25 percent of the payments were made to cover wage losses.[124]

Second, when the data on the recipients of the payments were analyzed, they showed that an increasingly larger percentage of the successive payments were made to doctors or hospitals. Among the first payments, slightly less than 10 percent were made directly to a doctor or hospital.[125] However, where there were five or more payments, nearly 20 percent were made to a doctor or hospital.[126] There was, of course, a corresponding reduction in the portion of the PIP payments that were made to the insureds. And, there was also a slight decrease in the relative percentages of payments that were made jointly to the claimants and the claimants' attorneys. The data on the recipients of payments are presented in Table 36.

122. CLRS NO-FAULT STUDY—INSURANCE CLAIMS SURVEY DATA, *supra* note 16.
123. *Id.*
124. *Id.*
125. *Id.*
126. *Id.*

TABLE 36

Percentage Distribution of PIP Payments
by Recipient of the Payments

SEQUENCE OF PAYMENTS	PIP CLAIMANTS	DOCTOR OR HOSPITAL	CLAIMANT AND CLAIMANT'S ATTORNEY	TOTAL
First Payment	83.1%	9.2%	7.7%	100.0%
				Base: 1,482
Second Payment	80.1%	12.8%	7.0%	99.9%
				Base: 483
Third Payment	81.4%	12.6%	6.0%	100.0%
				Base: 167
Fourth Payment	78.6%	15.7%	5.7%	100.0%
				Base: 70
Fifth or Final Payment	75.6%	19.5%	4.9%	100.0%
				Base: 41

VII. ATTORNEY REPRESENTATION

Interviews with attorneys indicated that in most instances lawyers in Massachusetts were advising both clients and potential clients to file their own PIP claims.[127] Accordingly, the data from the claim files survey which confirm that most PIP claims were made by insureds who were not represented by attorneys are not surprising. Among the claim files surveyed, it appeared that less than 15 percent of the PIP claimants were represented by attorneys.[128] As shown in Table 37, the converse of this meant that more than 85 percent of the claim files indicated that the claimants had not been represented by lawyers.

TABLE 37

Percentage Distribution of PIP Claimants by
Whether They Were Represented by Lawyers

First Notice From Attorney	7.2%
Attorney After First Notice	6.2%
Not Represented	86.6%
TOTAL:	100.0%
Base:	1,503

127. See A. Widiss, *Massachusetts No-Fault Automobile Insurance: Its Impact on the Legal Profession,* 56 BOSTON UNIVERSITY LAW REVIEW 323 at pp. 332-337 (1976).

128. CLRS NO-FAULT STUDY—INSURANCE CLAIMS SURVEY DATA, *supra* note 16.

The survey of the claim files showed that among the insureds whose claims were handled by lawyers, attorneys represented about half of this group from the outset.[129] The other claimants who were represented retained attorneys who became involved sometime after the insurance company received the first notice of the accident.[130]

The responses of the attorneys in the general survey of the bar in Massachusetts indicated that among those attorneys who were handling PIP claims, over 40 percent would only do so if there was a possible tort claim.[131] This, of course, should mean that typically the cases where PIP claimants were represented by attorneys would be those persons who suffered the relatively more serious injuries. This was borne out by the survey of the claim files. The average amount of PIP benefits paid to insureds who were represented by attorneys was $662.00,[132] and this was almost three times greater than the average PIP payment paid to claimants who were not represented by attorneys.[133]

Further analysis of the files of those claimants who were represented by attorneys showed that most of these claimants had sustained injuries that satisfied one or more of the thresholds which would allow the claimant to seek a tort recovery as well as PIP compensation.[134] Of the claim files that indicated an attorney had been involved, about half showed medical expenses in excess of $500.[135] One-third of the files indicated that the injury sustained in the accident included a fracture.[136] And there were also a number of files that recorded various other injuries that would satisfy another of the tort thresholds.[137] Taken together, and allowing for files in which more than one of the critieria for a tort suit were satisfied, about three-quarters of the PIP claimants who were represented by an attorney had sustained some type of injury that would have allowed them to assert a tort claim as well as the no-fault claim. Although there was no way to ascertain from the information in a PIP claim file whether such a tort claim had been made, it seems likely that in many instances the involvement of an attorney in these PIP claims was attributable to the possibility of a tort claim.

---

129. *Id.*

130. *Id.*

131. See A. Widiss, *Massachusetts No-Fault Automobile Insurance: Its Impact on the Legal Profession,* 56 BOSTON UNIVERSITY LAW REVIEW 323 at p. 333 (1976).

132. CLRS NO-FAULT STUDY—INSURANCE CLAIMS SURVEY DATA, *supra* note 16.

133. *Id.* Since the PIP insurance is limited to compensation for actual economic losses, it seems reasonable to assume that in most instances the lawyers did not influence the amounts paid by the insurance companies.

134. For a description of the Massachusetts tort thresholds, see the discussion in Chapter 1 at p. 10, *supra*

135. CLRS NO-FAULT STUDY—INSURANCE CLAIMS SURVEY DATA, *supra* note 16.

136. *Id.*

137. *Id.*

VIII. CONCLUDING OBSERVATIONS

The data compiled in this study of closed claim files provide considerable insight into how the PIP claims process was working in Massachusetts during the period studied. In reviewing the results of the claim files survey together with the information developed in the other segments of the CLRS Massachusetts No-Fault Study, one finds considerable empirical evidence to support the impressions of government regulators, insurance executives, and PIP claimants that no-fault automobile insurance in large measure achieved the objectives sought for the coverage. In addition, several more specific concluding observations are warranted.

One of the most interesting aspects of the no-fault claim files survey data is that the profile of the PIP claimants differs from that of the Massachusetts claimants whose files were surveyed in the DOT claims study. The differences between the two groups appear to indicate that the no-fault coverage affords indemnification for persons who were not compensated by automobile liability insurance under the tort system. Overall, when the PIP claimants are considered with respect to the type of accident, their status or role in the accident, and biographical characteristics such as age- they appear to more closely resemble the entire population of accident victims than did the claimants who were compensated under the liability coverage in the DOT survey of Massachusetts claim files.[138] Accordingly, the CLRS survey data indicate that the goal of providing insurance protection for accident victims who were not being compensated under the tort system is being achieved.

One of the significant issues for any insurance is the adequacy of the coverage in relation to the economic losses incurred by the claimants. The data from the CLRS study indicate that well over 90 percent of the persons who sustained injuries that led to PIP claims did not exhaust the $2,000 of no-fault insurance mandated by the Massachusetts legislation. In fact, about 93 percent of the claimants whose files were examined received less than $1,500 under the PIP coverage.[139] The principal reasons are, first, that a great majority of accident victims sustain relatively minor injuries that do not result in substantial economic losses,[140] and second, that many of the more seriously injured also receive indemnification for some portion of their economic losses from other sources.[141] Whether the percentage of PIP claimants who were fully indemnified for their economic losses by the PIP coverage is as high as 95 percent—as some of the data would seem to suggest—or somewhat lower, this survey demonstrates that even relatively

---

138. See generally Part II and Part III, *supra.*

139. See generally Part V, *supra.*

140. See generally Part IV, *supra.*

141. See generally A. Widiss, *Accident Victims Under No-Fault Automobile Insurance: A Massachusetts Survey,* 61 IOWA LAW REVIEW 1 at pp. 33-41, 46-50 (1976).

modest no-fault coverage can provide complete indemnification for the out-of-pocket losses of the great majority of the persons who are injured in automobile accidents. [142] However, having offered this observation, it is equally important to recognize two additional points.

First, the inflation which has been prevalent throughout the half-decade since the Massachusetts no-fault plan went into effect means that there has been a continuing erosion in the relative adequacy of the coverage—that is, the number of claimants whose economic losses exceed the $2,000 of no-fault coverage has been increasing as medical costs and wage losses have risen as a result of inflation.

Second, even though the PIP coverage and other existing collateral sources provide ample indemnification for the economic losses of something over 90 percent of the persons who are injured in automobile accidents, it should be remembered that the Massachusetts no-fault legislation was not designed to provide complete indemnification for all economic losses. Persons who are seriously injured can, of course, also seek indemnification for their uncompensated economic losses in a limited tort action, [143] and such persons usually have injuries which satisfy at least one of the thresholds that must be satisfied in order to seek general damages for pain and suffering as well as indemnification for out-of-pocket economic losses that are not covered by the PIP insurance. [144] This, however, does not mean that they will be assured indemnification. Indeed, the failure of the tort system to compensate the seriously injured has often been advanced as one of the serious shortcomings of liability insurance as a primary or only source of indemnification. The Massachusetts no-fault coverage was not designed to reach the problem of inadequate compensation for the very seriously injured beyond the point of assuring that all accident victims would be provided $2,000 of personal injury insurance protection.

The interviews with accident victims, which constituted one of the other major segments of the CLRS study, indicated that a substantial majority of those interviewees who had made PIP claims were generally pleased with the no-fault coverage. [145] These accident victims were specifically asked how satisfied they were with both the amounts they had been paid and the speed with which their claims had been paid by the insurance companies. In response to these inquiries over 85 percent of the respondents stated that they were either "satisfied" or "very satisfied ". The survey of accident claim files provides clear corroboration for the data compiled from the accident victim interviews.

142. See Part V-A, *supra.*

143. See the discussion of Tort Litigations in Chapter 1, at p. 10, *supra.*

144. *Ibid.*

145. See A. Widiss, *Accident Victims Under No-Fault Automobile Insurance: A Massachusetts Survey*, 61 IOWA LAW REVIEW 1 at pp. 52-53 (1976).

First, the comparisons between the amounts claimed and the amounts paid under the no-fault coverage disclosed that in most instances there were no differences. Over 98 percent of the medical expenses and over 90 percent of the wage losses were paid in exactly the amounts claimed.[146] In other words, the no-fault coverage was designed to indemnify actual economic losses, and it appears that the claimants were satisfied because they were compensated in the amounts they actually had to pay out or lost in wages.

Second, the data amply support the overall judgment that most PIP claims were expeditiously handled by the insurance companies. For example, slightly over 80 percent of the medical expense claims were paid within 30 days after the insurance company received the requisite supporting documents.[147] However, this survey did also disclose some instances where claims remained unpaid for extended periods of time. Approximately 10 percent of the claimants were paid only after periods ranging from two months to more than a year after the insurance company files indicated that the companies had received information documenting the amounts claimed.[148] This survey finding not only provides credible evidence that supports the criticisms voiced by some of the PIP claimants interviewed in the victim survey, but also justifies periodic monitoring of the payment patterns to assure that the goal of prompt payment is uniformly achieved.

Each of the segments of the CLRS No-Fault Study that preceded the claim files survey contributed some information which supported the conclusion that in most instances insureds are able to successfully assert PIP claims without the assistance of lawyers. Thus, it was not surprising to find that the data from the claim files on attorney representation showed that most claimants were not represented by lawyers. The relative success of the claimants in making their own claims without the assistance of counsel is indicated by the fact that among the files surveyed the insureds were overwhelmingly paid exactly what they claimed.[149]

The survey of the claim files also provides support for the conclusion that the Massachusetts no-fault personal injury coverage has generally not been abused by the insureds. The fact that in most instances the claims were paid by the insurance companies in the amounts requested by the insureds suggests that the companies claims personnel considered the claims to be justified and reasonable. Finally, it is also worth noting that this conclusion accords with comments made to the author by many insurance executives about the experience in Massachusetts with no-fault personal injury insurance. This takes an added significance in view of the fact that many of these insurance company executives also observed that this was not always the experience of their companies in regard to no-fault coverages in other states or in regard to property no-fault coverage in Massachusetts.

---

146. See Part V-B, *supra.*
147. See date presented in Table 30, *supra.*
148. See generally Part VI, *supra.*
149. See Part V-B, *supra.*

APPENDICES

MASSACHUSETTS NO-FAULT AUTO INSURANCE STUDY
COUNCIL ON LAW-RELATED STUDIES
CLOSED CLAIMS STUDY
BACKGROUND AND GENERAL INSTRUCTIONS

BACKGROUND

This study is being sponsored by the Council on Law-Related Studies, a non-profit independent foundation that supports and conducts research on law in action. It is designed to describe the handling of auto claims in Massachusetts after the implementation of the limited no-fault Personal Injury Projection coverage in 1971. In addition, some comparisons will be made with pre-no-fault BI amd UM claims that were surveyed by the Department of Transportation study in October, 1969.

CLOSED CLAIMANT FILES TO BE SURVEYED

1. TYPES OF CLAIMANTS to be surveyed are BI, UM, PIP Subrogation, PIP, and Med Pay. (Not covered are ADD, PPI, PD, comprehensive and towing. Also omitted is Subrogation other than PIP Subrogation, e.g., workmen's compensation or VA Hospital).

2. LOCATION OF ACCIDENT: All claimants of these types from accidents within Massachusetts are to be included in the survey. Only PIP claimants (and PIP claimants getting Med Pay) from accidents outside Massachusetts are to be surveyed. (BI and UM claimants from accidents outside Massachusetts should not be included. However, claimants living outside Massachusetts but injured inside Massachusetts should be included.)

3. FILES (OR SUBFILES) CLOSED IN OCTOBER, 1972 are the source of claimants to be surveyed. (Special arrangements to survey prospectively will be made for a company unable to locate October files for the retrospective survey.) Companies that keep only one claimant in a file will survey all files closed in October. Companies that keep several claimants in a single accident file but can identify individual claimants whose claims were closed in October will survey those claimants. Companies that keep several claimants in a single accident file and cannot identify individual claimant's closings will survey all claimants in files closed in October, including claimants whose claims were disposed of earlier than October.

Each company is to apply its own definition of closing to its files (whether before or after subrogation is complete on PIP cases, for example).

If your company's "month" for internal purposes does not coincide exactly with the calendar month of October, the "month" most closely corresponding to October should be surveyed.

If a file was closed in October, but has since been re-opened, the forms completed for its claimants should be filled out as though the reopening had not occurred, as though the survey took place on the closing date. Similarly, "after final" payments made without reopening the closed file should not be recorded for this survey.

4. DEFINITION OF CLAIMANT: A person should be considered a "claimant" and should be included in the survey whenever (s)he (or someone else) has indicated an injury (in an accident report, for example). For most companies, this will mean that a file number and reserve have been established. (For some companies, no file is created for such reports unaccompanied by actual claim papers. Special additional procedures will apply to those companies; the survey will include more than their closed-file claimants).

If more than one person (e.g., a family) has been treated as a single "claimant" for purposes of settlement, please consider it as more than one claimant for this survey and complete as many forms as there are individuals, allocating the expenses and payments among them.

5. FILE OPENED IN ERROR: If a file was erroneously created (e.g., claimant was not actually insured by your company) and closed when the error was discovered, it should not be surveyed.

DESCRIPTION OF FORMS

Form A is the PIP, Med Pay, and PIP Subrogation (Applicant) form. The form is a four-page folder; a separate form is to be filled out for each PIP claimant regardless of how many claimants there were in the accident.

Form B is the BI, UM, and PIP Subrogation (Respondent) form. The form consists of an accident cover sheet. (page 1) and a claimant form (pages 2 and 3). (The four-page folder has one blank page). It is used for accident information and data about the first claimant in the accident. Each additional claimant from the same accident should be handled on an additional Form C.

Form C is the additional claimant form for BI, UM, and PIP Subrogation (Respondent). The form is identical to the claimant portion (pages 2 and 3) of Form B. Where a single accident results in more than one claimant, it is not necessary to fill out an entire form B; the accident cover sheet (page 1) is applicable to all claimants, so only Form C should be completed for each claimant after the first one. All Form C's from one accident should be inserted into the Form B folder and clipped in place. IT IS IMPERATIVE THAT ALL SUCH FORMS B AND C BE KEPT TOGETHER WITH THE SINGLE ACCIDENT COVER SHEET FOR THEIR ACCIDENT.

GENERAL INSTRUCTIONS FOR COMPLETING FORMS

1. PRENUMBERED SQUARES -- If the squares have numbers pro-
    vided, circle the number that best describes the situation.
    Circle only one number per block of boxes unless the item
    indicates that you may circle one or more. (If two or
    more are equally applicable, circle the lower number unless
    more than one circle is permitted. Exception: Item 22
    on the PIP form, where the highest applicable number
    should be circled.)

    Be sure to read all possible answers before circling the
    best one.

2. UNNUMBERED SQUARES -- Each unnumbered square should be
    filled in with a digit. Use zeros to the left of a
    number with fewer digits than there are squares to be
    filled. (For example, a PIP total payment of $46 is
    to be entered as 0046 in the four-box block provided
    at item 51.)

3. INAPPLICABLE ITEMS -- A few items are inapplicable under
    certain circumstances. When this occurs, a line should
    be drawn through the block.

    Examples: (a)   No wage loss for a PIP claimant: Item 23,
                      "Date Wage Loss Information Sufficient to
                      Make First Payment," should be lined out.

                (b)   No co-defendant in claim for BI: Item 16,
                      "Other Company's Total", should be lined
                      out.

4. UNAVAILABLE INFORMATION -- If it is impossible to obtain
    the information requested from a file, please enter UK
    (for "unknown") for each unavailable item. Do not line
    through an item when information is unknown; use UK.

5. PLEASE NOTE: The forms are designed for an entry to be
    made in every block of squares. Some mark must be made
    for every item -- a circle made, a digit entered, "UK"
    noted, or a line drawn through because inapplicable.

    Exception -- Where an entire page or section is skipped,
    draw a line through the page or section rather than many
    lines through all items on the page in the section.
    (e.g., the BI section of the BI - PIP Subrogation form is
    not used for a PIP Subrogation claim and vice versa.)

    This policy should vastly reduce the change of inadvertant
    failure to complete the forms fully.

    Specific instructions for each item on the three forms
    follow.

SPECIFIC CODING INSTRUCTIONS

PIP, MEDICAL PAYMENTS, PIP SUBROGATION (APPLICANT)

1. COMPANY CODE -- To preserve confidentiality, these codes are not provided here; enter the code your company has been assigned.

2. CLAIM NUMBER -- Enter your company's claim identification number for this claimant.

3. DATE OF ACCIDENT -- Month, day, and year the accident involving this PIP claimant occurred.

4. DATE ACCIDENT REPORTED TO COMPANY -- Month, day, and year your company first became aware of the accident, whether by phone, in person, or by mail report. This may or may not be the date PIP #1 was received. If PIP 1 or another communication is not date stamped, add two days to the date on it.

5. DESCRIPTION -- Enter the number that best describes the accident from the list attached at the end of these instructions. Please note that "claimant" means the person making the claim in question - not necessarily an "insured" under your company's policy. Note also that different codes apply to accidents due to the claimant's vehicle's negligence than to those due to another's negligence. Accidents on private property (including parking lots) are also coded differently from those on public streets and highways.

6. NUMBER OF MOTORIZED VEHICLES INVOLVED -- Enter the number of motorized vehicles in the accident. If there were nine or more, enter 9. A motorized vehicle is any vehicle (including any trailer) designed for operation on a public highway by any power other than muscular power.

7. LOCATION -- Indicate whether the accident occurred in Massachusetts (#1) or elsewhere (#2).

8. BASIS OF COVERAGE OF PIP CLAIMANT:

   A. Indicate whether the claimant was:

   #1, the named insured under your company's policy,

   #2, a member of the named insured's household, or

   #3, an "other insured." This would include a pedestrian hit by your insured's car, a non-household member passenger in your insured's car, or an assigned claim.

   B. Indicate whether your company's insured vehicle was (#1) or was not (#2) involved in this accident. #1, "our vehicle," includes all claims by occupants of and by pedestrians hit by your insured's vehicle. #2, "not our vehicle," is the "other vehicle" coverage and includes claims made by your

insured and his household as pedestrians or occupants of
some other car. #2 also includes all assigned claims.

It is obvious that <u>any</u> claim by one of your insureds
derives from your company's policy insuring the insured's
vehicle - otherwise, your insured would not be yours. This
<u>does not mean</u> that any claim by your insured is based on "our
vehicle;" the key is <u>what vehicle was in the accident</u>, not
what vehicle was covered by your company's policy.

C. Indicate whether this claimant was an assigned claim
(#2) or not (#1).

D. Indicate whether this claimant was a pedestrian (#2)
or not (#1). "Alighting from" claimants are not pedestrians

9. TYPE OF VEHICLE CLAIMANT WAS OCCUPYING -- Circle the number applicable to the vehicle the claimant was occupying at the time
of the accident. #1, Private Passenger, includes light trucks
used as private passenger vehicles (e.g., light pickups not
used in business, pickups with campers). Private passenger
vehicles insured as part of a fleet are still #1. Pedestrians
are #7, None. Taxis are #1.

10. STATE OF REGISTRATION OF VEHICLE CLAIMANT WAS OCCUPYING --
Indicate whether the registration was Massachusetts (#1) or
other (#2). #3, Not Applicable, includes claimants not in
registered vehicles (pedestrians, cyclists).

11. CLAIMANT'S STATUS -- Indicate whether the claimant was a driver
(#1) or a passenger (#2) in or on a motorized vehicle or whether
he was not in or on a motorized vehicle (#3, Other).

12. TOWN OR CITY OF RESIDENCE -- Please write out in full and
legibly; a coder will have to work from your handwriting.

13. HOUSEHOLD STATUS OF CLAIMANT IN HIS OWN HOUSEHOLD -- Circle the
category that best describes this claimant's status within his
own household. THIS ITEM IS NOT TO BE SKIPPED; please give your
best judgement based on the information available from the file.
You should be able to indicate at least whether the claimant
was a male or a female, for example. Examples:

#1. A married man living with his wife in his own residence.
#2. A married woman living with her husband in her own residenc
#3 & #4. A son or daughter (married or single) living with
one or both parents.
#5. A single, divorced, separated, or widowed male, with or
without children, living in his own residence (roomer or
boarder included).
#6. A single, divorced, separated, or widowed female, with
or without children, living in her own residence (roomer
or boarder included).

#7. A father, uncle, nephew, etc., who lives in the residence of a relative.

#8. A mother, aunt, niece, etc., who lives in the residence of a relative.

Note that each claimant's household status has nothing to do with the status of others in the accident. Each claimant is to be considered individually. A carload of women injured might be all "wives," #2; or a carload of teenagers injured might be all "sons," #3.

4. AGE -- Enter the claimant's age (at his last birthday before the accident). A child under one year is 00. Estimate if necessary and write "est." underneath.

5. OCCUPATION -- Enter the code for the claimant's occupation from the list of codes attached after the BI and UM claimant sheet instructions. Illustrations are given, but you will have to use your judgment as to which occupational code best describes the claimant.

6. HOW WAS FILE CLOSED? -- Circle the category that best explains why no payment was made to this claimant for PIP.

#0. Payment was made -- Some payment (not necessarily all that was asked for) was made.

<u>CLAIMANT DID NOT SEEK PAYMENT</u>

#1. PIP#1 Never Returned -- For any reason your company never got PIP #1, whether or not the form was given to the potential claimant.

#2. Claim not pressed -- Although PIP #1 was returned, it was not sufficient to make payment (for any reason); since the necessary information was never supplied, the file was closed. Or, PIP #1 indicated "no injury."

<u>CLAIMANT SOUGHT PAYMENT, BUT WAS DENIED, BECAUSE:</u>

#3. No Injury -- No payment was made because the claimant was never injured and had no "reasonable and necessary" medical expenses as a result of the accident.

#4. No Policy Coverage -- The policy has lapsed or was cancelled or the like. Do <u>not</u> use this code for workmen's compensation, alcohol, etc. Even though the policy is written not to cover these and they might be construed to be "no policy coverage;" they should be entered as #6-#10, <u>not</u> as #4.

#5. Loss Under Deductible -- A deductible applied to the named insured or his household that was larger than the potential recovery.

#6. Non-cooperation -- The Claimant refused to cooperate (e.g., would not allow a physical exam or submit his tax records if self-employed).

#7. Workmen's Compensation -- Claimant was entitled to workmen's compensation which covered all his loss, PIP none.

#8. Alcohol/Drugs -- The Claimant contributed to his own injury while under the influence of alcohol or a narcotic drug.

#9. Felony -- The Claimant contributed to his own injury while committing a felony-or seeking to avoid lawful apprehension or arrest by a police officer.

#10. Intentional Injury -- The Claimant contributed to his own injury with the specific intent of causing injury to himself or others.

NOTE: If no payment was made, skip to the medical payments section,
        item #1.

17.   DATE PIP #1 RECEIVED -- Month, day, and year PIP #1 was receive
      If not date-stamped, add two days to the date on the form itsel
      If none received, so note. If its equivalent was received,
      give its date, and write "equivalent."

18.   DATE MEDICAL INFORMATION SUFFICIENT TO MAKE FIRST PAYMENT --
      Month, day, and year information became sufficient to make the
      first medical payment made to this claimant. In a typical
      case, this might be the day   a medical bill was received.
      Less commonly, it might be the day a doctor verified to the
      adjustor's satisfaction that an expense was "reasonable and
      necessary." Or it might be the day the report from your
      company's own physical exam of the claimant was received.

19.   FORM OF MEDICAL INFORMATION REQUIRED -- Circle the highest numbe
      applicable.
          #1.   Only PIP 1 (or not form at all) was asked. This covers
                payment based on a phone call.
          #2.   A medical bill from the claimant was required in addi-
                tion to PIP 1.
          #3.   The PIP 2 Medical form was required from the doctor,
                hospital, or other medical institution.
          #4.   Some other, additional information was required, for
                example: an affidavit, deposition, or physical exam.

20.   DATE WAGE LOSS INFORMATION SUFFICIENT TO MAKE FIRST PAYMENT --
      Analogous to item 18, but for wage loss rather than medical
      expense. Month, day, and year information became sufficient
      to make the first wage loss payment of this claimant. This
      might be the day PIP #1 was received or the day the employer
      verified the loss.

21.   DATE(S), AMOUNT(S), AND TYPE(S) OF PAYMENT(S) MADE -- For each
      payment made, enter (A) the month, day. and year of payment
      (the date on the draft), (B) the amount paid (round to nearest
      whole dollar), (C) the type of loss(es) included - circle one
      or more, and (D) the person paid (to whom the draft was made
      payable) - claimant (#1), doctor or hospital (or other medical
      person or institution) (#2), claimant and claimant's attorney
      (jointly) (#3)."Claimant" includes claimant's relative or next
      friend.

      As many lines should be completed as there were payments made.
      If fewer than five were made, draw a line through the unused
      boxes. If more than five were made, enter only the final date,
      but the balance of all the payments (five through the final one
      and circle all the types included as well as all the payees.

      Finally, enter the total payments made.

. NUMBER OF PHYSICAL EXAMS BY INSURER -- Enter the number of medical exams made by your company (not by claimant's own doctor). Enter from zero to nine; if more than nine, enter 9.

. ATTORNEY REPRESENTATION -- Was the claimant represented by an attorney at the time of final payment? If not, circle #1. If yes, indicate whether the attorney entered the case before (#3) or after (#2) first notice of the claim.

4. SUIT FOR PIP BENEFITS -- If either the claimant (in small claims court, for example) or his attorney brought suit in connection with the PIP (not BI, UM or some other) claim , circle #2, Yes. If not, #1, No.

5. CLOSURE TYPE -- Circle whether or not a release was taken.

6. NUMBER OF DAYS HOSPITALIZED -- Enter the total number of days spent in a hospital. These need not be consecutive days, but each one must be at least an overnight stay.

7. INJURY CODE -- This need not be completed for fatalities. Circle the single most appropriate description for the non-fatal injury. Circle only one number per line; if there was more than one injury of a given kind, circle #2, Multiple. Examples:
   A fractured arm and neck whiplash would be #8 for "fracture," #5 for "strain," and #1 (none) for "bruise" and "cosmetic." Where internal injuries have been sustained, circle #6 (body) in the "strain" line. Where fractures of more than one bodily member are sustained, circle #2 (multiple) in the "fracture" line.

8. SERIOUS INJURY OR DEATH UNDER PIP STATUTE -- Circle as many as apply to this injured claimant.

9. OTHER ECONOMIC LOSSES -- These are the expenses (other than medical and wage loss) allowed by the PIP statute, services that would have been performed by the claimant but for his injury and for which payment was in fact made other than to a family member.

   A. SERVICES LOST -- Circle what services were replaced.

   B. DATES OF REPLACEMENT SERVICES -- Enter the number of days of services. If none, enter 000.

   C. TOTAL COST OF REPLACEMENT SERVICES -- Enter both the amount claimed and the amount paid (rounded to the nearest whole dollar).

TE: In 29C through 33, enter both the amount claimed and the amount paid or allowed; this device reveals any disputes over amounts due.

However, do not use the columb of "AMOUNT PAID UNDER PIP" to indicate losses above the PIP limit as opposed to losses in dispute. For example, if the claimant received two months of replacement services costing $2500, enter $2000 claimed and $2000 paid if there was no dispute. If the cost of replacement services was disputed, enter the amount claimed (e.g. $2500) and the amount paid (e.g. $1950).

0. WAGE/INCOME LOSS:

  A. CLAIMANT'S EMPLOYMENT STATUS -- At the time of the accident the claimant was:
    #1. Employee -- employed by some one else.

    #2. Self Employed

    #3. Unemployed -- seeking employment but not employed.

    #4. Not employed -- not seeking employment (e.g., a student).

  B. CLAIM PRESSED -- If the claim was not pressed, circle whether this was because there was no work loss or because wage continuation paid at least 75%. If the claim was not pressed, skip to Q30H and enter 0000 there.

  C. NUMBER OF WORK DAYS LOST -- Enter the nearest whole number from 001 to 999. Enter the number allowed by the adjuster if there was a dispute.

  D. WEEKLY WAGE/INCOME -- Enter the average weekly wage (at the time of the accident or during the preceeding 52 weeks), rounded to the nearest whole dollar. Enter the amount allowed by the adjuster if there was a dispute.

  E. TOTAL LOST WAGES/INCOME -- (This should equal 30C times 30H but may not if a fraction of a lost day was allowed.)

  F. 75% of TOTAL LOST WAGE/INCOME -- Enter 3/4 of 30E.

  G. AMOUNT COVERED BY WAGE CONTINUATION PLAN -- Enter 0000 if none.

NOTE: In some cases an adjuster may not have followed this procedure to compute PIP wage loss. If not, check the box so indicating.

  H. NET LOSS -- 30F minus 30G; enter 0000 if negative.

1.   TOTAL MEDICAL LOSS -- Enter the total of all expenses.

2.   FUNERAL EXPENSES -- Enter 0000 if none.

3.   SUBTOTALS - Add 29C, 30H, 31 and 32.

4.   LESS APPLICABLE DEDUCTIBLE -- Enter 0000 if none.

5.   TOTAL AMOUNT OF PAYMENTS -- 33 minus 34.   (This should equal #21 total).

NOTE: Check the box provided if there were economic loss(es) (not pain and suffering) above the PIP limit.

6.   SUBROGATION DECISION -- Indicate whether subrogation was sought and, if it was not, why it was not.

7.   DATE REQUEST MADE -- Month, day, and year request sent to other insurer.

8.   AMOUNT SUBROGATED -- Do not include the handling percentage (unallocated expense) but do include allocated expense.

9.   ARBITRATION -- Whether arbitration was used to settle the claim. Either statutory or pursuant to agreement is #2, yes.

10.   DATE SUBROGATION RECEIVED OR DENIED -- Month, day, and year payment was received; if no entry of the exact date, the date of the transfer plus two days.

11.   AMOUNT RECEIVED -- Enter the amount and whether this figure is the actual amount received or your best estimate. Enter 0000 if none. Include allocated expense, but not unallocated (handling percentage).

MEDICAL PAYMENTS SECTION

NOTE: Item 1, but only item one, is to be completed for <u>all</u> claimants
Items 2 through 4 are to be completed only for those claimants who
received some payment from med. pay.

1. COVERAGE LIMIT-- Enter the coverage limit. Write UK if unknown

2. TOTAL PAYMENTS-- Enter the amount paid from the med pay coverage
    to the date of searching the file.

3. STILL OPEN?-- Enter whether the coverage is still making payment
    or not.

4. PRIOR PIP MECICAL PAYMENTS REALLOCATED TO MEDICAL PAYMENTS?--
    Indicate whether earlier PIP payments earmarked at that time for
    medical expenses were later reallocated to wage loss so as to
    allow them to be paid by med. pay. instead. Check #3, Cannot Be
    Determined, if this is not clear from the file.

ACCIDENT DESCRIPTION - CODES

(Item 5, PIP, Med Pay, & PIP subrogation [Applicant] form.)

PEDESTRIAN OR BICYCLIST

01. Crosswalk or intersection   02. Dart out, mid block
0A. Alighting from car.

VEHICLE - STREET OR HIGHWAY

03. Other vehicle rear-ended Claimant
04. Claimant rear-ended other vehicle

05. Other vehicle backed into Claimant
06. Claimant backed into other vehicle

07. Other vehicle violated traffic signal
08. Claimant violated traffic signal

09. Other vehicle pulled away from curb
10. Claimant pulled away from curb

11. Other vehicle on wrong side of road
12. Claimant on wrong side of road

13. Other vehicle on left.
14. Claimant on left.

15. Other vehicle changed lanes
16. Claimant changed lanes

17. Other vehicle left turning- at intersection
18. Claimant left turning at inter-section

19. Other vehicle left turning - no intersection
20. Claimant left turning - no intersection

21. Other vehicle made improper turn
22. Claimant made improper turn

23. One car accident (includes hit-ting stationary object, but not pedestrian.
24. Other

PARKING LOT - PRIVATE PROPERTY

25. Other vehicle rear-ended Claimant
26. Claimant rear-ended other vehicle

27. Other vehicle backed into Claimant
28. Claimant backed into other vehicle

29. Other

[Claimant is to be coded by the actions of his car even if he was not driving: e.g., even if claimant was a passenger, #06, "Claimant changed lanes," is appropriate.]

AUTOMOBILE CLAIMS SURVEY
CLOSED P.I.P. CASES

FORM A

P.I.P., MEDICAL PAYMENTS, P.I.P. SUBROGATION (APPLICANT)

1. COMPANY CODE

2. CLAIMANT (SUB-) FILE NUMBER

ACCIDENT INFORMATION

3. DATE OF ACCIDENT

Month	Day	Year

4. DATE ACCIDENT RE-
   PORTED TO COMPANY

Month	Day	Year

5. DESCRIPTION

6. NUMBER OF MOTORIZED
   VEHICLES INVOLVED

7. LOCATION

Mass.	Other
1	2

8. BASIS OF COVERAGE OF PIP CLAIMANT

Named Insured	Member of Named Insured's Household	Other
1	2	3

9.

Our Vehicle	Not Our Vehicle
1	2

10.

Not Assigned Claim	Assigned Claim
1	2

11.

Not Pe-destrian	Pedes-trian
1	2

12. TYPE OF VEHICLE CLAIMANT WAS OCCUPYING

Priv. Pass	Com'l.	Public	Bi-cycle	Other	None
1	2	3	4	5	6

13. STATE OF REGISTRATION OF VE-
    HICLE CLAIMANT WAS OCCUPYING

Mass.	Other	Not Ap-plicable
1	2	3

14. CLAIMANT'S STATUS

Driver	Passenger	Other
1	2	3

CLAIMANT'S PERSONAL DATA

15. TOWN OR CITY
    OF RESIDENCE

16. AGE

17. OCCUPATION

18. HOUSEHOLD STATUS OF CLAIMANT IN HIS OWN HOUSEHOLD

Husb.	Wife	Son	Dgtr.	Single Head Of Household		Other Relative	
				Male	Female	Male	Female
1	2	3	4	5	6	7	8

CLAIM INFORMATION

19. HOW WAS FILE CLOSED?

Payment was Made	Claimant Did Not Seek Payment		Claimant Was Denied Payment Because:							
	P.I.P. #1 Never Returned	Claim Not Pressed	No Injury	No Policy Coverage	Loss Under Deductible	Non-coop-eration	Exclusions			
							Work. Comp.	Alcohol/ Drugs	Felony	Intent. Inj.
0	1	2	3	4	5	6	7	8	9	10

(IF NO PAYMENT WAS MADE, SKIP TO PAGE 4, ITEM 58)

20. DATE P.I.P #1 RECEIVED (ESTIMATE IF NECESSARY)

Month	Day	Year

NO PIP 1 RECEIVED [ ]

21. DATE MEDICAL INFORMATION SUFFICIENT TO MAKE FIRST PAYMENT

Month	Day	Year

22. FORM OF MEDICAL INFORMATION (CIRCLE HIGHEST APPLICABLE)

PIP 1 or No Form	Cl's Med Bill	PIP Med Form (PIP 2)	Other
1	2	3	4

23. DATE WAGE LOSS INFORMATION SUFFICIENT TO MAKE FIRST PAYMENT

Month	Day	Year

DATE(S), AMOUNT(S), AND TYPE(S) OF PAYMENT(S) MADE:

24. DATE(S) · **25. AMOUNT(S)** (WHOLE DOLLARS ONLY) · **26. TYPE(S)** · **27. PAYMENT MADE TO:**

	Month	Day	Year		Amount	Med.	Wage	Other	Claim-ant	Doc.or Hosp.	Cl. & Cl.'s Attorney
A. FIRST PAYMENT				$		1	2	3	1	2	3
B. SECOND PAYMENT (IF ANY)				$		1	2	3	1	2	3
C. THIRD PAYMENT (IF ANY)				$		1	2	3	1	2	3
D. FOURTH PAYMENT (IF ANY)				$		1	2	3	1	2	3
E. IF FIVE OR MORE, ENTER FINAL DATE & BALANCE OF PAYMENTS				$		1	2	3	1	2	3
						Med.	Wage	Other	Claim-ant	Doc.or Hosp.	Cl. & Cl.'s Attorney

28. TOTAL (SHOULD EQUAL #51). $ _____

29. NUMBER OF PHYS. EXAMS BY INSURER

30. ATTORNEY REPRESENTATION AT FINAL SETTLEMENT OR CLOSING

Not Repre-sented	Represented	
	First Notice From Atty.	Atty After First Notice
1	2	3

31. SUIT FOR PIP BENEFITS

No	Yes
1	2

32. CLOSURE TYPE

No Rlse.	Rlse.
1	2

INJURY INFORMATION

33. NO. OF DAYS HOSPITALIZED

34. SERIOUS INJURY OR DEATH UNDER PIP STATUTE (CIRCLE ONE OR MORE)

No Serious Injury or Death	Med. Ex. Over $500	Any Frac-ture	Loss of Body Member	Perm. & Serious Disfig.	Loss of Sight or Hearing	Death
1	2	3	4	5	6	7

35. NON-FATAL INJURY CODE (CHECK ONLY ONE PER LINE)

	None	Mult.	Head	Face	Neck	Body	Back	Limb	Ot
Fracture	1	2	3	4	5	6	7	8	
Strain	1	2	⊠	⊠	5	6	7	8	
Bruise	1	2	3	4	5	6	7	8	
Cosmetic	1	2	3	4	5	6	7	8	

ANALYSIS OF PIP LOSS(ES)

OTHER ECONOMIC LOSSES

36. SERVICES LOST

None	Housewife	Other
1	2	3

37. DAYS OF REPLACEMENT SERVICES

38. TOTAL COST OF REPLACEMENT SERVICES - - - - - - - - - - - - - $

AMOUNT CLAIMED UNDER PIP

(WHOLE DOLLARS ONLY)

AMOUNT PAID

$ | | | | |

(WHOLE DOLLARS ONLY)

WAGE/INCOME LOSS

39. CLAIMANT'S EMPLOY-MENT STATUS

Employee	Self-Emp.	Unemp.	Not Emp.
1	2	3	4

40. CLAIM PRESSED?

Yes	No, because:		(IF NO WAGE CLAIM, SKIP TO 46)
	No days lost	Wage Cont.	
1	2	3	

41. NO. OF WORK DAYS LOST

42. WEEKLY WAGE/INCOME

$ | | | |

(WHOLE DOLLARS ONLY)

AMOUNT CLAIMED UNDER PIP   AMOUNT ALLOWED

43. TOTAL LOST WAGES/INCOME - - - - - - - - - - - - - - - $ | | | | $ | | | |

44. 75% OF TOTAL LOST WAGES/INCOME - - - - - - - - - - - - $ | | | | $ | | | |

(CHECK IF WAGE LOSS FIGURED DIFFERENTLY [ ])

45. AMOUNT COVERED BY WAGE CONTINUATION PLAN (0000 IF NONE) - - - - - - - - - - - - - - - - $ | | | | $ | | | |

AMOUNT CLAIMED UNDER PIP   AMOUNT PAID

46. NET LOSS (44 MINUS 45; IF NEGATIVE ENTER 0000) - - - - - - - - - $ | | | | $ | | | |

47. TOTAL MEDICAL LOSS - - - - - - - - - - - - - - - - $ | | | | $ | | | |

48. FUNERAL EXPENSES (0000 IF NONE) - - - - - - - - - - - - - - - - $ | | | | $ | | | |

49. SUBTOTALS (38 + 46 + 47 + 48) - - - - - - - - - - $ | | | | $ | | | |

50. LESS APPLICABLE DEDUCTIBLE (0000 IF NONE) - $ | | | |

51. TOTAL AMOUNT OF PAYMENTS - - - - - - - - - - - - - - - - - - - (SHOULD EQUAL #28 TOTAL) - - - $ | | | |

CHECK IF THERE WAS ECONOMIC LOSS ABOVE PIP LIMIT [ ]

PIP SUBROGATION INFORMATION

52. FINAL SUBROGATION DECISION

Subroga-tion Sought	No Subrogation Sought, because:		
	Claimant At Fault	Amount Too Small	Other
1	2	3	4

(IF NO SUBROGATION, GO TO MED PAY SECTION)

53. DATE FINAL REQUEST MADE

Month	Day	Year

54. AMOUNT REQUESTED (not including handling percentage)

$ | | | |

55. ARBITRATION

No	Yes
1	2

56. DATE SUBROGATION RE-CEIVED OR DENIED

Month	Day	Year

57. AMOUNT RECEIVED (not including handling percentage)

$ | | | |

[ ]actual   [ ]est.

MEDICAL PAYMENTS COVERAGE

(COMPLETE #58 FOR ALL CLAIMANTS;
#59—#61 WHERE PAYMENT WAS MADE)

61: PRIOR P.I.P. MEDICAL PAYMENTS
REALLOCATED TO MED. PAY?

58. COVERAGE LIMIT

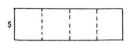

$

59. TOTAL PAYMENTS
(TO DATE)

$

60. STILL OPEN?

Yes	No
1	2

No	Yes	Cannot be Determined
1	2	3

CLOSED CLAIMS STUDY

FORM B

BI, UM, PIP SUBROGATION (RESPONDENT) ACCIDENT COVER SHEET

PLEASE COMPLETE ONE ACCIDENT COVER SHEET FOR EACH ACCIDENT, THEN ONE
CLAIM FORM FOR EACH BI, UM OR PIP SUBROGATION CLAIMANT IN THAT ACCI-
DENT. THE FIRST CLAIMANT FORM IS ATTACHED TO THIS COVER SHEET AS PP.
2 and 3. ADDITIONAL ONES ARE FORM C.

1. CLAIM FILE NO.   2.   CO. CODE   3. ACCIDENT DATE   4. ACCIDENT REPORT DATE

Month	Day	Year

Month	Day	Year

5.   LOCATION OF ACCIDENT   6.   ACCIDENT   7.   NO. OF MOTORIZED
                                      DESCRIPTION   VEHICLES INVOLVED

     (CITY OR TOWN)_____

8.   INSURED VEHICLE   9.   STATE OF REGISTRATION
                                 OF INSURED VEHICLE

Priv. Pass.	Com'l.	Public	Motor-cycle	Bicycle	Other	None
1	2	3	4	5	6	7

10. CITATION - YOUR INSURED   (CIRCLE LOWEST APPLICABLE)

Drunk Driving	Reckless Driving	Hit & Run	Susp. or no License	Speed	Stop or Light	Other Viol.	None Rpt'd.
1	2	3	4	5	6	7	8

11.   POLICY LIMITS
      PER PERSON/   PER ACCIDENT

B.I. $ [   ] $ [   ]

U.M. $ [   ] $ [   ]

MED.
PAY. $ [   ]

CLAIMANT FORM BODILY INJURY -- UNINSURED MOTORIST -- PIP SUBROGATION (RESPONDENT)

2. COMPANY CODE

1. CLAIMANT (SUB-) FILE NO. _____

3. CLAIMANT'S TOWN OR CITY
(IF SUB, PIP CLAIMANT'S TOWN) _____

4. WAS CLAIM MADE?

(IF NO, END FORM HERE)

Yes	No
1	2

5. CLAIM REPORT DATE

Month	Day	Year

6. CLAIM TYPE

BI	UM	SUB
1	2	3

(IF SUB, SKIP TO ITEM 41)

7. AGE

8. OCCUPATION

IDENTIFICATION

9. CLAIMANT STATUS

Driver		Passenger		Pedes-trian	Motor-cyclist	Bi-cyclist	Other
Other Car	Our Car	Other Car	Our Car				
1	2	3	4	5	6	7	8

10. CLAIMANT'S HOUSEHOLD STATUS

Husb.	Wife	Son	Dgtr.	Single Head of Household		Other Rela	
				Male	Female	Male	Fema
1	2	3	4	5	6	7	8

11. CLAIMANT VEHICLE

Priv. Pass.	Com'l.	Public	Motor-cycle	Bi-cycle	Other	None
1	2	3	4	5	6	7

12. CITATION TO CLAIMANT (CIRCLE LOWEST APPLICABLE)

Drunk Driving	Reckless Driving	Hit & Run	Susp. or no License	Speed	Stop or Light	Other Viol.	Nor Rpt
1	2	3	4	5	6	7	8

13. HOW WAS FILE CLOSED?

Payment Was Made	No Payment Was Made Because:							
	Claim Not Pressed	Insured Less than 50% at Fault	No Injury	Loss Under Threshold	NO Policy Coverage	No Right of Action	Defense Verdict	B.I. Released After P.D. Paid
O	1	2	3	4	5	6	7	8

SETTLEMENT

14. GENERAL DAMAGES? (CIRCLE ONE OR MORE)

NO	YES.					
	$500 Medical	Fracture	Body Member	Disfig-urement	Deaf, Blind	Death
1	2	3	4	5	6	7

15. THIS COMPANY'S TOTAL THIRD-PARTY PAYMENTS TO CLAIMANT

$

16. OTHER COMPANY'S TOTAL CO-DEFENDANT CONTRIBU-TION (THIRD-PARTY)

$

17. DATE FINAL PAYMENT TO CLAIMANT; DATE CLOSED, NO PAYMENT

Month	Day	Year

18. CLOSURE TYPE

Rlse.	No Rlse.	Open End Rlse.	Closed No Pymt.
1	2	3	4

19. THIS COMPANY'S INTERIM PAYMENTS

Date of First Payment		
Month	Day	Year

20. AMOUNT OF INTERIM PAY-MENTS (BY THIS COMPANY)

$

21. NO. PAYMENTS EXCLUDING FI PAYMENT (BY THIS COMPANY)

22. ATTORNEY REPRESENTATION AT FINAL SETTLEMENT OR CLOSING

Not Represented	REPRESENTED							
	No Suit		Suit					
	1st Notice from Attny	Attny After 1st Notice	Settled before trial	dis-continued	Settled during trial	Lost	Won	
							Verdict	Liability
1	2	3	4	5	6	7	8	9

23. DATE OF SUIT FIL

Month	Day	Year

(IF CLOSED NO PAYMENT, END FORM HERE)

INJURY AND LOSS

PMANENT INJURY OR DEATH

al	Disability			None
	Perm Total	Perm Partial	Perm. Disfig	
	2	3	4	5

FOR FATALITIES ONLY:

25. NO. OF DEPENDENTS (INCLUDING SPOUSE)

26. AGE OF DEPENDENTS

Spouse	1	2	3

NON-FATAL INJURY CODE (CHECK ONLY ONE PER LINE)

	None	Mult.	Head	Face	Neck	Body	Back	Limb	Other
ure	1	2	3	4	5	6	7	8	9
n	1	2	✕	✕	5	6	7	8	9
e	1	2	3	4	5	6	7	8	9
cic	1	2	3	4	5	6	7	8	9

WAGE LOSS -- HOSPITAL STAY

28. No. of Days Hospitalized

29. No. of Work Days Missed

30. No. of Days of Future Wages Lost (after settlement)

31. Weekly Income $

ECONOMIC LOSS

Medical $

Wages/Income $

Other Economic Loss (Not Pain and Suffering) $

Total $

LOSS OF SERVICES

36. Services Lost

House Wife	Self-Empl.	Other	None
1	2	3	4

37. Days of Replacement Services

·38. Total Cost of Replacement Services $

39. PERCENTAGE REDUCTION FOR COMPARATIVE NEGLIGENCE

_____ %

40. PIP BENEFITS RECEIVED BY CLAIMANT (FROM ANY COMPANY)

$

P.I.P. SUBROGATION

(COMPLETE ONLY IF FINAL PIP 5 WAS RECEIVED)

43. SUBROGATION DECISION

ATE FINAL SUBRO. RE-
UEST RECEIVED (PIP 5)

Month	Day	Year

42. AMOUNT REQUESTED (not incl. handling percentage)

$

Payment Made	No Payment Made			
	Insured Not Legally Liable	Insured Not Covered	Insured's Limits Exhausted	Oth-er
1	2	3	4	S

ARBITRATION

no	yes
1	2

45. DATE PAYMENT MADE OR DENIED

Month	Day	Year

46. AMOUNT PAID (not incl. Handling percentage)

$

(IF THERE IS MORE THAN ONE RE-QUEST FOR SUBROGATION ARISING FROM A SINGLE PIP CLAIM, ENTER THE FIRST ONE IN BOXES, ADDI-TIONAL ONES ALONGSIDE OR ON A BLANK PAGE.)

CHAPTER 6

MASSACHUSETTS NO-FAULT:
A NOTE ON SOME CHANGES IN THE LAW
AND IN RATE LEVELS

Randall Bovbjerg*

On an August day in 1967, the legislators in the Massachusetts House of Representatives broke into applause[1] after they became the first legislative body in the United States to pass a no-fault insurance bill.[2] The bill subsequently died in the Massachusetts Senate under a threat of a veto. Four years later, after an insurance rate freeze, a blue-ribbon commission report, a new governor, and much political jockeying,[3] "personal injury protection" no-fault insurance, known as PIP, made its debut in Massachusetts. What emerged from this process was an insurance industry consensus bill,[4] drafted by the Massachusetts Independent Brokers and Agents Association, that provides much lower benefits for wage and medical loss than had the 1967 bill and that is less restrictive on tort remedies that may still be used.[5] The perceived success and adjudicated constitutionality of PIP[6] encouraged the enactment of a no-fault property damage coverage, Property Protection Insurance, or PPI, which took effect one year later, on January 1, 1972.[7] Since then, additional modifications of the statutory no-fault schemes have been made,[8] but the basic no-fault concept for personal injuries remains in place.

*Research Attorney, Program on Legal Issues in Health Care, Duke Law School. Associate Director, Massachusetts No-Fault Auto Insurance Study, from 1971-73. A.B., 1968, University of Chicago; J.D., 1971, Harvard Law School. The author is indebted to Professor David F. Cavers for editorial advice and assistance.

1. Interview in 1971 with the then ex-Representative in the Massachusetts Legislature, now Governor, Michael S. Dukakis.

2. R. Keeton & J. O'Connell, BASIC PROTECTION FOR THE TRAFFIC VICTIM (1965).

3. P. Gillespie & M. Klipper, NO-FAULT: WHAT YOU SAVE, GAIN, AND LOSE WITH THE NEW AUTO INSURANCE 37-55 (1972). This account, though undocumented and argumentative, makes the best presentation of events relating to the enactment of the Massachusetts law. See also Rafalowitz, *The Massachusetts "No-Fault" Automobile Insurance Law: An Analysis and Proposed Revision,* 8 Harv. J. Legis. 455, 460-63 (1971).

4. P. Gillespie & M. Klipper, *supra* note 3, at 49.

5. A Massachusetts auto accident victim may sue for special damages (medical, wage, and other economic losses) not paid by the $2,000 PIP coverage and for general damages (pain and suffering) if the injury (a) necessitated medical bills exceeding $500, (b) was a fracture or loss of a body member, or (c) resulted in loss of sight or hearing, in permanent and serious disfigurement, or in death. Mass. Gen. Laws Ann. ch. 231, Section 6D (Supp. 1975). The Keeton-O'Connell coverage was $10,000, but pain and suffering were recoverable in tort only in excess of $5,000, so insurers were required to offer an optional no-fault "pain and inconvenience" coverage. R. Keeton & J. O'Connell, *supra* note 2, at 283, 274-75, 285-86.

6. Pinnick v. Cleary, 360 Mass. 1, 271 N.E. 2d 592 (1971).

7. Mass. Gen. Laws Ann. ch. 90 Section 340 (Supp. 1975).

8. Changes have resulted both from legislative and administrative actions. For example, a 1973 amendment, effective Jan. 1, 1975, allowed subrogation among PPI insurers of Massachusetts drivers. Mass. Gen. Laws Ann. ch. 90, Section 340 (Supp. 1975); and Insurance Commissioner John G. Ryan exempted motorcyclists from PIP.

Massachusetts has a long history of very expensive auto insurance. Its bodily injury claims frequency (claims per hundred insureds) was traditionally not merely the country's highest, but fully three times the national average.[9] It is not surprising, therefore, that from the beginning, the Massachusetts no-fault debate has centered on questions of auto insurance premiums and rating. Pocketbook issues were the mainspring of reformist sentiment; concern for prompt claims payment, reduced tort litigation, and other hoped-for no-fault benefits was distinctly secondary.

In 1967, having rejected no-fault, the legislature did respond to the immediate reform pressures by prohibiting increases in premiums for the compulsory bodily injury liability insurance.[10] The rate freeze not only saved motorists money, but also motivated insurers to take the lead in the quest for a viable no-fault plan.

A special insurance commission was created in April, 1968, to make over-all reform recommendations. A majority report in January 1970 presented six proposals but none offered significant relief or commanded a consensus; in fact, no fewer than five minority reports were filed.[11] In the 1970 gubernatorial campaign, no-fault automobile insurance, endorsed in both party platforms and by many news media, became a major issue, with the question of rate savings holding center stage. To the PIP bill introduced early in the session, the legislature tacked on two popular amendments—one making insurance virtually noncancellable and the other mandating a 15 percent cut in all auto insurance rates, not just those under PIP. As many of their proponents doubtless hoped, these provisions caused insurer support for the measure to evaporate rapidly, and a number of the larger companies threatened to leave the state altogether unless the bill were vetoed.[12]

Despite this threat, Governor (and Republican candidate) Francis W. Sargent signed the bill on August 13, 1970, in the full glare of campaign publicity and television lights, then charged the legislature to make the PIP package more palatable. Revisions, passed only 11 days later, watered down the noncancellability provision, but left untouched the 15 percent across-the-board rate cut.[13] A group of insurance companies sued to invalidate it, the governor was returned to office, and emergency preparations were made behind the scenes for a state-run insurance pool.[14] Only a few days after the election, on November 9, 1970, the Massachusetts Supreme Judicial Court held the rate reduction unconstitutional as to all property coverages.[15] This assured continued availability of insurance coverage, but considerably lower rate savings.

9. Data suplied by the Insurance Information Institute, Boston, Mass.

10. P. Gillespie & M. Klipper, *supra* note 3, at 41.

11. *Id.* at 44.

12. *The Boston Globe,* Aug. 14, 1970, at 1, col. 5 (hereinafter cited as *"Globe"* or *"Evening Globe"*).

13. Act of Aug. 23, 1970, ch. 744, [1970]. Mass. Acts & Resolves ch. 610, codified in Mass. Gen. Laws, Ann. ch. 1975. Sections 22E, H.(Supp. 1975).

14. Interview in 1973 with then Insurance Comm'r John G. Ryan. See also P. Gillespie & M. Klipper, *supra* note 3, at 55.

15. Aetna Casualty & Surety Co. v. Comm'r of Insurance, 358 Mass. 272, 263 N.E. 2d 698 (1970).

PIP thus took effect with the mandated reduction applying to bodily injury coverages, including no-fault. Though the rate savings were pegged at 15 percent, PIP's exact impact on premiums is difficult to quantify. For one thing, the state's 15 rating districts—each composed of areas with roughly equal loss experience and charged equivalent premiums—were reshuffled just as PIP took effect, and two-thirds of the towns and cities moved into higher brackets.[16] Similar district realignments continued in later years. Comparison is also made difficult because there was no precise equivalent to PIP before 1971. Moreover, individuals' actual premium charges vary widely, reflecting such factors as drivers' age, commuting distance and model of car. Consequently, year-to-year rate comparisons are probably best made with aggregate or average figures. Furthermore, the change in a motorist's insurance expense was only partly a function of PIP. Premium increases in 1971 on non-PIP coverages (the bulk of insurance costs) counteracted PIP's reductions.[17]

The rating picture was further clouded by another court decision, invalidating the 1970 rate freeze as unconstitutionally confiscatory.[18] This meant that the immediately pre-PIP rates were artificially low as a result of the 1970 rate freeze. Hence an appropriate comparison between 1970 and 1971 rates is not with any actual change in those rates (the journalistic and political focus), but rather with the reduction in 1971 rates from what compulsory rates should have been in 1970. It is generally conceded that the frozen rates were 20-30 percent too low,[19] so that PIP in fact probably achieved rate savings on the order of 35-45 percent in its first year.

Even so, the 1971 rates turned out to be too high. They had been computed under the erroneous assumptions that (a) claims would rise 30 percent because fault was no longer a prerequisite and (b) payouts would not be dissimilar to those made under the fault system.[20] In actuality, both factors turned out to be substantially lower under PIP.

In Massachusetts, auto insurance rates are set by the Insurance Commissioner on an industry-wide basis after hearings on the insurers' requests for the upcoming year's rates. These rates then become the fixed price for all companies doing business in the state, except for occasional year-end rebates by some mutuals. This lack of rate competition is sometimes cited as another reason for Massachusetts' high premiums. Steps to allow some competition did not come until early 1974[21]—much later in the no-fault saga.

In the fall of 1971, even the insurance companies acknowledged that 1972 PIP rates should be lower than 1971's—by 18.5 percent.[22] Governor Sargent pushed for a 27.6 percent decrease, and ex-Representative, now-Governor Michael S. Dukakis, the sponsor of

16. See P. Gillespie & M. Klipper, *supra* note 3, at 103.

17. *Id.* at 95.

18. Insurance Rating Bd. v. Comm'r of Insurance, 359 Mass. 111, 268 N.E. 2d 144 (1971).

19. See McNary, "No-Fault P.D.", *Insurance Advocate* 3 (Mar. 4, 1972). Another useful comparison would be between the actual rates for 1971 and the rates which should have been set for 1971 if the fault system had continued.

20. P. Gillespie & M. Klipper, *supra* note 3, at 98-99.

21. *Globe,* Jan. 16, 1974, at 1.

22. *Globe,* Nov. 5, 1971, at 1.

the original no-fault proposal, testified in favor of a 50 percent cut.[23] After extensive rate hearings in November, 1970, Insurance Commissioner John G. Ryan determined that the 1971 PIP coverage had been overpriced and ordered both prospective and retrospective adjustments.[24] Rates for 1972 were reduced by 27.6 percent and the insurers ordered to provide a 35 percent reserve for the rebate of overpayments of 1971 PIP premiums, the actual rebate being set later at 25.9 percent.[25] The reserve for rebates withstood constitutional attack by the insurers.[26]

For the next four years, the PIP rate showed further small declines, despite considerable wage and medical price inflation that affected the cost of benefits paid. The statewide average dropped from $40.23 in 1972 to $39.54 for 1973 and 1974 and to $36.10 in 1975.[27] Rates for 1976 showed only a 2 percent rise for bodily injury coverage,[28] though insurers are now suing for higher rates.[29] Statewide averages conceal more dramatic changes in high-rate districts and for high-risk classes of policyholders. Thus, in Boston, drivers over 25 enjoyed a rate decline from $99 in 1971 to $45 in 1975 while the rates for under-25 male owners with no driver training fell from $318 to $146.[30] Moreover, if a rate index were constructed taking the state wide average premium in 1951 as 100, the index would have reached 239.5 in 1967 when rates were frozen. Projected from 1967 to 1975 on a straightline basis, the rate index would have reached 310. Projected on a 6 percent curve to 1975, it would have climbed to 404.5. Instead, thanks to no-fault, it had fallen to 131.[31]

Of course, a report of Massachusetts insurance rating requires a look at the other side of the premium coin—claims experience, the frequency and average amount of claims paid. In PIP's immediate aftermath, it was obvious that both bodily injury claims frequency and amount had declined drastically. However, early estimates had to rely on incomplete data and suffered from lack of knowledge of how large and how long the "tail" of later or deferred claims payments would be,[32] especially since claims in larger cases are expected to be entered more slowly than smaller ones.[33] Later tabulations continued to

23. *Globe,* Nov. 13, 1971, at 5.

24. *Globe,* Dec. 15, 1971, at 1.

25. Comm'r of Insurance, Opinion, Finding and Order, Dec. 13, 1971; *id.* Oct. 11, 1972. With interest, the rebate came to 27.6%. For authorization of the orders, see Mass. Acts & Res. 1971, ch. 977.

26. Employers' Commercial Union Ins. Co. v. Comm'r of Insurance, 362 Mass. 34, 283 N.E. 2d 849 (1972); *Globe,* June 6, 1972, at 1.

27. Supplement to Statement of R.E. Keeton before the Massachusetts State Commission on Insurance, Hearings on H.R. 1272 and other bills, July 23, 1975, Exhib. 4 (hereinafter cited as Keeton Statement) (data supplied by Massachusetts Automobile Rating and Accident Prevention Bureau).

28. *New York Times,* Jan. 24, 1976, at 22, col. 7.

29. *Globe,* Jan. 20, 1976, at 35.

30. Keeton Statement, *supra* note 27, Exhib. 2.

31. *Id.* Exhib. 3.

32. A survey by the Massachusetts Insurance Department of PIP and BI Liability claims paid in the first nine months of 1971 showed a 51.5% decline from 1970 in BI paid claims. See also *Globe,* Nov. 16, 1971 at 1, (total claims, paid and incurred, down 34%).

33. The average cost per claim dropped 60.6%—from $419 in 1970 to only $165 in 1971. *Id.*

show a marked drop in claims frequency (both paid and incurred). From 134,000 claims in 1970, the number of bodily injury claims fell to only 77,000 in 1971.[34] Claims figures for 1973 show 63,000; for 1974, 59,000.[35] Claims paid and incurred are similarly down—from about $113 million in 1970 to $56 million in 1971, $55 million in 1973, and $52 million in 1974.[36] Thus the total savings seems to be on the order of 50 percent—roughly equal, not to the actual reductions under PIP from 1970 rates, but to the drop from what those rates would have been but for the unconstitutional pre-PIP rate freeze.

Property damage rates have had a very different history. From the beginning, PPI has failed to duplicate the premium savings of PIP, whose "no-fault" label it shares. The first year of PPI, 1972, saw no-fault property damage rates rise an average of about 10 percent above the 1971 levels,[37] though Insurance Department figures showed that nine of ten motorists would have had to pay a higher premium without PPI—because increases would have been still greater had the fault system been continued.[38]

Actually, any expectation of rate reductions comparable to those achieved by PIP would have been unrealistic since PPI, unlike PIP, could not achieve such savings as reduced payments for pain and suffering. Its chief attraction from the motorist's standpoint was that PPI allowed him to adapt his insurance coverage to his needs, while insulating him from tort liability for property damage negligently inflicted on another Massachusetts motor vehicle. For damage sustained by his own vehicle, the car owner was offered three options:[39] Option 1, essentially first-party collision insurance; Option 2, recovery for damage shown by the insured to have been caused by the fault of an identified driver—the recovery to be from the insured's own insurer; and Option 3, self-insurance coupled with the requirement, also applicable to the other two options, of $5,000 in property damage liability insurance covering damage not exempt from tort liability, such as damage in Massachusetts to out-of-state motor vehicles and to non-vehicular property.[40]

Option 1, offered with $50 and $100 deductibles, was appealing to those auto owners for whom their cars represented important investments; Option 2, with the same deductibles, protected against some fault-caused damage, at a much lower cost; and Option 3, for a still lower cost, permitted the owner of the aging car—and the owner in a high tax

34. The data, which have been rounded, are from Massachusetts Automobile Rating and Accident Prevention Bureau, Memorandum No. 5, "Development of Compulsory Coverage A Losses" (Aug. 1975). Coverage A includes both PIP and personal liability for injuries not covered by PIP within the prescribed $5,000—$10,000 limits.

35. *Id.*

36. *Id.* The data must be read with a view to the fact that each year the number of claims and the amounts paid and incurred alter as new claims are filed and claims already filed are dropped. Thus, the 1970 data are drawn from the 5th annual report on that year's claims; and 1971 data, from the 4th report on 1971 claims; 1973 data, from the 2nd report on 1973 claims; and 1974 data, from the 1st report on 1974 claims. The shrinkage from year to year in a given year's claims is not inconsiderable and, of course, serves to accentuate the post-PIP drop in claims.

37. P. Gillespie & M. Klipper, *supra* note 3, at 107.

38. *Evening Globe,* Jan. 28, 1972, at 1; *Globe,* Jan. 29, 1972, at 1.

39. Mass. Gen. Laws Ann. ch. 90, Section 340 (Supp. 1975).

40. *Id.* at par. 2.

bracket—to take his chances with other Massachusetts vehicles.

There was a small increase in the statewide average rate for property liability coverage for 1972 which was largely offset by a decrease for 1973. Small increases in collision coverage occurred in 1972, when Option 1 began, and in 1973, but none in 1974. There were no changes in Option 2 from 1972 through 1974.[41] In 1973, however, an amendment was adopted which sharply altered the basic nature of the law.[42] Effective January 1, 1975, the amendment granted subrogation rights to property damage insurers, to be enforced by compulsory arbitration. Even though in theory the tort exemption remained, an Option 1 or Option 2 insurer, who, as a first-party insurer, had paid a claim resulting, in its investigator's opinion, from the other driver's negligence, could claim against that driver's property damage insurer. Moreover, this statutory subrogation was extended to claims of damage caused by Option 3 insureds.

This amendment brought the fault principle back into property damage insurance. Its most serious impact was on Option 3. Because the compulsory property damage liability insurance now had to protect against these new subrogation claims at a time when repair costs were escalating,[43] its cost (on a statewide average basis) rose 165.3 percent in 1975 and 10.1 percent more in 1976.[44] In dollar terms, its statewide average cost rose to $46.51, a modest sum compared to its cost in high-risk districts. Morever, the ability of Option 1 and Option 2 insurers to allocate some of their losses by subrogation to compulsory property damage insurance meant reductions in the rates for those options. As a result, even after the sharp increase in compulsory property damage rates, insureds under Options 1 and 2 had net increases on a statewide basis in 1975 which reached 10 percent in only one category.

In these circumstances, Option 3 became meaningless; Option 2 (premiums for which had plummeted) cost only $3.00 additional on a statewide average basis. As a result of a shift to Option 2, losses that Option 3 would have met by self-insurance have thus come into the insurance system, amounting to between $20 and $30 million in terms of premiums, according to a knowledgeable estimator. Moreover, not only does the insurer have to meet the administrative costs of subrogation, but its incentive to hold down claims is diminished where it can pass on the losses to other insurers. The insured, of course, will always elect the most complete restoration of accident damage when he does not have to meet the bill.

Rapidly rising property damage claims, not merely under PPI but under "comprehensive" (fire and theft) coverage as well-reflected in a statewide average rate increase of

41. For these data, see Keeton Statement, *supra* note 27, Exhib. 4.

42. Mass. Gen. Laws Ann. ch. 90, Section 340 (Supp. 1975). Claims, if not settled, must be resolved by arbitration. *Id.*

43. "How It Works in Massachusetts," *U.S. News & World Reports,* Jan. 3, 1972, at 29; *Boston Herald Advertiser,* July 13, 1975, at A1.

44. For the 1975 data, see Keeton Statement, *supra* note 27, Exhib. 4. Data for 1976 were supplied by letter from Mr. L.H. Devers, Mgr., Massachusetts Automobile Rating and Accident Prevention Bureau, dated March 25, 1976.

Data on rates and costs in the remainder of this paragraph and the next are from the same sources.

38.6 percent in 1975[45] —brought the situation to a crisis. The insurance industry reacted in August, 1975, with a mammoth proposal to increase aggregate premiums by about one-third—$244 million over the 1975 total of about $600 million, mainly for property damage coverages.[46] Bodily injury (including the no-fault coverage) accounted for only $59 million of the rise sought. The counter-reaction was swift. Legislation raised property damage deductibles to $200 and made other changes[47] that cut the proposed increase approximately in half, though an additional upward adjustment brought the total request up to $186 million.[48] The new Insurance Commissioner, James M. Stone, however, allowed only a $76 million rise for property damage, of which only $33 million was attributable to PPI—a 10 -12 percent rise.[49] Early in 1976, insurers announced that they would seek further increases in court.[50] They had backed away from earlier predictions that insufficient rates would force them to cease doing business in the state.[51]

The seeming need for very much higher property damage premiums has been laid at the door of the PPI no-fault coverage, and a serious legislative repeal campaign is under way. It is noteworthy, however, that the dissatisfaction does not seem to focus on the no-fault concept *per se,* since no-fault as applied to bodily injury is not challenged. The costliness of the retreat from the no-fault principle by the subrogation amendment which undermined Option 3 is little recognized, but other features of the 1970's insurance reforms are seen as trouble-makers. Policies are more difficult to cancel,[52] and bad risks remain in the overall rates through the assigned risk pool.[53] Insurers must pay property claims within 15 days and so have little time or incentive to investigate them beforehand.[54] Property damage must be paid for whether or not the damage is actually repaired.[55] Finally, "totaled" cars must be paid for at book value, rather than market value.[56] Thus a stolen battered-up car (not repaired with previous insurance payments) may yield a profit to the owner; at best this is a disincentive to prudent theft-consciousness and at worse an inducement to fraudulent connivance in theft or fire.

Hostility to PPI prompted the legislature to create, in early 1976, a Special Commission on Auto Insurance Reform, on which some industry and public representatives sit with its legislator members. However, before any Commission report has been received, it seems likely that legislative action will have preempted the Commission's function. On

45. *Id.*

46. *Globe,* Sept. 23, 1975, at 24.

47. Mass. Acts & Res. ch. 707 (Nov. 26, 1975), amending Mass. Gen. Laws Ann., ch. 90, Section 340 and ch. 175, Sections 113B, 113C, 113H, 1130 (Supp. 1975).

48. *Globe,* Dec. 2, 1975, at 1.

49. *Globe,* Dec. 31, 1975, at 1.

50. *Globe,* Jan. 20, 1976, at 35.

51. *Globe,* Dec. 4, 1975, at 3.

52. The first law restricting cancellation, Mass. Acts & Res. 1970, ch. 670, led to such strong industry complaint that it was repealed and a less drastic measure substituted in the same session. *id.* ch. 744, adding Sections 22E-22H to Mass. Gen. Laws Ann., ch. 175 (Supp. 1975).

53. For the assigned risk pool plan, see *id.* ch. 90, Section 34N, ch. 175, Section 113H.

54. *Id.,* ch. 90, Section 340, par. 5.

55. *Id.* at par. 3.

56. Mass. Acts & Res. 1973, ch. 630, Section 1.

April 21, 1976, Governor Dukakis outlined a set of proposals designed to preserve a revised property damage no-fault law,[57] and on May 18, the co-chairman of the Joint Committee on Insurance (who also co-chaired the Special Commission) announced the measures they plan to introduce to supersede property damage no-fault.[58]

The principal features of the Governor's recommendations are (1) merit rating, basing property damage insurance rates on fault; (2) as determined under objective standards watched over by a Motor Vehicle Board of Appeals; (3) mandatory first-party insurance to be preserved, with settlements required within 15 business days, but subrogation to be abolished and actual market value substituted for book value for stolen and "totaled" cars; (4) law enforcement against auto thefts to be tightened; and (5) insurers to pay repair shops directly only after repairs have been made and the deductible has been certified as paid, unless the insured retains the privilege of receiving cash by paying a substantially higher premium.

The Joint Committee's proposals, which counsel to the Governor has characterized as "a good package, basically,"[59] have, as their principal features, (1) a rough-hewn form of merit rating, prescribing dollar surcharges on insurance premiums to penalize specified driving convictions;[60] (2) a retention of the $5,000 compulsory property liability insurance; (3) the required offering of an optional first-party insurance, with no deductibles, for negligent damage to the insured's auto, provided the insured can identify the other party and was himself found less than half at fault;[61] (4) rights of subrogation preserved for first-party insurers without the compulsory arbitration now required; (5) auto repair shops may exceed original estimates only with "the oral or written" consent of the insured and must join with him in certifying that any deductible amount was actually paid; (6) mandatory jail sentences for second and third auto theft convictions;[62] and (7) open competition in insurance rate-making, with some regulatory authority power in the In-

---

57. Governor Dukakis, appearing before the Special Commission on Automobile Insurance, outlined his proposals in a statement released on April 21, 1976. The released statement was accompanied by a two-page summary of twenty specific recommendations for legislative action. For an incomplete summary of his proposals, see *Globe,* April 22, 1976, at 3.

58. For incomplete summaries of the Joint Committee proposals, see *Globe,* May 19, 1976, at 1; *Boston Herald-American,* May 19, 1976, at 3.

59. See *Globe, supra* note 58, at 1.

60. The surcharge for a drunken driving conviction is $200; for driving to endanger, $100; for accidents due to insured's fault, $50. The Insurance Commissioner may set additional surcharges for repeated offenses. See *Herald-American, supra* note 58.

61. This coverage resembles Option 2 under the present law except that, under the latter, waiver of deductibles and of comparative negligence increased the premium. Presumably, insurers under the proposed plan may also offer this coverage without waivers for a lower premium.

62. The same provisions—7-day sentences for juveniles, 60 days for adults—appear in a Judicial Committee bill. Since Massachusetts is probably the most advanced state in doing away with detention for Juveniles and since its jails for adults are already overcrowded, one wonders how such a provision would be implemented.

surance Commissioner to check abuses.[64]

The Joint Committee's statement warned motorists not to expect "immediate, dramatic reductions" in premiums,[64] a caution that seems more clearly justified than its hope that rates could begin to stabilize for good drivers by 1977. An amendment allowing insurers to pay market value for stolen or "totaled" cars would strengthen the package, but even an improved bill seems unlikely to stem the tide of increasing property damage premiums. Their share of the state's auto insurance bill has moved, as Governor Dukakis noted, from "roughly the same total" as that of bodily injury in 1970 to $700 million of 1976's $900 million total.[65]

If the bill is enacted as proposed, it will be interesting to observe its impact on the Massachusetts courts. If optional first-party coverage were to attract a high proportion of motorists, the present low level of property damage actions might well continue, absent a marked increase in inter-insurer suits. But with all Massachusetts drivers carrying $5,000 in compulsory property insurance coverage to pay third-party tort claims, motorists might well shrink from assuming the extra expense of the first-party coverage, despite its advantages. If so, property damage actions may return in volume to the courts.[66]

Before no-fault, all Bodily Injury claimants were able to seek compensation for pain and suffering. It is widely supposed that such awards also helped pay for property damage, for which there was then no compulsory insurance.[67] Compulsory property damage no-fault failed in large measure because, at least in the Massachusetts context and in diluted form, it could not hold down rates by reducing claims or containing motorists' desire to pass on to insurers the soaring costs of auto repair. If the revised coverages and other remedial tactics proposed by the Joint Committee (and largely embodied in the final legislation [68]) also prove ineffective, their failure might in time lead to a strict form of no-fault property coverage.

63. Since insurance companies are now suing to set aside the 1976 rate structure, the success of competition in bringing down rates seems problematical. The Insurance Commissioner and the Governor's counsel are reported as skeptical. See *Globe, supra* note 58.

64. *Id.*

65. The data and quotation are from Governor Dukakis's statement, *supra* note 57.

66. After PIP went into effect, both Superior and District Courts experienced sharp drops in the number of entries claiming damages for both bodily injury and property damage, but a slight rise occurred in cases claiming PD damages only. See Bovbjerg, *The Impact of No-Fault Auto Insurance on Massachusetts Courts,* 11 N.E.L. Rev. 325, 343-48 (1976). After PPI, cases alleging property damage, with or without bodily injury, in post-PPI accidents fell 91.8% in a large Middlesex County District Court and 88.5% in the Middlesex County Superior Court. *Id.* at 350-51.

67. *See, e.g.*, P. Gillespie & M. Klipper, *supra* note 3, at 38. This does not mean that all or most pre-no-fault property damage was covered *sub rosa* as bodily injury. Indeed, fully half of the 1970 premium dollar went to PD liability or collision coverages. *Id.* at 94, 107.

68. See the following Addendum by Professor David F. Cavers on the 1976 AMENDMENTS TO THE MASSACHUSETTS NO-FAULT AUTOMOBILE INSURANCE ACT.

ADDENDUM

THE 1976 AMENDMENTS
TO THE
MASSACHUSETTS NO-FAULT AUTOMOBILE INSURANCE ACT

The Act Relative to Motor Vehicle Insurance, signed by Governor Dukakis on August 4, 1976, became effective immediately as Ch. 266 of the Acts of 1976, but its provisions relating to the issuance of insurance policies apply to policies issued to become effective January 1, 1977. This summary does not purport to be complete, and its arrangement does not follow the Act's.

Section 7 substitutes a new Section 34 *O*, the section providing for property damage insurance. Compulsory property liability insurance up to $5,000 is retained, and every insurer issuing such policies must also offer collision coverage and limited collision coverage.

1. *Collision Coverage.* The insurer is to pay either to the insured (or to a repair shop if the insured so indicates in writing) collision losses to the insured vehicle, subject to a $200 deductible, up to its "actual cash value," the benefits to be payable without regard to "fault of any kind." As a condition to continuing such coverage in effect after paying "total damage," the insurer may require that the vehicle pass a safety inspection test. The insurer shall also provide a no-deductible coverage, without regard to the comparative negligence of the insured not exceeding 50% for cases like those described below.

2. *Limited Collision Coverage.* This follows Option 2 in the repealed law covering damage to the insured vehicle, subject to a $200 deductible and without regard to the operator's comparative negligence not in excess of 50%. Four cases are covered, all involving identified operators. (a) The insured is entitled to recover in tort, taking "all steps necessary to preserve the insurer's right of subrogation." (b) Damage caused to the insured vehicle while parked. (c) Damage caused when the insured vehicle is struck in the rear by another vehicle moving in the same direction. (d) Damage caused by a vehicle operated at the time by a person convicted of operating under the influence of alcohol or a narcotic, driving down a one-way street, operating at an excessive rate of speed, or "of any similar violation of the law of any other state." Recovery is barred if the insured operator is also convicted of like violations when the damage was incurred.

The insured may recover regardless of whether he could have recovered in tort against another. The insurer paying for total damage may require the safety test noted above. An option must be offered permitting a $100 deductible. This may be refused on the basis of the insured's accident or driving record but not "because of age, sex, race, occupation or principal place of garaging." Other provisions relate to coverages with no deductibles and higher deductibles.

Insurers are forbidden to make payment under either collision coverage until receipt of a claim form stating that the repair work described in an appraisal has been completed. Payment must be made within 7 days after receipt of the form, unreasonable refusals exposing the insurer to double damages and attorneys' fees. If the insured elects not to repair the vehicle, the insurer shall decrease the actual cash value by the amount of the damage. A claimant may bring an action for a property damage liability claim or a limited collision claim against the tortfeasor.

Section 18 amends Ch. 175 by substituting a new Section 113 *O* and adding a new Section 113 *P*.

3. *Fire and Theft Coverage.* The new Section 113 *O* provides that all fire and theft (or comprehensive) coverages shall pay for loss or damage to the insured vehicle up to its actual cash value less a $200 deductible (for which a $100 deductible may be substituted) unless refused solely on "the basis of claims paid." No deductible shall apply to damage to glass. Provision for higher valuations shall be made if the insurer may inspect the vehicle. Payment on a claim for theft coverage shall not be made until the police receive a sworn statement from the insured relating to the theft. Provisions with respect to repair work and to an election not to repair parallel those for the collision coverages.

Merit Rating

Section 113 *P* provides for the establishment of a merit rating plan by the commissioner of insurance after hearing. Surcharges are prescribed for negligence exceeding 50% of the cause of an accident and on account of convictions of moving violations. The first surchargeable accident in a 3-year period costs $50. Additional surcharges for first convictions are specified below:

(a) $200—operating while under the influence of intoxicating liquor, marijuana or narcotic drugs, depressant or stimulating substances. This is payable even though the person charged has been assigned to a driver alcohol education program.

(b) $100—operating a motor vehicle recklessly, or negligently to endanger.

(c) $25—speeding and other moving traffic violations.

Surcharges for additional accidents and convictions shall be established in the merit rating plan. A driver's policy is charged if the actual driver is one who is "authorized to drive" or "customarily drives" the insured vehicle.

Credits shall be established for accident-and-conviction-free insureds. All "surcharges collected are credited to insureds entitled to credits pursuant to a formula promulgated by the commissioner" of insurance.

Certain accidents will be presumed not to be based on fault: damage to a parked car; insured's car struck from rear; damage by "flying gravel, missiles or falling objects"; and an accident caused by a hit-and-run driver if the insured reports to the police within 48 hours.

The insurer shall determine whether an insured should be surcharged for fault in excess of 50%. An aggrieved insured may complain within 30 days to a board of appeals which, if it denies the complaint, thereby gives the insured a right to a hearing. If, after hearing, the board finds the surcharge does not comply with its standards, it shall order the surcharge vacated. Any person aggrieved by a board order may appeal to the superior court in the complainant's county. The court shall give a summary hearing and affirm or reverse the board's order. Its decision shall be final.

Section 1 inserts in Ch. 6 a new Section 182 captioned "Motor Vehicle Insurance Rating Board". This creates within the registry of motor vehicles a board composed of the registrar, as chairman, the commissioner of insurance, and the attorney general. The board shall appoint a director and shall formulate a plan for the collection of all data pertaining to motor vehicle accidents, policy claims, and violations needed for the implementation and operation of merit rating. The board and insurance companies doing business in Massachusetts shall have access to criminal record information, the board to aid in developing its plan, the companies for information as to motor vehicle violations. Both must comply with the regulations of the criminal history systems board. The board's expenses shall be apportioned among the companies.

Section 3 amends Ch. 12 of the General Laws by adding, *inter alia,* Section 11 *F* authorizing the attorney general to intervene on behalf of any group of consumers in matters involving rates and charges by any insurance company doing business in Massachusetts.

Insurance Rate Regulation

Section 19 amends the General Laws by striking out Ch. 175 *E* and inserting a new chapter, "Regulation of Rates for Motor Vehicle Insurance." This chapter is almost half the length of the rest of the Act and its summarization here is impracticable except in the most general terms. The chapter represents a sharp departure from its predecessor which implemented provisions by which the commissioner of insurance set motor vehicle rates for the industry. The new law sets broad standards with which rates must comply and factors which must be taken into account. The commissioner, however, shall establish a classification of risks including a designation of at least 15 territories.

The commissioner, after hearing, may determine that, for any territory or class of insurance, competition is either "(i) insufficient to assure that rates will not be excessive" or "(ii) so conducted as to be destructive of competition or detrimental to the solvency of insurers," he may fix the relevant rates for a period of not more than one year which may be renewed.

Extensive provisions are designed to prevent any insurer or rating organization from monopolizing or attempting to monopolize or combine or conspire with any other person to monopolize the business of insurance or any part thereof.

Insurers and rating organizations acting for them are required to file their manuals of classifications, rules and rates, rating plans and modifications thereof at least 45 days before their effective dates. The commissioner may, and shall on the motion of the attorney general, order a hearing on any such filing, suspending it for 45 days. He may either approve or disapprove, but the premiums may be allowed to go into effect under bond.

The commissioner may once a year set rules for the production by the companies of information guides outlining in approved language the various coverages available to consumers and their approximate differences in cost. A guide must be forwarded to every person insured or solicited by a company.

Violations of the chapter are punishable by a fine of not over $10,000 for each offense or by up to one year's imprisonment, or both, or subject to a civil penalty of not over $1,000 for each offense (the issuance or negotiation of a single policy being an offense) in an action brought by the commonwealth.

The supreme judicial court for the county of Suffolk (namely, a single justice of the state's supreme court) has jurisdiction to enforce and to review all orders of the commissioner.

Assigned Risk Plan

Section 15, amending Ch. 175, Section 113 *H*, sets up a "governing committee" appointed from insurance companies and from associations of insurance producers to prepare and administer a reinsurance plan for assigned risks. The same section is further amended by Section 16 to deny insurers the right to issue motor vehicle policies unless they participate in an approved plan. The rates filed under the plan for "risks with no accidents based on fault" exceeding 50% or "convictions of moving violations of motor vehicle laws in the most recent three year period shall approximate as closely as the commissioner approves the rate levels used. . .for such risks not insured in the plan." The plan's rules shall forbid increases in the percentage of policyholders reinsured in the plan by territory "over the percentage reinsured as of" January 1, 1976. The commissioner may relieve companies threatened with insolvency by continuation of the plan's obligations.

Procedure for Small Property Damage Claims

Section 20 amends Section 21 of Ch. 218 by authorizing the chief justice of the district courts to make rules providing for "a simple, informal and inexpensive procedure" to determine contract or tort claims not exceeding $400 except that the "said dollar limitation shall not apply in an action for property damage caused by a motor vehicle and for a review of judgments upon such claims."

Section 21 amends the same section to provide, *inter alia,* that, for hearing claims for property damage by a motor vehicle, the procedure shall provide for all such claims to be heard one evening every other week and on one Saturday in the alternate weeks, unless the parties agree otherwise. Section 23 provides that, if any such action is removed to the district court by the insurer and the unpaid party recovers judgment, the insurer shall also be assessed costs and reasonable attorney's fees.

Towing, Salvaging, and Crushing Operations

Section 5 adds a new Section 246 to Ch. 90, forbidding the removal of an abandoned or stolen motor vehicle from a public way or place without the owner's consent or the written permission of the police. A tow vehicle must be licensed specifically for towing service. A salvage yard or junk yard must obtain a bill of sale or title from such a vehicle's owner, to be surrendered to the registrar of motor vehicles within 3 days.

Owners of machines designed to crush motor vehicles must list the machine with the registry and before destroying any motor vehicle, the machine owner must remove its identification number for submission to the registrar. A salvage or junk yard selling crushed or mutilated motor vehicles for reprocessing must submit the identification number and plate to the registry. Transports are to carry lists of vehicles transported, copies along with identification plates to be sent to the registry.

Upon convictions of violations of these sections, any related licenses shall be forfeited and offenders punished by fines of not less than $1,000 or imprisonment for not less than two years, or both.

David F. Cavers
Professor of Law, Emeritus

Harvard Law School

PART II
THE FLORIDA STUDY

JOSEPH W. LITTLE
Director

CHAPTER 7

NO-FAULT AUTO REPARATION IN FLORIDA: AN EMPIRICAL EXAMINATION OF SOME OF ITS EFFECTS

Editor's Note: Reproduced from *University of Michigan Journal of Law Reform,*
Volume 9, Fall 1975, Number 1.

NO-FAULT AUTO REPARATION IN FLORIDA:
AN EMPIRICAL EXAMINATION OF
SOME OF ITS EFFECTS

Joseph W. Little*

SUMMARY OF RESULTS

Any useful evaluation of the no-fault concept must test whether or not programs such as the Florida Automobile Reparations Reform Act accomplish the goals claimed for them before their enactments. Ordinarily, these goals will be to correct alleged deficiencies in the predecessor reparations systems. In a simple system in which everything else remained constant, testing whether success had been achieved would be easy. One would merely measure specified parameters before the reform measure was introduced and compare these baseline measurements to measurements made afterwards. In Florida of the early 1970's, however, nothing remained constant. The population was burgeoning as was the number of motor vehicles on the highways (rising from 5,360,302 registered vehicles in 1971 to 6,382,298 in 1973). Furthermore, this was a period of extreme inflation in the United States and Florida and of rapidly advancing medical costs, it was a period in which shortages of petroleum-based energy supplies first had tangible effects on the incidence of motor vehicle crashes, and it was a period that saw major revisions in Florida's court structure. In sum, no-fault was introduced into the midst of substantial general change, making it extremely difficult to establish baselines for comparative measurement. In such periods, comparisons must be made between what occurred under the no-fault plan and what would have occurred had the superseded system remained in effect. Thus, for example, in comparing insurance costs one must ask what the difference is between no-fault costs and costs as they would have been had there been no change, instead of asking what the difference is between no-fault costs and costs as they were before no-fault came into effect.

To evaluate Florida's no-fault system, five hypotheses were posited and tested for validity. These hypotheses and the inferences that may be drawn concerning them are summarized below. Before examining them, however, the reader may gain some perspective in evaluating their importance from the following remarks. The basic complaints about the third-party insurance-based tort reparation system concerned unnecessary costs, unfairness in allocation of benefits, inefficiency in disbursement of benefits,

---

* Professor of Law, University of Florida. B.S., 1957, Duke University; M.S., 1961, Worcester Polytechnic Institute; J.D., 1963, University of Michigan.

and certain systemic defects, such as unnecessary congestion of court dockets. A crucial point in evaluating any reform movement is to acknowledge that none of these factors is independent of the others. For example, to reduce total costs, including amounts paid out in benefits, and to expand coverage for benefits may be inconsistent goals. On the other hand, to reduce the portion of the costs consumed within the system and to expand benefits may be quite consistent. It follows, therefore, that a no-fault revision should be carefully designed with predetermined goals in mind and should thereafter be evaluated on the basis of performance in achieving those goals.

The Florida Automobile Reparations Reform Act was designed to reduce the costs incurred in transferring money from insurance premium payers to beneficiaries and to expand coverage for personal injury benefits. It was also designed to produce more fairness in the allocation of benefits to injured victims, to eliminate delays in the receipt of benefits and to reduce the proportion of personal injuries that result in litigation. The Florida law also contained property damage no-fault provisions, which had parallel goals. Although the property damage provisions were invalidated by the Florida Supreme Court, sufficient experience had accrued to permit a report on that aspect of the law. To test how well these goals were achieved in the first two years of the new system's operation, data were gathered from sample populations to test the following hypotheses about the workings of no-fault. A brief summary of the conclusions of this study will be given for each one.

> Hypothesis 1: *That no-fault will reduce the amount of litigation arising out of automobile crashes in comparison to the tort system.*

The Florida no-fault system utilizes a tort threshold that was intended to keep relatively minor personal injury cases out of the courts. Data from Alachua and Dade Counties from 1972 and 1973 suggest that the Florida system can reduce the frequency of personal injury litigation measurably. Nevertheless, insurance companies complain that the law is being abused by use of artifices to defeat thresholds, particularly in Dade County, with a resulting increase in the number of suits being filed. No data are available in this study nor are there any known to the author that quantify this phenomenon.

In contrast to the personal injury experience, insurance claims data suggest that property damage no-fault has had little effect on the frequency of law suits, mainly because claims involving only property damage always have been settled by negotiation with very little ensuing litigation. No marked change was seen.

> Hypothesis 2: *That the distribution of claims arising out of motor vehicle crashes between third-party and first-party modes will shift strongly toward first-party modes in a no-fault system.*

The Florida no-fault law mandated that both first-party and third-party personal injury insurance and third-party property damage insurance be carried by covered motorists. First-party property damage insurance remained optional. Experience under no-fault showed a very substantial shift from third-party to first-party claims for both personal injury and property damage coverages. Differences in costs between the two claim modes give importance to this otherwise modest finding. It appears clear that first-party personal injury payments are less inflated by nuisance value and that first-party claims cost less to process than third-party claims. Therefore, a third-party to first-party shift implies cost savings. However, no such difference in costs appeared in the property damage data.

> Hypothesis 3: *That the amount of time required for processing claims and receiving benefits will be shorter in a no-fault system as compared to a tort system.*

The data suggest that the amount of time elapsing between dates of crashes and settlement dates of personal injury insurance claims was not noticeably affected by no-fault. Furthermore, as to those claims that wound up in court, no important diminution occurred in the amount of time elapsing between the dates suits were filed and the dates of settlement. Nevertheless, one may not properly infer that no benefit in speedier claims processing inured to personal injury victims. In fact, a marked diminution in the amount of time elapsing between crash dates and dates of receipt of first payments did occur, indicating that victims are more likely to receive some recovery earlier, when their needs may be greatest.

In contrast, the time required to settle property damage claims actually increased under no-fault and the time required to receive first payments did not diminish.

> Hypothesis 4: *That the allocation of benefits in accordance with ascertainable losses will be more equitable in a no-fault system than in a tort system.*

Personal injury insurance claims data under no-fault show that more claims are settled in amounts much closer in value to verified medical losses than in the superseded tort system. This suggests that the nuisance value of relatively minor claims has been reduced, which arguably creates a more equitable settlement process so far as these claims are concerned. Whether severely injured victims are more adequately compensated under the no-fault system cannot be decided from the data available in this study.

In contrast to the personal injury experience, property damage insurers showed no tendency to pay insurance claims in amounts greater than verified damages under either no-fault or the superseded system. Therefore, with respect to property damage claims, no-fault property damage reparations appear to be no more equitable than was the tort system.

> Hypothesis 5: *That a no-fault system costs less to operate than a tort system.*

This hypothesis is phrased as it is because, from a political point of view, costs and insurance rates are the factors that generate the most attention. Nevertheless, this hypothesis is ambiguous until one clearly specifies the goals sought by no-fault. Data obtained in this study suggest that three changes occurred in connection with personal injury insurance rates and benefits in the sample populations in the first two years of no-fault: (1) the amount of premiums paid per registered vehicle diminished; (2) the amount of benefits paid per registered vehicle increased; and (3) the ratio of benefits to premiums increased. One may infer from these results that coverage for personal injury benefits was expanded and that the cost of processing claims was reduced. Different effects appeared in the property damage data: (1) the amount of premiums paid per vehicle increased; (2) the benefits paid per registered vehicle increased; and (3) the ratio of benefits to premiums also increased, but only slightly. Hence, although coverage for property damage benefits did expand, the expansion was not accompanied by important reductions in processing costs.

Of special interest to lawyers is the fact that the proportion of insurance claims that gave rise to litigation fell from about 9 percent in 1971 to about 2 percent in 1973. Lawyer participation in all personal injury settlements fell from involvement in about 25 percent of the claims in 1971 to about 11 percent in 1973; however, their participation in third-party claims actually increased from about 37 percent in 1971 to about 45 percent in 1973. A strong shift from third-party to first-party claims, which have a much lower lawyer involvement, accounted for the overall drop in lawyer participation.

In summary, the results of this study suggest that no-fault systems such as the Florida Reparations Reform Act can produce changes in the methods by which reparations are made to injured victims of motor vehicle crashes and in how much these benefits cost. Whether or not the changes detected in the sample populations studied herein are beneficial is, of course, for the political processes to determine. Whether or not one would want to rely upon the results of this study alone to predict that similar results would occur in other populations is a matter of judgment. At the very least, however, a methodology has been established that can be used in making more extended tests in Florida or elsewhere.

This article discusses certain aspects of reparations systems that can be described by statistical parameters, but it does not attempt to evaluate whether or not pervasive sociological changes may result from legal modifications of the concept of fault. It may be that any erosion of fault as a legal concept will result in a decline in individual responsibility. The fact that some members of the bar and some members of the medical profession allegedly regularly engage in conspiracies to defeat the $1,000 medical expense threshold of the Florida statute could be cited as evidence of such deterioration. Nevertheless, this writer doubts that a cause-and-effect relationship exists between no-fault and the corruption of professionals. It is more likely that the corruption of professionals helped to create the need for no-fault and that the abuse of no-fault, if it exists, is merely the reassertion of an underlying condition that has not been cured. No system should be evaluated solely on the basis of abuses perpetrated by those who are supposed to tend and nurture it. Sooner or later the professions must effectively police themselves and, if they do not do so, then the populace should through the law.

For convenience, the following report is divided into three parts. Part I presents some historical and background material that introduces the succeeding more technical discussion. Readers well-informed about no-fault may choose to skip this part. Part II contains data and analyses describing some of the effects of no-fault which were felt in the courts. Finally, part III contains similar information describing the effects of no-fault upon the operation of the motor vehicle insurance claim payment system.

I. History and Background

In the mid-1960's, no-fault automobile reparations became a topic of nationwide interest primarily through controversy stirred up by a proposal for a *Basic Protection Plan for the Traffic Victim*[1] produced by Professors Robert Keeton of Harvard University and Jeffrey O'Connell of the University of Illinois. The Keeton-O'Connell plan proposed a new accommodation among tort law, third-party liability insurance, and first-party insurance. Tort liability for automobile crash claims is eliminated if the pain and suffering damages would not exceed $5,000 and other tort damages would not exceed $10,000, and compulsory first-party insurance for actual losses up to $10,000 is added.[2] Presumably, the great numbers of costly tort claims whose value is less than these thresholds would be replaced by first-party claims in the exact amount of compensable damages. Unlike third-party tort actions, the first-party claims would be made against the insureds' own insurance companies.

Massachusetts became the first state to adopt a law based upon the Keeton-O'Connell plan when its no-fault statute[3] took effect on January 1, 1971. Florida was the next to follow when the Florida Automobile Reparations Reform Act[4] went into effect on the first day of the next calendar year. Since that time, twenty-one more states have enacted some variant of no-fault law,[5] not all of which are patterned as closely after the Keeton-O'Connell plan as are the laws of Massachusetts and Florida.[6]

The no-fault principle as it is embodied in any of these plans carries with it certain basic assumptions that give it legitimacy and preference over the

---

[1] R. Keeton & J. O'Connell, Basic Protection for the Traffic Victim (1965) [hereinafter cited as Basic Protection].

[2] *Id.* at 9.

[3] Mass. Ann. Laws ch. 90, § 34A *et seq.* (1975).

[4] Fla. Stat. Ann. §§ 627.730-.741 (1974).

[5] As of September 1975, states may be placed in the no-fault categories as follows: Mandatory no-fault add-on to unchanged tort system: Delaware, Maryland, Oregon, and Texas. Optional no-fault add-on to unchanged tort system: Arkansas, Minnesota, South Dakota, and Virginia. No-fault with abrogation of tort liability up to thresholds: Colorado, Connecticut, Florida, Georgia, Hawaii, Kansas, Kentucky, Massachusetts, Michigan, New Jersey, New York, Nevada, Pennsylvania, and Utah. Saskatchewan would fit under the first of the three categories and Puerto Rico under the last.

[6] Delaware, for example, enacted what is called an "add-on" no-fault provision. Under this plan no-fault insurance is added on to the existing system without eliminating tort liability. For a complete description of the system and an evaluation of its workings, see Clark & Waterson, *"No-Fault" in Delaware*, 6 Rutgers-Camden L.J. 225 (1974).

tort system. These assumptions include: (1) that the amount of litigation arising out of automobile crashes will be reduced; (2) that the distribution of personal injury claims arising out of motor vehicle crashes between third-party and first-party modes will shift strongly toward first-party modes in a no-fault system as compared to a tort system; (3) that the amount of time required for processing claims and receiving benefits will be shorter in a no-fault system as compared to a tort system; (4) that the allocation of benefits in accordance with ascertainable losses will be more equitable in a no-fault system than in a tort system; and (5) that a no-fault system will cost less to operate than a tort system. The purpose of the study reported herein is to test whether the Florida law has produced these desired changes in the operation of Florida's automobile crash victim reparation system.

The reparations reform statute brought the following changes to Florida law. Owners and registrants of certain classes[7] of motor vehicles, including especially passenger automobiles, are required to pay reparations to persons[8] injured by a crash while occupying an insured vehicle without regard to who was at fault in causing the crash or injury. This obligation of car owners to make reparations to occupants is known as the Personal Injury Protection obligation (PIP obligation).[9] The no-fault PIP obligation includes coverage for medical, hospital and other health-related expenses, and loss of earnings during disability up to a maximum aggregated PIP liability of $5,000.[10] No-fault payment for funeral expenses up to $1,000 also is included.[11] Florida law requires that these first-party obligations be secured by appropriate insurance policies or other approved security measures.[12] The law also mandates that liability insurance coverage be provided.[13] So long as PIP obligations are properly secured, owners, registrants, operators and occupants of insured vehicles are exempt from tort liability for the economic consequences of bodily injuries suffered by a person involved in a crash involving an insured vehicle up to the aggregated total of $5,000 in payable PIP benefits, unless aggregated PIP medical benefits exceed $1,000 or death of the claimant or his permanent injury ensues.[14] Recovery for "pain, suffering, mental anguish, and inconvenience"

---

[7] The principal class of covered motor vehicle is the passenger automobile. Certain classes are exempted from the no-fault reparations law including heavy trucks, commercial vehicles, motorcycles, and vehicles not registered in the state. FLA. STAT. ANN. § 627.732(1) (1974).

[8] Four classes of persons are entitled to PIP benefits. They are (1) owners of insured vehicles while occupying the insured vehicle anywhere in the United States, or while occupying any motor vehicle within Florida, or if, while a pedestrian within Florida, hit by a motor vehicle; (2) certain relatives of owners of insured vehicles who have the same protections as do owners unless covered as owners of insured vehicles themselves; (3) other occupants of insured vehicles while within Florida; and (4) Florida residents who are pedestrians hit by the insured vehicle within Florida. FLA. STAT. ANN. § 627.736(4)(d) (1974).

[9] FLA. STAT. ANN. § 627.736 (1974).

[10] FLA. STAT. ANN. § 627.736(1) (1974).

[11] FLA. STAT. ANN. § 627.736 (1)(c) (1974).

[12] FLA. STAT. ANN. § 627.733(3) (1974).

[13] FLA. STAT. ANN. § 627.733 (1974).

[14] FLA. STAT. ANN. § 627.737(1) (1974).

is abrogated unless one of the above three conditions prevails.[15] These conditions are known as tort thresholds; if they are surpassed, the bar to tort liability is removed. The Florida law also included no-fault property damage provisions,[16] which are discussed in part III *B* below.

In summary, the following situation prevails under Florida's no-fault law. A typical PIP claimant may recover up to $5,000 in no-fault benefits on a first-party insurance claim without regard to who was at fault in causing the injury. If the claim does not exceed a tort threshold, then PIP benefits are exclusive, with no remaining tort liability. If the claim exceeds a tort threshold, then the claimant is entitled both to collect PIP benefits as his expenses accrue and to bring suit in tort against an appropriate tortfeasor. If a tort recovery were obtained, the insurer who made the PIP payments would be entitled to reimbursement,[17] theoretically leaving the successful tort claimant with a full tort recovery in addition to whatever benefits accrued from having had the use of PIP monies as expenses were incurred.

Briefly reviewing no-fault purposes,[18] one may first say that no-fault PIP coverage and the personal injury tort exemption were intended to limit total recoveries to the amounts of proven PIP losses in cases where actual losses fell below the $1,000 threshold. The effect should be to eliminate

---

[15] FLA. STAT. ANN. § 627.737(2) (1974). As the law is enacted, the "pain and suffering" tort exemption-threshold section reads as follows:

> In any action of tort brought against the owner, registrant, operator or occupant of a motor vehicle with respect to which security has been provided as required . . . or against any person or organization legally responsible for his acts or omissions, a plaintiff may recover damages in tort for pain, suffering, mental anguish, and inconvenience because of bodily injury, sickness, or disease arising out of the ownership, maintenance, operation, or use of such motor vehicle only in the event that the benefits which are payable for such injury . . . or which would be payable but for any exclusion deductible . . . exceeded one thousand dollars or the injury or disease consists in whole or in part of permanent disfigurement, a fracture to a weight-bearing bone, a compound comminuted, displaced or compressed fracture, loss of a body member, permanent injury within reasonable medical probability, permanent loss of a bodily function, or death. Any person who is entitled to receive free medical and surgical benefits shall be deemed in compliance with the requirements of this subsection upon a showing that the medical treatment received has an equivalent value of at least one thousand dollars. Any person receiving ordinary and necessary services normally performed by a nurse from a relative or a member of his household shall be entitled to include the reasonable value of such services in meeting the requirements of this subsection.

Id.

In Lasky v. State Farm Ins. Co., 296 So. 2d 9 (Fla. 1974), the Supreme Court of Florida invalidated all thresholds except $1,000 medical expenses, death, and permanent injury on grounds that the other classifications

> cannot reasonably be said to rest on a rational basis but are clearly arbitrary and unreasonable, and for that reason this provision . . . denies equal protection of the laws. . . .

Id. at 21.

[16] FLA. STAT. ANN. § 627.738(2) (1974).

[17] FLA. STAT. ANN. § 627.736(3) (1974).

[18] *See generally* BASIC PROTECTION, *supra* note 1.

the nuisance value of small claims and thereby have them settled at lower costs. Because in Florida a preponderance of pre-no-fault personal injury claims were settled for amounts under $1,000 (even as inflated in payments),[19] substantial savings to consumers, presumably in the form of lowered premiums, should ensue. The savings should accrue both from reduced payments and from lessened administrative costs. In addition, the settlement of claims should be speeded up and fewer cases should make their way into the courts. Second, no-fault should favorably affect benefits received by victims whose injuries exceed the tort exemption threshold. PIP-covered victims would recover up to $5,000 whether or not they were at fault and whether or not the other party was at fault (subject to subrogation if a tort recovery is obtained subsequently). Severely injured victims, having the $5,000 PIP recovery to rely on, would be in a better bargaining position with respect to a liability defendant and, presumably, could increase the amount of recovery either through negotiation or trial. Crowded dockets supposedly had coerced needy victims to accept less than adequate settlements in many pre-no-fault cases involving severe injuries. (This latter point has never been documented in Florida and in fact may not have been prevalent in that state because its dockets move relatively quickly.) Thus, no-fault was supposed to bring faster and more equitable settlement of claims at a lower cost.

II. No-Fault Reparations in the Courts

One purpose of this study was to examine the effect of the Automobile Reparations Reform Act in the courts. It intended to assess the impact upon the court machinery itself and upon the citizen-consumers of court services. The experimental design called for only empirical data obtainable from court records of litigated cases. No attempt was made to evaluate budgets or other financial data or to engage in interviews with judges, clerks or other court personnel.

The typical sequence of events in a suit arising out of an automobile crash is: crash, filing suit, pleadings, trial, and judgment. The sequence can be interrupted and halted at any point by settlement. The duration of the time period between each step of the sequence is quite variable with no definite upper limit, except between crash and filing suit which is limited to four years for personal injury claims[20] and three years for property damage claims arising before January 1, 1975,[21] and four years thereafter.[22] The other periods are apparently governed by the usual delays needed to develop the cases, delays for tactical reasons, and delays stemming from congestion in court calendars and inefficient administration. Advocates of no-fault reparations systems have argued that no-fault recoveries will remove cases from court dockets, thereby alleviating congestion and allowing

---

[19] *See* Table 14 *infra.*

[20] FLA. STAT. ANN. § 95.11(4) (1960), *as amended,* FLA. STAT. ANN. § 95.11(3)(a) (Supp. 1975).

[21] FLA. STAT. ANN. § 95.11(5)(c) (1960).

[22] FLA. STAT. ANN. § 95.11(3)(h) (Supp. 1975).

for speedier disposition of cases that are brought to court. Florida's $1,000 medical expense threshold presumably would operate to achieve that result. This study was designed to determine two basic facts: (1) whether the number of automobile tort suits is reduced; and (2) whether measurable effects on the duration of the time periods between the stages of the cases can be discerned. Because the effects of congestion are not limited to automobile tort cases, a complete study would cover all types of cases appearing in the courts. Nevertheless, because of the resource limitations of this study, detailed examination of court records was limited to automobile tort cases.

Court records of suits filed in the years 1969 through 1973 were selected as the data sources for evaluation. Suits filed in 1971 and before represent the pre-no-fault sample, suits filed in 1972 represent the no-fault transition period, and suits filed in 1973 represent the stable no-fault period. In a sense, however, none of these samples is a pure reflector of the intended period. For example, some suits filed in 1971 represent crashes from an earlier time (up to four years earlier for personal injury claims) and some of them will remain in litigation well into the no-fault era. Similarly, suits filed in 1972 and 1973 will include holdover cases from the pre-no-fault era. Hence, all selected samples will be influenced to some extent by both pre-no-fault and post-no-fault factors.

During the period of this study several changes were made in Florida law that could independently affect the measurements being made, including a fundamental restructuring of Florida's court system. Prior to January 1, 1973, Florida's trial courts were comprised of circuit courts of general jurisdiction,[23] county courts with jurisdiction limited to demands not exceeding $500 in value in cases at law,[24] civil courts of record in counties of population 450,000 or more[25] with jurisdiction not to exceed $5,000,[26] and a miscellany of other subordinate courts. Preliminary records searches indicated that very few, if any, (none were found) tort claims arising out of automobile crashes, whether personal injury or property damage, were filed in the county court in Alachua County, the situs of the court records portion of this study. (Some Dade County data are also reported.) On January 1, 1973, a revised court structure became effective, abolishing all courts inferior to circuit courts except the county courts.[27] Owing to the jurisdictional limits of the various courts, most personal injury litigation would be expected to fall within the circuit courts' jurisdiction both before and after the change. Unfortunately, this is not entirely true in counties of 450,000 population or more because some unknown number of personal injury suits were filed in civil courts of record prior to their abolition on January 1, 1973. As a consequence, the analysis of Dade County court

---

[23] FLA. CONST. ANN. art. V, § 6(3).

[24] FLA. STAT. ANN. § 34.01(1) (1961).

[25] Ch. 21819, § 1, [1943] Fla. Laws Gen. 276 (codified at FLA. STAT. ANN. § 33.01 (1961)), (repealed Jan. 1, 1973).

[26] Ch. 11357, § 1, [1927] Fla. Laws Extra Sess. 45-46 (codified at FLA. STAT. ANN. § 3302 (1961)) (repealed Jan. 1, 1973).

[27] FLA. CONST. art. V, § 1. S.J. Res. 52-D, 1971, adopted 1972, created the judiciary article to the Florida constitution.

filing practices was confounded, as shall be seen. Nevertheless, the changed court structure is believed to have had little effect on the principal portions of the study conducted in Alachua County, which never had a civil court of record. Although the jurisdiction of the county court in Alachua County was increased from $500 to $2,500[28] in 1973, that change appears to have had little if any impact upon filings of personal injury cases in circuit courts. The only feasible automobile crash personal injury jurisdiction of the county courts would be in suits exceeding a no-fault tort threshold (or exempted suits) and not exceeding $2,500 in the *ad damnum* claim.[29] Presumably, such personal injury claimants would always demand a sum in excess of $2,500, thus forcing the case into circuit court. In contrast, the $2,500 jurisdiction of county courts is sufficient to satisfy many demands for property damages only. It also far exceeds the $550 threshold that governed property damage claims up to the time the Florida Supreme Court invalidated the property damage no-fault provisions.[30] Since claims involving only property damage often would not exceed $2,500, one would expect most property damage claims to migrate to county courts. However, this study shows that relatively few claims for property damage only were ever filed in circuit courts. Prior to 1971, these claims made up about 3 percent of the tort filings in circuit court; in 1971 they rose to 7.5 percent; and in 1972 and 1973 they fell to around 5.0 percent.[31] Furthermore, on July 11, 1973, the Florida Supreme Court, in *Kluger v. White*,[32] invalidated the property damage tort exemption, thereby in effect removing the threshold entirely. While this decision restored the pre-no-fault litigation potential for claims involving only property damage, the increased county court jurisdictional amount should attract practically all such litigation away from the circuit courts where personal injury claims are litigated.

One additional modification of the law during the course of the study must be mentioned. In *Lasky v. State Farm Insurance Co.*[33] the Florida Supreme Court invalidated certain portions of the no-fault personal injury threshold, leaving intact only a $1,000 threshold for medical expenses, permanent injury, and death. Because several thresholds were dispensed with (permanent disfigurement, a fracture to a weight bearing bone, a compound, comminuted, displaced or compressed fracture, loss of a body member, and permanent loss of a bodily function),[34] one would expect *Lasky* to restrict further the number of suits being filed. The data requirements for testing such a restriction far exceed the capabilities of this study. More-

---

[28] Fla. Stat. Ann. § 34.01(1) (Supp. 1974).

[29] While it was not possible to make exhaustive studies of the county court cases, a sample of 1974 cases indicated only about 2 percent of the cases filed in that court involved automobile crashes and all of those cases involved only property damage. (5,453 cases were filed in 1974. In the sample of the last 300 filings, seven involved motor vehicle crashes.)

[30] *See* text accompanying note 32 *infra*.

[31] *See* Table C1 *infra*.

[32] 281 So. 2d 1 (Fla. 1973).

[33] 296 So. 2d 9 (Fla. 1974).

[34] Fla. Stat. Ann. § 627.737 (1974).

over, since *Lasky* was decided relatively early in the life of the new law,[35] it seems unlikely that many cases were affected.

The court-based portion of this study supplies information to help test the following two of the several hypotheses set forth earlier:

> Hypothesis 1: *That no-fault will reduce the amount of litigation arising out of automobile crashes in comparison to the tort system.*

and

> Hypothesis 3: *That the amount of time required for processing claims and receiving benefits will be shorter in 'a no-fault system as compared to a tort system.*

For convenience the following court study is divided into two sections, one entitled Court Docket Study and the second entitled Court File Study. The docket study is limited to an examination of the number of cases being filed; the file study examines data from a large number of individual files. Information obtained from the docket study pertains mainly to Hypothesis 1; whereas the file study pertains mainly to Hypothesis 3. Information from the Insurance File Study[36] is used to augment the court data as appropriate.

A. Court Docket Study

The Court Docket Study includes an examination of court dockets for years 1969 through 1974 in the circuit courts of Alachua and Dade Counties. Alachua County contains about 125,000 people and is located in north central Florida. Dade County is the most populous county in the state, exceeding a million inhabitants, and lies in the southeastern tip of the peninsula. To an extent, therefore, these two courts represent small rural and large urban populations respectively. This is not a totally accurate representation, however, since Gainesville, the major north central Florida town with an urban population of about 100,000 people, is located in Alachua County. For that reason, the Alachua County courts may more precisely represent small city populations.

To a large extent, an examination of various data counts can reveal useful information about how the no-fault law is affecting the courts. Tables C1 and C2 present data from both Alachua and Dade Counties for the years 1969 through 1973. These data and statistics are explained in the following text.

Row 1, Civil Suits Filed, is a simple compilation of all civil suits of any description whatever filed during the study years. Row 2, Motor Vehicle Tort Suits Filed, is a compilation of all tort suits arising out of motor vehicle crashes filed during the study years. The information in Rows 1 and 2 was obtained from court records.

Row 3, Percentage of Motor Vehicle Tort Suits to the Total Number of Civil Suits, is computed by dividing the number of motor vehicle suits in

---

[35] The case was decided on April 17, 1974, two years and four months after the law went into effect. Rehearing was denied on May 28, 1974. 296 So. 2d at 9.

[36] *See* part III *infra.*

TABLE C1
ACTUAL AND EXPECTED ALACHUA COUNTY COURT FILINGS

TOTAL	1968	1969	1970	1971	1972	1973	1974
1 Civil Suits Filed	—	1,190	1,376	1,563	1,684	1,943	2,257
2 Motor Vehicle Tort Suits Filed	—	105	113	156	122	74	125
3 Percent of Motor Vehicle Tort Suits to Total	—	8.8	8.2	10.0	7.2	3.7	5.5
4 Registered Passenger Vehicles	42,725	45,632	47,905	52,442	56,640	59,508	N.A.
5 Crashes Reported	2,950	3,421	3,759	4,018	4,408	4,943	4,484
6 Crashes Per 100 Registered Vehicles	6.9	7.5	7.8	7.6	7.8	8.3	—
7 Suits Per 100 Crashes (Adjusted)	—	3.30	3.15	4.01	2.90	1.66	2.65
8 Expected Suits	—	103	116	125	136	151	152
9 Excess Suits (Actual Minus Expected)	—	+2	−3	+31	−14	−77	−27
10 Cumulative Excess 1971 & After	—	—	—	+30	+16	−61	−88
11 Cumulative Expected Suits 1971 & After	—	—	—	125	261	412	564
12 Percent Deviation From Expectations	—	—	—	+24.0	+6.1	−14.9	−15.6

[N.A. = Not Available]

TABLE C2
ACTUAL AND EXPECTED DADE COUNTY COURT FILINGS

TOTAL	1968	1969	1970	1971	1972	1973	1974
1 Civil Suits Filed	—	6,821	8,352	8,620	8,210	—	—
2 Motor Vehicle Tort Suits Filed	—	3,806	4,660	4,827	4,280	5,518	7,390
3 Percent of Motor Vehicle Tort Suits to Total	—	55.8	55.0	56.0	52.1	—	—
4 Registered Passenger Vehicles	613,676	658,284	673,134	719,351	770,222	815,147	N.A.
5 Crashes Reported	52,762	52,179	56,474	56,170	59,170	65,475	57,852
6 Crashes Per 100 Registered Vehicles	8.6	7.8	8.4	7.8	7.7	8.0	N.A.
7 Suits Per 100 Crashes (Adjusted)	—	7.25	8.57	8.54	7.42	N.A.	N.A.
8 Expected Suits	—	4,150	4,297	4,455	4,562	N.A.	N.A.
9 Excess Suits (Actual Minus Expected)	—	−344	+363	+372	−282	N.A.	N.A.
10 Cumulative Excess 1971 & After	—	—	—	+391	+109	N.A.	N.A.
11 Cumulative Expected Suits 1971 & After	—	—	—	4,455	9,017	N.A.	N.A.
12 Percent Deviation From Expectations	—	—	—	+8.8	+1.2	N.A.	N.A.

[N.A. = Not Available]

Row 2 by the total number of civil suits in Row 1. This ratio measures the relative burden placed on the courts by motor vehicle suits. Note that this relative burden varies only from about 10 percent to about 4 percent in Alachua County, but soars to over 50 percent in Dade County for years 1969 through 1972. The change in the number of Dade County suits reflects the court reorganization of 1973, abolishing the civil court of records and placing its cases in the circuit courts. Even with this discontinuity, comparison between Dade and Alachua County data give a hint that Dade County is a more litigious place. (If true, this could be the result of either litigation-minded plaintiffs or refractory defendants.)

Data in Rows 4 and 5, obtained from the Florida Department of Public Safety, indicate the number of registered passenger vehicles (Row 4) and the number of crashes reported (Row 5) in each county and each year. In a sense, these data represent gross litigation potential.

Row 6, Crashes Per 100 Registered Vehicles, is obtained by dividing the numbers of crashes (Row 5) by the numbers of registered passenger vehicles (Row 4). This parameter serves as a refined measure of litigation potential. Note that it is the most stable quantity in the table, varying only between a low of 6.9 in Alachua County and a high of 8.5 in Dade County over all the years in question.

Row 7, Suits Per 100 Crashes, is obtained by dividing the number of motor vehicle tort suits in a given year (Row 2) by the average of the number of crashes reported in the preceding and current years. The average number of crashes for the two years, rather than simply the number of crashes in the current year, was selected for this analysis because the median delay between suit and crash exceeded one-half year in all years except 1969. Thus, the number of suits filed in a given year is affected strongly by both the current and preceding year. To some extent, this parameter measures the litigiousness of the crash populations. Detected changes in it that are associated with the introduction of the no-fault law would suggest some connection between no-fault and the proclivity of crash victims to bring suit. The trends established in Row 7 suggest that some change may be in the making. Note also that the Dade County crash population appears to produce more than twice as much litigation per crash as does the Alachua County crash population.

Post-1971 trends in the number of motor vehicle suits (Row 2) and the number of suits per 100 crashes (Row 7) signal a reduction in the amount of litigation. This in turn suggests that no-fault does reduce litigation. On closer inspection, however, it is apparent that 1971 was itself an unusual year, particularly in Alachua County, in that the number of suits took a leap above the immediately preceding years. An explanation for this could be that uncertainties about the consequences of the impending no-fault law caused lawyers to file suits in the latter half of 1971 (the last pre-no-fault year) that ordinarily would not have been filed before 1972. Since the no-fault bill was passed in the 1971 spring session of the Florida Legislature (filed in the office of the Secretary of State on June 24, 1971),[37] there was

[37] Ch. 71-252, [1971] Fla. Laws Gen. 1355, 1371.

enough time for lawyers to file pending cases ahead of the January 1, 1972, effective date of the new law. Consequently, the reduction in cases in 1972 and 1973 could indicate no more than that cases ordinarily expected to be filed then had been filed earlier. In an attempt to account for this early suit possibility, the parameters in Rows 8 through 12 were generated.

Rows 8 through 12 can be explained as follows. If there were only a redistribution of law suits among years 1971 through 1973 and no real change in the numbers being filed, then the total number filed during those three years ought to be the same as the total number that would have occurred had the no-fault law not passed. If, on the other hand, a real decrease in the number of suits was experienced, then the total number of law suits filed during the three years ought to be less than the number that would have been projected upon continuation of past trends. The number of suits that would have been produced by such a continuation was estimated as follows. First, the number of suits per 100 crashes (as defined for Row 7 above) was computed for 1969 and 1970 and then the average for the two years was taken. This average is the parameter that establishes the assumed stable pre-no-fault trend. Next, this 1969-70 value was multiplied by the average of the number of crashes in the current and preceding years for each year after 1970 to obtain the expected number of suits shown in Row 8. Then, this expected number of suits was subtracted from the actual number of suits (Row 2) to produce a parameter called Excess Suits shown in Row 9. This parameter indicates the change in number of suits each year compared to the number that would have been expected based upon pre-no-fault experience. As can be seen, both Alachua County and Dade County experienced an anticipatory jump in 1971 and each experienced a sizeable decrease in 1972, the first year of the no-fault era. Note that fewer than the expected number of suits continued to be filed in Alachua County in 1973 and 1974, whereas the opposite trend appeared in Dade County. Unfortunately for this study, the Dade County Civil Court of Record formerly having jurisdiction of damage suits up to $5,000 was abolished effective January 1, 1973,[38] throwing its cases into circuit court. Whether or not this transfer accounts for the reversal of expectations in the Dade County circuit courts in 1973 and 1974 cannot be told from available data.

The analysis may be extended to average out the effects of the anticipating jump in suits as follows. First, the parameters Excess Suits (Row 9) and Expected Suits (Row 8) were accumulated over the years beginning with 1971 and placed in Rows 10 and 11 respectively. Next, the parameter Percent Deviation was computed by dividing accumulated excess suits by accumulated expected number of suits to produce a parameter measuring cumulative deviation from cumulative expectations. This parameter is displayed in Row 12. As can be seen, the 1971 anticipation in Alachua County was associated with about a one-fourth rise in suits over expectations. The total effect of this jump had not been erased by the end of the first no-fault year (1972), but by the end of the third no-fault year (1974), not long term

---

[38] *See* notes 23-29 and accompanying text *supra.*

deviation appears to be stabilizing at about 15 percent fewer suits than would have been expected without no-fault. The Dade County data showed a similar pattern through 1972 but with a much less extreme jump in 1971. This perhaps suggests that the Dade County lawyers were at that time more sophisticated in their knowledge about the impending no-fault law than were Alachua County lawyers. As pointed out above, the Dade County data for 1973 and 1974 are not comparable to those of the earlier years because of the 1973 change in court structure.

Tables C1 and C2 and the textual explanation of them demonstrate the association between the introduction of no-fault and changes in the number of cases being filed in Alachua and Dade Counties. General comments may be helpful. First, lawyers in both areas seemed to anticipate the new law by filing suits in 1971 earlier than they ordinarily would have, presumably because of uncertainties about the effects of the new law on the right to sue.[39] Data on time lapses between crash dates and suit dates corroborate this "speeding up" in 1971, which had the effect of increasing the number of motor vehicle tort suits filed in 1971 (Row 2), increasing the relative court burden imposed by them (Row 3), and increasing the number of suits per 100 crashes in Alachua County (Row 7). All of these effects were more strongly felt in Alachua County than in Dade County. In 1972 and 1973 the number of suits diminished rapidly (Row 3) in Alachua County, producing the opposite effect from that seen in 1971. While a reduction of suits occurred in Dade County in 1972, the effect of abolishing the civil court of record confounded the analysis thereafter. Because the effects in the latter two years could have been produced either by a real change in litigation practices or by delayed consequences of early suits in 1971, a routine for comparing the actual amount of litigation in 1972 and 1973 with the amount that would have been expected had the no-fault law not occurred was developed (Rows 8 through 12). This analysis suggests that the introduction of no-fault was associated with a genuine decrease in litigation culminating in about 15 percent fewer Alachua County suits in the aggregate for years 1971 through 1973 than would otherwise have been expected (Row 12).

That the number of motor vehicle tort suits appears to be diminishing compared to what would have been expected in the absence of the no-fault law also can be inferred from data obtained from insurance files. In a total sample of 1291 claims, the proportion of personal injury claims that was settled or otherwise disposed of without suit increased from 91.6 percent in 1971 to 94.8 percent in 1972 and to 96.6 percent in 1973. In a smaller sample of more serious claims, the respective percentages ranged from 93.8

---

[39] Interestingly enough, the same phenomenon seemed not to occur or to be less pronounced with the introduction of Delaware's no-fault law. Clark & Waterson, *"No-Fault" in Delaware,* 6 RUTGERS-CAMDEN L.J. 225, 232 (1974) (especially Table I). Two factors might account for the difference. One is that the Delaware statute of limitations is two years instead of Florida's four, thereby reducing the opportunity for early filing. The other is that Delaware's law does not have a tort exemption. Hence, there may have been less apprehension among members of the bar.

percent in 1971 to 95.0 percent in 1972 and to 93.5 percent in 1973. This principally reflects a marked supplanting of third-party claims with first-party claims that is clearly shown in the analysis of the insurance claim data. Of the much smaller numbers of more serious injuries that gave rise to third-party tort claims, the proportions that end up in suit actually increased. From the larger sample, the percentage of third-party insurance claims that resulted in suits rose from 10.7 percent in 1971 to 14.3 percent in 1972 and to 39.3 percent in 1973. In the smaller sample, suits in third-party insurance claims rose from 9.3 percent in 1971 to 23.3 percent in 1972 and to 32.7 percent in 1973. Because of the great decrease in third-party insurance claims, however, the actual number of suits decreased by about 50 percent, tending to corroborate the trends being established in the Alachua County circuit courts.[40]

This analysis suggests that no-fault does reduce the amount of litigation arising out of automobile crashes in comparison to the tort system. Quantifying the extent and importance of the change in terms of how effectively the courts are able to perform their functions would require a study extending over more years and data of a kind different from that available herein.

B. Court Files Study

The preceding section showed that the Florida no-fault law appears to be reducing the number of law suits stemming from motor vehicle crashes. In a sense, it concentrated upon the courts as an institution. This section attempts to measure some of the effects felt by the litigant-consumers of the services provided. In obtaining information for this part of the study, the court records of all of the closed suits arising out of motor vehicle litigation filed in the Alachua County circuit courts in the years 1969 through 1973 were individually examined.[41]

A preliminary question asked of the files was what causes of action are alleged in suits involving motor vehicle crashes. Presumably, most pre-no-fault suits would involve third-party actions of one kind or another and the data gave no surprises on this score. In each year a majority of the claimants alleged negligence as the cause of action, with only a sprinkling of survival and wrongful death actions. Of more significance is the fact that of 169 cases filed in Alachua County circuit courts in 1972 and 1973, only

---

[40] A more positive statement cannot be made since a fairly sizeable number of insurance claims remained unsettled when the data gathering phase of this project was completed. While adjustments could be made for certain analyses in the insurance portion of this paper, the statistics presented here were computed on the unadjusted data.

[41] A sample of suits filed in the Dade County circuit courts was also selected for examination. Sampling was necessary because of resource limitations. The sample selected was composed of all the suits assigned to one specific judge. This particular sample was selected because the judge's personal filing system was so organized as to facilitate greatly the research work. While such a sample has a potential for bias if the particular judge's trial practices were to vary importantly from the norm, nevertheless, having it available made it possible to obtain some measure of the Dade County situation. Unfortunately, due to this judge's death and other difficulties the 1973 data have not been obtained.

two were in the nature of suits against a no-fault insurer. Hence, it appears that no appreciable volume of contractual claims against no-fault carriers is springing up to replace the missing tort actions.

TABLE C3
DISTRIBUTION OF DAMAGE ALLEGATIONS
ALACHUA COUNTY SUITS
[Numbers represent percentages of total claims filed.]

	1969	1970	1971	1972	1973
Personal Injury Only	49.5	52.0	45.6	53.4	74.2
Property Damage Only	3.3	2.9	7.5	5.8	4.8
Personal Injury & Property Damage	44.0	41.2	38.8	26.2	14.5
Survival & Wrongful Death	3.3	3.9	8.2	14.6	6.5
n=	(93)	(102)	(147)	(103)	(62)

As was expected, most motor vehicle suits involved personal injuries either as the sole claim or in conjunction with a property damage claim. How the cases were distributed over various types is shown in Table C3. While the number of cases is too small to draw firm conclusions, it appears that a significant change has occurred in the proportion of suits that join claims for both personal injury and property damage (these decreasing from 44 percent in 1969 to 14.5 percent in 1973) and suits involving only property damage (jumping in 1971 and subsiding to about twice pre-1971 levels in 1972 and 1973). Although the reasons for these changes are not certain, the following explanation can be offered. Most claims joining personal injuries and property damage would involve occupants who were also the owners of the damaged car. Nonowners would not be asking for property damages and nonoccupants would not be asking for personal injury damages. In connection with crashes occurring after January 1, 1972, the tort threshold would cut out some injury claims, leaving only a property damage claim for which there has been no threshold since mid-1973.[42] Furthermore, most property damage claims would drop out of the circuit courts because of the $2,500 jurisdictional minimum. The net effect of these changes could produce the varied distributions seen in the data. In any event, it is important to note that the cases involving only property damage do not constitute a major portion of the litigation. One ancillary observation that might be made is that the litigable issues in property damage cases normally would involve fault and not damages, whereas personal injury cases would be more likely to involve both fault and damages or damages only. Hence, claims involving only property damage are not likely to be as demanding of the courts' time and resources as are personal injury cases.

Because court files were found to be unreliable as sources of information about damages suffered and payments made, the speed of processing claims was the only direct impact on consumers that could be measured with some

---

[42] *See* Kluger v. White, 281 So. 2d 1 (Fla. 1973).

degree of confidence from data contained in the court files. The bar graphs
in Figures C1 through C4 depict median values of relevant time lapses
experienced in Alachua County lawsuits. The median value, the value for
which one-half of the individual measurements are larger and one-half
smaller, is less sensitive to extreme values than is the arithmetic average
value (the mean). Because some cases filed in each year were still unsettled
when data were last gathered, the median of the cases that are settled
represents the true median of all the cases better than does the mean and
therefore has been used as the pictorial parameter. Under each bar graph
is placed the mean (in parentheses) and the number of cases in the sample.
Medians and means are measured in days.

Figure C1
TIME ELAPSED : DATE OF CRASH TO DATE SUIT FILED

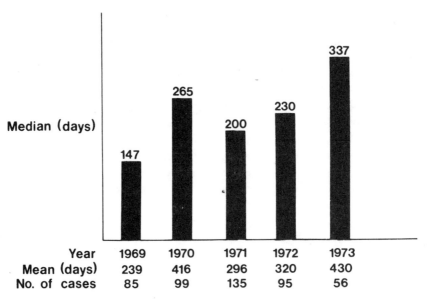

Year	1969	1970	1971	1972	1973
Mean (days)	239	416	296	320	430
No. of cases	85	99	135	95	56

Figure C1 depicts the amount of time elapsing between the date of crash
and the date suit was filed. The only upper constraint on this measurement
is the four-year statute of limitations on negligence actions.[43] Combining
all the data from all years into one population showed that one-half of the
motor vehicle crash suits were filed within about eight months and only 12
percent remain to be filed after two years. The bar graphs are inconclusive,
but suggest a definite trend toward lengthening the median value of this
delay beginning in 1971. Note that the apparent increase in delay between
crash date and suit date occurred at the same time that a marked decrease
in numbers of suits being filed occurred. Several factors could be at play.

---

[43] *See* note 20 *supra.*

One is that the 1971 statistic was artificially shortened by early suit filing behavior in anticipation of the law's coming into effect. Another could be that no-fault is working as promised by weeding out minor cases that were always filed relatively quickly and leaving the more serious cases that litigants can now develop more slowly with the support of PIP benefits. Other than these inferential time lapse data, however, no data are available to substantiate that supposition.

Figure C2
TIME ELAPSED: SUIT DATE TO ANSWER DATE

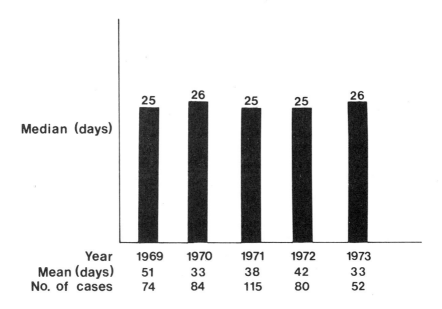

Year	1969	1970	1971	1972	1973
Mean (days)	51	33	38	42	33
No. of cases	74	84	115	80	52

Figure C2 depicts the amount of time lapsing between suit dates and answer dates; this remained practically constant across the years in question. Perhaps it is informative that the median and means of these values regularly exceed the maximum period of twenty days permitted by the Florida Rules of Civil Procedure.[44] This suggests either that motions of one kind or the other are often interposed[45] or that courts regularly extend this limit. If the latter is true, it also suggests that the workload of the courts might be lightened by extending the prescribed period to thirty days and then stringently adhering to it absent unusual circumstances.

The time lapses between crash dates and the dates that the trial began, and between suit dates and trial dates, were also measured. So many suits were settled prior to trial, however, that too few were left in the Alachua

---

[44] FLA. R. CIV. PRO. 1.140(a).

[45] The filing of a proper motion suspends the answer date until ten days "after notice of the court's action." *Id.*

County samples to produce reliable statistics descriptive of these measurements.

Whether or not settlement practices were modified by the no-fault law also has some bearing on the effectiveness of the act. Table C4 depicts the distribution of the suits according to various time-of-settlement categories. Lumping all the suits from all study years into one sample shows that settlements fall into three main groups. Between 10 and 20 percent of the suits are settled after suit is filed and before an answer is made. About one-half are settled after answer but before a trial date is set and about 20 percent are settled after a trial date is set but before trial. Only about 10 percent actually go to trial and reach judgment. While there is some variability in the data across the years, no particularly meaningful trend is discerned unless it is that fewer cases after no-fault are settled prior to an answer having been filed. This would be consistent with the supposition that many nuisance value cases have been dropped out of court by no-fault, leaving a preponderance of more serious cases.

TABLE C4
TIME-OF-SETTLEMENT CATEGORIES
ALACHUA COUNTY SUITS
[Numbers represent percentages of the total
number of settlements.]

	1969	1970	1971	1972	1973
Before Answer	17.6	14.9	14.3	12.1	9.7
Before Trial Date Set	53.8	47.5	39.5	57.9	59.7
After Trial Date Set	22.0	26.7	34.7	19.6	21.0
At Judgment	6.6	10.9	11.6	10.3	9.7
n=	(91)	(101)	(147)	(107)	(62)

Once suit is filed, there appears to be no discernible change in the amount of time it takes to reach settlement through whatever processes are involved. Lumping all the data from all years into one population showed that about 50 percent of the cases were settled within nine months after suit was filed in the Alachua County courts and only 3.8 percent remained unsettled after two years in court. The bar graphs of Figure C3 show no important change over the years.

Figure C4 depicts the total amount of time lapsing in lawsuits between crash dates and settlement dates. Combining all the data from all years into one population showed that about 40 percent of the cases were settled by the end of one year in court and that about 27 percent remained unsettled at the end of two years. While there was some variation from year-to-year, no trend that could be attributed to no-fault appeared to be in the making.

How members of the Florida bar were accommodating to the tort exemption thresholds in pleading cases was a matter of incidental interest to the study. In Alachua County in 1972, the pleadings in about one-third of the cases to which the law applied contained clear allegations that thresholds had been surpassed. In two instances, defendants had pleaded

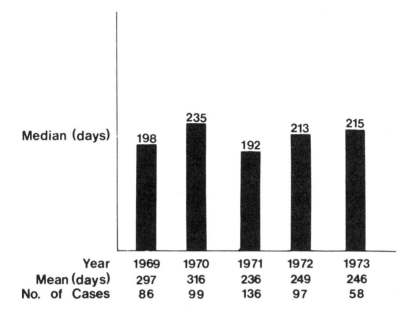

Figure C3
TIME ELAPSED : SUIT DATE TO SETTLEMENT DATE

Year	1969	1970	1971	1972	1973
Mean (days)	297	316	236	249	246
No. of Cases	86	99	136	97	58

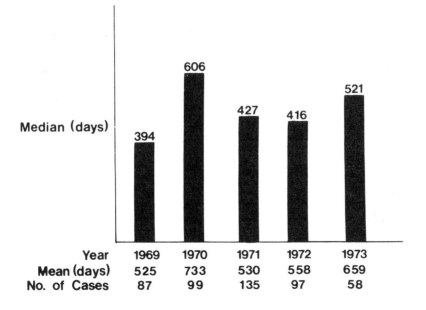

Figure C4
TIME ELAPSED : DATE OF CRASH TO DATE OF SETTLEMENT

Year	1969	1970	1971	1972	1973
Mean (days)	525	733	530	558	659
No. of Cases	87	99	135	97	58

thresholds as affirmative defenses, leading to amended complaints. By 1973 the incidence of affirmatively alleging the surpassing of thresholds had dropped to less than 10 percent, all of these being in amended complaints. The conclusion to be drawn from this seems to be that the thresholds are being treated as matters of affirmative defenses and therefore waivable if not pleaded in the answer. While there is no reported litigation on the issue, the correct rule would seem to be that the thresholds are matters that may be raised in defense at any time before judgment, or even on appeal if the courts were to treat them as pertaining to subject matter jurisdiction.

Another incidental aspect of Florida trial practice is that a liability insurance company may be named as a party defendant. This aspect of Florida's jurisprudence runs contrary to normal rules in tort cases and stems from a series of judicial innovations beginning with *Shingleton v. Bussey*[46] in 1969 and carrying forward to *O'Hern v. Donald*[47] in 1973. Stated in basic contract law nomenclature, these holdings classify injured crash victims as intended beneficiaries of liability insurance contracts, who, as such, have the right to sue liability insurance companies directly. *O'Hern* carried the development to the extent of stating flatly that proceeds obtained in suits brought against insurance companies for excess liability over policy limits (for tortiously refusing settlement within limits) are payable to the injured party, no matter in whose name the suit is brought.[48]

Beginning with *Shingleton* in 1969, the frequency with which insurance companies were named as defendants in Alachua County suits advanced as follows: 28 percent (1969); 61 percent (1970); 72 percent (1971); 81 percent (1972); and 66 percent (1973). Because it is apparent on the face of these statistics that plaintiffs' lawyers have found joining insurers to be a useful trial practice, there is no simple explanation for the reduction in 1973. It could be as follows. Every crash population involves some number of insured and uninsured vehicles. No-fault thresholds bar suits in crashes involving many *insured* vehicles, but if a motorist is uninsured for any reason, he will not be protected by thresholds.[49] Hence, the thresholds eliminate some portion of the population of insured defendants but eliminate none of the uninsured defendants. Consequently, a smaller proportion of

---

[46] 223 So. 2d 713 (Fla. 1969).

[47] 278 So. 2d 257 (Fla. 1973). It is worth noting that in conversation with the author, insurance company representatives generally expressed the belief that the *Shingleton* and *O'Hern* decisions were more damaging to their interests than was the enactment of the no-fault law.

[48] 278 So. 2d at 259.

[49] Uninsured motorists would fall into two categories: those who are required to provide security under the Act and have not (FLA. STAT. ANN. § 627.733 (1974)), and those who are not required to provide security. The latter group includes most visitors from other states, owners of commercial vehicles, and owners of motorcycles. As to the former uninsured group, the Act explicitly states that there "shall be no immunity from tort liability." FLA. STAT. ANN. § 627.733(4) (1974). Owners in this group are also made personally liable for payment of PIP benefits. *Id.* As to the latter uninsured group, the tort exemption never applies. FLA. STAT. ANN. § 627.737(1) (1974). Those owners also are not liable for the payment of PIP benefits.

the suits remaining under the no-fault law involve insured defendants and proportionately fewer insurance companies are available to be joined.

III. No-Fault Reparations in the Insurance Claims System

A. Personal Injury Claims

While a typical trial lawyer's conception of the automobile crash reparation system is likely to be influenced only by suits that come into the legal system for resolution, such a view is exceedingly narrow insofar as Florida experience goes both before and 'after the introduction of the Automobile Reparations Reform Act. Data from the insurance claim study show that about 75 percent of all insurance claims were settled without lawyer involvement in 1971, the last pre-no-fault year, and that this nonlawyer involvement advanced to about 85 percent in 1972 and to about 89 percent in 1973. While lawyer involvement per claim of all types fell off as indicated, the involvement of lawyers in bodily injury liability claims increased from 36.9 percent in 1971 to 45.7 percent in 1972 and 44.2 percent in 1973. Concomitantly, lawyer involvement in first-party claims decreased from 11.1 percent in 1971 to 8.6 percent in 1972 and to 5.8 percent in 1973. Because of a shift from third-party to first-party claims, overall lawyer involvement per claim diminished. Furthermore, the frequency of the filing of lawsuits also diminished—about 9.4 percent in 1971, to 3 percent in 1972 and to 2 percent in 1973.

Therefore, a complete picture of the operation of the reparation system is to be obtained from an examination of the insurance claims system and not merely from examining those few claims that arrive in lawyers' offices or the even fewer that wind up in court. To be totally comprehensive, one would need also to look at injuries for which no insurance claims are ever made, but such an undertaking was beyond the capabilities of this study.[50]

In preparation for presenting various analyses, the data samples and sampling methodology will first be described. Two insurance companies allowed their settled claims files to be used as data sources for the study. In each case the companies left experimental design, file selection, and file examination entirely to the researchers. The general experimental design called for selecting a sample of crashes that occurred in 1971 (the last pre-no-fault year) to represent the pre-no-fault situation, a sample of crashes that occurred in 1972 (the first no-fault year) to represent the transition period, and a sample of crashes that occurred in 1973 to represent the stable no-fault period. One of the companies was a relatively large insurer in the state and the other relatively small. The project was not able to examine every claim made against either of the companies during the three year period. Accordingly, the following sampling procedure was developed.

---

[50] The Council on Law-Related Studies also sponsored a study of the Massachusetts no-fault law that may shed some light on the subject. The study by Professor Alan I. Widiss of the University of Iowa is to be published in 1975 or 1976.

From the smaller company, every claim file opened in respect to crashes that occurred during February and March for each of the three years was selected as part of the sample. For the larger company, every claim file opened in a single designated regional office in respect to crashes that occurred during the same two months was selected. Owing to the difference in size of the companies, the sizes of the two samples are about equal. Once a particular claim file was identified as a member of a study subsample, every individual claim within the file became a part of the study. For example, a single file could have one or more third-party personal injury claims, one or more first-party personal injury claims, and one or more property damage claims. Once the file was selected all the claims would be coded into the study.

Because crashes occurring in a two month period are used to represent a twelve-month phenomenon, how representative these samples are of the total crash population may be asked. Nothing known to the researcher suggests that February and March differ significantly from the remainder of the year. These particular months were selected with several goals in mind, one being to facilitate the completion of the study. The earlier in the respective years the crashes occurred, the sooner the claims would be settled and the sooner the results of this study would be available. A second reason was that these months are somewhat representative of the two seasons of Florida: the winter tourist season by the February data and the remainder of the year by the March data. A second question of representation arises because samples are used to represent the entire state's performance. On this point it should be observed that the state-wide sample is distributed among the counties in rough approximation to the population distribution.[51] On the other hand, the regional sample is very strongly in-

---

[51] Comparative distributions across the ten most populous Florida counties and the unscreened claims population are shown below:

County	Percentage of Population Distribution by County (estimated 1974)[1]	Percentage of Unscreened Claim Population by County
Dade	17.1	5.0
Broward	10.0	2.2
Pinellas	7.9	1.5
Hillsborough	7.1	4.3
Duval	6.9	41.4
Palm Beach	5.6	2.0
Orange	5.1	3.4
Brevard	3.0	0.6
Escambia	2.7	1.4
Volusia	2.5	1.5
	68.0	63.3

[1] DEPARTMENT OF ADMINISTRATION, STATE OF FLORIDA, FLORIDA ESTIMATES OF POPULATION JULY 1, 1974, STATE, COUNTIES AND MUNICIPALITIES (1974).

Although the unscreened claim population is strongly skewed toward the Jacksonville experience in Duval County and slightly toward the less populous counties,

fluenced by the population concentration in Jacksonville and Duval County. Analyses from this regional sample showed few marked differences between it and the state-wide sample, so one may infer that the regional sample is a fair reflection of state-wide experience. Unfortunately, not enough data are available to make extensive county-by-county comparisons. Consequently, the insurance claims files data do not reflect the unusual practices that are said to exist in Dade County.[52]

When initial analyses were made of the data collected in the samples described above, it was found that the percentage of personal injury claims was so small that the number needed to be augmented in order to have a sufficient sample to describe relatively serious crashes. Accordingly, new samples were drawn following the format described above, except that the time frame was extended to cover crashes occurring in the months of February through May in each of the three years and files were selected only if they contained at least one personal injury claim on which payments totalling $200 or more had been made. Once a closed file was selected under this modified procedure, all personal injury claims therein were coded, and all property damage claims were ignored. Hereinafter the original samples are referred to as the "unscreened" sample to indicate that there was no screening out of small claims, and the second samples are referred to as the "screened" samples to indicate that they are skewed toward more severe personal injury claims by the exclusion of many claims that were settled for amounts less than $200. Although separate analyses have been run on the data collected from each company, the data and statistics presented herein derive from samples created by merging the data from the two. This makes for economy in presentation and was done only after it was determined that the trends established in the merged samples do not differ in kind from the trends established in the individual samples. Reference will be made both to the unscreened and the screened samples as necessary and appropriate.

Several steps have been taken to eliminate data that would unnecessarily confound the comparisons between no-fault and pre-no-fault experiences. One such step was the removal from the analyses of cases to which the no-fault law did not apply in the 1972 and 1973 crashes or would not have applied had the law been in effect in the 1971 crashes. This removed claims involving occupants of out-of-state and commercial vehicles. Another step was to remove claims in which some payment for property damage was included in the personal injury payment. A third step was to remove claims in which more than one claimant was compensated in a single payment. Unless stated otherwise, all of the data and statistics represent samples that have been filtered in this way. While this study contains data from more

---

it should be borne in mind that it is composed of two subpopulations, one drawn state-wide and the other mainly from the Jacksonville area. The component state-wide claim population is distributed much closer to the state-wide individual population and the trends established by analyzing that data alone corroborate the trends established in the unscreened population. Consequently, the unscreened claim population appears to be reasonably representative of the state-wide experience.

[52] *See* discussion of Rows 3 and 7 of Tables C1 and C2 *supra*.

than 2,000 personal injury claims, the reader should be cautioned not to overgeneralize the results of the various analyses that will be presented. The study contains a great many variables, such as different crash years and different claim modes, and, since the data are subdivided for comparative analyses, the subsample sizes often become small. When this happens, the representative character of the results can be questioned. In order that the reader will be aware of the need for caution, subsample sizes are stated in all tables and figures. The nomenclature "n=xxx," where "xxx" indicates the number of cases in the particular subsample, is used throughout.

The insurance claims data and analyses will now be used to test some of the hypotheses set forth earlier.

> Hypothesis 2: *That the distribution of personal injury claims arising out of motor vehicle crashes between third-party and first-party modes will shift strongly toward first-party modes in a no-fault system.*

Given the revised structure of the Florida law, the question is not whether such a shift would occur but rather how large the shift would be. Data and statistics in Tables I1 through I3 allow for a close estimation of the size of the shift. If uninsured motorists' claims are placed in the third-party category and the remaining unsettled cases are apportioned to third-party and first-party categories in the same proportions as the settled cases are apportioned, then the insurance data (Table I1) show a transfer from about a 60 percent third-party to 40 percent first-party split in 1971 to about a 20 percent third-party to 80 percent first-party split in 1973.

TABLE I1

DISTRIBUTION OF INSURANCE CLAIMS AMONG
THIRD-PARTY, FIRST-PARTY AND OTHER MODES

	1971	1972	1973
Total Personal Injury Claims	418	455	471
	(100%)	(100%)	(100%)
Third-Party Claims	235	118	70
	(56.2%)	(25.9%)	(14.8%)
First-Party Claims (Med. Pay, PIP)	164	323	326
	(39.2%)	(70.9%)	(69.2%)
Uninsured Motorists & Others	13	6	10
	(3.1%)	(1.3%)	(2.1%)
Unsettled & Unclassified	6	8	65
	(1.4%)	(1.8%)	(13.8%)

Related to the change in distribution of claims is the effect that the no-fault law has had on the insurance-buying practices of the motoring populace. Assuming that the portion of the population that is involved in crashes is representative of the total insurance-buying population, one may examine these buying practices from data available in the insurance claims samples.

It should be borne in mind that these data exclude persons who fail to buy any insurance since they are not reflected as policy holders in the insurance files. Of the insurance policies against which claims in this study were filed during the three years, 0.2 percent had no bodily injury liability coverage, 49 percent had 10-20 coverage, about 11 percent had 25-50 coverage, 9 percent had 50-100 coverage, 12 percent had 100-300 coverage, 0.4 percent had 300-500 coverage, and about 19 percent fell into some other category.[53] No important change was noted among the individual distributions for the three years of the study. In contrast, a marked difference in first-party insurance buying habits has occurred as the statistics in Table I2 show. The proportion of insurance buyers that chose not to purchase any first-party protection fell from 16.2 percent in 1971 to 2.1 percent in 1972 and to 2.4 percent in 1973. This change was expected since the no-fault law mandated the purchase of PIP first-party coverage for a large portion of the Florida motoring public. What may be noteworthy is that about 75 percent of the insured motorists purchased both PIP and medical payment coverage in 1972 and 1973, thus giving them first-party protection beyond that required under the law.

TABLE I2

DISTRIBUTION OF FIRST-PARTY INSURANCE COVERAGES

[Numbers represent percentages of total.]

	1971	1972	1973
None	16.2	2.1	2.4
Med. Pay	83.7	1.9	3.6
PIP	N.A.	21.8	17.3
PIP & Med. Pay	N.A.	74.2	76.7
n=	(1120)	(1680)	(1506)

As is the case in most states, Florida law authorizes insurance companies to make insurance available at special rates to motorists "who are in good faith entitled to but who are unable to procure such insurance through ordinary methods."[54] Drivers commonly fall into such an assigned risk plan because of a prior unlawful or dangerous driving experience. An examination of the data underlying Table I2 indicates that the proportion of drivers falling into the assigned risk category increased from just under 10 percent in 1971 to about 20 percent in 1972 and to slightly less than 18 percent in 1973. Although data in this study do not in themselves explain this increase, it may simply represent the decrease in numbers of motorists who were uninsured in 1971.

Perhaps a more useful way to gauge the shift in the distribution of claims from third-party to first-party modes is to examine the number of claims

---

[53] The meaning of the coverage categories is as follows. The first number indicates the amount of personal injury liability coverage (in thousands of dollars) provided in respect to a single injured person and the second number indicates the amount of personal injury liability coverage provided in respect to all injuries in a single crash. Thus, 10-20 coverage provides liability protection in an amount up to $10,000 for a single injury and up to a total of $20,000 in a single crash. Liability for claims exceeding those limits is uninsured.

[54] FLA. STAT. ANN. § 627.351(1) (1974).

per crash of the respective types. Because it was not feasible to trace claims from particular crashes, it was not possible to obtain a direct measure in this manner from these data. Nevertheless, a representative parameter was devised that allows for comparisons across years even though it does not give an absolute measure of claims per crash. This representative parameter is obtained by dividing the number of claims in each of the three unscreened files (Table I1) by the number[55] of motor vehicle crashes reported in the state in the three respective years.[56] To avoid confusing these ratios with the actual number of claims per crash, the ratio computed for each year was normalized to the ratio computed for the 1971 data. The value of this is to allow the reader to concentrate on the changes occurring in the various parameters rather than to concentrate on size alone.[57] If only closed claims are included in the calculations, the numbers shown under part A of Table I3 are generated. If the unsettled claims in Table I1 are allocated between first-party and third-party modes in the same proportions as settled claims in the 1972 sample are distributed, then the numbers in part B of Table I3 are generated. It can be seen from these statistics that the total number of personal injury claims per crash remained relatively stable, although a slight reduction occurred in 1973. Nevertheless, both parts A and B demonstrate a substantial shift from first-party to third-party claims, thus corroborating the results of Table I1 in a slightly different way.

TABLE I3

RATIOS OF PERSONAL INJURY CLAIMS PER REPORTED CRASH
[Normalized to 1971 total claim figure.]

	1971	1972	1973
A. Closed Claims			
Total Claims per Crash	1.00	0.99	0.76
Third-Party Claims per Crash	0.60	0.28	0.15
First-Party Claims per Crash	0.40	0.72	0.61
B. All Claims*			
Total Claims per Crash	1.00	1.00	0.86
Third-Party Claims per Crash	0.60	0.28	0.19
First-Party Claims per Crash	0.40	0.72	0.67

*The sixty-five unclosed claims were allocated between third-party and first-party modes in the same proportion as closed 1972 claims.

---

[55] The data in Table I1 and Table I4 include all claims and not just those from crashes subject to the no-fault law. Later analyses apply only to the portion of the claims to which the no-fault law is applicable or would have been for 1971 data had the law been in effect.

[56] Reported Florida crashes for years 1971 through 1973 were 249,227; 272,479; and 325,237 respectively. Figures obtained courtesy of the Florida Department of Highway Safety and Motor Vehicles.

[57] For example, if numbers of claims in a three-year period were 1,150; 1,285; and 1,407, there appears to be a change but the size of the value tends to underplay it. If instead the data are normalized to the value of the first year by dividing each number by 1,150, then the series becomes 1, 1.12, and 1.22. The new series shows at a glance that the second and third years exceeded the first by 12 percent and 22 percent respectively. The normalizing technique is useful where the amount of change is important but the absolute sizes of measurements are not, as here.

In summary, it is apparent that Florida's no-fault law has led to a substantial shift away from third-party liability claims and to first-party contractual claims, at least in the population of claims in this study. If the costs of dispensing first-party money are indeed less than those of dispensing third-party money, as this study suggests, this shift should represent either a net gain to the beneficiaries or a net savings to premium payers or both.

Hypothesis 3: *That the amount of time required for processing claims and receiving benefits will be shorter in a no-fault system as compared to a tort system.*

Three parameters were generated to measure processing times. They are:

TC = Amount of time (in days) elapsing between the date of the crash and the date a claim was filed with the insurance company.

TF = Amount of time (in days) elapsing between the date a claim was filed and the date the first payments were made to the claimant.

TS = Amount of time (in days) elapsing between the date the claim was filed and the date the claim was settled.

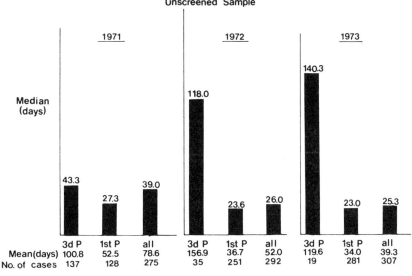

Figure I1
TF—TIME ELAPSED : PERSONAL INJURY CLAIM TO FIRST PAYMENT
Unscreened Sample

In the figures are displayed three bars depicting each of the three parameters defined above. The first bar represents the population of third-party claims, the second bar represents the population of first-party claims, and the third bar represents the population of all the claims obtained by merging these two subpopulations. The median value is depicted by the bars because that statistic is less sensitive to uncertainties stemming from the unsettled cases than is the mean value. Means and numbers of cases in each sample are stated beneath the bars and data depicting both unscreened and screened population samples are presented. (It should be recalled that the unscreened sample purports to represent the population of all personal injury claims,

Figure I2
TS – TIME ELAPSED: PERSONAL INJURY CLAIM TO SETTLEMENT
Unscreened Sample

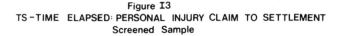

	3d P	1st P	all	3d P	1st P	all	3d P	1st P	all
Mean(days)	23.2	90.0	105.6	177.8	87.5	99.0	206.4	92.3	103.7
No. of cases	141	130	281	39	263	308	24	286	317

whereas the screened sample is skewed toward more serious injuries because a selected claim file had to have at least one claim for which payments
of \$200 or more were made. Third-party claims are those made under
bodily injury liability coverage, whereas first-party claims are those made
under medical payments and PIP coverages.)

No-fault has been associated with a slight diminution in the amount of
time taken to file claims for both third-party and first-party modes in both
the unscreened and screened populations. In general, the mean filing time

Figure I3
TS – TIME ELAPSED: PERSONAL INJURY CLAIM TO SETTLEMENT
Screened Sample

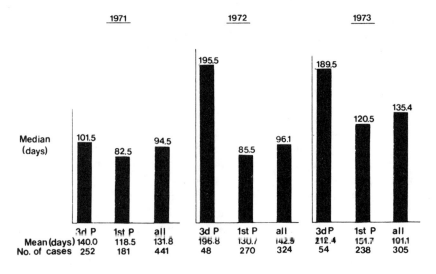

	3d P	1st P	all	3d P	1st P	all	3d P	1st P	all
Mean(days)	140.0	118.5	131.8	196.8	130.7	142.5	212.4	151.7	101.1
No. of cases	252	181	441	48	270	324	54	238	305

TABLE 14A
TC — TIME TO FILE PERSONAL INJURY INSURANCE CLAIMS

A. Unscreened Sample

	Third-Party Claims			First-Party Claims			All Claims		
	1971	1972	1973	1971	1972	1973	1971	1972	1973
Median (days)	8.0	6.2	6.8	12.0	8.5	8.9	9.6	8.3	8.5
Mean (days)	13.2	10.8	14.2	17.9	15.0	14.0	15.3	14.3	13.8
n =	(150)	(43)	(27)	(130)	(272)	(291)	(297)	(321)	(326)

B. Screened Sample

	Third-Party Claims			First-Party Claims			All Claims		
	1971	1972	1973	1971	1972	1973	1971	1972	1973
Median (days)	7.6	6.5	11.0	9.4	9.5	6.6	8.3	9.0	6.8
Mean (days)	9.3	9.7	26.1	13.7	17.2	13.0	11.9	15.9	15.8
n =	(270)	(60)	(56)	(193)	(290)	(241)	(472)	(350)	(310)

is more than one week and less than two weeks, as is shown in Table I4A. One deviation from a rather uniform trend is to be seen in the 1973 screened sample, which suggests that an increase in time to file third-party claims occurred. A slight downward movement in time to file first-party claims is consistent with the no-fault law's requirement that legitimate PIP losses be paid as they accrue.[58] Coupled with the shift from third-party to first-party claims, this provides some overall reduction in filing times.

Data in this study indicate that, in general, beneficiaries are receiving first payments slightly sooner after the filing of a claim than they were before the no-fault law became effective. Figure I2 shows that the delay in receiving a first payment diminished in both the first-party and all claims subpopulations of the unscreened population. The reverse trend is true for third-party claims; under no-fault it takes longer than before for liability claimants to receive the first payment. This, too, was consistent with expectations. The no-fault tort exemption shifted all of the minor third-party claims over to first-party modes, leaving only the more serious claims in the third-party mode. Since these claims are more costly to insurers, they are more likely to be disputed on various legal grounds. Accordingly, working out settlements takes longer on the average than before. It should be borne in mind, however, that these third-party claimants should now be receiving PIP benefits under first-party coverages while they are awaiting settlement of the third-party claims. (That the trends depicted in Figure I1 for the unscreened population also appeared in the screened population can be seen from data in Table I4B.)

TABLE I4B
TF — TIME TO RECEIVE FIRST PERSONAL INJURY
PAYMENT [SCREENED POPULATION]

	Third-Party Claims			First-Party Claims		
	1971	1972	1973	1971	1972	1973
Median (days)	83.5	102.5	136.5	37.3	25.3	29.1
Mean (days)	117.2	145.9	133.9	68.0	44.4	50.0
n =	(248)	(47)	(52)	(177)	(257)	(231)

	All Claims		
	1971	1972	1973
Median (days)	57.9	29.7	34.8
Mean (days)	95.3	62.5	69.4
n =	(431)	(309)	(295)

Interestingly enough, the time taken to settle claims in all subpopulations increased between pre-no-fault 1971 and no-fault 1973. This phenomenon, depicted in Figures I2 and I3, shows that before no-fault was introduced the time taken to settle was substantially greater in the screened population than in the unscreened population. It was to be expected that third-party

---

[58] The no-fault law provides that "Benefits due from an insurer   shall be . . . due and payable as loss accrues, upon receipt of reasonable proof of such loss. . . ." FLA. STAT. ANN. § 627.736(4) (1974).

settlement times would increase for the same reason that times to receive first payments on third-party claims increased, but the slight lengthening of settlement time in the first-party mode does seem unusual. It is perhaps explained by a more relaxed attitude about the need to settle on the part of first-party insurers, especially since the no-fault law gives first-party insurers a right of subrogation to third-party recoveries made by beneficiaries.[59]

Owing to the change in the pattern of claim modes, it is difficult to conclude from these analyses that claimants are better or worse off under no-fault than before with regard to speed of claims and processing. Nevertheless, on balance the speeding up of the receipt of first payments appears to be a favorable result for claimants.

> Hypothesis 4: *That the allocation of benefits in accordance with ascertainable losses will be more equitable in a no-fault system than in a tort system.*

While it would be desirable to gauge the equity in the competing reparation systems, equity cannot be measured solely by statistics describing insurance payments made to injured victims. Such a determination would also require knowledge of the extent of harm done and the extent to which it had been ameliorated by the benefits received. Because knowledge about harm done and needs could not be obtained in this study, the following discussion must necessarily be restricted to benefit payments made.

Data and analyses are presented for both unscreened and screened subsamples and for first-party and third-party recovery modes. By observing the allocation of numbers of cases between the recovery modes, particularly in the unscreened subsample, the reader may note again the switch from the third-party to the first-party mode that already has been seen.

To facilitate the analyses, several new variables are defined as follows:

> Verified Medical Expense = Total amount of medical expense claimed as verified by documentation in the insurance claim file.
> Total Personal Injury Payment = Total amount of the payment made to the claimant in settlement of a claim as verified by documentation in the insurance claim file.
> Extra Value = The difference between the total payment made to the claimant and the verified medical expenses. It represents the amount by which the settlement exceeded verified medical expenses.
> R = The ratio obtained by dividing the Total Personal Injury Payment by Verified Medical Expenses. R shows the multiplier effect between these two parameters.

Total Personal Injury Payment measures the total amount of insurance payments being made to injured victims of motor vehicle crashes. Observ-

---

[59] The Florida law provides for subrogation reimbursement after a third-party settlement has been made or judgment received by the first-party claimant. FLA. STAT. ANN. § 627.736(3) (1974). For a commentary on how this procedure works under the Florida law, see Note, *Insurer's Rights of Reimbursement Under Florida's No-Fault Law*, 26 FLA. L. REV. 534 (1974).

ing any changes in the distribution and size of this variable would allow
one to make a determination as to whether the introduction of no-fault has
been associated with any overall changes in patterns and sizes of payments.
Verified Medical Expense represents ascertainable out-of-pocket losses
associated with the injury. It was initially intended to include a variable
to measure wage losses, but this quantity was not found to be regularly
and reliably stated in insurance claim files. Insurers are more confident
using medical costs as the gauge of the true value of a claim. Hence, Verified
Medical Expense, representing documented medical expenses, is used as a
gauge of injury severity. Extra Value, the difference between the two foregoing variables, in a sense represents the value of the claim in excess of the
verified medical payments. If there is any nuisance value component in a
total payment, it will show up in this variable. Note, however, that the mere
existence of a positive Extra Value does not assure that the total payment
exceeds some actual measure of true worth of the claim. Also included
within it would be wage and other monetary losses plus whatever sum might
represent the value of the pain, suffering and inconvenience experienced by
the claimant. The fourth variable, R, represents a factor by which one
would multiply Verified Medical Expenses to estimate the settlement worth
of a personal injury claim.

TABLE I4
PERCENTAGE DISTRIBUTIONS OF TOTAL PERSONAL INJURY
PAYMENTS [UNSCREENED POPULATION]

	1971	1972	1973
$0 to $500	64.8	63.7	70.2
$500 to $999	10.4	9.7	9.0
$1,000 to $2,000	14.8	10.0	5.1
$2,000 & above	10.0	16.6	15.6
n =	(298)	(320)	(332)

The Total Personal Injury Payment distributions for the unscreened
population are shown in Table I4. Associated with the no-fault years of
1972 and 1973 is a trend toward greater proportions of cases in the payment brackets of $500 and below and $2,000 and above. The intermediate
brackets of $500 to $999 and $1,000 to $2,000 had proportionately fewer
cases. The shift to greater payments for more serious injuries is clearly seen
in the total payments distribution for the screened population (Table I5).

TABLE I5
PERCENTAGE DISTRIBUTIONS OF TOTAL PERSONAL
INJURY PAYMENTS [SCREENED POPULATION]

	1971	1972	1973
$0 to $500	41.9	38.4	28.8
$500 to $999	16.3	16.9	17.1
$1,000 to $2,000	21.1	16.9	16.2
$2,000 & above	20.7	27.7	37.9
n =	(473)	(354)	(309)

TABLE 16
PAYMENT DATA
Unscreened Population

	1971			1972			1973		
	VERMED*	TOTPAY**	EXTRA VALUE	VERMED	TOTPAY	EXTRA VALUE	VERMED	TOTPAY	EXTRA VALUE
Third-Party									
Mean ($)	403	1321	1076	1297	3749	3223	1956	5444	4037
Median ($)	93	344	300	840	2125	2220	953	3800	3050
Cases	(120)	(151)	(120)	(35)	(43)	(35)	(21)	(27)	(20)
First-Party									
Mean ($)	410	593	148	559	770	165	464	734	208
Median ($)	128	135	0	123	140	0	105	121	−7
Cases	(136)	(136)	(135)	(263)	(271)	(262)	(290)	(297)	(290)
All Claims									
Mean ($)	402	990	604	640	1174	527	610	1274	569
Median ($)	120	225	4	151	185	1	117	143	−5
Cases	(265)	(298)	(264)	(304)	(320)	(303)	(318)	(332)	(317)

*VERMED = Verified Medical Expense
**TOTPAY = Total Personal Injury Payment

TABLE I7
PAYMENT DATA
Screened Population

	1971			1972			1973		
	VERMED*	TOTPAY**	EXTRA VALUE	VERMED	TOTPAY	EXTRA VALUE	VERMED	TOTPAY	EXTRA VALUE
Third-Party									
Mean ($)	561	2495	1756	1407	5163	4100	2051	5760	3928
Median ($)	235	835	625	680	1970	1198	1365	4950	3225
Cases	(240)	(270)	(240)	(48)	(60)	(48)	(51)	(56)	(51)
First-Party									
Mean ($)	863	1224	238	1059	1444	285	1181	1858	672
Median ($)	423	498	0	484	570	0	545	850	13
Cases	(187)	(194)	(187)	(279)	(289)	(278)	(236)	(241)	(236)
All Claims									
Mean ($)	704	2083	1107	1109	2160	861	1391	2831	1427
Median ($)	302	710	125	508	673	4	673	1105	19
Cases	(432)	(473)	(432)	(329)	(355)	(328)	(297)	(310)	(297)

*VERMED = Verified Medical Expense
**TOTPAY = Total Personal Injury Payment

Note particularly the increase in the proportion of claims paid in amounts over $2,000 in 1973. These trends represent the type of change that would correct overpayments to minor claims and underpayments to severe claims, and suggest that no-fault is indeed correcting these inequities. Nevertheless, that such an explanation accounts for the changes cannot be definitely asserted from these data. It can be said, however, that this re-distribution is associated with the shift from third-party claims.

Tables I6 through I9 summarize the four variables defined above as they have been computed for various populations. In these tables the designation All Claims is used to represent the population of claims produced by merging the first-party and third-party claims into a single population. Furthermore, the presentations in Tables I8 and I9, displaying the total payment-to-medical expense ratio [R] have further divided the claim populations into those for which Total Personal Injury Payment was less than $1,000 and those for which it was greater than $1,000 and have also presented R for the parent population produced by merging the first-party and third-party claim populations.

A perusal of Tables I6 and I7 clearly shows the switch from third-party to first-party recovery modes. It also shows increases in Verified Medical Payments, Total Personal Injury Payments and Extra Value between 1971 third-party claims and those of later years. This was an expected conse-quence of the tort threshold's removal of many claims from the third-party mode.[60] The same general trend may be noted in the first-party payment data. In the first-party claims the increase in Total Personal Injury Payment is presumably attributable in part to general advances in the costs of medi-cal services and supplies[61] and in part to the fact that first-party PIP bene-fits under the no-fault law may include wage losses and the costs of ancil-lary services[62] that were not ordinarily compensable under pre-no-fault

---

[60] After Lasky v. State Farm Ins. Co., 296 So. 2d 9 (Fla. 1974), the remaining thresholds are: $1,000 or more in medical losses; death; and permanent injury. Presumably, the post-1971 third-party payments under $1,000 reflect permanent injuries.

[61] It may be that the increase in the mean of the Verified Medical Expense vari-able represents the increase in basic costs of medical services. If so the screened popu-lation of the Verified Medical Expense data shows an increase in the ratio from 1 to 1.23 and to 1.37 for years 1971 to 1973 respectively.

[62] Benefits payable under the no-fault law are:
(a) Medical benefits—All reasonable expenses for necessary medical, surgical, x-ray, dental and rehabilitative services, including prosthetic devices, and necessary ambulance, hospital, and nursing services. Such benefits shall also include necessary remedial treatment and services recognized and permitted under the laws of the state for an injured person who relies upon spiritual means through prayer alone for healing, in accordance with his religious beliefs.
(b) Disability benefits—One hundred percent of any loss of gross in-come and loss of earning capacity per individual, unless such benefits are deemed not includable in gross income for federal income tax pur-poses, in which event such benefits shall be limited to 85 percent, from inability to work proximately caused by the injury sustained by the injured person, plus all expenses reasonably incurred in obtaining from others ordinary and necessary services in lieu of those that, but for the injury, the injured person would have performed without

medical payments insurance coverages. The latter fact may also explain the increases in the Extra Value variable in the first-party populations. Note that while the mean value of this parameter is not zero in any first-party population, the median value of Verified Medical Expense is zero or close to it in all first-party populations. This indicates that a very large proportion of first-party claims is settled in the exact amount of verified medical payments. The same economy is not a characteristic of the third-party populations.

Comparisons among the values of the total payment-to-medical expense ratio [R], arrayed in Tables I8 and I9, highlight the relative economy of the first-party recovery mode. The tables show that the median of this variable is 1.0 or very near to it for every first-party subpopulation in both the unscreened and screened populations. This means that about one-half of all first-party claims is paid in amounts greater than the amount of verified medical payments and about one-half in amounts less. In contrast, the mean value of R for first-party began at about 1.0 for the 1971 pre-no-fault first-party claims and increased somewhat under no-fault. While this increase is seen both in the unscreened and screened populations (Tables I8 and I9 respectively), it is accentuated in the more seriously injured augmented population and in the claims of greater than $1,000 in the unscreened population. Presumably, this increase reflects the extended scope of losses covered under no-fault PIP insurance as compared with pre-no-fault medical payments insurance.

Even though wage losses and costs of certain other ancillary services are paid, no-fault PIP payments are not made for pain, suffering, and inconvenience. It is, of course, such quantities which are hard to prove and measure that give third-party claims their speculative value. One readily discerns this quality by comparing the sizes of the total payments-to-medical expense ratio [R] for third-party claims in Tables I8 and I9 to the sizes of R for first-party claims. The sizes of the median values of R for third-party claims are about four times those of their first-party counterparts and the mean values range from two to four times as large as the first-party mean values. These statistics suggest that a given injury, as measured by verified medical expenses, will be compensated from two to four times as much on the average under the third-party recovery mode as under the first-party mode.

These data and analyses have suggested that economy can be achieved by shifting personal injury claims from the third-party to the first-party mode, and that such a shift has occurred in Florida. The distribution of claims by total amounts paid (Table I4) also suggests that a greater percentage of claims now falls in each of the brackets of $500 and under, and $2,000 and above. If this indicates a trend away from overpayment of

income for the benefit of his household. All disability benefits payable under this provision shall be paid not less than every two weeks.
(c) Funeral, burial or cremation benefits—Funeral, burial, or cremation expenses in an amount not to exceed one thousand dollars per individual.
FLA. STAT. ANN. § 627.736(1) (1974).

TABLE 18

R: RATIO OF TOTAL PERSONAL INJURY PAYMENT TO VERIFIED MEDICAL EXPENSE [UNSCREENED POPULATION]

[X̄ = Mean   ME = Median]

Third-Party

	1971 Under $1000	1971 $1000 or More	1971 Combined	1972 Under $1000	1972 $1000 or More	1972 Combined	1973 Under $1000	1973 $1000 or More	1973 Combined
X̄	4.3	5.9	4.9	—	—	13.3	—	—	—
ME	2.0	4.4	3.2	—	—	4.0	—	—	—
n=	(79)	(41)	(120)	—	—	(35)	—	—	—

First-Party

	1971 Under $1000	1971 $1000 or More	1971 Combined	1972 Under $1000	1972 $1000 or More	1972 Combined	1973 Under $1000	1973 $1000 or More	1973 Combined
X̄	1.0	2.1	1.2	1.2	3.2	1.6	1.2	2.9	1.5
ME	1.0	1.0	1.0	1.0	1.1	1.0	0.8	1.0	1.0
n=	(111)	(24)	(135)	(213)	(49)	(262)	(251)	(39)	(290)

First & Third Totaled

	1971 Under $1000	1971 $1000 or More	1971 Combined	1972 Under $1000	1972 $1000 or More	1972 Combined	1973 Under $1000	1973 $1000 or More	1973 Combined
X̄	2.3	4.6	2.92	1.2	7.7	2.95	1.2	4.8	1.9
ME	1.0	3.5	1.0	1.0	1.6	1.0	0.9	2.1	1.0
n=	(197)	(67)	(265)	(223)	(80)	(305)	(258)	(59)	(317)

TABLE 19
R: Ratio of Total Personal Injury Payment to Verified Medical Expense [Screened Population]
[X̄ = Mean   ME = Median]

1971 Third-Party

	Under $1000	$1000 or More	Combined
X̄	4.8	8.7	6.7
ME	2.9	4.4	3.7
n=	(125)	(115)	(240)

1971 First-Party

	Under $1000	$1000 or More	Combined
X̄	1.2	1.9	1.4
ME	1.0	1.0	1.0
n=	(125)	(62)	(187)

1971 First & Third Totaled

	Under $1000	$1000 or More	Combined
X̄	2.9	6.3	4.4
ME	1.0	3.2	1.5
n=	(252)	(180)	(432)

1972 Third-Party

	Under $1000	$1000 or More	Combined
X̄	4.2	5.2	4.9
ME	3.5	3.9	3.7
n=	(12)	(36)	(48)

1972 First-Party

	Under $1000	$1000 or More	Combined
X̄	1.4	3.0	2.0
ME	1.0	1.0	1.0
n=	(176)	(102)	(278)

1972 First & Third Totaled

	Under $1000	$1000 or More	Combined
X̄	1.6	3.6	2.4
ME	1.0	1.3	1.0
n=	(189)	(139)	(328)

1973 Third-Party

	Under $1000	$1000 or More	Combined
X̄	3.5	4.0	4.0
ME	3.9	3.6	3.6
n=	(4)	(47)	(51)

1973 First-Party

	Under $1000	$1000 or More	Combined
X̄	1.6	3.2	2.3
ME	1.0	1.1	1.0
n=	(135)	(101)	(236)

1973 First & Third Totaled

	Under $1000	$1000 or More	Combined
X̄	1.6	3.5	2.6
ME	1.0	2.0	1.0
n=	(140)	(157)	(297)

minor claims and underpayment of severe claims, then no-fault is producing some of its promised equitable benefits. The general advance in the average size of the total payments-to-medical expense ratio [R] suggests that no-fault first-party claimants are being more adequately compensated for lost wages and ancillary services than were pre-no-fault first-party claimants. Presumably, little, if any, "nuisance value" has crept into these payments. At the same time, the mean value of R in the screened population dropped from 6.7 in 1971, to 4.9 in 1972, and then to 4.0 in 1973, suggesting that the relative magnitude of compensation for losses other than medical expenses is decreasing in third-party recoveries. Data in Table I7 show, however, that the absolute sizes of the mean values of both Verified Medical Expense and Total Personal Injury Payment have advanced markedly, giving a 1973 Extra Value of more than twice the 1971 value. Contrary to decreases seen in the size of R, this suggests that those claims which remain in the third-party mode are more adequately compensated than before.

Hypothesis 5: *That a no-fault system will cost less to operate than a tort system.*

Cost may be defined to mean several different things. One definition of cost might be the amount of money paid into the reparation system by purchasers of insurance policies; another might be the amount of money paid out to recipients of insurance settlements; and a third might be the ratio of the first two, representing a measure of the administrative cost efficiency of the transfer of money from premium payers to injured beneficiaries. Because each of these measures produces valuable information, all are used in the following analysis. To make meaningful year-to-year comparisons, the measurements have been normalized[63] to some invariate quantity.

While the most cogent means of making comparisons would be on the basis of costs per motor vehicle crash, it is possible that the reported number of motor vehicle crashes per actual crash might itself vary as a consequence of the introduction of no-fault, thereby artificially skewing some parts of the analyses.[64] Thus, to avoid possible error, the number of registered passenger motor vehicles[65] has been used as the normalizing parameter in the analyses that follow. It may be noted that parallel computations using reported vehicle crashes were made, producing trends that are totally consistent with those seen in the data and statistics presented herein.

To make this analysis, three new parameters were defined: premium paid per vehicle; benefits paid per vehicle; and ratio of benefits to premiums [B/P ratio]. If information describing all premiums and benefits paid per year in the state were available, the parameter "premiums paid per vehicle" would be computed by summing all premiums paid under the no-

---

[63] *See* note 57 and accompanying text *supra.*

[64] *See* text accompanying note 53 *supra.*

[65] According to the Florida Department of Highway Safety and Motor Vehicles, the total number of passenger vehicles registered in Florida for years 1971 through 1973 were respectively: 5,360,493; 5,933,501; and 6,382,298.

fault law (or paid in 1971 by motorists who would have been subject to the no-fault law had it been in effect that year) and dividing that sum by the number of vehicles registered to the motorists who paid the premiums. The trend in the premiums-paid parameter would establish whether the insurance costs per vehicle advanced or declined under the new law. The parameter "benefits paid per vehicle" would be computed similarly. Trends in the benefits-paid parameter would establish whether the no-fault law was associated with increasing or decreasing costs in terms of benefit payments. Finally, the benefits-to-premiums [B/P] ratio would be computed by dividing benefits by premiums. Trends in this parameter would indicate whether the reparations system was associated with greater or lesser efficiency in transferring money from premium payers to beneficiaries. A higher ratio would indicate the expenditure of proportionately less money in administrating the transfer.

Unfortunately, total amounts of benefits paid for the entire state of Florida are not available in this study. Nevertheless, data that are available may be used to estimate values for the parameters for each year in question. These estimates are made in the sections that follow. The reader should be aware that the samples from which the estimates are drawn are relatively small in some cases. For that reason the conclusions must be viewed as tentative and with caution.

Premiums Paid—In the absence of data describing the total amount of money paid for motor vehicle insurance by Florida motorists during the study years, a surrogate measure was devised as follows. First, profiles were developed for two motorists that would be assumed to be typical of the Florida motoring population insofar as their insurance costs were affected by the no-fault law. The selection of the profile criteria was judgmental and not empirical. Those criteria were stated as follows:

> Driver A: Male; married; 35 years of age; one insured vehicle; no drivers under age 25; no prior crashes or convictions; 1970 Chevrolet Caprice, four-door, airconditioned and automatic transmission.
>
> Driver B: Identical to A except for one at-fault crash creating $1,000 in personal injury liability during the preceding twelve months.

Second, because insurance prices vary from place to place, Jacksonville and Miami were selected as study areas under the assumption that they typified all areas of the state insofar as insurance costs were affected by the no-fault law. Third, an insurance package was specified as follows:

> Liability: $10,000 per injury/$20,000 total personal injuries per crash/$10,000 property damage per crash.
> Medical Payments: $1,000.
> PIP: $5,000 (Applicable only in 1972 and 1973.)
> Collision: $50 deductible and comprehensive.
> Basic Property Protection: (Applicable only in 1972 and part of 1973 because of the invalidation of the property damage tort exemption in 1973.)

Next, prices that would have been charged to drivers fitting the stated profiles in the two areas were obtained from the two participating insurance companies for each year from 1971 through 1973. Finally, the costs of the bodily injury insurance were averaged for the two companies, divided by the number of passenger motor vehicles registered in the state in each of the three study years, and normalized to 1971 costs. (Treating separately the data from the individual companies creates the same trends as are seen in the totaled data, so for economy in presentation, only the totaled data are used.) The normalized relative bodily injury insurance costs for Jacksonville and Miami are displayed in Table I10, showing identical decreasing trends in premium costs for 1971 through 1973.[66]

TABLE I10
RATIO OF COST OF BODILY INJURY
INSURANCE PACKAGES TO 1971 COST
Miami Area

	1971	1972	1973
Bodily Injury Insurance Cost	1	0.88	0.85

Jacksonville Area

	1971	1972	1973
Bodily Injury Insurance Cost	1	0.88	0.85

In summary, it appears from these data that the cost of bodily injury insurance per registered passenger vehicle diminished with the introduction of the no-fault law in Florida.[67] It is perhaps noteworthy that this apparent reduction occurred during a period when the trends in number of claims per registered passenger vehicle[68] and in the cost of medical services apparently were increasing.[69] It should also be noted, as will be demonstrated in part III *B*, that the property damage insurance costs per registered vehicle also were increasing during this period.

Benefits Paid—While the total amount of money paid out in benefits

---

[66] The initial insurance rate reductions did not necessarily reflect any gain in economy. The no-fault law itself mandated an immediate 15 percent rate reduction "calculated as a percentage of the combined financial responsibility rate . . . in effect at the time of the filing of the new rates required herein." FLA. STAT. ANN. § 627.741(2)(a) (1974). The financial responsibility law requires only liability insurance ($10,000 per injury/$20,000 two or more injuries per crash/$5,000 property damage per crash). FLA. STAT. ANN. §§ 324.151(a), 324.021(7) (1968). Therefore, no overall rate reduction was necessarily forthcoming in a complete insurance package that includes first-party coverages as did the insurance packages used in this study. Financial responsibility limits were changed to $15,000/$30,000/$5,000, effective July 1, 1975. Ch. 73-180, §§ 1, 2, [1973] Fla. Laws Gen. 366, *amending* FLA. STAT. ANN. § 324.021 (1968). That change does not affect the data in this study.

[67] Comparative 1974 and 1975 figures to those in Table I10 were respectively 1.04 and 1.09 for Miami and 0.96 and 1.00 for Jacksonville. As this paper is being prepared, Florida automobile insurance companies are seeking raises of about 20 percent. It should be observed, however, that this comes at a time when medical malpractice insurance costs are skyrocketing, and when Florida workmen's compensation insurance companies are seeking rate hikes, citing advancing medical costs as the reason. Gainesville Sun, Sept. 12, 1975, § B, col. 1.

[68] *See* Table I12 *infra.*

[69] *See* discussion of Table I13 *infra.*

during the study years is not available, a surrogate can be developed from the claims in the unscreened population, as follows. First, the claims for each year were divided into first-party and third-party categories to generate the distribution shown in Table I11.[70]

TABLE I11

ADJUSTED CLAIMS DISTRIBUTIONS*

	1971	1972	1973
Total Personal Injury Claims	291	320	369
Third-Party Claims	153	44	33
First-Party Claims	138	276	336

*These represent claims to which the no-fault law applied in 1972 and 1973 or would have applied in 1971, include no property component, and involve a single claimant.

Next the figures in Table I11 were divided by the number of Florida passenger vehicles registered in each year[71] to produce a surrogate number of claims per registered vehicle. Because resulting numbers may be used only for internal comparisons, they have been normalized to a common factor and presented in Table I12.

It should be pointed out that the trends seen in Table I12 can only be asserted with confidence to represent the populations in Table I11. In

TABLE I12

FREQUENCY OF CLAIMS PER REGISTERED
PASSENGER VEHICLE

	1971	1972	1973
Total Personal Injury Claims	1.00	1.01	1.11
Third-Party Claims	0.53	0.14	1.10
First-Party Claims	0.47	0.87	1.01

---

[70] As shown in Table I1 there were six, eight, and sixty-five unsettled cases respectively in years 1971, 1972 and 1973. In order to minimize skewing the results, particularly in the 1973 data, an accounting had to be made of these cases both from the point of view of whether the no-fault law applied to them and from the point of view as to whether they were first-party or third-party claims. The 1971 and 1972 data showed that about 70 percent of the cases each year were under no-fault and the remainder were not. Hence, 70 percent of the unsettled cases for each year were arbitrarily assigned to augment the unscreened sample as shown in Table I11. Next the newly assigned cases were allocated to first-party and third-party modes, as were the settled cases. The 1971 claims were distributed in accordance with the allocation of 1971 settled claims and the 1972 and 1973 claims were distributed in accordance with the allocation of 1972 settled claims. The 1973 unsettled claims were allocated according to 1972 allocations of settled claims in an attempt to avoid erroneous skewing away from third-party cases in 1973. The assumption was that 1973 unsettled cases were more likely to be third-party than first-party claims and that the 1972 and 1973 distributions should be nearly identical. Following this procedure, two unsettled cases were assigned to each settlement mode in the 1971 sample; one case to third-party and five to first-party in 1972; and six cases to third-party and thirty-nine to first-party in 1973. These numbers were incorporated into Table I11.

[71] See note 65 supra.

that population, the total number of claims per registered vehicle was rising from a relative value of 1.0 in 1971, to 1.01 in 1972, and to 1.11 in 1973. An increase, however, was to be expected since the percentage of insured motorists that carried first-party insurance had risen from 83.8 percent in 1971 to over 97 percent in 1972 and 1973. This, coupled with the fact that fault is not an issue in first-party recoveries, should have made more injured persons eligible for a recovery in the latter two years. Hence, the trends depicted in Table I12 are consistent with expectations.

The second and third rows of Table I12 show the division of the claims between first-party and third-party modes. The sum of the numbers in these columns equals the value in the first row for all personal injury claims. These data show that the relative frequency of third-party claims per registered vehicle decreased by a factor of four or five while the relative frequency of third-party claims per registered vehicle increased by a factor of slightly greater than two. Hence, Table I12 clearly shows the no-fault switchover from third-party to first-party claims.

By extending the data farther, surrogate relative measures for benefits paid per vehicle can be produced. These are obtained by multiplying the

TABLE I13

RATIO: BENEFITS PAID PER 1972 AND 1973
REGISTERED PASSENGER VEHICLE TO 1971
[Numbers are in dollars.]

	A. Claims Per Vehicle	B. Mean TOTPAY* Per Claim	C. Surrogate TOTPAY Claim Per Vehicle (A x B)	D. Surrogate TOTPAY Per Vehicle C(1) + C(2)	E. Ratio: Surrogate TOTPAY Per Vehicle to 1971 Figure
1971 Third-Party	0.53	1321	700(1)		
1971 First-Party	0.47	593	279(2)	979	1.0
1972 Third-Party	0.14	3749	525(1)		
1972 First-Party	0.87	770	670(2)	1195	1.22
1973 Third-Party	0.10	5444	544(1)		
1973 First-Party	1.01	734	741(2)	1285	1.31

*TOTPAY = Total Personal Injury Payments

relative numbers of first-party and third-party claims per vehicle for each year (data from Table I11 placed in Column A of Table I13) by the mean values of total payments made to first-party and third-party claimants in the unscreened populations in the respective years (data from Table I6 placed in Column B of Table I12). This computation produces a surrogate total payment per claim type per registered vehicle for each year (Column C, Table I12). Adding the first-party and third-party figures produces a surrogate total payment per registered vehicle for each year (Column D, Table I13). Finally, normalized surrogate measures of benefits paid per crash are produced by dividing this final sum produced for each year by the 1971 sum (Column E, Table I13).

It can be concluded from data in the first row of Table I12 and in Column E of Table I13 that, for claims included in the unscreened populations in this study, the number of claims per registered vehicle increased by about 11 percent between 1971 and 1973, and that the amount of benefits paid per registered vehicle increased by about 31 percent during the same period. This suggests that more people are receiving benefits in greater amounts under no-fault, thereby creating a more costly system. Such a conclusion may be erroneous for two reasons. One is that the cost of medical services advanced markedly during the three year period. This increase can be estimated by dividing the 1973 Verified Medical Expense by the corresponding 1971 value which produces a ratio of 1.52. This indicates about a 50 percent increase in medical costs.[72] Presumably increases would have occurred with or without no-fault. A second factor that suggests that no-fault may have held down total payments is the change in the value of the total payments-to-medical expense ratio [R] between 1971 and 1973. Data from the unscreened population in Table I8 show a drop from 2.9 in 1971 to 1.9 in 1973, representing a reduction of 34 percent.

For a complete analysis one needs to know what would have happened to the amount of money paid out in benefits had the no-fault law not been enacted. Such a finding would require examining the trends in a control population which was not affected by the no-fault law. While it would be possible to obtain a control non-no-fault sample from claims arising out of crashes involving commercial vehicles and out-of-state vehicles, not enough data from no-fault-exempt claims were obtained in this study to make valid comparisons. Nevertheless, one can generate a representative cost per vehicle measure for motorists exempted from the no-fault law by making several assumptions that allow use of the available data. Let it be assumed that without no-fault the 1971 distribution between first-party and third-party recovery modes would have held constant in succeeding years; that the number of claims per registered vehicle would not have increased; that medical costs would have increased; and that the value of the R would have held constant at 2.9. Calculations based upon these assumptions produce a non-no-fault 1973 representative total payments

---

[72] See Table I6 supra.

per registered vehicle value of $1,385. Dividing this by the comparable 1971 quantity[73] produces a normalized measure of 1.42, representing a 41 percent increase over 1971. Using this analysis, one can argue that the no-fault law, while paying benefits to about 11 percent more claimants, held the increase in total amount of payments in the unscreened sample to 31 percent, instead of the 41 percent increase that would have occurred otherwise.

Summary—Having derived these representative numbers for the premium costs (Table I10) and benefits paid (Table I13) per registered passenger vehicle, one may now arrange the premiums paid per vehicle, benefits paid per vehicle, and the benefits-to-premiums [B/P] ratios in a matrix, as below:

MATRIX A

	1971	1972	1973
Premium Paid Per Registered Vehicle	1	0.88	0.85
Benefits Paid Per Registered Vehicle	1	1.22	1.31
B/P Ratio	1	1.39	1.56

With respect to the particular population of claims under study, several important inferences can be drawn from this matrix. First, the premium cost per registered vehicle decreased for the first two years of no-fault. Second, the benefits paid per registered vehicle increased. Finally, the benefits-to-premium ratio increased markedly during the same period. To these may be added the earlier finding that the number of claims per registered vehicle also increased,[74] thereby spreading the benefits paid over a larger population of injured victims. To the extent that the sample population is representative of the entire state these findings reflect the performance of no-fault in Florida. They suggest that the hypothesis of more cost-effectiveness with no-fault should be accepted.

B. *Property Damage Claims*

Unlike the Keeton-O'Connell plan,[75] other no-fault proposals,[76] and the forerunner law in Massachusetts,[77] the Florida Automobile Reparations Reform Act included property damage as well as personal injury within its no-fault provisions.[78] Before the no-fault law was enacted, motor vehicle insurance purchasers had the options of purchasing contracts to cover third-party liability in respect to property damage caused to other people, to cover crash damage to the motorists' own motor vehicles regardless of fault, or to cover incidental damage. As an alternative the motorists could remain uninsured. The first-party coverage is commonly called "collision coverage" and typically is sold with deductibles of $50 and $100.

---

[73] The 1971 quantity is 979. *See* Column D of Table I13 *supra*.

[74] *See* Table I12 *supra*.

[75] *See* BASIC PROTECTION, *supra* note 1.

[76] *See* notes 2-5 *supra*.

[77] *See* note 3 *supra*.

[78] FLA. STAT. ANN. § 627.738 (1974), *ruled unconstitutional in* Kluger v. White, 281 So. 2d 1 (Fla. 1973).

Under the Florida no-fault property damage law, Florida owners and registrants of passenger vehicles were required to purchase property damage liability insurance [PDL][79] and to exercise one of three options as to first-party property damage coverage: they could purchase collision coverage [COLL] that would pay regardless of fault;[80] they could purchase a new basic property protection coverage [BPP] that would pay first-party benefits only if the loss was attributable to the fault of another no-fault insured driver;[81] or they could choose not to purchase first-party property damage insurance.[82] In all instances, including the last, a property damage tort exemption precluded the bringing of a tort claim against a no-fault insured third-party tortfeasor unless one of several property damage thresholds was surpassed. These thresholds were met when damages to the insured vehicle exceeded $550, the damaged vehicle was parked, the at-fault insured driver was engaged in "willful or wanton misconduct," or the at-fault vehicle was being operated without the consent of the owner.[83] The structure of these thresholds left each motorist to provide protection for damage to his own vehicle when the total loss was less than $550, although actual self-protection was not required. Hence, if a motorist chose not to obtain one of the first-party property coverages and suffered damage of less than $550 to his motor vehicle through the fault of another no-fault insured driver, then the no-fault law left the motorist no right to recover in any mode. One year and seven months after the Automobile Reparations Reform Act had been in operation, the Florida Supreme Court invalidated the property damage provisions on the ground that the tort exemption as applied in the situation just described totally deprived motorists of the right to sue, without sufficient justification or acceptable alternative.[84]

Fortunately for this study, the experimental design of the unscreened sample called for examining claims arising from crashes in the months of February and March of 1971, 1972, and 1973. This means that the last crash giving rise to a claim in this study occurred not later than three months and eleven days prior to the invalidation of the law.[85] It will be shown that claims involving only property damage were typically filed and settled following a crash in a period of time much shorter than that. Consequently, it is believed that the data in this study fairly represent the no-fault property damage reparations system as it was operating up to the time of invalidation.

---

[79] PDL insurance is required for covered motorists by virtue of their having to meet all the requirements of the Florida financial responsibility law, including the property damage portion. *See* note 66 *supra*.

[80] The Act referred to this as full coverage. FLA. STAT. ANN. § 627.738(2)(a) (1974). Deductibles were allowable as in collision coverage. FLA. STAT. ANN. § 627.738(3) (1974).

[81] The Act referred to this as basic coverage. FLA. STAT. ANN. § 627.738(2)(b) (1974). Deductibles were allowable as in collision coverage. FLA. STAT. ANN. § 627.738(3) (1974).

[82] FLA. STAT. ANN. § 627.738(1) (1974).

[83] FLA. STAT. ANN. § 627.730(4) (1974).

[84] Kluger v. White, 281 So. 2d 1 (Fla. 1973).

[85] Kluger v. White was rendered on July 11, 1973. *Id.*

The property damage portion of this study was an integral part of the experimental design that already has been explained in detail in connection with personal injury claims. As mentioned previously, the property damage claim population comes from the same total claim population that produced the personal injury unscreened population. The number of property damage claims was great enough that no augmentation by the inclusion of crashes from additional months was necessary. The format of the presentation of data and statistics will follow that used in the personal injury claim section without repeating the explanation of procedures and assumptions detailed there. One slight difference is that in some presentations mean values have been used as the key statistic rather than median values. This was believed to be justifiable because so few property damage claims remained unsettled that no important effect on the final mean values would be felt. Two other points need to be made. One is that the property damage claims used in this study arose out of crashes that did not include a personal injury. The rationale for this is the assumption that the handling of property damage claims associated with personal injury crashes would generally be strongly influenced by the handling of the personal injury claims. The second point is that only claims that were covered by the no-fault law (or would have been in respect to 1971 crashes had the law been in effect that year) are included in the analyses.

> Hypothesis 1: *That no-fault will reduce the amount of litigation arising out of automobile crashes in comparison with a tort system.*

It first should be noted that litigation involving only property damage was found not to be occurring in the circuit courts of Alachua and Dade Counties either before or after the implementation of the no-fault law. This in part reflects the jurisdictional hurdles of the circuit courts, but is entirely consistent with the premise that property damage claims themselves very infrequently result in lawsuits. The insurance claim data completely corroborate this assumption. As shown in Table D1, the proportion of claims settled without payment or by negotiation without suit always has been high: ranging from 97.4 percent in 1971 and 1972 to 99.4 percent in 1973. More detailed analysis showed that virtually the same distribution prevailed for both first-party and third-party claims. As a corollary, the data show

TABLE D1
DISTRIBUTION OF PROPERTY DAMAGE
SETTLEMENT MODES
[Numbers represent percentage of total.]

	1971	1972	1973
Closed Without Payment	4.1	8.1	0.1
Settled Before Suit Filed	93.3	89.3	99.3
Settled After Suit Filed	0.6	0.3	0.5
Settled at Judgment	0.6	0.1	0.1
Other	1.5	2.2	0.0
n=	(1172)	(1447)	(1341)

that the proportion of property damage insurance claims involving lawyers has always been small and apparently became smaller under no-fault. The percentage of claims in which lawyers apparently were not involved rose from 95.8 percent in 1971, to 97.8 percent in 1972, and to 98.7 percent in 1973.

In summary, these data and analyses suggest that property damage claims never have been burdensome sources of litigation and that the trend seems to be toward further limitation. Nevertheless, by comparison to the apparent changes occurring in personal injury claims, it may be concluded that the reduction in litigation caused by the no-fault property damage law was minimal.

> Hypothesis 2: *That the distribution of property damage claims arising out of motor vehicle crashes between third-party and first-party modes will shift strongly toward first-party modes in a no-fault system.*

Preliminarily, the insurance claim data as summarized in Table D2 show that motorists covered by the no-fault law made marked changes in their first-party property damage insurance-buying practices while the law was in effect. Prior to no-fault, motorists had the choice of selecting some collision coverage or choosing to remain unprotected. The data in Column 1 of Table D2 show that 14.3 percent of those in the unscreened crash population had not bought first-party insurance in 1971 while 85.7 percent had bought some form of collision coverage. Note that even the 14.3 percent were not self-insurers as against damage caused by other at-fault motorists. In 1973 the distribution shifted to 1.6 percent uninsured, 17.1 percent Basic Personal Protection (BPP) and the remainder collision or collision and BPP, and in 1973 the distribution shifted again to only 1.1 percent uninsured, 12.0 percent BPP and the remainder in the other categories. Several observations can be made about these data. One is, of course, that most motorists were persuaded to purchase some sort of first-party property damage coverage. Secondly, the BPP buyers were in effect only half-insured, in that this coverage did not protect against damage caused by the owner or suffered without fault of anyone. Finally, a majority of the motorists were persuaded to purchase both BPP and collision coverages. While this had the effect of eliminating the collision deductible when

TABLE D2
DISTRIBUTION OF FIRST-PARTY PROPERTY DAMAGE
INSURANCE COVERAGES
[Numbers represent percentages of total.]

	1971	1972	1973
None	14.3	1.6	1.1
COLL-$50 Deductible	59.2	1.0	0.7
COLL-Other Deductible	26.5	1.3	0.7
BPP	—	17.1	12.0
BPP & COLL	—	78.9	85.6
n=	(1175)	(1444)	(1344)

damage was done at the fault of another person and, perhaps, of adding certain elements to the recovery such as the rental cost of a replacement vehicle while repairs were being made,[86] the end result appears to be substantial overlapping coverage.

Having reviewed the changes in the structure of the law and the pattern of insurance-buying practices, one would expect a strong shift from third-party to first-party recovery modes between 1971 and the succeeding years. The statistics in Table D3 show that this occurred. Third-party claims fell from just less than 50 percent of the total to less than 20 percent in both succeeding years. In sum, therefore, Hypothesis 2 can be accepted as correct.

TABLE D3
DISTRIBUTION OF PROPERTY DAMAGE
CLAIMS BY TYPE
[Numbers represent percentage of total.]

	1971	1972	1973
Property Damage Liability (PDL)	47.4	14.8	17.3
Collision (COLL)	52.5	49.2	39.7
Basic Property Protection (BPP)	—	36.1	43.1
n=	(1178)	(1464)	(1344)

Hypothesis 3: *That the amount of time required for processing claims and receiving benefits will be shortened in a no-fault system as compared with a tort system.*

In testing this hypothesis the same three time measurements defined in the personal injury portion of the study[87] were used. The findings are displayed in Figures D1 through D3. As in the personal injury graphs, the first bar represents the population of third-party claims (PDL), the second bar represents the population of first-party claims (COLL in 1971 and COLL plus BPP in 1972 and 1973), and the third bar represents the population of all the claims obtained by merging the two subpopulations. The bars represent median values. Mean values and numbers of cases are presented below each bar.

An examination of Figures D1 through D3 reveals that no great speeding up of processing property damage claims occurred with the introduction of Florida's no-fault law. Looking at the bar for "all" claims in all three figures, one sees that while the time delay in filing a claim diminished from a median value of 7.6 days to a value of 5.0 days between 1971 and 1973, the time elapsed in making the first payment increased slightly from 6.3 days to 6.8 days, and the time elapsed in settling increased from 8.9 days to 12.4 days. The figures show that a major contribution to these increases came from the third-party claims, whereas the reduction for time of filing occurred in the first-party claims. The figures also suggest that a stabilized

---

[86] *See* FLORIDA NO-FAULT INSURANCE PRACTICE 160 (Fla. Bar Continuing Legal Educ. 1972).

[87] *See* part III *A supra*.

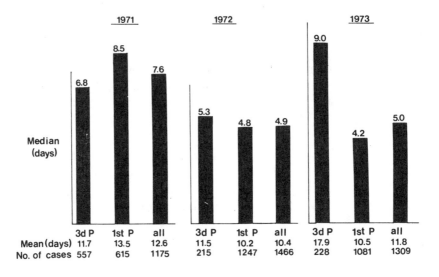

Figure D1
TC – TIME ELAPSED: CRASH TO PROPERTY DAMAGE CLAIM
Unscreened Sample

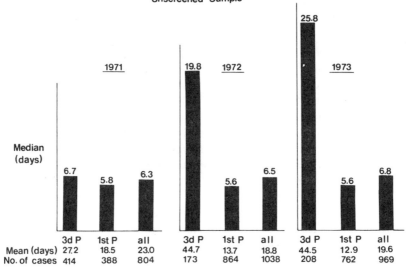

Figure D2
TF – TIME ELAPSED: PROPERTY DAMAGE CLAIM TO FIRST PAYMENT
Unscreened Sample

operation represented by the 1973 claims generally takes longer to process each claim than the transition operation in 1972.

An explanation for the marked increases in TF and TS for third-party claims is that the $550 threshold eliminated many of the minor claims from the third-party population leaving only only the more costly claims that require more investigation and are more likely to be contested. Hence, it is not surprising that processing the remaining third-party claims takes longer than before. Why there should be an increase in time to settle first-

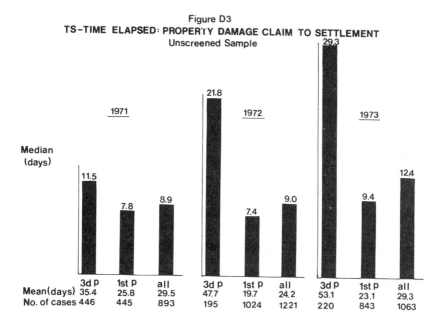

Figure D3
TS—TIME ELAPSED: PROPERTY DAMAGE CLAIM TO SETTLEMENT
Unscreened Sample

	3d P	1st P	all	3d P	1st P	all	3d P	1st P	all
Mean(days)	35.4	25.8	29.5	47.7	19.7	24.2	53.1	23.1	29.3
No. of cases	446	445	893	195	1024	1221	220	843	1063

party claims is a little more complex. More detailed analyses showed that the time to first payment and the time to settle collision claims actually diminished slightly between 1971 and 1973. The increase, therefore, is due to longer times taken to process BPP claims than COLL claims. To illustrate, the median values for TS were 8.7 and 11.2 days respectively for 1972 and 1973 BPP claims, whereas they were only 6.9 and 7.3 days for COLL claims in the same two years. Presumably, processing BPP claims took longer because of the necessity of determining that the damage was "caused by the fault of another resulting from contact between the insured vehicle and a vehicle with respect to which security"[88] was required under the no-fault law. In contrast, benefits under collision coverage were payable without respect to fault. Hence, it is apparent that the addition of an element of fault in first-party coverages runs counter to the general goal of speeding up payments and settlements.

In summary, these data do not suggest that the no-fault property damage law brought any advantage to consumers when contrasted with the superseded recovery modes. Therefore, Hypothesis 3 as it applies to property damage claims apparently must be rejected.

Hypothesis 4: *That the allocation of benefits in accordance with ascertainable losses will be more equitable in a no-fault system than in a tort system.*

Paralleling the personal injury analyses, several new parameters are defined as follows:

Verified Property Damage = Total amount of property damage claimed as verified by documentation in the insurance claim file.

---

[88] FLA. STAT. ANN. § 627.738(2)(b) (1974).

Property Damage Payment = Total amount of payment made to the claimant in respect to the property damage claim as verified by documentation in the insurance claim file.

Extra Value = The difference between Property Damage Payment and Verified Property Damage.

RD = The ratio obtained by dividing Property Damage Payment by Verified Property Damage. It represents the multiplier effect between the amount of damage and insurance payments.

Verified Property Damage is a measure of actual property damage repair bills and estimates, and Property Damage Payment measures the amount of money paid in respect to the claims arising out of crashes. Extra Value and RD are both measures of the difference, if any, between damages and payments which might reflect either equities or nuisance value inherent in property damage claims. It is largely these latter measures that pertain to equity in the allocation of benefits.

Table D4 presents statistics representing these measures. Starting first with Verified Property Damage, there is a general increasing trend over the three years of the study. Using the COLL data as a guide, the value of the general increase can be estimated to be 22 percent. It should be noted that after 1971 third-party claims have the highest Verified Property Damage value, whereas in 1971 COLL claims were greater. This switch undoubtedly reflects the influence of the property damage thresholds that has already been discussed.[89] Perhaps of more interest is the fact that BPP Verified Property Damage figures are substantially lower than COLL figures.

That a similar rising trend exists in Property Damage Payments is also shown by Table D4. Interestingly enough, the differences between COLL and BPP statistics diminish somewhat in this parameter. This is apparently accounted for by two factors. One is that most COLL policies carry a deductible with $50 being the most common amount.[90] The effect of this factor shows up clearly in the median values of Extra Value for COLL claims. A second factor was the ruling that reimbursement for rental cars used while damaged vehicles were being repaired was an allowable item of BPP recovery.[91] Although insurers were required to offer this coverage as an addition to normal collision coverages after 1972,[92] rental reimbursement in the past was not included under collision policies. These two factors—less frequent use of deductibles in BPP coverages and rental reimbursement—apparently accounted for the narrowing of the difference between COLL and BPP Property Damage Payment statistics.

The effects of deductibles and rental reimbursement presumably account

---

[89] *See* text accompanying notes 30-32 *supra.*

[90] The Florida Insurance Commissioner had recommended that BPP policies be written to be paid from a first dollar of damage basis rather than with deductibles because of a small difference in consumer cost of the two. INSURANCE COMMISSIONER BULLETIN OF OCTOBER 8, 1971, *reproduced in* FLORIDA NO-FAULT INSURANCE PRACTICE, *supra* note 86, at 159. No such recommendation was made in respect to collision coverage. Apparently, insurance companies and buyers followed this advice.

[91] FLORIDA NO-FAULT INSURANCE PRACTICE, *supra* note 86, at 159.

[92] *Id.* at 160.

TABLE D4
PROPERTY DAMAGE REPARATION PARAMETERS

	1971				1972				1973			
	Third-Party	COLL	BPP	ALL	Third-Party	COLL	BPP	ALL	Third-Party	COLL	BPP	ALL
Verified Property Damage												
Median ($)	198	318	N.A.	248	415	329	224	290	555	390	245	312
Mean ($)	309	479	N.A.	398	620	499	341	459	605	583	370	491
n =	(543)	(598)	(N.A.)	(1143)	(202)	(695)	(518)	(1418)	(198)	(522)	(577)	(1297)
Property Damage Payments												
Median ($)	188	251	N.A.	215	360	246	213	238	258	323	253	289
Mean ($)	332	439	N.A.	383	575	420	353	418	528	539	396	476
n =	(556)	(619)	(N.A.)	(1178)	(212)	(719)	(528)	(1463)	(231)	(533)	(579)	(1343)
Extra Value												
Median ($)	1	-50	N.A.	-3	0	-50	1	-3	-1	-52	0	-6
Mean ($)	17	-28	N.A.	-6	-15	-64	19	-27	4	-60	25	-12
n =	(541)	(598)	(N.A.)	(1141)	(201)	(694)	(518)	(1416)	(197)	(522)	(577)	(1296)
RD												
Median	1.0	0.86	N.A.	0.99	1.0	0.87	1.0	1.0	1.0	0.85	1.0	1.0
Mean	1.0	0.87	N.A.	0.95	0.97	0.76	1.06	0.90	1.0	0.82	1.05	0.95
n =	(541)	(598)	(N.A.)	(1141)	(201)	(694)	(518)	(1416)	(197)	(522)	(577)	(1296)

for the differences in BPP and COLL Extra Values and RD's statistics shown in Table D4. The Extra Value parameter and the RD parameter for both the third-party and "all" populations suggest that property damage claims typically carry little in the way of equity or nuisance value. Apparently, property damage losses are usually paid in the exact amount of the losses verified as having been sustained. Interestingly enough, the COLL population tends to undercompensate, presumably because of deductibles, and the BPP population seems to overcompensate, presumably because of the rental reimbursement feature. Combining these two populations with the third-party population produces a composite with slight undercompensation.

In summary, it appears that property damage claims have little in the way of either nuisance value or equities to create the speculative values and resulting system costs seen in personal injury claims. Consequently, it does not appear that a no-fault system in itself leads to a more equitable reparation system so far as property damage claims are concerned. Nevertheless, one factor not subjected to empirical testing in this study is worth mentioning. Under a pure fault system a motorist must purchase liability insurance that will protect him against damage done to vehicles owned by other motorists. Therefore, a person with an inexpensive vehicle must insure against possible damage to more expensive vehicles. However, a pure no-fault system, such as Florida's was not, would require only that each motorist insure against damage to his own vehicle. Hence, owners of inexpensive vehicles would presumably pay less. Under a threshold plan, as Florida's was, this advantage does not prevail.

> Hypothesis 5: *That a property damage no-fault system will cost less to operate than a tort system.*

A parallel analysis to that used in testing this hypothesis for personal injury no-fault reparations will be employed without reviewing the logic in detail. The next two subsections will develop representative values to be inserted in a premium-benefits matrix analogous to Matrix A generated in the discussion of personal injury claims. That care must be taken in generalizing the results seen in the sample populations needs repeating. Nevertheless, it should be observed that the property damage claim samples are much larger than the personal injury claim samples, permitting somewhat greater confidence in the validity of the results.

Premiums Paid—In the absence of data describing the total dollars paid in property damage premiums, it was necessary to resort to the typical premium procedure described in connection with personal injury claims.[93] Computed in accordance with that procedure, the normalized[94] relative property damage insurance costs for Jacksonville and Miami are displayed in Table D5. Unlike personal injury insurance costs, some difference in effects on rates was felt by drivers with previously clean records as compared with drivers with a prior crash. Interestingly enough, the increase in

---

[93] *See* part III *A supra.*
[94] *See* note 57 and accompanying text *supra.*

rates of the prior "good" drivers was greater than the increase for prior "bad" drivers. Overall the increase ranged between 15 percent and 17 percent in the Miami area and 11 percent and 13 percent in the Jacksonville area.[95] While data are not available to produce a true mean value, it will be assumed that a 14 percent increase typifies the motorists represented in the study populations.

TABLE D5
RATIO OF COSTS OF PROPERTY DAMAGE INSURANCE
PACKAGES TO 1971 COSTS
A. *Previously Clean Record Driver*
Miami Area

	1971	1972	1973
Relative Property Damage Insurance Costs	1	1.15	1.15

Jacksonville Area

	1971	1972	1973
Relative Property Damage Insurance Costs	1	1.17	1.17

B. *Driver with Prior Crash*
Miami Area

	1971	1972	1973
Relative Property Damage Insurance Costs	1	1.11	1.11

Jacksonville Area

	1971	1972	1973
Relative Property Damage Insurance Costs	1	1.13	1.13

The data in Table D5 indicate that the costs of Florida's no-fault property damage reparation system increased as measured simply by premiums paid. This should be contrasted to the downward trend in personal injury insurance costs as depicted in Table I10. However, other factors should be considered. One such factor is simply that more drivers elected first-party coverages than before as was shown in Table D2. Such extended coverage naturally adds more costs to consumers but these increased costs should eventually be reflected in increased benefits. The next subsection discusses such benefits.

Benefits Paid—In accord with the procedure explained in detail in the personal injury section,[96] calculations were made to produce representative benefits paid per vehicle in the unscreened property damage population. First, claims were allocated between first-party and third-party

---

[95] After the no-fault property damage provisions were invalidated, the pre-no-fault insurance system supplanted it. Interestingly enough, property damage premiums fell in 1974 and readvanced in 1975. Parallel 1974 and 1975 figures for Table D4 are as follows: Part A: Miami, 1.06 and 1.11; Jacksonville, 0.99 and 1.04. Part B: Miami, 1.08 and 1.13; Jacksonville, 1.0 and 1.05.

[96] *See* part III *A supra.*

modes.[97] Next, the number of claims in each category per year[98] was divided by the number of registered vehicles in Florida for the respective years.[99] Then the resulting dividends were normalized to the 1971 "all" claims statistic to produce the array of comparative frequencies of property damage claims per registered passenger vehicle shown in Table D6.

TABLE D6

COMPARATIVE FREQUENCY OF PROPERTY DAMAGE CLAIMS
PER REGISTERED PASSENGER VEHICLE

	1971	1972	1973
Total Property Damage Claims	1.00	1.13	1.01
Third-Party Claims	0.47	0.17	0.17
First-Party Claims	0.53	0.96	0.84

The statistics in Row 1 of Table D6 suggest a 13 percent rise in property damage claims per registered vehicle in the unscreened population in 1972 but with a return to the pre-no-fault frequency in 1973. Nevertheless, Rows 2 and 3 depict a substantial shift from third-party to first-party claims.

By combining claim frequency data from Table D6 and total property damage cost data derivable from information in Table D4, one may obtain the ratio of property damage benefits in 1972 and 1973 per crash per registered passenger vehicle to the comparable figure for 1971. The results are presented in Table D7. This analysis suggests that the payments per crash per registered vehicle in the unscreened claim population increased by 22 percent in 1972 over 1971, and by 24 percent in 1973 over 1971. With respect to benefits payments, therefore, the Florida no-fault property reparation system appears to have been more generous than the tort system.

As in the case of personal injury payments, a representative non-no-fault control can be generated by making certain assumptions. First, that in the absence of no-fault the third-party to first-party claim distribution would have continued as in 1971 and that increases in total property damage payments would have followed the trend set by the COLL claims in 1972 and 1973. Given these assumptions, a non-no-fault system would have seen Comparative Benefits declining to 0.96 in 1972 and then rising to 1.23 in 1973. Except for 1972, this very closely parallels the results depicted in Table D7.

Summary—Data from Tables D5 and D7 may now be arrayed by year to produce the first two rows of Matrix B below. The third row is computed by dividing the values of Row 2 by those of Row 1.

[97] *See* Table D3. COLL and BPP claims must be combined to obtain the total number of first-party claims.

[98] It was assumed that each closed claim file contained one claim for property damage only. Distributions between first and third-parties were made in accordance with the distributions of closed claims in each year.

[99] *See* note 66 *supra*.

TABLE D7
RATIO: PROPERTY DAMAGE BENEFITS PAID IN 1971 AND 1972
PER CRASH PER REGISTERED PASSENGER VEHICLE TO 1971 FIGURE
[Numbers are in dollars.]

	A. Claims Per Vehicle	B. Mean PD* Pay Per Claim	C. Surrogate PD Pay/Claims Per Vehicle (A x B)	D. Surrogate PD Pay Per Vehicle C(1) + C(2)	E. Ratio: Annual Surrogate PD Pay Per Vehicle to 1971 Figure
1971					
Third-Party	0.47	332	156(1)		
1971					
First-Party	0.53	439	233(12)		
1971					
Total				389	1
1972					
Third-Party	0.17	575	98(1)		
1972					
First-Party	0.96	392	376(2)		
1972					
Total				474	1.22
1973					
Third-Party	0.17	528	90(1)		
1973					
First-Party	0.84	465	391(2)		
1973					
Total				481	1.24

*PD Pay—Property Damage Payment

MATRIX B

	1971	1972	1973
Property Damage Premiums Paid Per Vehicle	1	1.14	1.14
Property Damage Benefits Paid Per Vehicle	1	1.22	1.24
B/P Ratio	1	1.07	1.09

The conclusion to be drawn from this information is that while both premiums and the size of property damage benefit payments increased under the Florida no-fault system, the benefits-to-premium [B/P] ratio also increased. This suggests that the no-fault system was somewhat more cost-efficient in transferring premiums paid to beneficiaries than was the superseded system.

AFTERWARD
1976 STATUTORY REVISION OF FLORIDA LAW

Joseph W. Little

Having allowed the Florida no-fault law to operate without legislative changes for more than four years, the 1976 Florida legislature made some important revisions. Two principal issues motivated the action. One was the recurring allegation that the $1000 medical expense tort exemption threshold was being abused by fraudulent practices, and the other was that, despite no-fault, insurance costs had risen to unreasonable levels. Much was made of the fact that the amount of the average tort recovery was markedly up. Not much was made of the fact that the number of tort claims was markedly down. Both results were exactly what should have been expected from a system that cuts the mass of cases out of the tort system, leaving only the most serious ones. Moreover, not much was made of the fact that more injured victims received reparations than ever before.

This being the mood of the legislature, it is not surprising that reform legislation took on a cost-cutting air. Staving off alternate attempts either to scrap no-fault altogether or to raise the medical expense tort exemption threshold to $3500, the legislature restructured the threshold to include only verbal categories.[1] Gone is the troublesome $1000 medical expense category. And, although the new threshold contains terms such as "loss of bodily member" and "permanent loss of bodily function" that have never been definitively defined in Florida, the new catch-all category of "serious non-permanent injury which has a material degree of bearing on the injured person's ability to resume his normal activity and life style during all or substantially all of a ninety day period" expresses an apparent intent to create a firm, meaningful threshold that should provide needed guidance to the courts.

The new verbal threshold should relieve the fraudulent pressures on the threshold. Not content to stop there, however, the legislature introduced several policing mechanisms. Included is a requirement that, upon request of insurers, physicians, hospitals and other treating institutions provide a statement sworn to under penalty of perjury attesting to the reasonableness

---

1. The new threshold requires injury or disease consisting "in whole or in part in":

    (a) loss of a body member, or

    (b) permanent loss of a bodily function, or

    (c) permanent injury within a reasonable degree of medical probability other than scarring or disfigurement, or

    (d) significant permanent scarring or disfigurement, or

    (e) a serious non-permanent injury which has a material degree of bearing on the insured person's ability to resume his normal activity and life-style during all or substantially all of the ninety day period after the occurrence of the injury, and the effects of which are medically or scientifically demonstrable at the end of such period, or

    (f) death.

F.S.A., § 627.737 (1976 revision).

and necessity of the treatment provided and to the fact that it was incurred as a result of the bodily injury alleged in the insurance claim.[2] Further enforcement is provided by making fraudulent violations of the Act a felony of the third degree. Particularly named as subjects for control are insured persons, insurers and insurance adjusters;[3] physicians and other health treating people;[4] lawyers;[5] and hospital administrators.[6] Finally, a Division of Fraudulent Claims is created to investigate complaints and make enforcement recommendations to prosecuting officers and licensing authorities.[7] The administrative and operating costs of this new agency are to be borne by insurers, who presumably will pass them on to policy buyers.[8] Attuned to the current vogue of halting bureaucratic expansion, the legislature limited the division to 25 employees and a $500,000 budget.[9]

A measure[10] taken to reduce the amount of tort recoveries was to prohibit direct tort actions against liability insurers. Direct joinder of insureds had been judicially authorized in Florida by *Shingleton v. Bussey*[11] and its progeny. The apparent reason for this move was a belief that juries bring in larger verdicts than are justified when insurers are joined as defendants and larger than would be rendered were insurers not named as defendants. That the reasoning is valid in a state with mandatory insurance is to be doubted. Fortunately, however, the legislature added a provision requiring liability insurers to file a statement in suits indicating their potential liability.[12] If the insurer claims a contractual defense, it may be joined,[13] and in any case it may be joined after the verdict is rendered.[14] The law does not specify what kind of notice is required to cause the insurer to file its statement.

The legislature also acted to clear up the badly confused state of the law[15] pertaining to no-fault insurers' rights of subrogation or reimbursement when the insured gains a tort recovery after having received no-fault benefits. To meet its cost-cutting goal of not over-compensating victims, the legislature could have either provided for full reimbursement of no-fault insurers or reduced the recovery obtained from tortfeasors by the amount of the no-fault benefits paid. Although it has some unfavorable connotations in terms of relieving tortfeasors of part of their proper burden, the Florida legislature selected the latter approach.[16] Presumably, the legislature was

---

2. F.S.A., § 627.736 (6) (b) (1976 revision).
3. F.S.A., § 627.7375 (1) (New, 1976).
4. F.S.A., § 627.7375 (2) (New, 1976).
5. F.S.A., § 627.7375 (3) (New, 1976).
6. F.S.A., § 627.7375 (4) (New, 1976).
7. F.S.A., § 629.989 (New, 1976).
8. F.S.A., § 629.989 (4) (New, 1976).
9. *Id.*
10. F.S.A., § 627.7262 (1) (New, 1976).
11. Shingleton v. Bussey, 223 So.2d 713 (Fla. 1969).
12. F.S.A., § 627.7262 (1) (New, 1976).
13. F.S.A., § 627.7262 (3) (New, 1976).
14. F.S.A., § 627.7262 (4) (New, 1976).
15. See, for example, Williams v. Gateway Insurance Company, 331 So.2d 301 (Fla. 1976).
16. F.S.A., § 627.736 (3) (1976 Revision).

persuaded that because liability insurance is mandatory, tortfeasors themselves do not pay anyway and also believed that the selected system has less cost-shifting expenses involved. Under the revised law, victims not barred by the exemption can prove their no-fault losses in tort suits, but the fact finders are to be instructed that such losses are not proper items of recovery. Whether or not juries will ignore these exhortations remains to be seen.

The legislature also moved to prohibit "stacking" of insurance coverages to obtain a total recovery exceeding the limits of any one policy.[17] Stacking pertains when one insured has several insurance policies on several cars, each covering the insured in a variety of situations. The practice has particular applicability to uninsured motorists coverages and has been used in Florida[18] and other states to obtain total recoveries in excess of the limits of any single policy. The new Florida provision eliminates this practice by limiting coverage to that provided in the policy covering the crash vehicle,[19] or, if none of the insured's vehicles are involved, to that available under any one of his policies.[20] So that drivers can insure themselves adequately against uninsured motorists, the revised legislation requires that the limits of uninsured motorist insurance be the same as the liability limits, unless the insured selects lower limits, and requires that limits up to $100,000 per person/$300,000 per crash be made available.[21] Under the new law, uninsured motorists' benefits are excess over no-fault benefits.[22]

In its cost cutting fervor, the legislature cut back mandatory liability coverage limits from $15,000 per person/$30,000 per crash to $10,000 per person/$20,000 per crash.[23] This seems a mistake that ought to be remedied at the first opportunity. The legislature also authorized no-fault deductibles of $250, $500 and $1000,[24] and added an authorized property damage deductible of $500 (or other amounts agreed by the parties and permitted under the insurer's approved rating plan).[25]

Under the revised law, insurers need not pay no-fault benefits when insureds are "charged with" specified disqualifying behaviors (intentional injury of oneself; driving under influence of liquor or drugs, or committing a felony).[26] This provision is likely to cause trouble because it leaves open the matter of what kind of charges are required. The revised law also authorized insurers to cease payments if a beneficiary "unreasonably refuses" to submit to physical examination.[27]

---

17. F.S.A., § 627.4132 (New, 1976).
18. See, for example, Sellers v. United States Fidelity & Guaranty Company, 185 So.2d 689 (Fla. 1966), on remand, 197 So.2d 832 (Fla. App. 1967).
19. F.S.A., § 627.4132 (New, 1976).
20. *Id.*
21. F.S.A., § 627.727 (2) (New, 1976).
22. F.S.A., § 627.727 (1) (New, 1976).
23. F.S.A., § 324.021‑(7) (1976 Revision).
24. F.S.A., § 627.739 (1976 Revision).
25. F.S.A., § 627.7377 (New, 1976).
26. F.S.A., § 627.736 (2) (1976 Revision).
27. F.S.A., § 627.736 (7) (b) (1976 Revision).

On the whole the 1976 legislation is positive. Although definitions pertaining to the now-critical verbal thresholds need more flesh, the trouble-filled dollar amount threshold has been removed and very strong measures against fraud have been put in place. A reasonable measure to eliminate overlapping of no-fault and tort recoveries was adopted, although it, too, may need later revision if juries ignore instruction that no-fault losses are not to be included in tort awards. Some of the peripheral measures such as lowering limits of mandatory liability coverage and raising deductibles may prove to be unwise.

PART III
THE DELAWARE STUDY

ROGER S. CLARK
Director

CHAPTER 8

"NO-FAULT" IN DELAWARE

by *Roger S. Clark** and *Gerald E. Waterson***

I. INTRODUCTION

Among the many proposals for "no-fault" automobile insurance under active consideration in various states, the type that has found most support among members of the organized bar is the "add-on" or "no-threshold" variety[1] of which the Delaware law is an early example.

---

* Professor of Law, Rutgers School of Law at Camden. B.A., LL.M. Victoria University of Wellington; LL.M., J.S.D. Columbia.
** Director, Rutgers Center for Computer and Information Services at Camden. B.S., M.S. Rensselaer; Ph.D. University of Pennsylvania.
Research assistance for this study was provided by Ann Gaughan, Matthew Jodziewicz and Peter Reinhart, students at the Rutgers School of Law at Camden. David Gwalthney of the Center for Computer and Information Services supervised the programming.
1. Comparing twenty state laws in force that sponsors have referred to as "no-fault," Professor Keeton placed them into two main groups, add-on statutes and partial-tort-exemption statutes.

> The add-on statutes merely add to the negligence system of reparations some kind of provision for no-fault insurance benefits—benefits payable by an insurer (or perhaps a "self-insurer") to an injured person without regard to fault. These statutes preserve all tort claims, though some of them provide for subrogation or offset to avoid double recovery for an item of loss.
>
> . . .
>
> In sharp contrast with add-on laws, partial-tort-exemption statutes change the basic character of the reparations system. The partial tort exemption eliminates tort claims for some injuries (those of less consequence), and other provisions of the statute provide benefits that are payable without regard to fault. These no-fault benefits are also available to those who suffer injuries of greater consequence, but persons in this group retain their tort claims as well—subject only to provisions designed to dovetail the two kinds of benefits and avoid double recovery for a single item of loss.

Keeton, *Compensation Systems and Utah's No-Fault Statute,* 1973 UTAH L. REV. 383, 386-87. The argument for a partial tort exemption made by Professors Keeton and O'Connell in their seminal work in the area, R. KEETON & J. O'CONNELL, BASIC PROTECTION FOR THE TRAFFIC VICTIM (1965), has been summarized this way by Professor O'Connell:

> The essential feature of the Basic Protection Plan is the elimination of the great mass of small and medium-sized tort claims. Because it is so difficult to know and/or to prove who was at fault in the typical automobile accident and to translate pain and suffering into dollars and cents, the variables involved in a negligence claim are almost immeasurable. The result is extensive and often protracted negotiations between motorists, their legal counsel, and the insurance adjustors to determine what payment, if any, should be made. An-

Editor's Note: Reproduced from *Rutgers - Camden Law Journal,* Volume 6, Fall 1974, Number 2.

The relevant legislation, commonly known as the Motorists Protection Act,[2] came into force on January 1, 1972. This study, which was funded by the Council on Law-Related Studies, attempts to assess the impact of the Act in its first two years of operation. It is a modest companion piece to the studies of "no-fault" automobile insurance in Massachusetts and Florida that are also being carried out under the auspices of the Council.[3] This study will offer a fairly comprehensive, but by no means complete, picture of the impact which the legislation has had on the system of automobile accident reparations in Delaware. Obviously it will be some years before the effect of the legislation becomes entirely clear. The empirical material in the study deals with the impact of the "no-fault" legislation on courts and lawyers.[4] The data was obtained from the pleading files of state and federal courts in Delaware,[5] and from a survey of Delaware attorneys, including those engaged in motor vehicle accident litigation.[6] We lacked the resources to do a massive study of insurance company files, but were able to supplement our data by discussions with state officials, lawyers, and insurance company supervisory personnel.

---

other result is that more money can be spent arguing over a claim than the claim would be worth, if paid. This consequent "nuisance" value often coerces an insurance company to pay an inflated value for a claim just to get rid of it. This means, of course, that a payment supposedly made to compensate for pain and suffering is often actually a payment to buy off the "nuisance" value of a "twinge in the back—or neck" whether real or imaginary.

O'Connell, *A Balanced Approach to Auto Insurance Reform: O'Connell Answers His Critics*, 41 U. COL. L. REV. 81, 82 (1969).

2. 58 Del. Laws ch. 98 [1971] (codified at DEL. CODE ANN. tit. 18, §§ 3902(a), (b), tit. 21, § 2118 (Michie Noncum. Supp. 1972)) [hereinafter referred to as "Motorists Protection Act" or "the Act"]. *See also* 58 Del. Laws ch. 353 [1972], *amending* DEL. CODE ANN. tit. 21, § 2118(a)(2)(b) (Michie Noncum. Supp. 1972) making special provisions for motorcycles. The Delaware law, which is discussed in Ghiardi & Kircher, *Automobile Insurance Reparations Plans: An Analysis of Eight Existing Laws*, 55 MARQ. L. REV. 1, 5-16 (1972), is based essentially on a bill floated by the Insurance Company of North America. For a discussion of the latter see Ross, *The INA Bill: A New Approach to Automobile Insurance*, 5 VALPARAISO L. REV. 557 (1971).

3. Preliminary reports on these two studies have appeared in Widiss & Bovbjerg, *No Fault in Massachusetts: Its Impact on Courts and Lawyers*, 59 A.B.A.J. 487 (1973); Little, *How No Fault Is Working in Florida*, 59 A.B.A.J. 1020 (1973).

4. Data runs were made on an IBM 360/67 computer located at Rutgers University at New Brunswick, using the Statistical Package for Social Sciences (SPSS) developed by Norman Nie, Dale H. Bent and C. Hadai Hull. This system was selected because it offered flexibility in the data format, allowed data transformation and file manipulation, and provided a comprehensive and easy to read output format without a great amount of coding. While a large variety of statistical programs are available on SPSS, we needed only the descriptive statistics portion and made no attempt to use inferential statistics.

5. *See* text accompanying notes 26-33 *infra*.

6. *See* text accompanying notes 76-77 *infra*; Appendix 3 *infra*.

II. THE DELAWARE LAW

The Delaware legislation is "no-fault" in the sense that it provides for compulsory first-party benefits,[7] but not in the sense that the right to sue in tort is abolished or limited by a partial tort exemption (or "threshold") requirement. It requires every owner of a motor vehicle registered in the state,[8] who operates or authorizes any other person to operate the vehicle, to obtain, *inter alia*, "Personal Injury Protection" (PIP)[9] insurance. This insurance provides

> compensation to injured persons for reasonable and necessary expenses for medical, hospital, dental, surgical, medicine, X-ray, ambulance or prosthetic devices, professional nursing and funeral services, and for loss of earnings and reasonable and necessary extra expense for personal services which would have been performed by the injured person had he not been injured, arising out of an accident involving such motor vehicle and incurred or medically ascertainable within 12 months of said accident. This compensation shall have minimum limits of $10,000 for any 1 person and $20,000 for all persons injured in any 1 accident. The compensation for funeral services . . . shall not exceed the sum of $2,000 per person.[10]

This coverage is applicable "to each person occupying such motor vehicle and to any other person injured in an accident involving such motor vehicle, other than an occupant of another motor vehicle."[11] The owner of a vehicle may elect to take "certain deductibles, waiting

---

7. *I.e.* benefits obtained by the insured (and passengers and others entitled) from his or her own insurance company without a showing of fault. Such coverage may be compared with typical "third-party" coverage in which an injured party must try to obtain damages from a "guilty" third-party's insurer. In the third-party situation, the potential plaintiff has no ongoing relationship with the insurer. *See generally* KEETON & O'CONNELL, *supra* note 1, at 343-50.

8. DEL. CODE ANN. tit. 21, § 321 (1953), requires every "motor vehicle, semi-trailer and pole trailer" to be registered. DEL. CODE ANN. tit. 21, § 101 (1953), defines "motor vehicle" as "every vehicle, as defined in this section, which is self-propelled, except farm tractors . . ." and defines "vehicle" as "every device in, upon or by which any person or property is or may be transported or drawn upon a public highway, excepting devices moved by human power or used exclusively upon stationary rails or tracks, and excepting trackless trolley coaches . . . ." The only significant group of vehicles normally garaged in the state but not included in the legislation appears to be a few hundred federal vehicles. Federal vehicles are not required to be registered in the states. State, municipal and county vehicles are regarded as included under the Act and insurance for them is purchased by the State Insurance Department.

9. The Act does not use the terms "Personal Injury Protection" or "PIP" to describe the first-party benefits, but the term is in common usage in the state and this usage has been followed herein in referring to PIP benefits.

10. DEL. CODE ANN. tit. 21, § 2118(a)(2) (Michie Noncum. Supp. 1972).

11. DEL. CODE ANN. tit. 21, § 2118(a)(2)(a) (Michie Noncum. Supp. 1972).

periods, sublimits, percentage reductions [and the like], applicable
to expenses incurred as a result of injury to the owner of the vehicle
or members of his household . . . ."[12]

The insured is required to be covered, apparently on a strict liability basis, for

> [c]ompensation for damage to property arising as a result of an accident involving the motor vehicle, other than damage to a motor vehicle, aircraft, water craft, self-propelled mobile equipment and any property in or upon any of the aforementioned, with the minimum limits of Five Thousand Dollars ($5,000.00) for any one accident.[13]

Unlike the Massachusetts plan,[14] however, the "no-fault" provisions
do not extend to damage to the vehicle itself, although the insurer must
offer the insured the opportunity to buy coverage, subject to maxima,
for damage to the insured's motor vehicle, including loss of use.[15]

One further compulsory feature of the legislation deserves mention. Prior to its passage, Delaware had only a typical financial responsibility law, entitled the Motor Vehicle Safety-Responsibility Law,[16]
aimed at insuring that tortfeasors were able to satisfy judgments.
While this law remains in effect, under the new legislation an owner
is additionally required to have coverage providing "[i]ndemnity from
legal liability for bodily injury, death or property damage arising out
of ownership, maintenance or use of the vehicle . . . ."[17] Since its

---

12. DEL. CODE ANN. tit. 21, § 2118(a)(2)(b) (Michie Noncum. Supp. 1972).
The intent of this provision is to enable people to avoid having to pay for double coverage (*e.g.*, Blue Cross/Blue Shield and PIP) for the same items. *See No-Fault Insurance—Hearings on S. 354 Before the Senate Comm. on the Judiciary*, 93d Cong., 1st & 2d Sess. 420-21 (1974) (remarks by Robert A. Short, Delaware Insurance Commissioner). The extent to which it is being used for this end in practice is unknown.

13. DEL. STAT. ANN. tit. 21, § 2118(a)(3) (Michie Noncum. Supp. 1972). The only criterion of responsibility in this subsection, which is separate from the general liability provision, is that the damage arise "as a result of an accident involving the motor vehicle." Presumably damage in excess of the $5,000 minimum (which is also the amount offered by the companies) is dealt with on normal fault principles. Query whether a plaintiff who proves fault and suffers sufficient loss can collect the $5,000 plus the full liability limits (minimum $5,000). A sensible interpretation of the section as a whole would seem to permit this.

14. MASS. GEN. LAWS ANN. ch. 90, § 34A (Cum. Supp. 1974).

15. DEL. STAT. ANN. tit. 21, § 2118(a)(4) (Michie Noncum. Supp. 1972).

16. DEL. CODE ANN. tit. 21, § 2901 *et seq.* (Michie Noncum. Supp. 1972). On the limited effectiveness of financial responsibility laws to insure that the defendant is worth suing see KEETON & O'CONNELL, *supra* note 1, at 102-09; A. WIDISS, A GUIDE TO UNINSURED MOTORIST COVERAGE 4-8 (1969).

17. DEL. CODE ANN. tit. 21, § 2118(a)(1) (Michie Noncum. Supp. 1972), *as amended* 59 Del. Laws ch. 179 [1973].

amendment in 1973, the legislation has made it clear that the required policy limits are those of the Motor Vehicle Safety-Responsibility Law—$10,000 for death or injury to one person, $20,000 for more than one, and $5,000 for property damage.[18]

One of the criticisms often made of the tort system is that the collateral benefits rule (which the Supreme Court of Delaware impliedly has held to be the law in the state)[19] permits some lucky plaintiffs to collect twice—for example, from a medical payments carrier as well as from the tortfeasor.[20] This type of windfall and its attendant waste to the system has been eliminated, at least as far as PIP and liability carriers are concerned.[21] While there is no threshold requirement for tort claims, the Act does provide that

> any person eligible for [PIP] benefits [or for damages to property other than a motor vehicle] is precluded from pleading or introducing into evidence in an action for damages against a tort-feasor

---

18. DEL. CODE ANN. tit. 21, § 2904(b)(2) (Cum. Supp. 1970).

19. *See generally* Yarrington v. Thornburg, 58 Del. 152, 205 A.2d 1 (1964). The rule has been explained thus:

> [T]he plaintiff who has been paid his salary or a pension during disability, or had his medical expenses paid for by another, or out of the proceeds of an accident insurance policy, may still recover full damages for those items from a defendant who is liable for the injury. To this extent, plaintiff may get double payment on account of the same items. The defendant wrongdoer should not, it is said, get the benefit of payments that come to the plaintiff from a "collateral source" (*i.e.* one "collateral" to the defendant).

2 F. HARPER & F. JAMES, THE LAW OF TORTS 1343-44 (1956) (footnotes omitted).

20. Medical payment coverage ("med-pay") was widespread in the past. Over 90% of the liability policies in force with the largest companies in the state in 1971 contained "med-pay" provisions. The extent of double payment is unknown, but we do know that some plaintiffs' attorneys advised their clients of their rights to more than one payment of the same bills in the case of overlapping coverage. Some companies made "med-pay" subrogable; some did not. The incidence of subrogation from the proceeds of damage suits was apparently small.

21. It is probably still possible to claim under PIP and again under some forms of accident insurance, such as that issued by automobile clubs to their members. Some difficulties survive which will probably lead to suit. For instance, there are problems concerning the collateral benefits rule and sick leave entitlements. The term "loss of earnings" is undefined in the statute but is interpreted both in § 4(2) of the Delaware Insurance Commissioner's Amended Regulation No. 9 Dec. 20, 1972, concerning the Delaware Motorists Protection Act, and in the policy form used in the state as "any amounts actually lost, net of taxes on income which would have applied by reason of inability to work and earn wages or salary or their equivalent that would otherwise have been earned in the normal course of an injured person's employment but not other income." Must an employee use up any sick leave entitlement before qualifying for PIP wage payments? What if he does use up his sick leave with the motor accident and then suffers an illness from another source? Can he now go back to the PIP carrier? *See* Current Legislation, *How Faultless are the No-Fault Statutes—A State Survey*, 13 B.C. IND. & COM. L. REV. 935, 942 (1972).

those damages for which compensation is available . . . without regard to any elective reductions in such coverage and whether or not such benefits are actually recoverable.[22]

The obvious intent of this subsection is to make sure that a person obtaining PIP benefits will not subsequently be able to recover the same compensation from the tortfeasor. The first-party insurer may, however, be able to recover the amount of the PIP benefits paid by it from the tortfeasor's carrier or from the injured party's workmen's compensation carrier in a subrogation action which is permitted by the law.[23]

An interesting side effect of this new prohibition of windfall judgments, suggested to us by some of those involved in drafting the legislation, is that juries may be encouraged to keep damage awards low. If the plaintiff is not permitted to prove special damages the jury will be prevented from operating on a multiplier principle to arrrive at a figure for pain and suffering. On the other hand, most of the lawyers and insurance people we interviewed felt that Delaware juries (and insurance companies and their lawyers engaged in settlement negotiations) never have operated in this way[24] and that the effect of not telling the jury the amount of the special damages is, therefore, minimal. There have been too few cases tried since the Act became effective to obtain any firm impressions on this point. Clearly, however, the dollar value of the special damages is only one of many methods by which a skillful plaintiff's attorney can inform the jury of a client's pain and suffering.

It is a curious commentary on the innate conservatism of lawyers that in a substantial proportion of the files we examined that bore post-"no-fault" accident dates, special damages, which presumably had already been paid by PIP insurers, were cheerfully pleaded. Furthermore, defense counsel failed to contest the pleading of such damages in a number of cases.

---

22. DEL. CODE ANN. tit. 21, § 2118(g) (Michie Noncum. Supp. 1972). The law says that the "person eligible" may not plead or prove special damages. May the defendant do so in an effort to minimize injury? It could be advantageous to do so on some occasions.

23. DEL. CODE ANN. tit. 21, § 2118(f) (Michie Noncum. Supp. 1972) states, "Insurers providing benefits described in subsections (a)(1), (a)(2), (a)(3) and (a)(4) shall be subrogated to the rights, including claims under any Workmen's Compensation law of the person for whom benefits are provided, to the extent of the benefits provided."

24. In spite of these protestations, it should be noted that there were a number of offers of judgment (see note 55 *infra*) recorded on the files that were for amounts that looked suspiciously like figures 2 or 3 times the special damages claims rounded off to the nearest 50 or 100. It was not possible to detect such a pattern in jury verdicts, however.

III. IMPACT ON THE COURTS

Our expectation was that there would be a significant drop in the number of cases filed in the courts. The figures did not bear this out. If a drop has in fact occurred, it has been small at best.[25]

Our court study covered the period from January 1, 1970 to December 31, 1973, two years prior and subsequent to the advent of "no-fault." It comprised an examination[26] of all the court files for motor vehicle bodily injury cases[27] filed during the relevant period in courts having appropriate jurisdiction. These courts are the courts of common pleas and the superior courts for each of the state's three counties, New Castle, Kent and Sussex, and the United States District Court for the District of Delaware. The superior court is the court of general jurisdiction in which the great bulk of the litigation took place. Indeed, the Superior Court for New Castle County in Wilmington, which serves the northern and most populous area of the state,[28] received most of the superior court litigation. In New Castle County the court of common pleas has concurrent jurisdiction with the superior court for claims not exceeding $3,000.[29] No jury trial is available in the New Castle Court of Common Pleas, but litigants desiring a jury trial may have their cases transferred to the Superior Court.[30] In Kent and Sussex Counties, the courts of common pleas have exclusive jurisdiction over claims not exceeding $3,000,[31] and jury trial is available.[32]

---

25. The argument that legislation like the Delaware statute will reduce litigation is plausible enough and we began with the hypothesis that it was true. It rests on "the fact, known from current experience with no-release settlements, that most people with minor injuries are reluctant to sue on liability grounds if their out-of-pocket expenses are paid." Ross, *supra* note 2, at 563. The difficulty is that the statistics indicate that no substantial reduction of litigation has taken place.

26. A copy of the work sheet used is contained in Appendix 1 *infra*.

27. For the sake of completeness the study included not only the typical cases where an injured victim (or estate) sued an alleged tortfeasor, but also any others where an action was brought as a result of someone suffering personal injury. The numbers of such cases turned out to be small—4 subrogation claims by uninsured motorist carriers, 11 claims by insureds against their uninsured motorist carriers and 1 claim by the United States under the Federal Medical Care Recovery Act, 42 U.S.C. § 2651 (1970).

28. According to the 1970 census, the total population of the state was 548,104. New Castle County had 385,856 people, 80,386 of whom were residents of the city of Wilmington. Kent County, whose courts are situated in the state capital, Dover, had a population of 81,892. Sussex County, with courts in Georgetown, had 80,356. 1 U.S. DEP'T OF COMMERCE, SOCIAL AND ECONOMIC STATISTICS ADMINISTRATION, BUREAU OF THE CENSUS, CHARACTERISTICS OF THE POPULATION, pt. 9 (Delaware) (1970).

29. $2,500 prior to August 3, 1973. 59 Del. Laws ch. 133 [1973].

30. DEL. CODE ANN. tit. 10, §§ 1361, 1362 (Cum. Supp. 1970).

31. $2,500 prior to August 3, 1973. 59 Del. Laws ch. 133 [1973].

32. DEL. CODE ANN. tit. 10, §§ 1581, 1681 (Cum. Supp. 1970).

There was little personal injury litigation in the courts of common pleas. Of the 1,766 cases filed during the years in question, only 106 were filed in the courts of common pleas and only 120 were filed in the United States District Court. The superior courts handled 1,322 cases in New Castle, 50 in Sussex, and 168 in Kent.[33]

The study originally contemplated drawing comparisons between the effect of the Act on urban and rural areas, but the figures for the southern counties of Sussex and Kent were too small to engender confidence in them as a source for statistical conclusions. The Sussex County files appeared to contain a higher proportion of cases than those in the other two counties involving collisions with livestock and one-car accidents where the plaintiff-passenger was trying to overcome the effects of the Guest Act.[34] It seems likely, therefore, that Sussex County contains a higher proportion than the other two counties of people who might have received nothing under the simple tort system, but who are at least receiving some PIP benefits under the "no-fault" Act.

TABLE I

CROSS-TABULATION OF DATE OF FILING SUIT BY DATE OF ACCIDENT
All Courts

Date Filed	Date of Accident						Total Filed in Year
	1968	1969	1970	1971	1972	1973	
1970	188	156	57	0	0	0	402
1971	4	232	152	48	0	0	436
1972	1	2	266	135	32	0	437
1973	1	3	9	285	142	47	491

In an effort to illustrate the impact of the "no-fault" legislation

---

33. Court by court tables appear in Appendix 2 *infra.*
34. *See* note 84 *infra.*

on the courts, the settlement process, and the amounts of settlements or awards, four tables analyzing different types of data have been compiled. Table I compares the date of accident-litigation filings with the date the accident occurred. There are several ways of approaching this data. One is to consider the total number of motor vehicle bodily injury cases filed in courts during each year—the "Total Filed in Year."[35] These raw figures seem to indicate that there has been little change in the four year period or, at most, that there has been a modest *increase*—most noticeable in 1973. They do not, however, take adequate account of the effect of the two year statute of limitations[36] and of the tendency of lawyers to delay in filing actions. Because of such delays the 1972 and 1973 filings still contain cases arising out of pre-"no-fault" accidents. Hence, the cross-tabulation lines on the Table are included. Diagonal lines have been drawn across Table I to highlight the significance of the number of filings made in the year of the accident and in the following year. The figures highlighted by the diagonal lines indicate that 32 actions concerning 1972 accidents were filed in 1972 and 47 actions for 1973

---

35. While the case load may appear small, it should be stressed that these are the figures for *all* litigation involving automobile accident personal injury cases. Such litigation in Delaware is not the industry that it is in Massachusetts or a typical larger metropolitan area. Totals for cases filed in each year are 402 in 1970, 436 in 1971, 437 in 1972 and 491 in 1973. To underscore the magnitude of its contribution to the sample, the corresponding figures for New Castle Superior Court are 289, 317, 337 and 379, respectively.

36. DEL. CODE ANN. tit. 10, § 8118 (Cum. Supp. 1970). In our study 46 cases were filed beyond the two year period. Apart from a few cases where the defendant successfully moved to dismiss on the basis of the statute, the files are seldom illuminating on how the plaintiff confronted the problem. One of the few that were explicable was a claim by the United States pursuant to the Federal Medical Care Recovery Act, 42 U.S.C. § 2651 (1970), which has a three year limitation. It might appear that there is something of a local custom not to plead the statute. Some instances perhaps can be explained by the effects of an interesting provision enacted in 1970 to try to encourage insurers to make periodic advance payments to injured plaintiffs, without such payments being treated as an admission of liability. DEL. CODE ANN. tit. 10, § 4318 (Cum. Supp. 1970), which states in part:

> Any person, including any insurer, who makes . . . an advance or partial payment, [as an accommodation to an injured person or on his behalf to others or to the estate or dependents of a deceased person . . . under . . . section 906(a)(2) of Title 18], shall at the time of the payment notify the recipient in writing of the statute of limitations applicable to such injury or death. Failure to provide such written notice shall operate to toll any applicable statute of limitations or time limitations from the time of such advance or partial payment until such written notice is actually given.

While there were occasional files in the court which indicated that credit was being given for advance payments, the practice of making such payments does not appear to have been widespread.

accidents were filed in 1973.[37]   Similar figures for 1970 and 1971 are 57 and 48, respectively.   For cases filed in the year *after* the date of accident, the figures show that 152 cases concerning 1970 accidents were filed in 1971, 135 cases concerning 1971 accidents were filed in 1972 and 142 cases for 1972 accidents were filed in 1973. Nearly all cases were filed within 2 years of the accident, as might be expected because of the statute of limitations.[38]   Overall, these figures suggest, at most, a slight drop in litigation.   This is most noticeable for 1972 cases filed in 1972, although some of that drop in volume was recouped in 1973.   The 47 cases filed in 1973 for 1973 accidents suggest that actions for 1973 accidents filed in 1974 could approach the level of the 1971 accidents filed in 1972, if the 1974 filings of 1973 accidents follows the pattern set by the 1972 cases filed in 1973.

During the course of the study, it seemed apparent that the statistics were pointing to an unexpected conclusion: that so far as litigation was concerned, the new law had made very little difference.   Accordingly, we thought that perhaps some other factor had affected the pattern of personal injury litigation in the state.   One hypothesis suggested was that for some reason unrelated to the "no-fault" law itself the number of potential plaintiffs had increased.   For example, if, for some reason twice as many people were able to sue as before, it could be argued that the "no-fault" legislation had had a noticeable effect since the actual number of suits remained the same.   There was no indication, however, of such an explanation.

In determining that there was no such explanation, the main factors that we considered were the number of vehicles on the road and the number of accidents, fatalities and injuries.   The number of vehicles registered in the state for the years in question was 302,914 in 1970; 309,879 in 1971; 316,666 in 1972; and 329,315 in 1973,[39]

---

37. These figures include 7 claims against PIP carriers, 3 of which were joined with suits against alleged tortfeasors.   All of the PIP claims were in the New Castle County Superior Court and all were filed in 1973.   Six had accident dates in 1972 and one in 1973.   None of these cases had been terminated by December 31, 1973.

38. DEL. CODE ANN. tit. 10, § 8118 (Cum. Supp. 1970).

39. These figures and those in note 40 *infra* for accidents and injuries reported to the State Division of Motor Vehicles were supplied by Mrs. Hattie W. Tarburton, Administrative Officer, Delaware Division of Motor Vehicles, Safety Responsibility Department, in letters to Roger S. Clark, Feb. 21, May 4, 1974.   The total in the text includes what are described as "Pleasures," "Commercials," "Recreational Vehicles," "Farm Tractors," "Motor Cycles," "Stock Cars," "Construction Tags" and "Farm Trucks," but does not include "Trailers."

an increase of a little over 9 percent between 1970 and 1973. One might expect a corresponding increase in the volume of accidents and injuries, but this did not occur. The number of accidents reported to the State Police for the years in question was 17,584 in 1970; 16,841 in 1971; 17,101 in 1972; and 17,271 in 1973. The number of fatalities was 152 in 1970; 117 in 1971; 133 in 1972; and 129 in 1973. The number of people injured was 5,651 in 1970; 5,604 in 1971; 5,673 in 1972 and 6,194 in 1973.[40] It appears that for sev-

---

40. Letter from Col. James L. Ford, Jr., Superintendent, Delaware State Police to Roger S. Clark, June 24, 1974. There is, however, some question about the reliability of the statistics. There are two parallel systems of reporting required by Delaware State Law. DEL. CODE ANN. tit. 21, § 4203(a) (Cum. Supp. 1970), which governs Col. Ford's statistics, provides:

> The driver of any vehicle involved in an accident resulting in injury or death to any person or property damage to an apparent extent of $100 or more shall immediately . . . report such accident to the nearest State Police Station except that when such accident occurs within the City of Wilmington, such report shall be made to the Department of Public Safety in that city.

The Motor Vehicle Safety-Responsibility Law, DEL. CODE ANN. tit. 21, § 2909(a) (Cum. Supp. 1970) provides:

> The Secretary of Public Safety shall require all persons involved in accidents [resulting in bodily injury or death or damage to the property of any one person in apparent excess of $100] to make reports of such accidents on forms furnished by the Department of Public Safety within five days from the date of such accidents, provided the person is sufficiently mentally and physically able to make such reports. In the event a person is unable to make such reports, then he shall be exempted under this section from making such report of accidents until such time as the disability is removed, at which time he shall make the report within five days from the date the disability is removed. . . .

DEL. CODE ANN. tit. 21, § 2910 (Cum. Supp. 1970) provides:

> The Secretary of Public Safety shall handle the filing of the standard forms as used in other States, for the estimating of the security required, and for the suspending, revoking and reinstalling of licenses and registrations as required by this chapter. . . .
> . . . The State Police shall help enforce this chapter.

Clearly a complete record is not kept. The number of accidents reported to the Department of Motor Vehicles under the latter statute is: 13,601 in 1970, 14,984 in 1971, 15,458 in 1972 and 15,615 in 1973. The number of injured persons reported is 4,074 in 1970, 3,165 in 1971, 3,348 in 1972 and 2,579 in 1973. Letter from Mrs. Hattie W. Tarburton, Administrative Officer, Delaware Division of Motor Vehicles, Safety Responsibility Department, to Roger S. Clark, Feb. 21, 1974. A copy of these figures was sent to the Superintendent of the State Police in an attempt to have the disparity between the two sets of figures explained. He replied:

> This data sheet which you included with your letter represents figures collected by the State Highway Department's Division of Financial Responsibility. The total number of accidents reported represents those which were reported to that division by the operators involved. Since the figure for total accidents is approximately 2,000 less than that reported by our department, it is obvious that not all operators are complying with the laws for reporting. The total accident figure 17,271 is the official total for 1973.

Letter from Col. James L. Ford, Jr., Superintendent, Delaware State Police, to Roger

eral years (at least until 1972) Delaware, like other states, experienced a drop in the rate of injuries resulting from accidents in relation to the number of vehicles registered and vehicle miles traveled.[41] Thus between 1970 and 1972, despite the rise in the number of vehicles, the number of injuries was more or less constant and the number of fatalities dropped—in other words, cars or roads seemed to be getting safer. The figures for 1973 showed a significant increase in injuries, notwithstanding the impact of the energy crisis in the latter part of the year. This surprising discovery led us to suspect that the increase might be due, at least in part, to some administrative change which had improved the collection of accident data.[42] We have not been able, however, to find any such change. It seems, therefore, that the number of actions commenced, at least with respect to 1972 accidents, has not been affected by the increased number of vehicles on the road, since the number of people injured has remained more or less constant. The number of suits (47) filed in 1973 with respect to 1973 accidents may be a little larger than might otherwise have been expected, had the number of reported injuries not increased that year. But no clear inferences can be drawn to explain this increase until the 1974 filing figures are available. It is clear, however, that neither the 1972 nor the 1973 filings were significantly distorted by the minor variations in the pool of potential plaintiffs.[43]

S. Clark, June 20, 1974. It would appear that some people fill out one of the two forms, some people fill out both—and some fill out neither. How many accidents and injuries go completely unreported is, of course, unknown. In addition, the Department of Transportation statistics in our possession, which were close to, but not identical with the State Police figures, constitute yet a third set of numbers of questionable validity.

41. The trend is documented by the annual publication U.S. DEP'T OF TRANSPORTATION, FATAL AND INJURY ACCIDENT RATES. For a description of the rates per thousand vehicles and the rates per 100 million vehicles, see *id.* at 14, 28 (1972); *id.* at 14, 36 (1970). The 1972 and 1973 Delaware fatality figures (*see* note 40 *supra* and accompanying text) are higher than those for 1971, but well below those for 1970. Department of Transportation figures for 1973 were not available at the time of writing. Nationwide figures for fatal accident rates per thousand vehicles have followed a consistent downward trend.

42. Our doubts were compounded by a feeling that something had to be wrong with the Division of Motor Vehicle figures (*see* note 40 *supra*) showing a sharp *drop* in the 1973 injuries. It may well be that the drop in the degree of compliance with reporting requirements associated with the enforcement of liability insurance provisions is a strange side effect of the PIP legislation. A similar phenomenon occurred in Massachusetts. *See* Coombs, *The Massachusetts Experience Under No-Fault*, 44 MISS. L.J. 158, 167-69 (1973).

43. The increased number of vehicles compared with the number of suits, however, ought to lead to a reduction in the cost of insurance for their owners. *See* text following note 100 *infra*.

It had been suggested to us that the constant rate of cases being filed could be partially attributed to an increase in complaints filed by out-of-state plaintiffs not eligible for PIP benefits. Drivers and passengers of vehicles registered in Delaware are covered by PIP wherever they are, but similar occupants of out-of-state vehicles involved in accidents in Delaware are not covered by PIP insurance. They have only a tort remedy unless they are covered by "no-fault" insurance in their home state. The data compiled, however, does not support this hypothesis. If anything, there has been a reduction in the number of claims filed by out-of-state plaintiffs. Files with relevant data were obtained on 1,521 pre-1972 cases and 220 post-"no-fault" cases. Of the pre-"no-fault" claims, 214 (or about 1 in 7) were made by out-of-state plaintiffs—most of these from Maryland, Pennsylvania and New Jersey. Of the post-"no-fault" complaints, 13 (or about 1 in 17) were filed by out-of-state plaintiffs. Thus in the post-"no-fault" sample, 207 out of 220 claims were by in-state plaintiffs, of whom most would have been entitled to some PIP benefits.[44]

---

44. A complete breakdown is as follows:

	Before 1-1-72	After 1-1-72	Row Total
Plaintiff In— Defendant In	1,016	162	1,178
Plaintiff In— Defendant Out	291	45	336
Plaintiff Out— Defendant In	158	9	167
Plaintiff Out— Defendant Out	56	4	60
Column Total	1,521	220	1,741

The characterization "in" or "out" was made on the basis of the party's residence at the time the suit was filed. It is not a perfect index of residence at the time of the accident, but that information was not in the files. Nor is it a perfect index of when the plaintiff was eligible for PIP payments. Quite apart from those who move in or out of the state between the two dates, there is the handful of out-of-staters driving or riding in in-state cars (and vice versa) at the relevant time. In one anomalous case a post-"no-fault" plaintiff, who was listed as "in" because of his address, was riding in an Air Force vehicle not registered in the state. He successfully claimed medical and wage loss in a tort action after establishing that he was not eligible for PIP. Such movements and anomalies probably tend to cancel one another out, and in any event their numbers are too small to affect the general validity of the point made in the text. One other item which is of some interest is the place of accident. We were able to get this information in 1,744 cases. A breakdown is as follows:

	Before 1-1-72	After 1-1-72	Row Total
New Castle	1,207	179	1,386
Kent	174	22	196
Sussex	90	12	102
Out of State	54	6	60
Column Total	1,525	219	1,744

One factor in the "no-fault" law itself that would support an expectation of a slight increase in the number of suits is the compulsory insurance feature of the law.[45]   In Delaware, as elsewhere, it is likely that the uninsured motorist is also the motorist least able to satisfy a judgment.   An increase in the percentage of insured vehicles might be expected to increase the pool of defendants worth suing and, consequently, to increase the number of suits.   The best estimate that can be made of the pre-"no-fault" percentage of insured vehicles (insured with a nudge from the Motor Vehicle Safety-Responsibility Law[46]) is 80-85 percent.[47]   This percentage ought to have increased since the passage of the new legislation, even though the state has not been able to devote considerable resources to the policing of the compulsory features of the Act.   Under the new law proof of insurance is required at registration time and when drivers are asked for their license and registration during traffic stops.[48]   The Division of Motor Vehicles re-

---

45. DEL. CODE ANN. tit. 21, § 2118(a)(1) (Michie Noncum. Supp. 1972).

46. DEL. CODE ANN. tit. 21, § 2941 *et seq.* (Michie Noncum. Supp. 1972), discussed in text accompanying note 16 *supra.*

47. We despair of getting precise percentages of vehicles insured before or after January 1, 1972.   Not only is it difficult to be confident about the insurance company figures for policies issued and in force, but also various state and federal agencies give somewhat different figures for the number of registered vehicles.   There are two relevant figures for insurance policies, those for "written exposure units" (policies in force at the beginning of the year or issued during the year) and those for "earned exposure units" (numbers of yearly premiums earned and paid during the year).   Thus if two different cars were each insured in the state for six months, they would turn up in the statistics as two written units but only one earned unit.   The numbers of earned units give a closer approximation of the number of vehicles insured at any one time than do those of written units.   A person insured on January 1 who cancelled on January 2 makes the "written" statistics, but is not insured if involved in an accident a few days later. If the number of written exposures is higher than the number of earned exposures, the disparity should reflect discontinued policies.   A lapsed policy normally means that the vehicle has become uninsured, although it may mean that the owner has junked it or moved out of state so that it is not being used on the Delaware roads.   The State Department of Insurance supplied the following written exposure figures for automobiles in 1971:

Automobile Registrations	Voluntary Business	Assigned Risk	Combined	Percent of Cars Insured
264,225	199,620	12,847	212,467	80.41

Letter from Everett E. Gale, Jr., Actuarial Supervisor, Delaware Department of Insurance, to Roger S. Clark, July 22, 1974.   In the same year the insurance companies reported to the Commissioner that they had "earned" 215,502 automobile premiums.   This suggests a slightly higher figure than 80%—hence our 80-85% estimate.   The percentage for vehicles other than automobiles may have been a little higher than this.

48. Noncompliance is punishable by a fine of not less than $300 nor more than $1000 and inprisonment for not more than 6 months.   DEL. CODE ANN. tit. 21, § 2118(j) (Michie Noncum. Supp. 1972).   A curious provision in the statute as origi-

ports that there is some evidence that people obtain insurance at the time of registration and then cancel their policies or, through non-payment, allow them to lapse.[49] This assertion seems borne out by the continued filing of a significant number of uninsured motorist's claims.[50] Other states with compulsory insurance laws have never reached 100 percent compliance.[51] A reasonable estimate is that by 1973 Delaware had never achieved much better than 90 percent compliance at any one time.[52]

---

nally enacted rendered it unlikely that many prosecutions would be brought since they involved a great deal of effort. It provided that "[t]he Superior Court . . . shall have exclusive original jurisdiction of any violation of this section . . . ." Motorists Protection Act, 58 Del. Laws ch. 98, § (k) [1971] *as amended* DEL. CODE ANN. tit. 21, § 2118(k) (Michie Noncum. Supp. 1972). Traffic cases are normally processed in justice of the peace courts, but legislation which confers criminal jurisdiction on such courts needs the "concurrence of two-thirds of all the members elected to each House." DEL. CONST. art. 4, § 28. Doubting that such a majority could be mustered, the proponents of the Motorists Protection Act conferred jurisdiction on the superior courts, since only a simple majority was required for this type of enactment. The section was amended in 1972 and jurisdiction conferred on the justice of the peace courts, 58 Del. Laws ch. 443 [1972], *amending* DEL. CODE ANN. tit. 21, § 2118(k) (Michie Noncum. Supp. 1972). According to State Police figures there were 395 arrests for violation of the section in 1973 (Letter from Col. James L. Ford, Jr., Superintendent, Delaware State Police, to Roger S. Clark, June 11, 1974), but it appears that very few of these were in fact prosecuted.

49. Letter from Mrs. Hattie W. Tarburton, Administrative Officer, Delaware Division of Motor Vehicles, Safety Responsibility Department, to Roger S. Clark, Aug. 22, 1973. The Department of Insurance supplied the following figures for written exposure units in 1972 (1973 figures were not available):

Automobile Registrations	Voluntary Business	Assigned Risk	Combined	Percent of Cars Insured
266,923	221,517	45,007	266,524	99.9

Letter from Everett E. Gale, Jr., Actuarial Supervisor, Delaware Department of Insurance, July 9, 1974. Earned exposure for the same year was reported as 227,770. This is of course considerably lower than the written exposure figure and is consistent with a significant number of policies being obtained for registration purposes and then being cancelled. Consequently, the percentage of automobiles insured at any one time was probably somewhere in the range of 85-90%.

50. In the 1972 accident year the companies reported paying 68 such claims and incurring 105, compared with 79 and 131 respectively the year before. No uninsured motorist suits for accidents occurring in 1972 or 1973 turned up in the court study. This is not surprising since all the earlier suits of this type had been filed close to or beyond the two year limitation period. One large company told us that its 1973 uninsured motorist cases were "well up" while another said that they were "down."

51. *See* U.S. DEP'T OF TRANSPORTATION, AUTOMOBILE INSURANCE AND COMPENSATION STUDY, DRIVER BEHAVIOR AND ACCIDENT INVOLVEMENT: IMPLICATIONS FOR TORT LIABILITY 201-13 (1970). It was estimated that in 1967 New York had approximately 93% compliance, North Carolina had 98% and Delaware had 80%. *Id.* at 212. The precise figures must be viewed with caution.

52. This is based on the material in notes 47 & 49 *supra* and the likelihood that

We might add that some cases turned up in which it was likely that the tortfeasor was uninsured. We encountered 4 cases that were subrogation claims by uninsured motorist carriers who had paid their insureds and were trying to recoup their losses. There were 11 claims by injured persons against their own uninsured motorist carriers.[53] 23 pre-"no-fault" and 5 post-"no-fault" cases were default judgments. It is highly unlikely that an insured defendant would suffer a default judgment. Finally, there were a few cases in which the plaintiff took a consent judgment for a round figure such as $1,000, which was considerably less than the special damages pleaded. Here, too, the inference may be drawn that the defendant was uninsured.[54]

The implicit lesson of these cases is that the absence of insurance does not necessarily mean that the plaintiff will not try to recover losses by suit, although it may well mean that, without uninsured motorist coverage, the endeavor to recover losses is doomed to ultimate failure. Since even in the past it was possible for an incident involving an uninsured motorist to appear in court statistics as a suit, an increase of 10 percent, for example, in insured defendants will not result in a 10 percent increase in potential plaintiffs. It is impossible to assess the precise extent to which the compulsory insurance provision has increased litigation in Delaware, but we believe, for the reasons discussed, that the resulting increase in litigation has been small. The compulsory insurance provision's impact is probably greater on the rate of financial recompense than on the volume of litigation. In any event, the lesson of the statistics clearly seems to be that, regardless of whatever else the legislation has done, it has not succeeded in discouraging very many of the Delaware residents who seek damages for pain and suffering.

The "no-fault" legislation *may* have had an impact on lawyers' filing practices. While most Delaware lawyers do not wait until the expiration of the statute of limitations to file, neither do they typically file immediately. In those cases in our sample having accident dates before January 1, 1972, the average time taken to file was 567 days from the date of the accident. Half of the cases were filed more

---

some improvement over the initial year would take place in the second year of the scheme.

53. A number of these uninsured motorist claims were dismissed because the attorney had overlooked the standard arbitration clause in this part of the coverage. One case had an accident date in 1968, 2 in 1969, 6 in 1970 and 2 in 1971.

54. A number of complaints were never served on the defendant. It is probable that at least some of these defendants not served were uninsured.

than 672 days after the accident. It was suggested to us that many cases will be filed close to the tolling of the statute of limitations since some lawyers are waiting to see what will happen to cases currently in litigation before deciding on a course of action. There appears to be no hard data to support this hypothesis, although it may help to explain why only 32 cases arising out of 1972 accidents were filed in the same year. There are obviously more cases yet to be filed involving 1972 and 1973 accidents. Some claims from those years are probably still in the hands of lawyers who are attempting to settle them without suit and others may not yet have been brought to a lawyer. It is also possible that clients who are receiving PIP benefits are less anxious about their tort action and will not be as insistent about seeing that the litigation is pursued, but this, of course, is also speculation. Probably the initial impact of the legislation is now spent. Lawyers, on the whole, are handling tort actions at about the same pace as before. Those who actively manipulated the court procedure, especially the taking of interrogatories and depositions,[55] as part of the settlement process are continuing to file early. Those who preferred to file suit only as a last resort, and close to the two year deadline, are doing just as they did before.

Although we concluded that the effect of the new legislation on the pattern of tort litigation has been minimal, we should mention another study that reached a different conclusion. In July 1973 the Delaware Insurance Commissioner's office conducted a survey of lawyers in the state believed to be engaged in plaintiffs' personal injury work. They were asked two questions:

(1) Approximately how many BI suits[56] did you file resulting from accidents occurring within 18 months previous to January 1, 1972?

(2) Approximately how many BI suits have you filed resulting from accidents that have occurred since January 1, 1972?[57]

---

55. Among the most striking features of the pre-trial proceedings were the efforts by plaintiff's counsel to smoke out the insurance company on the policy limits (DEL. SUPER. CT. (CIV.) R. 26(b)(2)); the careful way in which victims and their spouses appeared to have been schooled prior to the taking of depositions on how to present the evidence necessary to sustain an action for loss of consortium; and use of the offer of judgment procedure (DEL. SUPER. CT. (CIV.) R. 68) to force settlement. This latter procedure was used regularly by three Wilmington firms which handled a substantial amount of defendants' work. Few other practitioners in the state seemed to have heard of it.

56. *I.e.* bodily injury suits against alleged tortfeasors.

57. Questionnaire of July 3, 1973 and results supplied by Mr. Lewis Darlin, Legal Supervisor, Delaware Department of Insurance.

About 30 percent of those surveyed responded. The respondents' re-
plies yielded a total of 145 suits for the first period and 52 for the
second.[58] The figures can be interpreted as indicating a substantial
drop in litigation. In fact, when we compared these survey responses
with our court statistics the imbalance was even more striking. Our
court data showed that in fact by June 30, 1973, 560 BI suits had
been filed resulting from accidents occurring within the 18 months
prior to January 1, 1972, and only 106 had been filed relating to the
period after January 1, 1972. The Commissioner's survey appears to
have underestimated the relative proportion of cases filed with respect
to the earlier period! Nevertheless, these statistics are entirely consistent with our own conclusion that any drop that has occurred has
been small. The key to the discrepancy is the operation of the statute
of limitations and the habits of lawyers with respect to their delay in
filing. As has been mentioned, with respect to accidents occurring between January 1, 1970 and December 31, 1971, the average time
taken to file suits was 567 days and the median 627 days from the
date of the accident.[59] It seemed likely to us that most of the suits
"resulting from accidents occurring within 18 months previous to
January 1, 1972" had been filed by July 1973 (a three-year period),
whereas most of those "resulting from accidents that have occurred
since January 1, 1972" (an eighteen-month period) had not. A true
statistical comparison of the two periods reflecting the effects of filing
practices in relation to the statute of limitations was obtained from our
court data by determining the number of cases arising out of accidents
with dates between July 1, 1970 and December 31, 1971 that had been
filed by December 31, 1971, the end of that eighteen-month period.
These cases numbered 117. The other 443 filings had taken place
after the end of the eighteen-month period! The similarity in the numbers, 117 and 106, filed by the end of the comparable eighteen-month
periods "before" and "after," is consistent with our belief that any
drop in litigation has at best been small. Undoubtedly there are still
many 1972 and 1973 accident cases yet to be filed.[60]

---

58. *Id.*

59. *See* text accompanying note 55 *supra.*

60. Delay is a relative matter and Delaware does not suffer as much as other states.
See note 69 *infra* and accompanying text. But delay in filing and delay in the court system is the true explanation of the phenomenon noted by the Delaware Insurance Commissioner in testimony before a special committee of the Pennsylvania Legislature examining "no-fault" insurance. The Commissioner said that "[n]o lawsuits have been
brought to trial in Delaware in the 20 months since the 'reform' was instituted," and attributed this to psychological factors, stemming from the plan's quick payment of claims
submitted by accident victims. The Evening Bulletin (Philadelphia), August 29, 1973,
at 9, col. 2.

IV.   EFFECT ON THE SETTLEMENT PROCESS

It is probably too soon to see whether there has been any substantial change in settlement practices with respect to those cases finding their way into the courts.   Of the 1,772 cases in our sample, 1,110 had clearly been terminated.   Most of the rest were still wending their way through the process.   About 100 appeared to be "dead."   We assumed that these actions had lapsed for one reason or another, since for the past year or so no new paper had accumulated in their files. What follows is a cross-tabulation of the cases that had clearly been terminated showing the stage at which termination occurred.   The table permits comparison between pre-January 1, 1972 and post-January 1, 1972 cases.

TABLE II

WHEN CASE WAS TERMINATED

	Accidents Before 1-1-72	Cumulative Percentage (Before)	Accidents After 1-1-72	Cumulative Percentage (After)	Row Total	Cumulative Percentage Total
After Complaint Before Answer	155	14.73	16	27.59	171	15.41
After Answer Before Date Set	435	56.08	22	65.52	457	56.58
After Date Set	256	80.42	6	75.86	262	80.18
After Jury Drawn	11	81.46	0	75.86	11	81.17
After Trial Begun	23	83.65	0	75.86	23	83.24
Upon Judgment	164	99.24	13	98.28	177	99.19
Appeal	8	100.00	1	100.00	9	100.00
Column Total	1,052		58		1,110	

Note: 655 observations are missing.   Their files are still not formally "closed."   This group includes some cases that are obviously "dead."   In addition, 23 "before" and 5 "after" default judgments are included in the "Upon Judgment" figures.   In nearly all of these instances no answer was filed.

No blatant differences between the "before" and "after" groups could be discerned.   Obviously enough, some cases were settled almost immediately (after complaint but before answer), probably with some payment by the defendant.   In both the "before" and "after" groups, the largest subgroup contained cases that were terminated at the next stage (after answer but before date).   We did not keep precise figures, but it was apparent from the files that in most of these cases the taking of interrogatories and depositions provided the catalyst for the settlement process.   Most claimants who settled at this stage appeared to have received some recompense.[61]   The next group

---

61.   As one insurance claims supervisor told us, "Every claim has *some* value.   It may not be much—but *some* value."   On the role of the insurance adjuster as a "sharp

(settled after date set) reflects the impact of the pretrial conference in moving a few more cases towards settlement. A few of the pre-1972 cases were settled at the eleventh hour, either after the jury was drawn or the trial begun. Finally, there are the groups which were determined only upon judgment or on appeal. These small groups are, of course, of enormous significance for attorneys who most often must arrange settlements based on their knowledge of the cost of litigation and on their informed hunches about what might happen if their cases should reach the final stage of adjudication.[62] It probably includes a higher proportion of cases in which the plaintiff gets nothing.[63]

One might expect that out of curiosity both plaintiffs' and defendants' counsel would be interested in taking a few post-"no-fault" cases to trial in an effort to see how juries react to the absence of quantified special damages. Perhaps some of the small number of cases going to trial in the post-1972 period reflect this desire, but the numbers are too small to be of significance.[64] Again, there seems to have been little change with respect to settlement practices, but it is too early to be absolutely sure that the new law will have negligible effect.

It was possible to compare the number of cases filed in court and the number that went no further than the insurance companies' files. By the end of the period of this study, a total of 468 cases with accident dates in 1971 found their way into the courts.[65] Probably there will be another half dozen or so to come that, for one reason or another, escape the effect of the statute of limitations. This figure represents about 500 injured persons, since a few of the cases involved multiple plaintiffs who were injured together. In the accident year

---

but decent buyer of commodities," see H. ROSS, SETTLED OUT OF COURT: THE SOCIAL PROCESS OF INSURANCE CLAIMS ADJUSTMENT 66 (1970).

62. It has been suggested that it costs the nation's average defendant $819 in lawyer fees and $284 in expenses to take a case as far as a verdict—a figure which is highly significant in assessing the nuisance value of a case to the insurance company. U.S. DEP'T OF TRANSPORTATION, AUTOMOBILE INSURANCE AND COMPENSATION STUDY, AUTOMOBILE ACCIDENT LITIGATION 37 (1970). This figure, which does not include internal company costs of keeping a file open, is probably indicative of approximate costs in Delaware.

63. Even so, only 38 of the 177 cases finally determined at trial resulted in defendants' verdicts. Of these 33 were pre-"no-fault" cases.

64. Of the 13 post-January 1, 1972 cases concluded "upon judgment," 5 were default judgments for the plaintiff, 3 others were verdicts for the plaintiff and the other 5 resulted in defendants' verdicts. There *may* be a trend toward more defendants' verdicts, but the sample is too small to be more than "suggestive."

65. It was too early to do a similar comparison for 1972 and 1973 accidents because the statute of limitations had not run on all of them by December 31, 1973.

1971, evaluated as of March 31, 1972, the companies reported to the Insurance Commissioner that they had paid 1,552 bodily injury claims and had incurred 2,553 claims.[66] Some of the incurred claims that had not been paid then would no doubt become "paid" over the next couple of years, although it is unlikely that all of the claims will be paid.[67] The practice of listing claims as "incurred" seems to vary somewhat from company to company, and some injuries are listed as "incurred" even though there has never been contact with a potential claimant. This will normally occur when the company has been notified of the apparent injury by only its insured or the Division of Motor Vehicles. Hence the injuries marked "incurred" contain some cases that are highly unlikely ever to become "paid." In any event, if the paid claims are taken as the lower limit and the incurred claims as the upper limit, those cases reaching the court are somewhere between 20 and 30 percent of all claims made to insurers. This is a little higher than the national average.[68] This higher percentage may perhaps be traced to the absence of any log jam of tort cases in the Delaware courts.[69] The state and its citizens have not been so loath to use the courts, since they have not experienced the delays and frustrations of the litigation process that occur in more urban states.

V. Amounts Claimed and Received

We had hoped that the files might tell something conclusive about the effect of the legislation on amounts claimed and received. It was a forlorn hope.

A. Amounts Claimed

The information on amounts of damages pleaded was so sketchy

---

66. They had also incurred 1,708 and paid 1,184 "med-pay" claims. Any final accounting of the overall cost of the Motorists Protection Act system must consider the widespread pre-"no-fault" use of medical payment coverage. *See* note 20 *supra*. The methodology used in a recent attempt at an assessment of costs in Florida needs modification, in order to take into account this highly significant item, before it can be applied adequately in Delaware. *See* Brainard & Fitzgerald, *First-Year Cost Results Under No-Fault Automobile Insurance: A Comparison of the Florida and Massachusetts Experience*, 41 J. Risk & Ins. 25 (1974).

67. The figure for "incurred" includes all paid claims plus "potential" ones. For most companies this means ones for which a reserve has been made.

68. *See* U.S. Dep't of Transportation, Automobile Insurance and Compensation Study, Automobile Accident Litigation, A Report of the Federal Judicial Center for the Department of Transportation 253 (1970).

69. *See* the comparative state figures in The Institute of Judicial Administration, Calendar Status Study, 1973—Personal Injury Cases in *1974 Hearings, supra* note 12, at 359-65.

as to be unrevealing. The main reason for this is the Delaware Rules of Civil Procedure. While some practitioners do plead a specific sum for general damages in the *ad damnum* clause, this is in breach of Rule 9(g) of the Delaware Superior Court Civil Rules.[70] Under Rule 9(g), the defendant may demand notice of the amount the plaintiff is seeking, but the reply is not required to be filed with the court.[71] The rule is undoubtedly aimed at encouraging the settlement process rather than providing illuminating data for researchers.

Even the claims for special damages were not always entirely accurate. A few complaints did not contain the figure at all and merely requested "general and special damages." Others gave an amount but made it clear that further expenses were still being incurred.[72] The post-January 1, 1972 figures are also unreliable because of the practice of pleading special damages that have already been paid by a PIP carrier.[73]

B. Amounts Received

As noted above,[74] most cases are settled before trial, but the amount of the settlement is not usually recorded in the stipulation of dismissal. The most useful information on amounts received that could be gleaned was data on the settlement amount contained in 165 pre-1972 cases and 10 later ones. This group comprised cases that went to judgment[75] or cases in which the amount of settlement was revealed by the parties. The figures since 1972 are sufficiently sparse to be only "suggestive." This data is shown in Tables III and IV.

---

70. DEL. SUPER. CT. (CIV.) R. 9(g) provides:

Damages. A pleading, whether a complaint, counterclaim, cross-claim or a third party claim, which prays for unliquidated money damages, shall demand damages generally without specifying the amount, except when items of special damage are claimed, they shall be specifically stated. Upon service of a written request by another party, the party serving such pleading shall, within ten days after service thereof, serve on the requesting party a written statement of the amount of damages claimed; such statement shall not be filed except on order of the Court.

71. *Id.*

72. In the few cases that get to trial, the amount of special damages is normally agreed upon by pre-trial stipulation. We did not record information from this source, but future researchers may find the stipulations useful.

73. *See* text in paragraph following note 24 *supra.*

74. *See* text accompanying notes 61-63 *supra.*

75. Among those going to judgment were several examples of the action for loss of marital consortium. As mentioned earlier, this action is alive and well in Delaware. *See* note 55 *supra.* Of the consortium cases that went to trial, we noted one judgment each at $1,000, $2,500 and $5,000; 2 each at $500, $2,000 and $3,000; and 3 at $1,500—all good examples of a jury thinking of a round number when it has had to deal with something extremely difficult to put in dollars and cents terms.

TABLE III

INFORMATION ON ACCIDENTS BEFORE 1-1-72

Distribution of Amounts Settled by Agreement or Judgment

	No. of Cases	Cumulative Percentage
$1-250	4	2.4
$251-500	7	6.7
$501-750	5	9.7
$751-1,000	10	15.8
$1,001-1,500	21	28.5
$1,501-2,000	13	36.4
$2,001-2,500	8	41.2
$2,501-3,000	8	46.1
$3,001-4,000	12	53.3
$4,001-5,000	7	57.6
$5,001-10,000	26	73.3
$10,001-20,000	21	86.1
$20,001-50,000	11	92.7
$50,001-100,000	10	98.8
over 100,000	2	100.0
Total known	165	
Total not settled or unknown	1,379	
Total	1,554	

TABLE IV

INFORMATION ON ACCIDENTS AFTER 1-1-72

Distribution of Amounts Settled by Agreement or Judgment

	No. of Cases	Cumulated Percentage
$1-250	1	10.0
$501-750	1	20.0
$751-1,000	1	30.0
$1,001-1,500	1	40.0
$1,501-2,000	2	60.0
$2,001-2,500	1	70.0
$3,001-4,000	1	80.0
$5,001-10,000	1	90.0
over 10,000	1	100.0
Total known	10	
Total not settled or unknown	211	
Total	221	

It should be noted that the amounts include both general and special damages. Presumably the post-"no-fault" figures in nearly all cases are deflated by the previous payment of PIP amounts which would otherwise turn up in the tort claims. The figures do seem to suggest two things: first, the absence of a substantial number of "nuisance" claims both before and after "no-fault," and secondly, the absence of any startling change since the new legislation. The first inference is, of course, quite consistent with the very low number of cases being brought in the courts of common pleas and with the state's reputation for not being claims-conscious.

VI. IMPACT ON THE LEGAL PROFESSION

With a population of little more than half a million people, Delaware has a small bar. In July of 1973 we sent a questionnaire to the 372 attorneys listed in Martindale-Hubbell as members of the Delaware bar in private practice.[76] The list included nearly all of those who appeared as plaintiff's or defendant's counsel on the court files we had studied by then. The number of usable responses, 107, was somewhat disappointing.[77] Although a careful effort was made to keep the survey confidential, we believe, from discussions with several attorneys and from cover letters and comments from others who kindly took extra time to record their impressions, that the sample included most of those who do a significant amount both of plaintiff's and of defendant's work. Most of the respondents in fact did some personal injury work, although in the majority of cases it constituted only a small proportion of their total professional income. The questionnaire was sent to individuals, but it was apparent from some of the answers that "firm" responses had been received from some of the larger groups of lawyers practicing together. This sample of attorneys represented a range of years of practice from none to over thirty, with the largest cluster of practitioners in the 5-10 (27) and 10-20 (34) year range.

The questionnaire first asked a series of attitude questions to see whether the support of the bar that existed at the time of the passage of the legislation still continued. Most of the respondents favored re-

---

76. A copy of the questionnaire is reproduced in Appendix 3 *infra.*

77. But this return is about average for this type of research. The Federal Judicial Center in its study of automobile accident litigation for the Department of Transportation had a 32% return. *See* FEDERAL JUDICIAL CENTER, AUTOMOBILE ACCIDENT LITIGATION 4 (1970). In retrospect it probably would have been wiser to survey only those attorneys whose names had been obtained from the court survey. The survey questionnaire and cover letter attempted to make it clear that we were interested in the views of "the bar as a whole." A number of unanswered questionnaires were returned by attorneys engaged primarily in corporate work who courteously stated that they had no relevant views.

tention of the present "no-fault" system: 66.4 percent were in favor of continuing it, 26.2 percent were against, and the rest did not answer. Most did not want a change to threshold-type "no-fault": 61.7 percent were against such a change, 29 percent were for, and 9.3 percent gave no answer.

Secondly, the questionnaire tried to assess the loss of legal work that appeared to have occurred as a result of the "no-fault" legislation. It appears that in terms of personal injury work overall attorney activity and income have decreased somewhat. For example, in 1971, the year before "no-fault" began, 11.2 percent of the respondents derived half or more of their income from personal injury claims. In 1972, the percentage was 8.4. The percentage of respondents claiming less than 25 percent of their income from personal injury work increased from 55.1 percent in 1971 to 65.4 percent in 1972. The size of the sample must be appreciated in determining the significance of these changes. The actual number of people involved is small and reflects a tendency of those involved most deeply in this type of litigation to respond more readily. Those who had been affected by "no-fault" were changing their activities either by expanding into other fields of law or by increasing their time spent on other economic activities. The percentage of those anticipating a change to other fields of law was 32.1 percent; 16.7 percent said that they were increasingly engaging in other economic activities.[78]

Our survey instrument was not sensitive enough to quantify this change in terms of dollars and cents. But in response to the question "how would you characterize the impact of personal injury 'no-fault' on your practice since January 1, 1972?," the following answers were given: none, 36.4 percent; small, 32.7 percent; moderate, 21.5 percent; substantial, 7.5 percent.[79] Of those who were increasing their work in other areas, most indicated that they were expanding in the areas we listed as business, commercial, corporate, tax and civil (other than auto). A few were doing more criminal work, and even fewer checked off estate planning, wills, and real estate.

Again, it is clear that there has been some impact on the profession, but it does seem that the impact has been modest. With two possible exceptions,[80] no attorney claimed to have suffered a major

---

78. There was some indication in the data that those who do more defendants' work than plaintiffs' work were being affected more. This interpretation, however, was eventually rejected.

79. The percentages do not quite round out to 100, because one respondent wrote in "[s]mall to moderate," and another did not reply.

80. One respondent reported reducing the number of attorneys in his office and another decided not to hire additional people.

career setback as a result of the legislation. Those affected all seemed to be adapting by making some shifts into other areas.

A surprising number of attorneys reported helping clients to file PIP claims. Of the attorneys who responded, 45 maintained that they had helped clients to file a total of 942 PIP claims in the previous 18 months. The actual figure is suspect, since many of the attorneys answered in "round" numbers, such as 5, 10, etc. But these answers, as well as anecdotal discussions with attorneys, suggest definite activity in this area. Much of this assistance has apparently been rendered free of charge as a service for steady clients. The practice may never even come to the attention of the insurance company in claims in which the attorney has merely helped to fill in the forms and the client, rather than the lawyer, has forwarded them to the company. It seems quite common for a practitioner handling a third-party claim to fight the paper war—sometimes for a flat fee—also on the first-party claim. We understand that the actual work and profit from this line of activity is minimal.[81] A number of our respondents felt that the legislation could be improved by adding a provision for payment of attorney's fees by the company when the attorney has helped a client file a first-party claim—especially when the company has dragged its feet.[82]

VII.   What Does It All Mean?

In interviews with insurance company officials and officials at the Delaware Insurance Department, the view was continually expressed that "no-fault" was working in Delaware. Statistical evidence, however, puts this assertion into question at least so far as litigation is concerned. It is necessary to consider what really has been happening in Delaware. The remarks that follow attempt such an assessment.

There is no doubt that the Insurance Department and the companies have worked together to make the new system operate smoothly and in most instances to the public's benefit. The $10,000/20,000 minimum PIP limits are fairly generous.[83] People who suffer serious

---

81. Spangenberg, *No-Fault Fact, Fiction, and Fallacy*, 44 Miss. L.J. 15, 41 (1973), notes that "traditionally" lawyers have helped in making medical payments and collision claims without charge.

82. Section 6(b) of the Delaware Insurance Commissioner's Amended Regulation 9, Dec. 20, 1972, provides that "[PIP] benefits shall be payable within 30 days of the demand thereof by the claimant; provided, that reasonable proof of loss for which the benefits as demanded have been submitted to the PIP carrier." No penalty is prescribed for overdue payments. *Cf.* New Jersey Automobile Reparation Reform Act, N.J.S.A. 39:6A-5 (1972), which imposes a penalty for late payments.

83. *Cf.* Personal Injury Protection Act, Mass. Gen. Laws Ann. ch. 90, § 34A

injury are having their medical bills paid and are also receiving, subject to policy limits, lost wages and other services. This probably means that some do not need to rush into possibly unwise settlements of their bodily injury claims. They can wait until the injury stabilizes.

A higher proportion of injured people are entitled to make successful claims under the system. Injured passengers whose claims would often have been totally frustrated by the Automobile Guest Statute,[84] (which remains in force) and those who would formerly have had their claims defeated by an inability to prove negligence or by the doctrine of contributory negligence are now receiving payments under PIP. But in practice not everyone injured in an insured vehicle is recovering. The form of endorsement used in the state includes the following exclusions:

This insurance does not apply:

(a) while the motor vehicle is used as a public or livery conveyance unless such use is specifically declared and described in the policy;

(b) to any person who sustains bodily injury while occupying a motor vehicle located for use as a residence or premises;

(c) to bodily injury resulting from the radioactive, toxic, explosive or other hazardous properties of nuclear materials;

(d) to any person who sustains bodily injury due to war, whether or not declared, civil war, insurrection, rebellion or revolution, or to any act or condition incident to any of the foregoing;

(e) to any person who sustains bodily injury to the extent that benefits therefore are in whole or in part either payable or required to be provided under any workmen's compensation law;

(f) to any person while operatng the insured motor vehicle without the express or implied consent of the named insured;

(Cum. Supp. 1974), which sets a minimum of $2,000. A useful comparative table of different state laws appears in Keeton, *supra* note 1, at 385.

84. DEL. CODE ANN. tit. 21, § 6101(a) (1953), provides:

No person transported by the owner or operator of a motor vehicle, boat, airplane or other vehicle as his guest without payment for such transportation shall have a cause of action for damages against such owner or operator for injury, death or loss, in case of accident, unless such accident was intentional on the part of such owner or operator, or was caused by his wilful or wanton disregard of the rights of others.

A large number of prayers for relief in guest cases included a claim for punitive damages which also turns on the "wilful or wanton disregard" standard. We recorded only one instance going to judgment where punitive damages were clearly awarded. That was on an inquisition following the entry of default judgment. Special damages were $582, general damages were $8,000, and punitive damages were $5,000.

(g) to any person, if such person's conduct contributed to his bodily injury under any of the following circumstances:

   (i)   causing bodily injury to himself intentionally;

   (ii) convicted of driving while under the influence of alcohol or narcotic drugs; or

   (iii) while committing a felony.[85]

There is some doubt about the validity of the exclusions in clause (g) in the absence of any specific reference to such exclusions in the "no-fault" Act. The form was approved in apparent reliance on a provision in the Act authorizing coverage to be "subject to conditions and exclusions customary to the field of liability, casualty and property insurance and not inconsistent with the requirements of this section."[86] It has been suggested that "[e]xclusions (g)(ii) and (g)(iii) may be supported by some public policy considerations, but they do not appear to be 'customary' when compared to the typical automobile medical payments coverage endorsement now in use."[87] The actual number of persons affected by the exclusions is probably small, but we understand from discussions with attorneys that the alcohol exclusion has led to some disputes.

It is plain that litigation has not dropped off sharply, if at all, although attorneys seem to be doing less personal injury work. We suspect that attorneys may have somewhat overestimated the actual impact of the legislation on their practices. The most plausible explanation of what effect the legislation has had is that there has been a drop in the number of smaller, including nuisance, claims. Larger claims, however, are continuing to occupy attorneys' time. The litigious are still hiring lawyers and litigating. But under "no-fault," people are dealing with their own insurers in a non-adversary context and seem not to need much legal assistance beyond some help with filling in the forms. This is borne out by the paucity of claims against

---

85. Amendatory Endorsement for Personal Injury Protection for Automobile Liability Policies, Form A956, Pt. I, (1972) (this form states that it is based on the Delaware Motorists Protection Act).

86. DEL. CODE ANN. tit. 21, § 2118(e) (Michie Noncum. Supp. 1972).

87. Ghiardi & Kircher, *supra* note 2, at 8. Medical payments insurance is still being offered in Delaware by some carriers on terms not including such exceptions as those for PIP. *See* note 89 *infra*. Such exceptions are perhaps "customary" in other states with PIP laws, but the companies are empowered by statute to make the exceptions. *See, e.g.*, Massachusetts Personal Injury Protection Act, MASS. GEN. LAWS ANN. ch. 90, § 34A (Cum. Supp. 1974); New Jersey Automobile Reparation Reform Act, N.J.S.A. 39:6A-7 (Supp. 1974). PIP is presumably not "liability insurance" as that term is used in DEL. CODE ANN. tit. 21, § 2118(e) (Michie Noncum. Supp. 1972). Query whether it is "casualty insurance."

PIP carriers. The effect on lawyers thus is more noticeable than the effect on the courts. Lawyers are getting fewer small cases. With those claims that they do get, they are not earning the contingency fee that they would formerly have received on the special damages part of the judgment or settlement.

The preceding assessment is supported by insurance company figures which indicate a drop in the number of BI claims but a rise in overall claims activity (including PIP claims).[88] Of course, there was never a lawyer behind each BI claim in the past, but a decline in such claims probably represents a decline in lawyer-represented claims. Figures for 1973 were not available at the time of this study, but the figures for 1971 and 1972 show that the number of BI claims paid and incurred dropped from 1,552 and 2,553, respectively, in 1971, to 1,339 and 2,354 in 1972. The overall claims picture is a fascinating one that will gain further clarity only when more company data is available. PIP claims in 1972 were 1,810 paid and 2,744 incurred. The PIP paid figure of 1,810 does not quite represent the lower limit of people who have received something from the reparations system since it does not include out-of-state plaintiffs and others not eligible for PIP. Nor does the data on the number of BI claims paid represent the total number of traffic accident victims receiving something under the system's third-party liability provisions. It contains a presently indeterminable number of inter- and perhaps intra-company payments pursuant to the subrogation provision of the "no-fault" Act.[89]

---

88. Figures supplied by the Delaware Department of Insurance. In light of these figures, the responses to our attorney survey and the court data contained in Table I *supra*, the following undocumented claim by Leonard Ring, National President of the Trial Lawyers of America is just plain wrong:

> The Delaware Plan . . . has reduced claims by more than 70 per cent. Lawyer representation has been reduced to the same extent. . . . The Delaware experience has indeed proven that, where the victim has received his medical and wage loss, the incentive to make further claim is extinguished in all but the most serious cases.

Ring, *The Fault With "No-Fault,"* 49 NOTRE DAME LAW. 796, 825-26 (1974) (footnote omitted).

89. DEL. CODE ANN. tit. 21, § 2118(f) (Michie Noncum. Supp. 1972); *see* note 23 *supra*. Another interesting feature of the 1972 claims pattern was 178 paid and 247 incurred "med-pay" claims. We had assumed that medical payments coverage would no longer be offered because its field of operation would be covered by PIP. In fact some companies are still offering it as an option to their policyholders. The justifications for buying it seem to be two: first, it is a cheap form of coverage excess to PIP, and secondly, it is not made subject to all the exceptions applicable to PIP, *e.g.*, the drunken driving exception. *See* text accompanying note 85 *supra*.

The subrogation provisions are indeed perplexing. They seem to have found their way into the Act at the insistence of the smaller companies doing business in the state.[90] Allowing subrogation defeats part of the advantage of "no-fault" liability, at least as a matter of theory. The question of negligence must now be investigated by both carriers, where before it was investigated only by the BI carrier. Indeed, all the claims personnel interviewed mentioned the increased paperwork generated when two carriers are forced to work out the liability question.[91] It was even suggested that some PIP carriers might be inflating payments to their insured, knowing that in the end some other company would be liable.[92] The cost to the policy-holder of the subrogation operation has not yet been investigated. If companies were to fight one another seriously, to the extent of investigating liability carefully and going to court, the costs could be substantial. In practice, it is probably a minimal cost, because most "investigation" is done by means of telephoned statements obtained by in-house claims personnel. Inter-company settlement is done by phone and letter, with inter-company arbitration as a little used backup procedure. The trend towards the use of in-house claims personnel had begun before the legislation came into force and has simply been accelerated. Nev-

---

90. The State Insurance Commissioner has provided the following justification for the subrogation provisions:

> Delaware people believe that those who cause accidents should pay more. To assure that this happens, subrogation is a part of our law and I urge that it be provided for in S. 354. It is handled entirely in our State by intercompany arbitration. It is neither burdensome nor costly, yet, it does assure that careless drivers pay more for their insurance.
>
>   . . . .
>
> The rates in Delaware are based on driving record with benefit of subrogation between companies, that is no-fault benefits might be subrogated against the liability coverages that all of us are required to carry. Therefore, the dollars for no-fault, the dollars for liability are assessed against the responsible driver through the subrogation process rather than through suit.

1974 Hearings, supra note 12, at 416-17 (remarks of Robert A. Short, Delaware Insurance Commissioner). We suspect that "the people" haven't a clue what goes on, but that if they did they might have some reservations about the risks involved in being determined "careless," "responsible" or among "those who cause accidents" and "should pay more" in arbitration proceedings in which they usually play no part!

91. The new system increases paper work in another way—more people are paid by installment and more drafts must accordingly be processed.

92. We found one company (which has only a small share of the business in the state) whose claims personnel still actively buy up third-party claims for medical and other special damages from injured parties in cases of relatively clear liability—even though the "claimant" is eligible for PIP. Their reasoning is that they will eventually have to reimburse the PIP carrier through subrogation and that it is cheaper to pay in the first instance. One suspects that some lucky victims must be greatly surprised to find *two* insurance companies happily offering to "look after" them.

ertheless, in the case of two-car accidents, liability will need to be investigated by both insurance companies for the inevitable property damage claim, and the additional expense of BI investigations is minimal. The cost of investigating liability for property damage claims is, of course, one reason why some commentators argue that property "no-fault" should be introduced at the same time as personal injury "no-fault."[93]

The question of cost to consumers is another puzzling one. According to figures supplied by the Delaware Department of Insurance the "typical average driver" was able to transfer to the new system with no increase in the "basic package premium."[94] In November 1972 an order from the Insurance Commissioner to withdraw filings[95]

---

93. For a theoretical discussion of whether or not property damage should be dealt with on a no-fault basis, see Blum & Kalven, *Ceilings, Costs, and Compulsion In Auto Compensation Legislation*, 1973 UTAH L. REV. 341, 370-74. An early version of the Delaware bill included damage to the vehicle under "no-fault," but this was deleted in response to insurance company opposition.

94. Memorandum on Delaware Automobile Rates from Everett E. Gale, Jr., Actuarial Supervisor, Delaware Department of Insurance, to Robert A. Short, Delaware Insurance Commissioner, June 20, 1973 at 1. It states in part,

> The following compares a typical average driver at 10/20/5 limits of liability under the Fault System in Delaware and the same driver under the No-Fault System, as of 1 January 1972.

Fault System (31 Dec. 71)			No-Fault System (1 Jan. 72)		
BI	(10/20)	[$] 43	BI		[$] 38
PD	(5K)	36	PD	(5K)	36
MP	(5K)	10	PIP		11
UM	(10/20)	4	MP	(2K)	5
			UM		3
		[$] 93			[$] 93

[Key:

BI	Bodily Injury	
PD	Property Damage	
MP	Medical Payments ("med-pay")	
UM	Uninsured Motorist	

(10/20), (5K) minimum coverage limits of $10,000 for 1 person dead or injured, $20,000 for more than 1, and $5,000 for property damage required under the Motor Vehicle Safety—Responsibility Law, DEL. CODE ANN. tit. 21, § 2904(b)(2) (Cum. Supp. 1970). See note 18 *supra* and accompanying text.]

Note:

In order to compare a similar benefits level of coverage the maximum available benefit level of Medical Payments Coverage at $5,000, under the Fault System, was compared to the Personal Injury Protection Coverage with a maximum benefit level of $10,000 plus a $2,000 benefit level of Medical Payments Coverage, under the No-Fault system. Note that *no* increase in basic package premium occurred.

95. Delaware, like most states, gives its Insurance Commissioner power to regulate insurance rates according to various principles, of which the most important is that "rates shall not be excessive, inadequate or unfairly discriminatory. . . ." DEL. CODE

resulted in an overall reduction of 9.4 percent in the "typical liability package rate."[96] This reduction does not appear to have been
based on experience under the Act, because no coherent data was available at that time. Six months later, in April of 1973, further property
damage insurance reductions occurred.[97] On September 18, 1973, an
additional rate reduction was ordered by the Commissioner of Insurance based on data provided by the companies on their 1971 and
1972 accident experience. The Commissioner determined that, on the
average, bodily injury rates were 17 percent too high and property
damage rates were 10 percent too high.[98] In a subsequent press release on November 6, 1973, the Commissioner stated:

> The Insurance Department recently designed a statistical plan to
> analyze statistical data from auto insurers by means of computer
> programming. Upon completion of the computer run, it was
> learned that the traditional amount of reserve money set aside to
> pay claims was excessive—almost 20%. This excess has occurred
> since the advent of "no-fault" insurance and was fully anticipated
> by the Commissioner.
>
> This anticipation was based on one of the prime objectives
> of "no-fault"—to pay accident victims immediately for all out-of-
> pocket expenses, such as medicals, loss of wages, and subsequent
> services. With these expenses paid, most claimants do not find it
> necessary to go to court, thereby saving legal expenses, excessive
> verdicts, and unwarranted settlements. These savings, which are
> substantial, do not require the traditionally large reserves set aside
> prior to "no-fault." Therefore, the public should benefit by lower
> rates.
>
> In order to fully implement this rate reduction, [the Commis-
> sioner], on September 18, 1973, ordered all auto insurers and
> Bureaus representing various insurers to file new rates reflecting
> designated reductions, except those few companies who had already
> effected a reduction.[99]

We have not seen the "statistical plan" referred to in this release

ANN. tit. 18, § 2303(a)(2) (1953). The Commissioner does not himself promulgate
rates. Companies are required to file their rates with him. Upon review and a hearing
he may "issue an order specifying in what respects he finds that such filing fails to meet
the requirements of [the rating legislation], and stating when, within a reasonable period
thereafter, such filing shall be deemed no longer effective." DEL. CODE ANN. tit. 18,
§ 2305(a) (1953). Such an order is known as an "Order Withdrawing Filings."

96. Memorandum on Delaware Automobile Rates, *supra* note 94, at 2. The term
"liability" is apparently used to include all items of coverage.

97. *Id.*

98. Order Withdrawing Filings, Delaware Department of Insurance, September 18,
1973.

99. Office of the Insurance Commissioner, Press Release, Nov. 6, 1973.

but we have no reason to doubt the Commissioner's statement that rates were too high. Unfortunately, in light of what we have found about the continuation of substantially the same amount of litigation, any saving in the system can hardly be explained by reduced litigation. Furthermore, it is difficult to see why property damage rates should be too high as a result of "no-fault" savings. The main item of property damage is damage to other automobiles, and "no-fault" does not apply to damage to automobiles. Former Pennsylvania Insurance Commissioner Herbert Denenberg has suggested that one reason why a reduction was possible in Delaware is that rates were excessive even under the unadulterated fault system operative prior to January 1, 1972.[100] Industry data that would provide a definitive answer to the question is not presently available to researchers. The court study, however, indicates at least one way in which some cost reduction (and perhaps an overall system cost reduction) could be explained, namely that while litigation in the courts has remained about the same, the number of persons insured has increased. It follows that, with the increased size of the pool of contributors, the cost to each insured should be a little lower.[101] Otherwise, it is all very mysterious.

On the basis of the Delaware experience, one final point can be made about the question of the effects of an "add-on" as opposed to a partial tort exemption law. In a small, non-claims-conscious state the law has at most caused some reduction in the number of relatively trivial claims being made. Delaware did not have a mass of small claims in the courts before the new law was in effect, and it still does not. Whether the legislation would provide the necessary psychological incentives to discourage nuisance claims in a large claims-conscious jurisdiction is unproved. We strongly suspect that it would not, but the matter could only be settled on the basis of experience in such a state.

---

100. *1974 Hearings, supra* note 12, at 389 (statement by Herbert S. Denenberg, Pennsylvania Insurance Commissioner).

101. An interesting feature of the increased pool, in 1972 at least, was the large number who found their way into the assigned risk category compared with those insured the previous year. *See* figures in notes 47 and 49 *supra*. The assigned risk insureds were probably making fairly generous contributions to the pool. Assigned risk status carries with it a surcharge of between 10% and 50%. Del. Code Ann. tit. 21, § 2907(a) (1953).

APPENDIX 1

COURT STUDY WORK SHEET

NAME: _____

1. Docket Number & Court _____
   Date Examined _____
2. Date Suit Filed _____
3. Accident Date _____
4. Place of Accident _____
5. Plaintiff (or Defendant) in or out of state _____
6. Type of Action _____
   1. PI
   2. PD
   3. Survival
   4. Wrongful Death
   5. 1st Party No Fault
   6. Don't know
   7. Loss of services
7. Amounts claimed: PI — general _____
                  PI — special _____
                  PD _____
                  1st Party No Fault _____
                  Other _____
8. Date of Answer _____
9. When Was Case Settled? _____
   1. After Complaint Filed, But Before Answer
   2. After Answer, But Before Trial Date Set
   3. After Trial Date Set
   4. After Jury Drawn
   5. After Trial Began
   6. Upon Judgment
   7. Don't Know
   8. Appeal
10. Amount _____
11. Trial Date _____
12. Date Closed _____
13. Was a Counter Claim Made? _____
    1. Yes
    2. No
    3. Don't Know
    4. Not Applicable
    5. Other
14. Date of Counter Claim _____
15. Type of Action _____
    1. PI
    2. PD
    3. Survival
    4. Wrongful Death

     5. 1st Party No Fault
     6. Don't Know
16. Date of the Reply to the Counter Claim _____
17. When was the Counter Claim Settled? _____
     1. After Counter Claim Filed But Before Reply
     2. After Reply, But Before Trial Date
     3. After Trial Date Set
     4. After Jury Drawn
     5. After Trial Began
     6. Upon Judgment
     7. Don't Know
     8. Not Applicable
     9. Other
18. Date Counter Claim Settled _____
19. Amount Settled For _____
20. Plaintiff's Attorney _____

21. Defendant's Attorney _____

22. Remarks

APPENDIX 2

CROSS-TABULATION: DATE OF FILING SUIT BY DATE OF ACCIDENT

1.   U.S. DISTRICT COURT

Date Filed	Date of Accident						Total Filed in Year
	1968	1969	1970	1971	1972	1973	
1970	17	9	4	0	0	0	30
1971	1	19	23	4	0	0	47
1972	0	1	9	8	1	0	19
1973	0	0	3	12	7	2	24

Total Observed = 120

2. NEW CASTLE SUPERIOR

Date Filed	Date of Accident						Total Filed in Year
	1968	1969	1970	1971	1972	1973	
1970	147	100	42	0	0	0	289
1971	1	178	107	31	0	0	317
1972	1	1	214	97	24	0	337
1973	1	3	4	229	106	36	379

Total Observed = 1,322

3. NEW CASTLE COMMON PLEAS

Date Filed	Date of Accident						Total Filed in Year
	1968	1969	1970	1971	1972	1973	
1970	3	12	2	0	0	0	17
1971	0	9	4	7	0	0	20
1972	0	0	7	10	1	0	18
1973	0	0	0	8	8	5	21

Total Observed = 76

4. KENT SUPERIOR

Date Filed	Date of Accident						Total Filed in Year
	1968	1969	1970	1971	1972	1973	
1970	18	21	6	0	0	0	45
1971	2	20	13	6	0	0	41
1972	0	0	26	12	3	0	41
1973	0	0	2	24	13	2	41

Total Observed = 168

5. KENT COMMON PLEAS

Date Filed	Date of Accident						Total Filed in Year
	1968	1969	1970	1971	1972	1973	
1970	1	0	0	0	0	0	1
1971	0	0	1	0	0	0	1
1972	0	0	0	2	0	0	2
1973	0	0	0	3	3	0	6

Total Observed = 10

6. SUSSEX SUPERIOR

Date Filed	Date of Accident						Total Filed in Year
	1968	1969	1970	1971	1972	1973	
1970	2	12	0	0	0	0	14
1971	0	6	3	0	0	0	9
1972	0	0	8	6	3	0	17
1973	0	0	0	7	3	0	10

Total Observed = 50

7. SUSSEX COMMON PLEAS

Date Filed	Date of Accident						Total Filed in Year
	1968	1969	1970	1971	1972	1973	
1970	0	2	3	0	0	0	5
1971	0	0	1	0	0	0	1
1972	0	0	2	0	0	0	2
1973	0	0	0	2	2	1	5

Total Observed = 13

APPENDIX 3

ATTORNEY'S CONFIDENTIAL SURVEY

1. Given the opportunity, would you vote to continue Delaware personal injury "No-Fault" insurance as stated in 21 *Del. C.* § 2118?
   Yes ( )
   No ( )

2. Would you vote for some form of property damage "No-Fault" auto insurance?
   Yes ( )
   No ( )

3. Would you vote to increase the minimum 10/20 "No-Fault" coverage?
   Yes ( )
   No ( )

4. Would you vote to establish a threshold level of medical costs for soft tissue injuries below which a tort action would be barred?
   Yes ( )
   No ( )

5. How would you characterize the impact of personal injury "No-Fault" on your practice since January 1, 1972?
   None ( )
   Small ( )
   Moderate ( )
   Substantial ( )

6. If there has been an impact on your practice, in which area has there been an increase in the amount of time worked?
   Criminal ( )
   Estate planning, wills ( )
   Real estate ( )
   Business, commercial, corporate, tax ( )
   Civil (other than auto) ( )

7. Assuming no change in the present law, what will the effect on your practice be in the next three years?
   None ( )
   Small ( )
   Moderate ( )
   Substantial ( )

8. In 1971, approximately what proportion of your total case load was made up of auto personal injury cases?
   Under 1/4 ( )
   1/4 to 1/2 ( )
   1/2 to 3/4 ( )
   Over 3/4 ( )

9. In 1972, approximately what proportion of your total case load was made up of auto personal injury cases?
   Under 1/4 ( )
   1/4 to 1/2 ( )
   1/2 to 3/4 ( )
   Over 3/4 ( )

10. Did you do mostly plaintiff or defendant work?
    Pl.   (   )
    Def.   (   )
11. Approximately what proportion of cases were settled before suit was filed?
    Under 1/4   (   )
    1/4 to 1/2   (   )
    1/2 to 3/4   (   )
    Over 3/4   (   )
12. Approximately what proportion of cases was settled after suit was filed, but before trial?
    Under 1/4   (   )
    1/4 to 1/2   (   )
    1/2 to 3/4   (   )
    Over 3/4   (   )
13. Approximately what proportion of your income from the practice of law in 1971 was derived from personal injury claims?
    Under 1/4   (   )
    1/4 to 1/2   (   )
    1/2 to 3/4   (   )
    Over 3/4   (   )
14. In 1972, approximately what proportion of your income from the practice of law was derived from personal injury claims?
    Under 1/4   (   )
    1/4 to 1/2   (   )
    1/2 to 3/4   (   )
    Over 3/4   (   )
15. Are you increasingly engaging in other fields of practice to offset the actual or prospective impact of "No-Fault" insurance?
    To a substantial extent   (   )
    To a moderate extent   (   )
    To a small extent   (   )
    Not at all   (   )
16. Do you anticipate any such change as a result of "No-Fault"?
    Yes   (   )
    No   (   )
17. Are you increasingly engaging in other lines of economic activity to offset the impact of "No-Fault"?
    Yes   (   )
    No   (   )
18. Do you anticipate any such change?
    Yes   (   )
    No   (   )
19. Has your office, as a result of the impact of "No-Fault" insurance,
    Reduced the number of attorneys   (   )
    Decided not to hire additional attorneys   (   )
    Done nothing   (   )
    Other   (   )
20. Do you anticipate any measure such as described above?
    Yes   (   )
    No   (   )
    Please specify:

21. How long have you been admitted to practice?
    0-5 years   (   )
    5-10 years   (   )
    10-20 years   (   )
    20-30 years   (   )
    Over 30 years   (   )

22. In which county is your principal office located?
    New Castle   (   )
    Kent   (   )
    Sussex   (   )

23. What is your present mode of practice?
    Individual   (   )
    Partnership   (   )
    Firm   (   )

24. In 1972, was at least 3/4 of your income derived from the practice of law?
    Yes   (   )
    No   (   )

25. Approximately how many claims for personal injury "No-Fault" benefits have you handled since January 1, 1972?

26. Additional Comments:

DELAWARE NO-FAULT—
1974 and 1975 COURT FILINGS
ARISING FROM PERSONAL INJURY
INCURRED IN MOTOR VEHICLE ACCIDENTS

by Roger S. Clark

In order to see whether the pattern of litigation for 1974 and 1975 is similar to that reported in our Delaware study up to the end of 1973, we have examined the 1974 and 1975 filings in the Superior Court for New Castle County. Since over 70% of the motor vehicle bodily injury litigation in the state takes place in this court (see 6 *Rutgers-Camden Law Journal* at 233, note 35), there is no doubt that the pattern for the whole state is similar. The figures are included in the following table, which updates the table for New Castle County to the end of 1973 contained in 6 *Rutgers-Camden Law Journal* at 260. It should be compared with Table 1 for all courts to 1973.

365 suits arising from motor vehicle accidents involving personal injury were filed in the New Castle Superior Court in 1974 and 436 in 1975. There is no way to explain the figures other than that tort litigation is continuing, substantially unabated by the no-fault legislation. In particular, note that during 1974, 244 cases were filed arising out of 1972 accidents—the first year of no-fault. In 1975 no fewer than 258 cases were filed in respect of 1973 accidents. A comparable figure for the last year before no-fault is the 229 cases for 1971 accidents filed in 1973. (Incidentally, the rather large number of suits arising from 1973 accidents is consistent with the apparent increase in injuries on the Delaware roads that year notwithstanding the impact of the energy crisis. See the accident figures in 6 *Rutgers-Camden Law Journal* at 235.)

Once again, it does not seem possible to explain away the continuing volume of litigation on the basis of any unusual variation in the number of injuries occurring on the Delaware roads (*cf.* 6 *Rutgers-Camden Law Journal* at 235-236). The figures for injuries and fatalities reported to the police over the period of the study are now:

	Injuries	**Fatalities**
1970	5651	152
1971	5604	117
1972	5673	133
1973	6194	129
1974	5969	113
1975	6679	125

1975 was another record year for reported injuries, and this is consistent with the 39 suits already filed for the year. However, the full impact of the 1975 increase in injuries over 1974 will be felt in the filings during 1976 and 1977.

An interesting feature of the 1974 and 1975 filings is the increasing but still small amount of litigation activity involving insurance companies. It will be recalled that the 1973 filings in the State included 7 claims against PIP carriers, 3 of them joined with suits against alleged tort feasors. All of these actions were brought in the New Castle County Superior Court. (See 6 *Rutgers-Camden Law Journal* at 234, note 37.) The 1974 New Castle figures included 11 claims brought only against PIP carriers and 4 in which a claim against a PIP carrier was combined with one against the alleged third-party tort feasors. In addition there were 10 PIP subrogation claims by companies plus 3 more cases in which a subrogation action by an insurance company was joined with a bodily injury action against a third party. In 1975 there were 13 suits against PIP carriers only (in 2 of which uninsured motorist coverage was also alleged) and 16 in which a PIP carrier was sued along with an alleged tort feasor. 13 cases were subrogation actions by PIP insurers and in 5 additional cases a PIP insurer joined its subrogation claim with a tort claim by its insured.

The legislation has obviously generated some litigation of its own but the number of suits brought solely by (i.e., subrogation actions) or against (i.e., PIP claims) insurance companies is still small. Such suits do not explain the continuing volume of litigation in the 4 years of no-fault. The overwhelming majority of cases are third-party tort actions.

It is now clear that, whatever beneficial effects it has had, the Delaware legislation has not discouraged any significant number of potential tort plaintiffs from suing.

CROSS TABULATION OF DATE OF FILING
SUIT BY DATE OF ACCIDENT

MOTOR VEHICLE CASES ARISING
FROM PERSONAL INJURY
New Castle County Superior Court
Date of Accident

	1968	1969	1970	1971	1972	1973	1974	1975	Total Filed in Year
1970	147	100	42	0	0	0	0	0	247
1971	1	178	107	31	0	0	0	0	317
1972	1	1	214	97	24	0	0	0	337
1973	1	3	4	229	106	36	0	0	379
1974	0	0	0	3	244	97	21	0	365
1975	0	1	1	3	8	258	126	39	436

PART IV

THE MICHIGAN STUDY

THOMAS C. JONES
Commissioner of Insurance
State of Michigan

CHAPTER 9

No-Fault Automobile Insurance in Michigan
A Preliminary Study

By

THOMAS C. JONES, *Commissioner of Insurance*
State of Michigan

In October, 1972 after several years of study and intense debate, the Michigan legislature enacted, and Governor William G. Milliken signed, the most comprehensive no-fault automobile insurance law in the nation. [1] The law was implemented on October 1, 1973. Almost three years have elapsed since the implementation. Since the Insurance Bureau is presently analyzing several aspects of the law this study is a preliminary evaluation. The Bureau plans to complete a more thorough examination in the future.

Summary of the Michigan No-Fault Coverage

The mandatory or compulsory coverage for owners of motor vehicles in Michigan consists of three parts — Personal Injury Protection (PIP), Residual Bodily Injury and Property Damage Liability Insurance, and Property Protection Insurance (PPI).

Statutory first-party no-fault PIP coverage offers broad benefits and includes the following:

(1) unlimited medical and rehabilitation benefits;

(2) work or income loss benefits of up to $1,285 per month for a maximum period of three years;

(3) dependent survivor loss benefits of up to $1,000 a month for a maximum period of three years;

(4) replacement service benefits of up to $20 per day for a maximum period of three years for disabled accident victims and dependent survivors of death victims;

(5) funeral and burial expense benefits of $1,000.

The PIP benefits are required by statute to be coordinated with governmental benefits, e.g. social security benefits. [2]

It should be noted that income loss benefits have increased under the statutory cost-of-living provision from the original $1,000 per month to a current level of $1,285. [3] Potential aggregate income loss benefits per person have therefore increased from $36,000 to $46,260, an increase of 29 percent in three years.

Eligibility for PIP benefits is broad. In addition to protecting insured motorists, coverage extends to pedestrians and occupants of motorcycles and other vehicles when accidents involve automobiles. Even the family of an uninsured owner of an automobile is covered. Persons from other states injured in an accident in Michigan are eligible for PIP benefits if their insurer is licensed in Michigan or, if unlicensed, has voluntarily certified the coverage. Out of state persons are also covered if they are

---

1. Mich. Comp. Laws Ann. §§500.3101-.3179 (Supp. 1975).

2. Id., §3109(1).

3. Id., §3107(b).

hurt in a Michigan car, or as a pedestrian in Michigan. Michigan residents also are protected for PIP benefits while traveling in any other state and Canada. Exclusions from PIP coverage include the owner of a vehicle who does not purchase the mandatory coverage and who is injured in his own vehicle; a person injured in an automobile that he has stolen, or a non-resident who does not have coverage that has been certified by his insurer.

One technical question has arisen with respect to the third-party residual liability coverage. Section 3131 of the Act states . . . "In this state this insurance shall afford coverage for automobile liability retained by section 3135." Section 3135 provides that persons remain subject to tort liability for non-economic losses due to injuries resulting in death, serious impairment of bodily function, or permanent serious disfigurement. The two sections, when read together, can be interpreted to mean that residual liability coverage must be unlimited if the injury occurs in Michigan, but not in another state. On the other hand, section 3009 states that mandatory coverages need only be within the dollar limits set forth in that section.

To clarify the statute, a bill has been introduced in the Michigan legislature. [4] The bill would make clear that the residual liability coverage which must be purchased need not be unlimited, but that instead the dollar limits of section 3009 are applicable to that coverage as they are to other coverages.

The third portion of the mandatory coverage in Michigan is Property Protection Insurance (PPI). Property Protection Insurance benefits are payable without regard to fault to third parties for damage to tangible property, including damage to parked vehicles. The statutory policy limit for damage from any one accident is $1 million.

Tort liability with respect to accidents in Michigan involving damage to automobiles has been abolished for insured car owners. [5] The result is that the third party property damage liability insurance system for car damages has all but been eliminated. First party collision coverages, which are not mandatory, are offered by all auto insurers operating in Michigan, and collision options with inverse liability features are available to Michigan automobile owners.

The available coverages fall into three categories. Regular collision insurance is offered, which pays the owner of a damaged vehicle his loss after the subtraction of a stated deductible amount. Limited collision pays the loss only if the driver of the damaged vehicle was not at fault, and again after the subtraction of a stated deductible. Broadened collision pays regardless of which driver is at fault, but no deductible is subtracted if the insured is not at fault.

Constitutional Litigation

The no-fault statute has been subject to constitutional litigation. In *Shavers* v *Kelley* [6] the Wayne County Circuit Court upheld the tort restrictions of the act for personal injury but ruled invalid the abolition of tort liability for property damage. The intermediate appellate court affirmed the trial court [7] on these issues. In addition, several other issues are involved. The case is currently on appeal to the Michigan Supreme Court.

In another recent case, *O'Donnell* v *State Farm*, [8] the Michigan Court of Appeals rules unconstitutional the provision in the act requiring coordination of Personal Injury

---

4. Senate Bill 1266, 1976 Regular Session, Michigan Legislature.

5. Id.

6. CCH Auto. L. Rep. 91 8303 (Mich. Cir. Ct., Wayne County 1974).

7. Shavers v. Atty. Gen. 65 Mich. App. 355; 237 N.W.2d 325 (1975).

8. 70 Mich. App., NW2d No. 25429 (August 4, 1976).

Protection benefits and governmental benefits. The economic impact of these decisions, if allowed to stand, will be discussed later in this report.

Standards for Evaluation of Michigan No-Fault Experience

In analyzing the experience of the Michigan no-fault law it is important to review some of the original objectives sought in reforming the automobile insurance system. In June, 1971, Commissioner Russell Van Hooser opened testimony before a joint committee of the Michigan legislature. [9] His statement highlighted the deficiencies of the existing automobile tort liability insurance system as revealed by many studies, e.g. the two year study by the U.S. Department of Transportation. It is important to note that Commissioner Van Hooser did not mention the possibility of premium decreases. Similarly, in a special message on automobile insurance, as well as in his January, 1972 State of the State message, Governor Milliken emphasized the fact that although there might be some savings in premiums, the principal thrusts of the no-fault proposals he was supporting were to compensate accident victims more promptly and adequately, and to reduce the expense and delay of the tort liability system.

Commissioner Van Hooser in his testimony suggested the following priorities and standards against which various legislative no-fault proposals could be tested:

(1) Compensate injured persons adequately, promptly, and without regard to fault for medical expenses, wage loss and rehabilitation expenses.

(2) Reduction or elimination of the nuisance value of small claims.

(3) Reduction of the duplication and overlapping of benefits within the auto-insurance system and other systems. If the duplication is not reduced or eliminated, it should at least be subject to greater control by the consumer so that the consumer will have a corresponding control over his costs.

(4) Reduction or elimination of some of the other frictions and inefficiencies of the present system, such as the adversary relationship between insurer and injured party, court congestion, litigation expense, and overhead expense.

These standards outlined in 1973 remain relevant in evaluating the experience of the Michigan no-fault law.

Adequacy of Benefits

The Michigan no-fault law is fulfilling the objective of guaranteeing prompt, sure, and more adequate recovery of injury costs, including compensating many victims who would have been either undercompensated or received no benefits under the prior liability system. A recent study by the National Association of Independent Insurers (NAII) of catastrophe medical claims in Michigan offers striking evidence. A catastrophe medical claim was defined as an injury resulting in medical expenses exceeding $25,000. The study included the results of NAII member companies insuring approximately 43 percent of the private passenger automobiles in Michigan. The study covered the period from October 1, 1973 to December 31, 1975. A total of 443 claims in which NAII insurers have established reserves for medical expenses of $25,000 and over were reported for the time period. Aggregate reserves established for these claims amounted to over $32 million, with 21 percent of the claims reserved for more than $100,000. Table 1 summarizes such claims.

---

9. Russell E. Van Hooser, "Statement on Automobile Insurance". Before a Joint Meeting of Senate Commerce Committee & House Insurance Committee, June 7, 1971.

Table 1

Unlimited Medical No-Fault Claims in Michigan, October 1, 1973-December 31, 1975,
NAII Companies Distribution by Size of Reserve $25,000 and Over

Reserve	No. of Claims	% of Total	Amount of Reserve	% of Total	Amount Pd. to Date
$100,000 & over	91	21%	$17,660,902	54%	$3,127,019
$50,000-$99,999	102	23	6,344,882	20	2,077,193
$25,000-$49,999	250	56	8,296,985	26	4,424,449
Total	443	100%	$32,302,769	100%	$9,628,661

If all insurers writing automobile insurance in Michigan are considered, the number of victims with current catastrophic medical claims very likely exceeds 1000.

The NAII data were further analyzed by type of accident and injury. Table 2 itemizes the catastrophic medical claim cases by type of accident. [10]

Table 2

Unlimited Medical No-Fault Claims in Michigan, October 1, 1973-December 31, 1975,
NAII Companies Distribution by Type of Accident $25,000 and Over

Type of Accident	No. of Claims	Per Cent	Amount of Reserve	Per Cent
Multi-Car	100	38%	$ 7,329,920	34%
Single Car	82	32	8,784,533	40
Motorcycle	40	15	2,558,313	12
Pedestrian	38	15	2,971,986	14
Total	260	100%	$21,644,752	100%

Table 2 reveals that 32 percent of the catastrophe claims involved single vehicle accidents. These victims would have gone uncompensated under the prior tort system, or at most, would have received modest amounts of medical payments, typically a maximum of $1000. The average reserve for such single vehicle cases under no-fault exceeds $87,000.

The distribution of catastrophic medical claims by type of injury and the average age of accident victims is shown in Table 3. [11]

Table 3

Unlimited Medical Claims in Michigan, October 1, 1973-December 31, 1975,
NAII Companies Distribution by Type of Injury $25,000 and Over

Type of Injury	Number	Amount of Reserve	Average Age (Years)
Brain Damage	61	$ 8,115,484	25
Quadriplegic	12	1,906,449	30
Paraplegic	20	2,881,974	24
Other	256	12,182,458	34
Total	349	$25,086,365	32

---

10. The number of total claims in Table 2 does not agree with the total number of claims in Table 1 since not all companies reported the type of accident.

11. The number of total claims in Table 3 does not agree with the total number of claims in Table 1 since not all companies reported the type of injury.

The seriousness of the injuries and the relative young average age of the accident victims (age 32) vividly demonstrates the need which is being met by no-fault. Some insurers have expressed concern that the cost of unlimited medical benefits may be prohibitive. While a detailed study by the Insurance Bureau has not been completed, it is interesting to note that on the basis of its study the NAII estimates the total cost of medical claims exceeding $25,000 in Michigan is $8 per car.

Perhaps the most dramatic impact of the Michigan no-fault law has been the provision for comprehensive rehabilitation. Critically injured persons are assured immediate access to all necessary rehabilitation treatment. A substantial number of cases are already in or scheduled to enter the best rehabilitation centers in the country, and several insurers have established their own rehabilitation units. An effective rehabilitation program is not only essential in returning seriously injured persons to productive lives, but also reduces future medical and wage loss claims. An excerpt from a recent letter to the editor of a Michigan newspaper from a family relating their experience is illustrative:

"... No fault has been a godsend to our family over the past 28 months. At that time our 18-year-old son was very seriously injured in a collision between his motorcycle and a car. The no-fault insurance our boy carried on his car at the time has helped us keep our heads above water.

I wouldn't attempt to list all the expenses it has paid, but I will name a few. It paid for his wheel chair, crutches, leg braces, shoes and even for the labor attaching the braces to his shoes. It paid for the driver's training to enable our son to get his driver's license, with the use of hand controls, as his legs were paralyzed in the mishap. Also it paid for the hand controls on his car and pick-up truck.

Our agent even gave me to understand I could submit a bill for caring for my son after he returned home from an eight-month stay in the hospital. Needless to say I didn't feel that was necessary; having him home was payment enough. No fault picked up the medical bills that our medical and hospital insurance didn't quite cover. And, when necessary, it will also pay 85 per cent of lost gross earnings.

No fault cannot save and restore lives, but it certainly helped our son over what could have been a pretty rough rehabilitation." [12]

Reduction or Elimination of Nuisance Value of Non-serious Claims

A complete evaluation of the effectiveness of the "threshold" in the law in eliminating minor non-serious injury tort liability cases is premature. However, evidence is growing that the threshold has resulted in a significant decline in the number of minor tort liability claims and liability suits filed.

Data collected by the Michigan Association of Insurance Companies (MAIC) from their member companies indicate a substantial reduction of private passenger automobile bodily injury liability claims since 1973. Liability claims decreased from 163,369 in 1973 (includes three months of no-fault) to 21,553 in 1975 — a decline of 87 percent. The MAIC companies write approximately 50 percent of the private passenger automobile insurance business in Michigan. As will be discussed later in this study, the number of automobile negligence cases filed in circuit courts in Michigan is also declining.

---

12. Letter to the Editor, Bernice Weber Dorr, *Grand Rapids Press*, Feb. 27, 1976.

Reduction of Duplication and Overlapping of Benefits

Commissioner Van Hooser highlighted the problems of duplicating and overlapping of auto insurance and other benefits in 1971:

> Such duplication increases the cost of the present system and encourages overutilization of medical services and malingering. Much of the duplication in the present system is beyond the control of the consumer and arises out of the conflict between systems designed to pay benefits directly to the injured without regard to fault (like sick leave, group health insurance, personal accident and health insurance, automobile medical payments insurance, social security and medicare) and the liability insurance system which is designed to pay benefits to third parties injured through the negligence of the insured. Much of the duplication could be reduced by making automobile insurance excess over existing coverages. If the duplication is not reduced or eliminated, it should at least be subject to greater control by the consumer so that the consumer will have a corresponding control over his costs. [13]

In order to reduce duplication, the Michigan legislature mandated coordination of automobile no-fault PIP benefits and other collateral governmental benefits such as workmen's compensation, social security, etc. This provision while assuring adequate compensation, reduces aggregate automobile insurance premiums. As previously mentioned, the Michigan Court of Appeals has ruled in the *O'Donnell* [14] case this provision unconstitutional. Actuaries of the Insurance Bureau have estimated that if the *O'Donnell* decision stands, the added costs to the automobile insurance system may be as high as $25 million per year. Moreover, the decision would have a major premium redistributive effect. [15]

In 1974, the Michigan legislature acted to give automobile insurance consumers more control over duplication of no-fault benefits and other private sources of accident and health insurance. A new section, Section 3109(a), was added requiring all automobile insurers to offer an option, at reduced premiums, of deductibles and exclusions for PIP benefits reasonably related to other health and accident coverage. Potential aggregate no-fault premium savings, if all insureds elected the option, were estimated by the Insurance Bureau to be 80 to 100 million dollars per year.

Under guidelines promulgated by the Insurance Bureau all automobile insurers are offering "coordinated coverage" or wrap-around options whereby PIP benefits are secondary and supplementary to other private health and accident insurance. Premiums for the coordinated option for PIP coverage are reduced 50 percent resulting in an average reduction of 10 to 15 percent in the total auto insurance premium depending on coverage elected, classification, etc.

Precise data on the utilization of the coordination option by insureds is not yet available. However, a survey of eleven insurers writing a substantial portion of automobile insurance in Michigan was conducted in April, 1975 by the Consumer Affairs Department of the United Automobile Workers. [16] The eleven companies estimated the percentage of their total policies and renewal business which was coordinated with other private accident and health insurance. The percentage that was coordinated by the eleven companies varied from a low of 5 percent to a high of 80 percent. Significantly, several companies reported that the percentage of policyholders electing the option on new applications and renewals was increasing. For example, one insurer estimated that 45 percent of its total Michigan business was coordinated but 80 percent of its new business was coordinated.

---

13. Van Hooser, *supra* at p. 9.

14. See fn. 8.

15. See p. 12 for a further discussion.

16. UAW Consumer Affairs Department, "Utilization of Coordination Option in Michigan," unpublished, April, 1975.

The UAW study noted that utilization of the coordinated option was likely to be significantly affected by consumer education concerning the option, and the efforts made by the company or its agents to disclose and explain the option. The UAW study concluded:

> Consumers like and use the option when available to reduce the direct cost of auto insurance. The data clearly indicates that (except in a couple of instances) a significant proportion of consumers utilize. the option. The proportion of new applicants using the option is especially high.

> The high usage is especially significant since consumers do not reject but must specifically ask for the option on forms provided by insurers. [17]

The UAW survey was completed ten months after all insurers were required to offer the option. Not all policyholders would have been offered the option because of the staggered renewal policy dates of insurers.

Reduction or Elimination of Frictions and Inefficiencies of Tort System

One of the major, but controversial objectives of no-fault was to reduce litigation and thereby reduce court congestion. This objective is clearly being realized. Table 4 records the number of automobile negligence cases filed in circuit courts in Michigan from 1971 through June, 1976. The declining trend is evident and the decrease of cases filed of nearly 20 percent from 1975 is very impressive. It should also be recognized that the circuit court data include many cases that are based on accidents filed before the effective date of the no-fault law which makes the case reduction even more impressive. It is reasonable to expect a further decline in automobile negligence suits in the future with corresponding savings accruing to the Michigan auto insurance consumer and taxpayer. The important no-fault objective of reducing the costs related with court congestion will continue to result in important cost reductions.

Table 4

Michigan Circuit Court Auto Negligence Cases Filed, January, 1971-June, 1976

Period	Auto Negligence Cases	Percentage Change
Jan., 1971-Dec., 1971	11,295	
Jan., 1972-Dec., 1972	13,118	+16.1
Jan., 1973-Dec., 1973	12,952	− 1.3
June, 1973-June, 1974	12,580	− 2.9
June, 1974-June, 1975	12,582	+ 0.0
June, 1975-June, 1976	10,079	−19.9

A full analysis of the efficiency of the Michigan no-fault system has not been completed. Sufficient time has not elapsed since the effective date of the law. Automobile insurers experienced no interruption in operations in the change-over to no-fault; they continue to handle liability claims and tort suits arising out of the previous liability insurance system which results in added costs to the system which will wash out as time goes on. It may be noted, however, that a recent study of the Florida no-fault law — a law which is much more modest than that of Michigan — the benefits-to premium ratio increased markedly. [18] Thus, the no-fault system in Florida was found to be more cost-efficient, i.e. consumers received more benefits per premium dollar. There is no reason to believe that the Michigan no-fault system is less efficient than that of Florida, and indeed it should prove to be more efficient.

17. *Id.* at p. 3.

18. See Joseph Little, "No-fault Auto Reparation in Florida: An Empirical Examination of Some of its Effects," 9 Mich. J. L. Reform 1 (1975).

No-Fault Property Damage

Perhaps the most controversial aspect of the Michigan no-fault law has been the property damage provisions. The Insurance Bureau has received consumer complaints concerning the liability to hold negligent drivers "responsible" for collision damages. However, the Insurance Bureau also received numerous complaints under the previous property damage tort liability system. Under the previous system only about one-third of the automobile collisions resulted in payment under the property damage liability system, and most of those were the result of subrogation, after payment of a collision insurance claim.

The Bureau has also received complaints from innocent insureds who have had to bear a deductible for collision damages. Such complaints have risen largely from insureds whose insurers do not offer first-party inverse liability coverage insuring such deductibles. The majority of insurers operating in Michigan are covering such losses. However, from the consumer's point of view insuring "first dollar" car collision losses may be inefficient. Whether insured under a third party property damage liability insurance system or a first party collision system, deductibles provide savings to the consumer. By offering deductibles on first party inverse liability, total premiums to the individual policyholder may be reduced.

Major savings in premiums were not expected in the shift from the property damage liability insurance system to a first party collision insurance system. The transfer to a single system of compensating for collision losses has undoubtedly produced some efficiencies, e.g. savings resulting from the elimination of subrogation, but an analysis of the cost efficiency of the no-fault property damage system in Michigan has not been undertaken. The Florida study found that the no-fault property damage system previously in effect in Florida, which was only a partial system, was still more efficient than the property damage liability insurance system. [19]

One significant result of the Michigan first-party no-fault collision insurance system has been the redistribution of the premium burden for auto collision damages. First party collision insurance is priced in relation to the value of the vehicle. Owners of higher priced vehicles in Michigan pay relatively larger premiums than owners of older, lower valued vehicles. Thus more equity was introduced into the system. The "ability to pay" principle is absent in the pricing of liability insurance. Owners of older cars in Michigan also have the option of not purchasing collision coverage. Under the previous system of financial responsibility, owners could not avoid the purchase of property damage liability insurance.

Analysis of Overall Premium and Rate Levels

Serious observers and proponents of the Michigan no-fault law did not expect, or predict in 1973, a substantial reduction or significant change in the total or overall automobile insurance system costs. Rather, most parties agreed that total costs within the bodily injury reparation system would be distributed more fairly. That is, cost reductions were expected due to lowered legal and other system expenses and the reduction of payments for non-economic loss for minor injuries, but such reductions were expected to be offset by increases in costs to compensate the additional number of injured persons whose injuries were not covered under the tort system, and increases in costs associated with more adequate compensation of seriously injured persons. Similarly, overall cost reductions for car damages were not expected, but rather a more equitable distribution of such costs among drivers would occur.

---

19. *Id.* at p. 61. The property damage provisions of the law were held unconstitutional by the Florida Supreme Court. Kluger v. White, 281 So.2d 1 (Fla. 1973).

The data the Insurance Bureau has accumulated thus far would lead to the conclusion that the effect of no-fault on overall real system cost in Michigan was to lower it somewhat. Premium levels were remarkably stable from 1973 through the summer of 1975 when premium increases began to be implemented. The most important external factor affecting overall rates and premiums has been the pace of national inflation.

Inflation since 1971 has caused the Consumer Price Index to rise by more than 40 percent, and it has increased almost 30 percent since October 1, 1973. More importantly, the cost indices associated with items covered by automobile insurance have increased at an even greater rate than the Consumer Price Index.

Five inflation variables which particularly affect automobile insurance premiums are medical care costs, automobile repair and maintenance, wage levels, automobile crash parts prices and the maximum work loss benefit. The indices of the variables are shown in Table 5. As can be observed, since 1972 medical care costs increased 45 percent, auto repair and maintenance costs arose 39 percent, wage levels increased 35 percent, the maximum work loss benefit increased 29 percent and auto crash parts prices jumped an alarming 87 percent. Exhibit 1 shows the combined effects of these five auto insurance cost components and indicates how much premiums should have increased. The combined index increased 40 percent from 1972 to 1976. In contrast, overall auto insurance rate levels in Michigan have increased more modestly, with most insurers in Michigan currently (as of June, 1976) at rate levels 20 percent higher than in 1971. [20]

It is apparent that no-fault has reduced the aggregate cost of insurance in Michigan.

This conclusion is reinforced when Michigan rates are compared with country wide rates. Exhibits 2 and 3 portray rate level changes in Michigan and the average national increase in rates. Michigan rates were about 15 percent higher in January, 1976 than in January, 1972. The average national increase was about 22 percent.

Premiums for Selected Drivers and Changes in Distribution of Premiums

Rates and premiums for individual drivers, as distinguished from average rate levels, vary considerably. Furthermore, the rate classification systems of auto insurers in Michigan are not uniform. One beneficial result of the Michigan no-fault system has been to shift the premium burden, generally lowering rates in urban areas and for the poor and elderly. As a group retirees have gained the most in savings since the risk exposure for work loss is minimal and some medical benefits are provided under Medicare. As noted earlier, the *O'Donnell* decision, if upheld, would eliminate a portion of these savings. These shifts in premium distribution was shown clearly in the "Consumer's Guide to Automobile Insurance" issued by the Insurance Bureau in 1974. [21] The guide published rates for the largest twenty four automobile insurers writing in Michigan for six separate risk categories covering a variety of income, dependency and territory situations.

Another sample review of premium rates for selected risks was recently completed. The sample covered rate changes from the pre-no-fault period (September, 1973) to March 1, 1976 and included four companies writing a combined 44 percent of the automobile insurance premiums in Michigan. Two risks were studied for the four companies — a married couple, age 35 with no children of driving age, and a retired couple, age 67. Two territories, Detroit and Dearborn (suburban Detroit) were included.

---

20. The energy crisis in 1974 resulted in a temporary decrease in the number of miles driven, deaths, accidents and injuries. Inflation offset these factors and these variables started to increase again in 1975.

21. Michigan Department of Commerce, Insurance Bureau, "Consumer's Guide to Automobile Insurance in Michigan".

Table 5

Comparison of Relative Inflation

Year	Medical Care Inflation (Detroit Average)	Auto Repair & Maint. Inflation (National Average)	Wage Inflation (Detroit Average)	Maximum Work Loss Benefit (Michigan)
1972	$1.00	$1.00	$210.35	
1973	1.03	1.04	246.39	1,000
1974	1.11	1.11	240.29	1,111
1975	1.26	1.28	242.69	1,213
1976	1.45	1.39	284.10	1,285

For every dollar spent on auto repair in 1972, one dollar and thirty-nine cents ($1.39) must be spent in 1976.

Exhibit 1: Combined Auto Insurance Cost Component Inflation

$2.00

$1.00

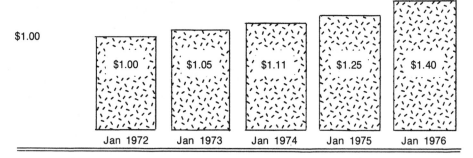

| Jan 1972 | Jan 1973 | Jan 1974 | Jan 1975 | Jan 1976 |

Combined effect of medical care inflation, auto repair inflation, and wage inflation on the auto insurance premium components.

Exhibit 2: Increase in Auto Premiums (Actual National Average)

$2.00

$1.00

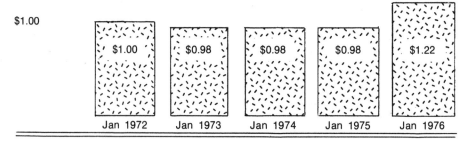

| Jan 1972 | Jan 1973 | Jan 1974 | Jan 1975 | Jan 1976 |

For every dollar spent in the United States on auto insurance premiums in 1972, one dollar and twenty two cents ($1.22) is spent in 1976.

Exhibit 3: Increase in Auto Premiums (Michigan Estimated Average)

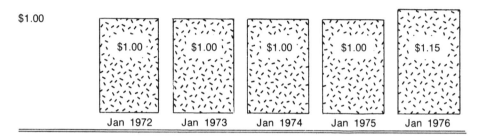

For every dollar spent in Michigan on auto insurance premiums in 1972, one dollar and fifteen cents ($1.15) is spent in 1976.

The rates for bodily injury coverage for a married couple for the four companies decreased in both territories. Table 6 shows that in all eight cases rates decreased, with the reductions ranging from 2 to 27 percent. Rates for bodily injury coverage decreased more dramatically for retirees. Table 7 shows that rates for all four companies and territories decreased. In six cases the decreases were 20 percent or more, and in the remaining two cases, the decreases were 13 percent and 17 percent respectively. These decreases in bodily injury premiums occurred despite inflationary conditions and the significant increase in coverage and benefits under the no-fault system.

A comparison of rates for the compulsory, or minimum, coverages indicates that the magnitude of rate decreases are even larger. Tables 8 and 9 show the percentage change in rates for minimum or compulsory coverage. The difference in the size of the reductions is largely accounted for by the fact that property damage liability for damage to cars is no longer a compulsory coverage under the present no-fault system.

A comparison of rate changes for full coverage automobile insurance, including optional collision and comprehensive insurance, is shown in Tables 10 and 11. Full coverage rates have increased in the same time period of September, 1973, to March 1, 1976, for three of the four companies. The percentage increases for the entire period ranged from no change to an increase of 29 percent. During this period, the increases in virtually every instance were a result of the substantial increases in rates for collision and comprehensive insurance which have been subject to extreme inflationary pressures during the same period.

Table 12 illustrates that the rate increases observed from the inception of no-fault is a direct result of this rate increase in collision and comprehensive insurance, the optional coverages under no-fault. These coverages increased from fifty to ninety-nine percent for the four companies. Since collision and comprehensive premiums make up almost two thirds of the cost of full coverage, one can clearly see that they will dominate overall rate changes. Therefore, any reduction in no-fault bodily injury rates is more than offset by rate increases in the optional coverages. Without the no-fault related reduction in bodily injury rates, rate increases for full coverage would have been substantially greater than they were during the period ending March 1, 1976.

Table 6

Percentage Change in Premium Rates for Bodily Injury Coverage
for Married Couple* in Two Territories for the Period
September 30, 1973 (Pre-No Fault) to March 1, 1976**

	Detroit	Dearborn
Company A	−14%	−4%
Company B	− 2%	−4%
Company C	− 2%	−8%
Company D	−27%	−7%

* Married couple; age 35; no children over 15; husband earns $12,000-$16,000 annually; drives to work six miles one way; annual mileage 12,000; no accidents or violations in three years; and has a 1972 (or 1973, 1974 for the respective years in the period) Chevrolet Impala.

** Bodily Injury coverage for pre-no-fault period includes Bodily Injury Liability of 20,000/40,000; Uninsured Motorists and $1,000 Medical Payments. No-fault Bodily Injury coverage includes coordinated Personal Injury Protection and Residual Bodily Injury Liability of 20,000/40,000.

Table 7

Percentage Change in Premium Rates for Bodily Injury Coverage
for Retired Couple* in Two Territories for the Period
September 30, 1973 (Pre-No Fault) to March 1, 1976**

	Detroit	Dearborn
Company A	−22%	−17%
Company B	−24%	−26%
Company C	−20%	−23%
Company D	−26%	−13%

* Retired couple; age 67; no children; no earned income; drives less than 7,500 miles per year; no accidents or violations in three years; and has a 1972 (or 1973, 1974 for the respective years in the period) Chevrolet Impala.

** See note 2, Table 5.

Table 8

Percentage Change in Premium Rates for Minimum or Compulsory Coverage
for Married Couple* in Two Territories for the Period
September 30, 1973 (Pre-No Fault) to March 1, 1976**

	Detroit	Dearborn
Company A	−31%	−29%
Company B	−31%	−32%
Company C	−26'	−27%
Company D	−41%	−29%

* See note 1, Table 5.

** Minimum coverage for pre-no-fault period includes BI/PD Liability of $20,000/40,000/10,000; Uninsured Motorists and $1,000 Medical Payments. No-fault mandatory coverage includes coordinated Personal Injury Protection (PIP); Residual Liability 20,000/40,000; and Property Protection Insurance.

Table 9

Percentage Change in Premium Rates for Minimum or Compulsory Coverage
for Retired Couple* in Two Territories for the Period
September 30, 1973 (Pre-No Fault) to March 1, 1976**

	Detroit	*Dearborn*
Company A	−36%	−37%
Company B	−46%	−47%
Company C	−40%	−41%
Company D	−40%	−33%

* See note 1, Table 6.
** See note 2, Table 7.

Table 10

Percentage Change in Premium Rates for Full Coverage
for Married Couple* in Two Territories for the Period
September 30, 1973 (Pre-No Fault) to March 1, 1976**

	Detroit	*Dearborn*
Company A	+ 5%	+ 6%
Company B	+25%	+29%
Company C	+12%	+ 7%
Company D	+12%	+20%

* See note 1, Table 5.

** Full coverage for pre-no-fault period includes BI/PD Liability of $20,000/40,000/10,000; Uninsured Motorists; $1,000 Medical Payments; $100 Deductible Collision; and Comprehensive. No-fault full coverage includes coordinated Personal Injury Protection (PIP); Residual Liability 20,000/40,000; Property Protection Insurance; Uninsured Motorists; $100 Broad Collision and Comprehensive.

Table 11

Percentage Change in Premium Rates for Full Coverage
for Retired Couple* in Two Territories for the Period
September 30, 1973 (Pre-No Fault) to March 1, 1976**

	Detroit	*Dearborn*
Company A	+ 1%	0%
Company B	+15%	+18%
Company C	−14%	−14%
Company D	+17%	+18%

* See note 1, Table 6.
** See note 2, Table 9.

Table 12

Percentage Change in Collision and Comprehensive Premium Rates
for Married Couple* in Two Territories for the Period
September 30, 1973 (Pre-No Fault) to March 1, 1976

	Detroit	*Dearborn*
Company A	+50%	+50%
Company B	+90%	+99%
Company C	+52%	+42%
Company D	+59%	+73%

* See note 1, Table 5.

Insurance Industry Experience in Michigan

Overall statewide loss ratios in Michigan for all automobile insurers were relatively stable for the years 1972-74. In 1975, insurers suffered losses higher than those in previous years largely due to the substantial increase in the inflation rate. Table 13 displays the statewide loss ratio for all coverages for personal passenger automobiles for the years 1972 through 1975.

Table 13

Michigan Automobile Insurance Experience
Personal Passenger Automobiles, 1972-1975

	1972	*1973*	*1974*	*1975*
Earned Premiums	$706,072,098	$767,989,927	$813,280,921	$790,999,122
Incurred Losses	477,119,182	494,649,790	526,413,786	612,510,031
Loss Ratio	.676	.644	.647	.774

As can be seen in Table 13, the loss ratio increased almost 13 points in 1975, from 64.7 percent to 77.4 percent, which resulted in an underwriting loss for the industry. The large increase in loss ratio for 1975 was not unique to Michigan, but was a national phenomenon reflecting the national inflation.

The experience in Michigan also reflects the rampant inflation of automobile repair costs. Data collected since 1973 by the Michigan Association of Insurance Companies for Michigan-based insurers, making up about 50% of the automobile insurance market, show that while the loss ratios for the mandatory coverages in Michigan remained relatively stable through 1975, loss ratios for non-mandatory collision and comprehensive coverage soared in 1975. Total earned premiums for the mandatory coverages for these companies actually decreased! Table 14 records premiums earned, losses incurred and loss ratios for Michigan mandatory coverage and collision and comprehensive coverage for Michigan-based insurers for the years 1973 through 1975.

Summary

It is clear that the Michigan No-Fault Law is meeting all of its intended objectives. Automobile accident victims are being compensated more adequately and promptly for their medical, wage and rehabilitation expense. Litigation is being reduced. Needless and expensive duplication of benefits is decreasing. More equity in the distribution of benefits and premiums has been introduced in both the automobile bodily injury and property damage insurance system.

Although overall premium rates were not expected to decrease, the evidence is that No-Fault in Michigan has, in fact, lowered real costs. Inflation has raged in the almost three years since No-Fault was enacted, with the Consumer Price Index increasing almost 30 percent. Michigan auto insurance rates were constant for about four years until they began to rise in the summer of 1975. As of July, 1976, rates in Michigan are about 20 percent higher than in 1971. Moreover, the rate increases in Michigan have been lower than those experienced in most other states. This decrease in real costs is more dramatic when viewed in terms of the significant increase in coverage and benefits under the Michigan No-Fault system. Michigan policyholders enjoy more protection per premium dollar than in any other state in the country.

Table 14

Earned Premiums, Incurred Losses and Loss Ratios for Michigan
Mandatory Coverage (PIP, PPI, RI), Collision and Comprehensive
1973-1975, MAIC

	1973	1974	1975
Earned Premiums			
Mandatory......................	$226,854,043	$205,497,108	$193,059,802
Collision	94,991,039	127,576,377	130,344,877
Comprehensive	39,137,858	42,634,197	44,904,625
Incurred Losses			
Mandatory......................	146,385,286	130,282,579	133,810,047
Collision	70,022,908	96,287,712	111,642,813
Comprehensive	26,591,525	31,269,316	44,775,291
Loss Ratios			
Mandatory......................	64.7%	63.4%	69.3%
Collision	73.7%	75.4%	85.7%
Comprehensive	67.9%	73.3%	99.7%

Appreciation is expressed to Mr. Dennis F. Reinmuth, Mr. Robert H. Rowe, Mr. Lee N. Smith, and Mr. James D. Jones for their assistance in the preparation of this article.

INDEX

Accident Victims

See also Accidents
Claimants
Claims
Economic Losses
Non-Claimants

Massachusetts

Survey, 15-86

Accidents

See also Accident Victims
Claimants
Claims

Massachusetts

Consequences, 35
Number of vehicles involved, 57, 193-194
Place of occurrence, 28-29, 181
Reduction in, 156-161
Reporting required, 23-24
Statistics, 15, 34-35, 132
Types of, 191-196

Attorneys

See Lawyers

Bicyclists

Massachusetts

Role in accidents, 30, 33, 57, 188,
195-196

Claim Files

See also Claims

Delaware

Surveyed, 334

Florida

Surveyed, 289-291

Claim Files—continued

Massachusetts

Classified, 180
Closed with payment, 190
Closed without payment, 190
Defined, 176
Survey, 173-245
Surveyed, 95-99, 177

Claimants

See also Claims
Economic Losses
Non-Claimants
No-Fault Insurance

Massachusetts

Age, 181-183
Attitudes towards insurer, 55-56
Attorney representation, 70, 219-221
Biographical characteristics, 179-183
Collateral sources, use of, 48-56, 60-62
County of residence, 179-181
Denial of claims, 190-191
Dissatisfaction with amount of payment,
64-70
Dissatisfaction with speed of payment,
66-70, 214
Economic losses, 62
Family status, 187-188
Hospitalization, 200
Medical expenses, 48-60, 200-201, 206
207, 219
Medical insurance, 60-62
Medical treatment, 59
Occupations of, 183-186
Options affecting number of payments,
217
Role in accident, 30, 32-34, 57, 125,
188, 194-196
Satisfaction with amount of payment,
64-66, 67-70, 207-208
Satisfaction with speed of payment,
66-70, 211-216